CARS OF THE THIRTIES AND FORTIES

CARS
OF THE THIRTIES AND FORTIES

MICHAEL SEDGWICK

BEEKMAN HOUSE
NEW YORK

Typeset by Ytterlids Sätteri AB, Falkenberg, Sweden.

Colour reproduction by Reproman AB (using the Jemseby method), Gothenburg, by Kvalitets-Kliché AB, Gothenburg, and by Örebro Offset Service, Örebro, Sweden.

Printed by Legatoria Editoriale Giovanni Olivotto, Vicenza, Italy.

First English edition published by Hamlyn. This edition is published by Beekman House, a division of Crown Publishers, Inc., by arrangement with AB Nordbok.
a b c d e f g h

5th printing, 1986
ISBN 0-517-32051-7

CARS OF THE THIRTIES AND FORTIES has been originated, designed, and produced by AB Nordbok, Gothenburg, Sweden. The book is the result of close cooperation between the author and the Nordbok art and editorial departments.

Artwork: Syed Mumtaz Ahmad, Jeremy Banks, Rick Blakey, Gerry Browne, Steve Cross, Sue Edlundh, Anders Engström, Inger Eriksson, Marie Falksten, Nick Framer, Per Fischel, Ferenc Flamm, Vince Griffin, Lars Jödahl, Susanne Kolman, Hans Linder, Sergio Albert Marquis, Eddie Mitchell, Lennart Molin, Chris Mynheer, Yusuke Nagano, Barry Needham, David Penney, Holger Rosenblad, Dave Staples, Ed Stuart, Ulf Söderqvist, Roland Thorbjörnsson.
Nordbok would like to express its sincere thanks to Curt Borgenstam and Björn Eric Lindh for their advice and assistance. The following have also been of great assistance in providing illustration reference material from which new artwork has been produced by the Nordbok studios: *The Autocar* (pages 68, bottom and centre right; 77 top; 100; 130; 131; 137 lower right; 154; 155; 156; 157; 196; 197; 201, left; 205; 206; 207; 212; 213; 223; 224; 225; 229; 230; 231; 233); *Autohistorica* (pages 12; 20; 21; 132; 142; 214); *Motor* (pages 13 top right; 15 top; 44; 45; 59, centre right; 63, top right; 70; 71; 101; 139, bottom; 146; 147; 151 centre right; 186; 187; 192 top; 194; 199; 200; 201 right; 208; 209; 210; 211; 220).

Colour photography
Nicky Wright: Pages 18; 23; 25; 29; 31 bottom; 40; 42 centre; 47 top and centre; 50 top left and right, centre right; 51; 54 top centre, bottom; 55; 58 bottom; 59; 67 top right; 70; 74; 78; 79 top right, bottom; 82; 83 top right, centre left and right; 86 centre left, bottom; 87; 89; 92; 93; 94 right; 96; 100; 103; 106; 107 bottom; 128 top left; 129 top left and right; 133 top right, centre; 136; 137; 140; 141; 145 top left, bottom; 148 top left, bottom left and centre; 149; 163; 165; 167 top left and right, centre left; 168; 176 top right, centre right; 195 bottom; 198; 199; 202; 203 bottom; 206; 210 top; 214–215; 218 top left; 219 centre, bottom; 222 top left, centre; 226 centre right; 227.
Peter Haventon: Pages 22; 32; 34; 35; 42 top left and right; 46; 47 bottom; 50 centre left; 54 top left and right; 58 top left and right, centre; 66 bottom; 67 top left, centre left and right; 71 bottom left and right; 83 top left; 86 top left and right; 90; 91; 94 left; 95 left; 96 bottom; 101; 107 top; 128 top right (Collection Raffay, Hamburg); 132 top left and right; 133 top left; 145 top right; 148 top right; 167 centre left; 169; 176 centre left; 195 top; 203 top, centre; 210 centre; 211; 218 top right; 219 top; 222 top right; 226 top left and right, centre left.
Neill Bruce: Pages 10 top; 66 top; 71 centre left and right; 75; 86 centre right; 139 bottom; 144; 148 centre right; 162.
Fiat: Pages 10 bottom; 11 top; 15; 164.
National Motor Museum: Pages 43; 118; 121.
Holden: Page 176 top left.
Automobil Chronik: Page 39.
Wieslaw Fusaro: Pages 14; 30; 102; 105; 104; 152.

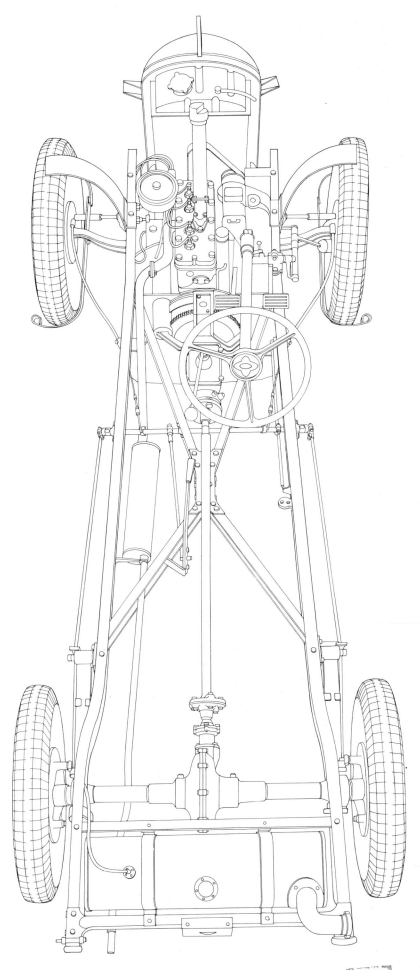

Preface

Nostalgia for the 1930s has not – until recently – extended to the automobile. Moistening of the eyelids accompanies talk of Model T Fords, Prince Henry Vauxhalls, Austin Sevens, chain-driven Mercedes, even the sedate little Citroën Cloverleaf. But Singer Nines and Opel Kadetts – never.

We would probably prefer to forget the decade. Nobody has forgotten the era of *Brother, Can You Spare A Dime*, of Al Capone, of the rise of the Nazis, of the Soviet purge trials, and of that fearsome instrument, the theatre organ. In any case, even dedicated motorists are hardly likely to wax sentimental over vehicles forced to soldier on beyond their appointed time, held together by parts from other breeds. My own thirties' cars were a motley assortment: £20 ($55) worth of Morris Eight, for instance, or a £35 ($100) Wolseley Hornet exhumed from a bed of nettles at the back of a country garage.

Yet both these ancients, already well beyond their majority, gave several thousand miles of trouble-free motoring. They merited no maintenance – and they received none, beyond the replenishment of the necessary fluids, a check on tyre pressures, and, in the Wolseley's case, the fitting of oversize retreads at the back to make it go round corners. To enthusiasts of the 1950s, they were junk, and to that generation (now well into middle age) junk they remain. To such folk, Senior Packards, Duesenbergs, 328 BMWs, 3.5-litre Delahayes, V12 Lagondas, straight-eight Alfa Romeos, and Georges Roesch's Talbots stand out as bright spots in an arid generation. The rest is best consigned to limbo and the scrap merchant.

Only recently has sentiment taken over, and now, cars of the thirties are "preserved", an unhappy term which suggests immurement in heated garages and echoing museums. This must be the wrong fate, for these hitherto unloved machines appeal to the "collector" on two grounds. The first militates against the whole investment trend, for people chose such "special interest" vehicles because they are easily drivable by modern motorists and can be made to conform with most of the stringent safety laws of our times.

Secondly, such cars arouse sentimental associations in a rising generation, as the sort of vehicles their parents drove. The new intake of enthusiasts can't afford Rolls-Royces, Duesenbergs, and Bugattis at today's inflated prices. Even if they could, there aren't enough to go round. Bugatti statistics remain a big question mark, but one doubts if two thousand cars left Molsheim in the last pre-Second World War decade. Rolls-Royce made about twenty-five hundred 40/50s (if one includes American production) in the same period, and 470 Model-J Duesenbergs were turned out between 1929 and 1937. In any case, if you fancied a running J for less than a grand, you should have snapped it up some time between Pearl Harbor and 1950.

Even less memorable, perhaps, are the austere years that followed the Second World War, when everything was rationed, power cuts were the results of coal shortages rather than industrial disputes, the black market yielded anything from a kilogram of butter to an apartment or a new 4CV Renault, and cigarettes were the most valid tender in Occupied Germany.

Beneath these miseries, nonetheless, ran a current of optimism. Things were bound to get better. Some time one's name would be at the top of the waiting list (in Britain it was a matter of six years for a popular model). Fuel would soon be off the ration, and there was even the hope of something better than that abominable Pool, with no measurable octane at all. And if the new model we studied covetously through the dealer's showroom window became an export best seller, would there be such fringe-benefits as an increased foreign travel allowance?

But though we ground along at a laboured 40 mph (65 km/h) in our twelve-year-old sedan, we weren't assailed from all directions. Nobody complained of smoky exhausts (just as well, as most of the oil exited that way). Nobody suggested that the bumpers wouldn't stand a 5 mph head-on impact. A motorist was not yet, by definition, either a sure accident statistic or a contributor to somebody else's accident. Parking in cities was discouraged and never easy, but a Londoner with an office in Kensington and a morning's business in Kingston did the trip by car. Only Americans had parking-meters, and radar was aviation's business, not the speed-cop's.

True, we were a long way, even in 1950, from the zenith of the passenger automobile. The magic ton (160 km/h) was the preserve of sports cars and big sedans with lots of litres underhood, and in any case the tyres of the period weren't up to sustained stretches at such speeds. In most countries one was content to cruise at 50–55 (say 85 km/h), and to put 40 miles or 65 kilometres into an hour was good going. Gears still had to be shifted, and low called for a neat double-clutch action. Heaters, where fitted, were of the "all or nothing" species, and the revolting suction wiper was not entirely confined to American cars. One also worried about oil pressure; gauges were still common practice in Europe, to be ignored at one's peril and a costly repair bill. This rule was so dinned into us that we missed the infuriating instrument when "idiot lights" took over, probably because we suspected the latter of being inoperative until the awful moment when white metal became the sole lubricant!

The twenties can safely be summarized from the automotive viewpoint – electric starters, four-wheel brakes, balloon tyres, coil ignition, cellulose, and chromium plate, with Weymann's flexible fabric bodies and the cyclecar as the prime Lost Causes. If one were to nominate a "long-term" Lost Cause, it would have to be the straight-eight engine, though this phenomenon would reach its zenith in the early 1930s. Alas! it was more than necessary, didn't fit into 1938's styling idiom, and had been consigned to limbo by 1954.

The thirties are not so easy. One could talk of the triumph of hydraulic brakes, except that they were far from universal by the outbreak of the Second World War. Of famous makers wedded to mechanicals, there were a whole army, from Renault (who regarded hydraulics as an extravagance) to Rolls-Royce (who mistrusted them). With independent suspensions one would be on safer ground, though again, there were numerous dissidents, not to mention a degree of uncertainty as to why one should use them anyway. The cheap sports car? Strictly a British preserve, and in any case, the French had mastered this art by 1924, only to discard it.

Then there is the question of styling. If this means the integration of chassis and body, then what were the Lanchester brothers doing in 1900? If it means the evolution of elegant coachwork, then we'd certainly have been better off without stylists; the cost accountants of the 1930s were bad enough.

Pure transportation is a little nearer the mark. Statistically, only 1 Italian in 182 had a car in 1929, while the ratio was 1 in 112 by 1939. Similar increases were recorded in other nations. Yet, curiously, production dropped; in 1929, the six major car-producing countries of the world (the United States, France, Canada, Britain, Germany, and Italy) turned out over 5.6 million units. The total in 1939, by contrast, was down to just under 5 million, though this was due solely to a substantial drop in the United States, which produced a good seventy per cent of the world's cars. Elsewhere an upward trend was detectable.

Maybe the real truth is the acceptance of the automobile as part of our lives. Subtly the attitude changed, and nothing, to my mind, expresses this change so exactly as the conversation incorporated in a German primer I studied in my schooldays. Whether it was written by a German in Germany or by a German-speaker resident in England is immaterial. There stood the words in bald Gothic type: *"Haben Sie ein Auto?" "Ich habe kein Auto."*

A logical enough answer in the mid-thirties, when car ownership was general only in the United States, and many who could afford the luxury were content to do without. But it would certainly have been the wrong one in 1950. By that time, if the respondent had a car, he would have told you the make, type, and year, and added a few laudatory or damnatory comments on the manufacturer and the local agent as well. If he hadn't, there would have been a few qualifying phrases, such as, "I used to run an Opel, but it was requisitioned in 1944, and I'm still two years down the waiting list", or "What do you expect. Do you know how many litres a month we get on our ration card?" Necessity might breed a race of armchair-shoppers, or resign some motorists to the idiosyncrasies of a time-expired, sixth-hand 1933 sedan, but the car was as safe a topic of conversation as the weather in England or politics in Greece.

How was it done? The much-derided cost accountants may have given us chromium plate instead of nickel, plastic instead of timber, and idiot lights instead of proper circular gauges with every unit graded. Presswork may have replaced craftsmanship, while the skilled engineer no longer rebuilt your engine: the factory did it and gave you a replacement unit "while you wait". But they also administered their painkillers: clash-proof synchromesh, power brakes, one-shot lubrication that dispensed with grease guns, controlled ventilation, pushbutton radios, pneumatically operated antennae. True, in place of handy hood latches you had a nasty little bent wire linkage that ran from dash to grille, and you groped for the dipstick in a seemingly bottomless cavern with fixed sides, but how often, nowadays, did you have to lift the hood? With fixed-rate servicing it was cheaper to let the garage do it. And did you pause to think that when Rover first furnished a dipstick at all in 1912, it was considered revolutionary?

Do the forties fit in at all? Here is an even trickier period, since an attempt to study them in isolation from what followed is comparable to that maddening character who hums the first bar of a piece of music and has forgotten the rest. Much of what happened between 1945 and 1950 marks the consolidation of ideas tried – and largely accepted – between 1935 and 1940. For the rest, one gets tantalizing glimpses of a new era of sophistication: three figure maxima as a commonplace, disc brakes, automatic transmissions, tubeless tyres, the space frame, and the *granturismo*. The fascination of the forties lies in the admixture of old and new, and also in the hopefuls (Invicta, Tucker, and Rovin, for instance) which invariably appear in times of shortage. These hopefuls breed the best Lost Causes, and the pity of most of them is that they are wholly irrelevant to mainstream thinking and, thus, have to be omitted.

Of course, one cannot cram the whole spectrum of automobiles and automobilism in a crucial twenty-year period into a few pages. If one stresses the sporting aspect, one is accused of being pro-British. A study

7

of handling would lay overmuch stress on Italian makers, and sophisticated suspensions spell Germany, be it the Germany of Stresemann, Hitler, or Adenauer. Stylistic progress and pain-killers are an integral part of the American saga.

One must also pursue a hazardous course between mass-produced tinware (which everybody drove) and the exotics, from Ferrari to Franklin, which are much more fun, but less relevant to the story. If I have erred on the side of the Big Battalions, I can only explain that I was nearly thirty years old before I even saw a Duesenberg, and many a German of my age has never encountered a Maybach outside a museum or a vintage-car rally. Many of the super-cars made vital contributions to the development of the automobile – Daimler and Packard in the evolution of the multi-cylinder engine, for instance. But in other respects, such vehicles remain peripheral to the main theme.

As for sports cars, they would not have existed had the standard article not been cured of its childhood foibles. The great American raceabouts of Stutz and Mercer came about because Ford and Overland had attained uniformity, and the well-to-do wanted something different. Herbert Austin may have innovated nothing with his Seven, but soon, people wanted baby cars that went faster, so Austin made them. Morris sought to beat Austin at his own game, so he made the overhead-camshaft Minor, evolved by Cecil Kimber into a long line of MGs. The cycle, of course, continues. By 1946, American cars were so dull, comfortable, uniform, and reliable that it wasn't enough for press departments to churn out commercials of the "sky seems brighter" type as yet another opiate. Those who wanted to recapture the fun of driving bought MGs and Jaguars, thus forcing the native industry into a race of pony-cars which furnished a different kind of fun – standingstart acceleration of the sort one normally associated with hot-rods.

Maybe certain makes and models have been overstressed. This is because they paved the way for others. They didn't necessarily invent anything. One links modern independent front suspensions with Vincenzo Lancia in 1922, and the American "boulevard ride" with General Motors's knees of twelve years later.

These were the leaders, and it matters very little that the 1898 Decauville – or for that matter John Henry Knight's 1895 experimental car in its definitive four-wheel form – had independent front suspension. One is brought down to reality by the hard truth: the Decauville's rear end was totally unsprung, and in any case, everyone went on using leaf springs quite happily for another quarter of a century.

One final thought. Not many thirties cars are fun to drive, unless one finds a decayed specimen with idiosyncratic tendencies. Of mine, the 1938 Fiat suffered from a freeze-prone front suspension, and the 1937 MG would fry the soles of one's feet off in a traffic jam. The same went for a contemporary SS Jaguar I used to drive, if only because, with a low-slung frame, the exhaust pipe was right up against the floorboards. They did, however, possess one redeeming feature. Any intelligent driver could master them quickly; and this is a lot more than can be said of many popular machine from the sixties, a generation which bred much unforgiving machinery.

Chapter 1

THE HERITAGE OF THE TWENTIES

The 1930s have been summarized as "the age of planned obsolescence and pure transportation".

This is a facile summary which will not bear too close a scrutiny. Planned obsolescence was certainly implicit in the whole cycle of the mass-produced automobile, whose expectation of life decreased from eight or nine years to about six by 1939. Development, however, marched far more slowly in the inter-war period; if, in 1914, a 1900 Benz would have been totally unsuited for everyday motoring, there were, in 1939, probably more than two million Model T Fords of 1927 and earlier vintage still in daily use, not to mention comparable numbers of 501 Fiats, 5CV Citroëns, and Austin Twelves from the same period. Those who slate the expendability of the 1930s automobile should also consider that force of circumstances condemned it to a prolonged existence comparable to that of Jonathan Swift's Struld-brugs. Outside the United States sound 1939 models still had a modest transportation-value twenty years later, while in countries with inadequate industries and heavy import restrictions – East Germany, for instance, or New Zealand – they were condemned to soldier on far longer. A 1939 Chevrolet Master coupé encountered by the writer on an Auckland used-car lot in 1964 had depreciated no more than twenty per cent in a quarter of a century!

As for the role of "pure transportation", this had long been assumed in the United States, where the industry's first million year had been in 1916. In the last pre-Depression season of 1929, America's factories had turned out 4.5 million units. In 1930, $600 (£120) bought a new Ford Fordor sedan; the customer who preferred the smoothness of six cylinders could have them on a Chevrolet for another $75. If Britain and France still lagged behind, either country had an annual potential of a cool 250,000 units; further, they could sell these at prices accessible to the middle class, if not as yet to workers, whose weekly pay packets seldom exceeded $25 (£5).

Nor is it fair to say that the Great Depression placed a major brake on the spread of the automobile. In the matter of new-car sales, it certainly did; Morris's deliveries fell from 63,522 in 1929 to 43,582 in 1931, and Fiat's even more dramatically from 42,780 to 16,419. Chevrolet, whose first million year had been 1927, were down to barely 300,000 in the dark atmosphere of 1932. The slump had, however, less effect on actual ownership; wherever possible, motorists either hung on to their existing vehicles or bought secondhand. This state of affairs was clearly reflected in the United States, where a seventy-five per cent drop in new registrations was balanced by a fall of only ten per cent in licences issued.

In fact, 1929's stock market crash would serve as a spur to the industry; in order to stay in business, manufacturers had to provide more for less money. Purists might lament the cheese-paring influence of the cost accountant, but retail prices fell steadily from 1930 to 1938's "little recession", when a cut-back in demand was compensated by the loss of production necessitated by the exigencies of rearmament in most countries. Already, shop capacity was being redeployed to meet the requirements of the fighting services, with "shadow factories" being set up in Britain and Germany, and even the Americans questing additional sources of aero engines.

Britain and the United States, with their relatively stable economies, offer perhaps the best yardsticks. At the beginning of our decade, the Chevrolet Six offered mechanical brakes, a beam axle at either end, a "crash" gearbox calling for double-clutch techniques, and fixed disc wheels on which only the rims were demountable. Its 1936 counterpart cost £20 ($100) less, yet the brakes had been given hydraulic actuation, the front wheels were independently sprung, all wheels were demountable, and the presence of synchromesh on the two upper gear ratios made for painless shifting. Better still, wood had virtually been eliminated from the body structure, even if the price of freedom from rot and distortion was drumming at high speeds. The 1930 Morris Minor sedan, priced at £130 ($650), had indifferent stopping power, an overhead camshaft motor which offered considerable performance potential at the cost of complicated maintenance, and most of the other 1920s characteristics encountered on the Chevrolet, the demountable rims apart. Yet, for a couple of pounds more in 1936, the British motorist was offered the immortal Series I Eight, hydraulics, sliding roof, and all. It was, admittedly, a pedestrian side-valve, but its servicing needs were minimal, and it was 5 mph (8 km/h) faster than any stock Minor.

One paid, of course, in terms of individuality. The Chevrolet looked like most other American cars, down to the fashionable fencer's-mask grille on which the bow-tie badge survived as identification. Facias were now designed by stylists rather than engineers; while the home mechanic still enjoyed the convenience of a sideways-opening hood, he would not enjoy it much longer. The alligator type with its fixed sides was on the way. The Morris might adhere more closely to the traditional idiom, but its sedan bodywork was a direct crib of the 1932 Model Y Ford (and thus of the contemporary V8 from Dearborn), the curious wasp-waisted dashboard with its postage-stamp size instruments was hardly a delight, and the "honeycomb" radiator was strictly a dummy, concealing a cheap tubular affair a few inches further aft.

9

Fiat evolution, 1919–30. (*Top left*) A 501 roadster of the type made from 1919 to 1926, (*bottom*) a complete car and a chassis of the 990-cc 509 family spanning the years 1925–29, and (*top right*) the six-cylinder 521, the company's regular big-medium type from 1928 to 1931. This is by no means even a partial model sequence, for though the 501 ran to 1.5 litres (a favoured size in Europe), the 509 was almost a true baby, even if its 102-in (2.6 m) wheel-base allowed plenty of room for four people, and with a 22-hp overhead-camshaft engine, it was more undergeared than under-powered. Top speed was a round 50 mph (80 km/h), whereas 45 mph (72 km/h) was the 501's comfortable limit. As a general provider to the Old World, with steady sales in countries from Norway to Spain, Fiat could not afford a mistake. And in 1928, it seemed sensible to pursue the medium-six market with the American-looking 2.5-litre 521, even if up to now Giovanni Agnelli had been reluctant to take on the massed battalions of Detroit.

After twenty years of quality cars, he was not immediately ready to attack the mass market. The 501 sold eighty thousand units in 7½ years, but it was never cheap: even in 1925, a Briton paid the price of two Morris-Cowleys, and it wasn't by any means all import duty. The car sold on the strength of its uncannily smooth and indestructible side-valve motor, giving a modest 24–27 hp. Front-wheel brakes would not be added until 1924, ignition was by magneto, and both steering wheel and gearshift were on the right. Central shift (but not left-hand drive) arrived on the 509, as did excellent

coupled four-wheel brakes. At the same time, Fiat, like most other Italian makers, opted for a Rolls-Royce shape of radiator instead of the "pear" which they'd initiated (and seen widely copied) way back in 1911. By contrast, the 521 was purest American, its four-speed transmission apart. It looked like a De Soto or Plymouth, wheels were disc or wire, a coil replaced the magneto, and left-hand drive was standard. Output was 50 hp, and the 521 managed to sell nearly twenty-three thousand units in four seasons. The company would persist hopefully with American-type flathead sixes until 1936, but despite a wide choice of wheel-base, tune, and body style, many Europeans preferred to buy American or opt for something smaller. The 522 (and its long wheel-base companion, the 524) replaced the 521 during 1931, but a three-year run barely attracted ten thousand buyers, despite the attraction of hydraulic brakes, and the final 527s (1934–36) accounted for precisely 260.

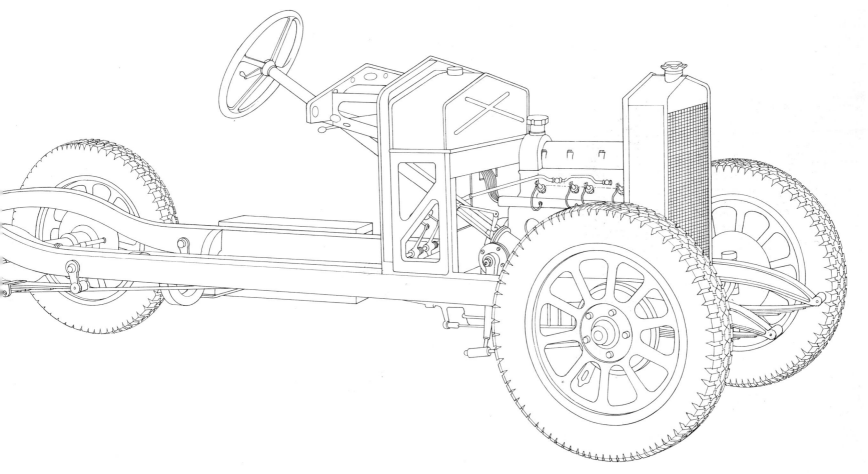

The 1920 Stutz, in some ways atypical of its country and period, has an entirely typical side-opening, two-piece hood. The advantages are immediate accessibility to, and plenty of room to work with, any part of the motor. However, one could only work on one side at a time, the catches were awkward, and the hood was heavy.

One-piece hoods (*opposite*) were one of the refinements of the thirties. The use of a dash-mounted radiator on the 1936 Fiat 500 (*top right*) ruled out underhood battery stowage and gave a short sloping nose which swung forward and could be lifted off. (It also had to be removed to insert the starting handle, an infernal nuisance when one stalled in traffic with a flat battery.) The German Ford Eifel, in 1937 form (*bottom*), offered almost equally good accessibility thanks to traditional un-streamlined fenders and deep hood sides, while rearward opening was safe enough so long as the catches held. On the 1940 Chevrolet (*top left*), however, the "alligator" hood took on its standard form for years to come and reveals its inherent failings. The fender line has now swept up to cylinder-head level, and lateral accessibility is tricky for the short-armed. Getting at anything below spark-plug level isn't easy with the normal tool kit.

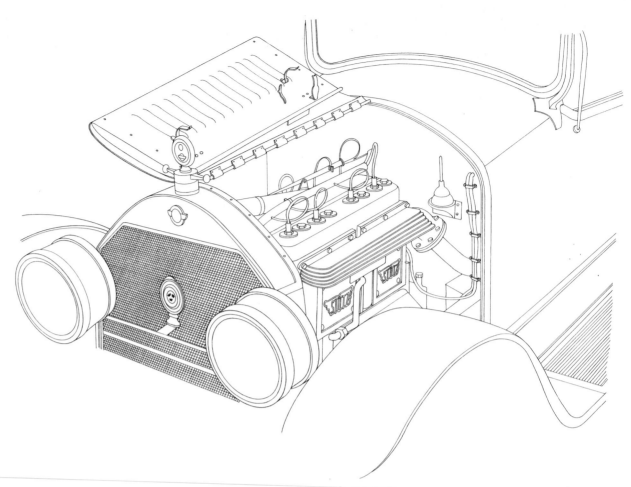

The Chevrolet and the Morris – and parallel efforts such as the 8CV Citroën, the 1.2-litre Opel, and the Fiat 508 – were, admittedly, by-products of the Depression. They signalized, however, the acceleration of a process that had gathered momentum in the previous decade as mass-production techniques spread across the Atlantic.

The advance was gradual. One may doubt if any European maker of the 1920s had a genuine potential of 100,000 units a year, and even in 1939, the ranks of the six-figure firms were probably limited to Austin, Citroën, Fiat, Morris, and Opel. But the ingredients were there; the moving assembly line, general practice in the United States by 1917–18, dominated the European cheap-car scene thirteen years later. Hot on the heels of Ford, Chevrolet, and Willys-Overland had come the re-doubtable André Citroën in 1919. Morris had moved into the big league by 1924, and so had Opel in Germany with their copy of Citroën's 5CV. Fiat's first cheap baby, the 509, appeared in 1925. Edward G. Budd's all-steel closed bodies had been a reality in the United States by the 1918 Armistice, and within a decade, his methods would find footholds in Britain (the Morris-sponsored Pressed Steel Company) and in Germany (Ambi-Budd of Berlin). In France, Citroën had been making *tout acier* sedans since 1924.

Along with new, sophisticated means of manufacture had come a serious campaign to tailor the automobile to the needs of the laity. The First World War had opened the Old World's eyes to the internal combustion engine and had bred a new generation of drivers – from both sexes. These recruits might as yet be unable to afford their own transportation, but all the ingenuity of Agnelli, Ford, Morris, Opel, and the rest would have been of no avail had the end-product remained complicated and capricious, as it still tended to be in 1914.

It has been said of the "Edwardians" that they made the automobile work perfectly. This they did, but the issue has been confused by the vast depreciation of money since those days. Seen through the eyes of the 1970s, a complete Rolls-Royce Silver Ghost touring car at £1,500 (say $7,500) seems a sensational bargain – it is too easy to forget that this probably represents about £60,000 ($120,000) in present-day currency. It is even easier to discount the truth: only a tiny fraction of the day's motorists could have afforded cars of the calibre of the Royce, the bigger Mercedes, or American giants like the Pierce-Arrow and the Locomobile 48.

Further, this "perfection" of running was available only to a good driver backed by a good mechanic. Most big thoroughbreds of the day were capable of 70 mph (110 km/h), if not over-bodied, while high gearing assured a reasonable thirst – for all its 7.4-litre motor the Silver Ghost would average 16 mpg (14.5 lit/100). One had learnt to take electric lighting for granted at these exalted levels, and even outside the United States electric starters were in fairly general use. Also in evidence – albeit in Europe only – was the quick-detachable wheel, though American makers considered this too unwieldy for the distaff side and would cling obstinately to fixed wheels and demountable rims right up to 1931. Further, wheel-changes were a pressing problem, for narrow-section tyres running at high pressures on rough surfaces had a hard life, and 2,000 miles (say 3,000 km) were considered a reasonable distance for a cover. The standard source of ignition was the high-tension magneto, a contraption beyond the understanding of the average layman.

Engines still turned slowly, with narrow rev ranges. The average touring unit of 1914 idled at 400–500 rpm and was eating its guts out at 1,600. Even the big Vauxhall, a high-speed unit by the standards of the day, was doing just that speed at 60 mph (100 km/h) in high gear. Hence, few family tourers of the period were blessed with measurable acceleration, the indirect gears being regarded as emergency adjuncts

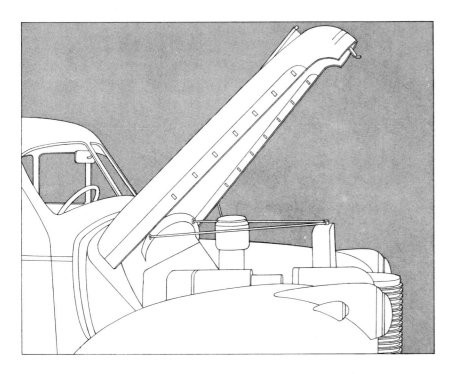

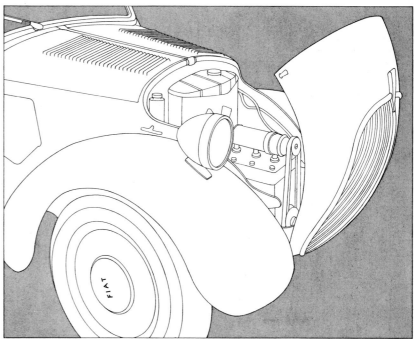

for hills or heavy city traffic. The tendency to "hang on" to top played havoc with early clutches. Progress during the 1920s can be shown by comparing Fiat's cheap 1.8-litre Zero of 1912–14 with the 990-cc 509 made in the 1925–29 period. The older car delivered its 19 brake horses at a round 1,800 rpm, whereas the 509 gave 22 bhp at a 3,400 rpm that would have horrified an Edwardian motorist. He would also have been horrified by the fierce buzzing noises emitted at 50 mph, but then he, unlike his 1929 counterpart, had no interest in the traffic-light Grand Prix.

The old Fiat Zero was capable of a respectable 45 mph (75 km/h), but even at these modest velocities, its owner had even worse problems than the limitations of early electrics or poor roads. It was far worse for the conductor of a Prince Henry Vauxhall or an Alfonso Hispano-Suiza. Even in the 1950s, such cars were physically capable of keeping up with modern traffic; what they could not do was stop in a hurry, for their two-wheel brakes called for intelligent anticipation at speeds of 60 mph or more. Little better was the foot-operated transmission brake, which produced either a rude smell or retardation on a dramatic scale, followed by side-slip and interesting consequences to the drive line.

The best hand-built coachwork of the period was superbly executed but almost invariably open; closed styles were confined to formal limousines and "doctor's coupés" (two-passenger cabriolets with winding windows and rumble seats). The traditional paint-and-varnish finish gave great depth of colour; it also required regular cleaning and renewal, if it were to retain its pristine glory. Brightwork, in brass or nickel, was quick to tarnish and the bane of a chauffeur's life.

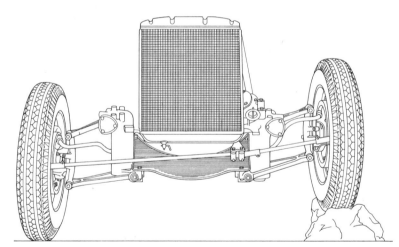

(*Top*) Belgian decline. Making luxury cars, mainly for export to Britain, didn't pay in the depressed 1930s. In 1925, however, Minerva of Antwerp had been riding the crest of the wave, with beauties like this 6-litre sleeve-valve six with coachwork by Erdmann & Rossi of Berlin. But most Minervas carried formal limousine coachwork, so sales slowly dwindled until the company was forced to amalgamate with Imperia in 1936.

The front end of 1937's Fiat 508C (*bottom*). No publicity man could resist the posed shot on a boulder to show how the coils and swinging arms kept the chassis horizontal. The Fiat handled beautifully (if one were careful with tyre pressures), but those coils in their oil-filled dashpots could freeze in sub-zero weather, with most interesting consequences!

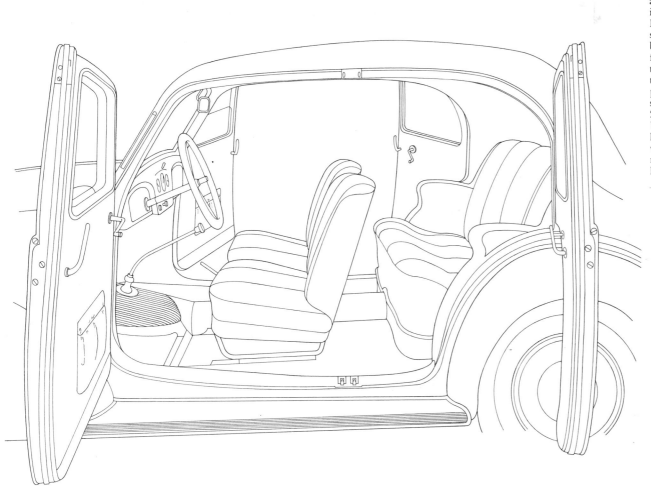

The Fiat 508 C of 1937 had easy all-round access for four on a wheel-base of only 95 in (2.4 m), as this illustration (*left*) shows. Luggage lived behind the rear seat: the space wasn't shared by the spare wheel but was only accessible from inside. Unfortunately, the pillarless doors soon distorted, and then rattles and draughts were the order of the day. Fiat even applied the pillarless principle to a long-chassis six-seater edition (wheel-base was 108 in or 2.7 m) which became popular as a taxi. Unusually for a long and narrow car, it handled as well as the short model, only, with an abbreviated hood, one had to remember that most of the vehicle was behind one!

In Italian, *balilla* means "plucky little one": most people today have forgotten the association with Fascist youth movements! Of the two 508 Fiats shown here, only the 1932–33 three-speed 508 (*bottom*) is a Balilla, though the name was often applied to early 508C *Millecentos* as made between 1937 and 1952. The original Balilla was a boxy little car with a lot of 1929 De Soto in its styling. One didn't expect synchromesh on a cheap baby in 1932, and its gravity feed from a dash-mounted fuel tank would never be allowed in our safety-conscious times, and on 995 cc and 20 hp, 60 mph (95–100 km/h) were possible only downhill – until first the backyard tuners and then the factory laid hands on the car, transforming it into the delightful 36-hp 508 S sports two-seater with overhead valves. But the Balilla's short-stroke engine was unburstable – maximum power was nominally developed at 3,400 rpm, but 4,000 were entirely safe. Later four-speeders with synchromesh (1934) carried the story through to 1937, and Balillas were built under licence in France (Simca), Germany (NSU), Czechoslovakia (Walter), and even, briefly, in Spain.

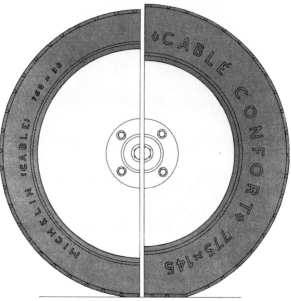

Tyre development. The sectional drawing (*above*) shows the difference between the early low-pressure type and the "balloon", first seen in 1923. The distance from axle to ground is the same in both cases, owing to the greater deflection of the modern version, which is on the right. Significantly, the low-pressure tyre, which was not new — Palmer had made "giant" tyres for formal carriages before the First World War — was offered in early days with the beaded edge, though Dunlop had a straight-side type (*left*) available. With straight-sided tyres the inside of the wheel itself was modified.

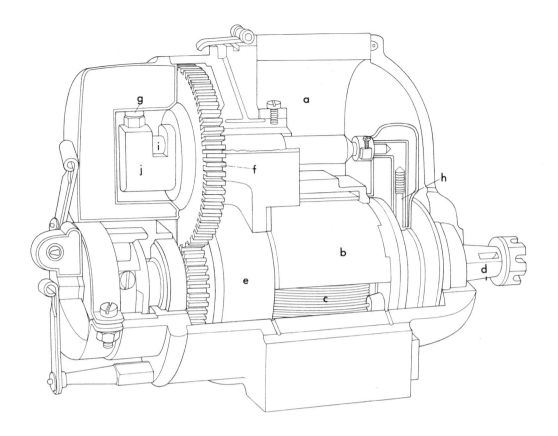

Not that the spread of mass production transmitted Packard or Rolls-Royce quality to the middle-class sector of the market. What it did was to render the vehicle more acceptable practically to folk whose engineering knowledge was nil, and who could not afford "motor servants". Their prime requirement was to get from A to B more freely, more comfortably, and, if possible, more cheaply.

Hence, manufacturers of the 1920s administered pain-killers in place of the superb workmanship of the Golden Age. Engine speeds went up, giving the driver greater control of his machine. Power units were given full-pressure lubrication, which meant (in theory) only occasional toppings-up with oil, and the unintelligible magneto gave way to the simple battery and coil. By 1919, electric lighting had become a "must", even if the more dedicated cost-cutters clung to such crudities as Ford's magneto-driven headlamps (still available in 1925) and the acetylene illuminations found on French cyclecars, quite simply because full electrics would have landed the vehicles in a higher taxation class. In the same period, the electric starter progressed from being a high-cost option in Europe to a standard fixture, omitted at the maker's peril. Such a state of affairs had, in any case, obtained in the United States since 1915.

Starting-handles caused broken arms; inadequate anchors caused skids and fatalities. Hence, brakes received major attention during the decade. True, four-wheel brakes had been known in 1910, but an early preference for the uncoupled type (remember Austin Sevens in the 1920s!) had done nothing to increase their popularity. Thus, in 1919, France's Delages and Hispano-Suizas were virtually the only cars with a brake drum on each wheel, even if Duesenberg's advanced hydraulics lay only a year in the future. The speed with which the new idiom spread can best be assessed from the annual design summaries published in *The Autocar*. These, admittedly, covered only cars on the British market, but they are none the less illuminating. Four-wheel brakes received no mention in 1922, yet a year later, 28.5 per cent of all models had them as standard. The percentage rose to 47 in 1924, and 75 in 1925. In 1927, the last time a statistical breakdown was deemed necessary, only 6 per cent held out against progress, this despite the fact that only a short while back correspondents in the journal were inveighing against the idea as "an invitation to reckless high speed". But then Britain was rather a special case; she was bedevilled with a blanket speed limit of 20 mph (32 km/h) and would continue to be so beset until 1930.

Tyre life had also to be extended. Nineteen twenty-three saw the first wide-section, low-pressure "balloon" tyres, capable of absorbing the impact of a baulk of timber at 20 mph. "Balloons" were, in fact, claimed as the panacea for almost everything: better comfort on rough roads, less stress for the axles, longer tyre and chassis life, and freedom from skids thanks to superior road contact. Unfortunately, this new development coincided with front-wheel brakes, with results that were sometimes peculiar.

Early contracting-type front-wheel brakes were dirt-prone and not a great improvement on the two-wheel systems they replaced. Worse still, the manufacturers failed to recognize that the addition of anchors to front axles not designed to take the additional torque was an invitation to disaster. Add the extra weight of the new "balloons", and the result was the dreaded "shimmy", a disease worse than the side-slip of earlier days. It was not until 1927 that revised axle and steering layouts had eliminated the teething troubles of the new combination.

Next to receive attention was bodywork. In those days of composite wood-and-metal construction, open tourers were cheaper to make; they were also a great deal lighter. They were not, however, truly all-weather bodies, for all the elaborate arrangement of side-curtains affected by

Damn-the-cost luxury at its best, 1930. Rolls-Royce's Phantom II (*left*) was launched at the 1929 Shows, and was conservative in that its makers clung to six cylinders at a time when Isotta Fraschini had been making straight-eights for a decade, and so had Duesenberg. Output from the 7.7-litre overhead-valve motor was "sufficient" (in fact, about 120 hp in 1930), and with reasonable bodywork, 90 mph (145 km/h) were possible. The car stopped superbly, thanks to the Hispano-type servo brakes. As even the short chassis measured 144 in (3.6 m) between wheel centres, there was plenty of room for the ultimate in coachwork, such as this sporting sedanca de ville (Americans would call it a town car) with the semi-cycle fenders, step plates instead of running boards, and the sidemounted spare wheels then fashionable. Cost? Anything from £2,900 to £3,300 ($14,500–$16,500), at a time when a working man with a job could expect to bring home £3 ($15) a week.

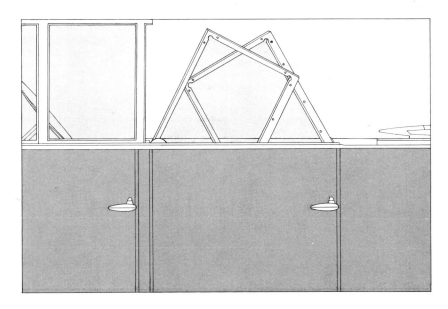

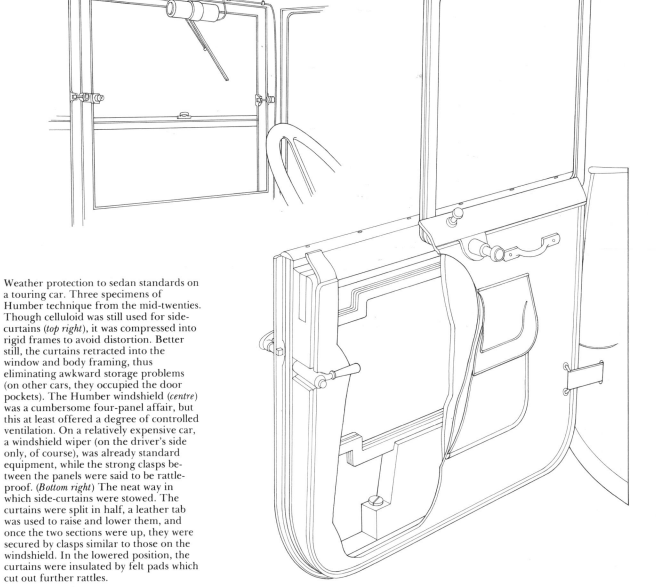

Weather protection to sedan standards on a touring car. Three specimens of Humber technique from the mid-twenties. Though celluloid was still used for side-curtains (*top right*), it was compressed into rigid frames to avoid distortion. Better still, the curtains retracted into the window and body framing, thus eliminating awkward storage problems (on other cars, they occupied the door pockets). The Humber windshield (*centre*) was a cumbersome four-panel affair, but this at least offered a degree of controlled ventilation. On a relatively expensive car, a windshield wiper (on the driver's side only, of course), was already standard equipment, while the strong clasps between the panels were said to be rattle-proof. (*Bottom right*) The neat way in which side-curtains were stowed. The curtains were split in half, a leather tab was used to raise and lower them, and once the two sections were up, they were secured by clasps similar to those on the windshield. In the lowered position, the curtains were insulated by felt pads which cut out further rattles.

such makers as Humber in Britain, which, like the American "California" tops, added weight and defeated the whole object. Lancia's detachable top, to be replaced by a canvas affair in summer, presented storage problems.

Little better were the early "all-weather" (five-passenger convertible sedan) styles affected by Britons and Frenchmen alike. These styles resulted in even heavier weights, and the top was a two-man affair, whatever catalogues claimed. Thus, only a sizable price differential could keep the tourer in its position of pre-eminence.

There were, of course, closed bodies available on inexpensive chassis. Most American makers were offering permanent-top sedans by 1918 – at a price. Even in 1921, the differential could be as much as eighty per cent: compare the $1,695 asked for a Maxwell sedan with the $995 asked for the tourer. The Ford at $760 was cheap enough, but it could not compete with open cars at $415. A Buick Six with a $1,795 price-tag was elevated into the luxury class if winter comforts were required.

In 1922, Hudson's breakthrough on the Essex Four, with a mere $300 differential between open and closed models, paved the way to a new era. By 1927, only $5 separated a tourer from the cheapest five-passenger sedan.

With Europe's smaller volume sales, of course, such minimal differentials were not viable, though the same trend was reflected in the fact that the prices of open and closed Morris-Cowleys fell by twenty-six per cent between 1925 and 1931. Purchasers of the more expensive Oxford fared rather better; only four per cent was slashed off tourers, but

thanks to the new Pressed Steel plant, sedans became twenty-five per cent cheaper.

Low prices generate demand, and further demand forces them still lower. By 1928, eighty-five per cent of all new cars sold in the United States carried closed bodywork, and some interesting price patterns were emerging. While Ford and Chevrolet still sold enough roadsters and tourers to list these as bargain-basement items, the cheapest Buicks, Essexes, Graham-Paiges, Hudsons, and Oldsmobiles – to name but a few breeds – were coaches (two-door sedans). In some cases, the open-car package was jazzed up with wire wheels and dual side-mounted spares to justify the extra manufacturing cost of what was fast becoming a special-order item, retained in the catalogue to keep faith with the customers. Hupmobile charged a $145 premium for a roadster and a whopping $175 for a phaeton; even the four-door sedans were cheaper.

Thus, the open models were slowly phased out. Buick, who had sold nearly 41,000 phaetons in 1925, broke 10,000 of this style for the last time in 1927, while only 4,650 of the 53,000 Chryslers made in 1931 carried open bodies. Ford disposed of over 200,000 Model A roadsters in 1929, but even the Depression cannot alone account for the total of 15,000 roadsters and phaetons sold in 1932. Henceforward, the celluloid side-curtain would be virtually confined to sporting machinery. Attempts to revive it on both sides of the Atlantic after the Second World War – Dodge's Wayfarer and the Morris Minor – met with a cool reception, both cars soon acquiring proper wind-up windows.

(*Left*) Handwork is much in evidence on the Volvo body line in 1929. The composite construction is obvious: it was a case of fitting together a series of fairly small panels, since Volvo, still a modest outfit, had no large presses. If the tempo of this factory scene seems leisurely, one must remember that Volvo's total production of sixes that year was precisely 386 units.

(*Opposite, top*) Anatomy of a family automobile at the beginning of our period. In fact, Volvo's PV652 was fairly advanced for its time, with its hydraulic brakes, the one feature which stamps it as essentially early thirties rather than vintage. For the rest, there is little one would not have encountered any time from about 1923 onwards–a simple channel-section frame with four cross-members, a semi-elliptic leaf spring at each corner, and a front-mounted engine driving the rear wheels. Unit gearboxes had, of course, long been majority practice (and pretty well universal on mass-produced cars) but engines still sat well back behind the front axle centre-line, and thus space was wasted.

(*Opposite, bottom*) Making a car, 1929. This drawing from Volvo shows the assembly of chassis and body, and their ultimate marriage. In those pre-unitary days, the two elements had to do a fair amount of travelling before they came together. Not that new methods necessarily put a stop to this: in unitary times, the press-work specialists were often responsible for the entire chassis-body structure, which was then transported to the official "factory" to receive its engine, transmission, axles, and running gear. Interesting is the adoption of a moving assembly line in a small venture.

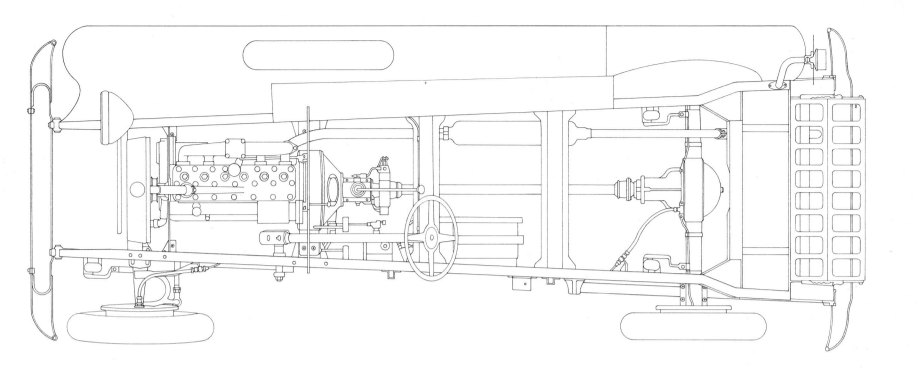

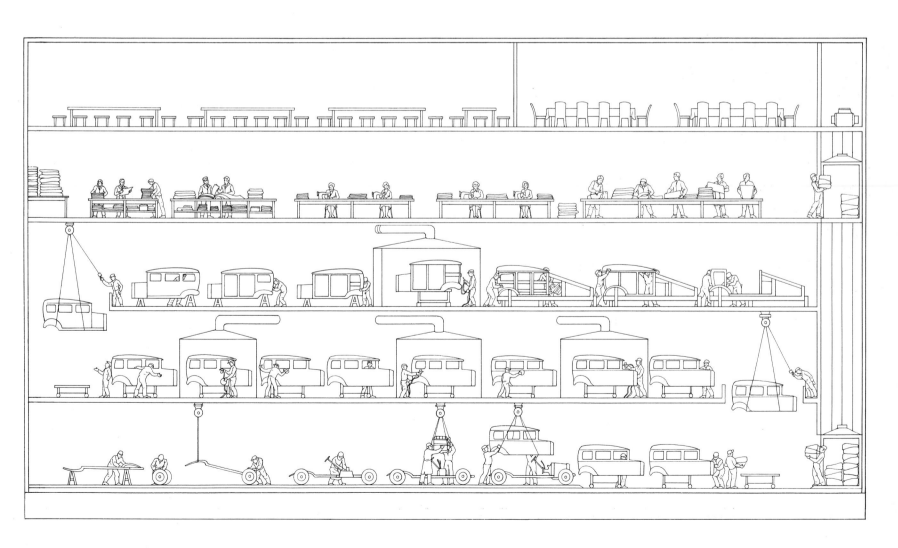

Terribly, terribly British, or what the Anglo-Saxons do best. (*Left*) The 1930 M-type MG Midget. The body was fabric covered, flimsy (it only cost its makers £6.50 or $32.50), and claustrophobic with the top up, actual output from the 847-cc overhead-camshaft engine was a mere 20 hp, and the two-bearing crankshaft wasn't exactly adamantine. However, 60–65 mph (100–110 km/h) were yours for a mere £185 ($925), and as the basis was Morris Minor, there were parts and service in every English town. The office (*bottom*) is a little cramped, and the vee windshield doesn't really help. This example has black-face dials of obvious Morris origin: later ones had white faces. The gearshift is awkward: a quick change from low to second can impale one's hand against the facia, a good reason why later clients often chose the fourspeed option with MG's famous remote lever.

The MG sold. The 21-hp Speed Model Sunbeam four-door coupé (*opposite*) didn't, largely because its main competitor was Talbot of London, a member of the same group and more dynamic in design and marketing. Neither firm considered rationalization, so by 1935, when this car was made, the receivers were in. The Sunbeam combined elegance, handling, and a comfortable cruising speed of 70 mph (112 km/h). The trouble was that not many people had £800 ($4,000) to burn, and there was plenty of choice in this sector – Alvis and Lagonda as well as Talbot.

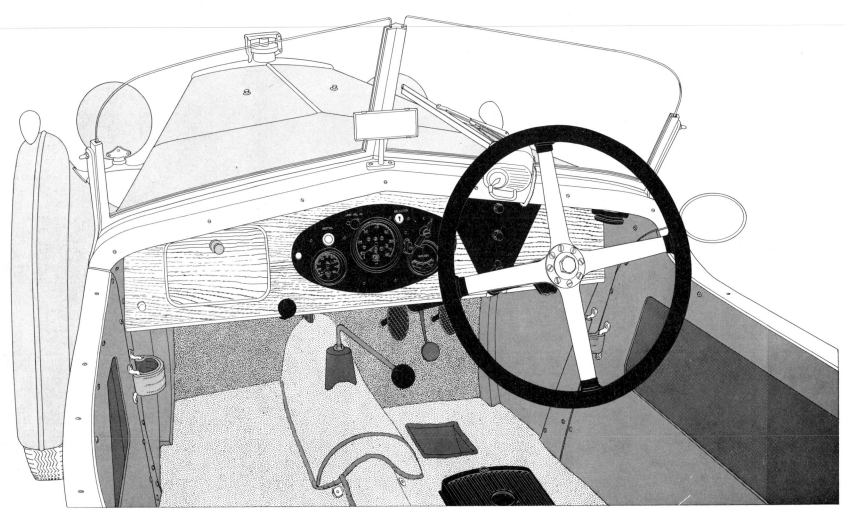

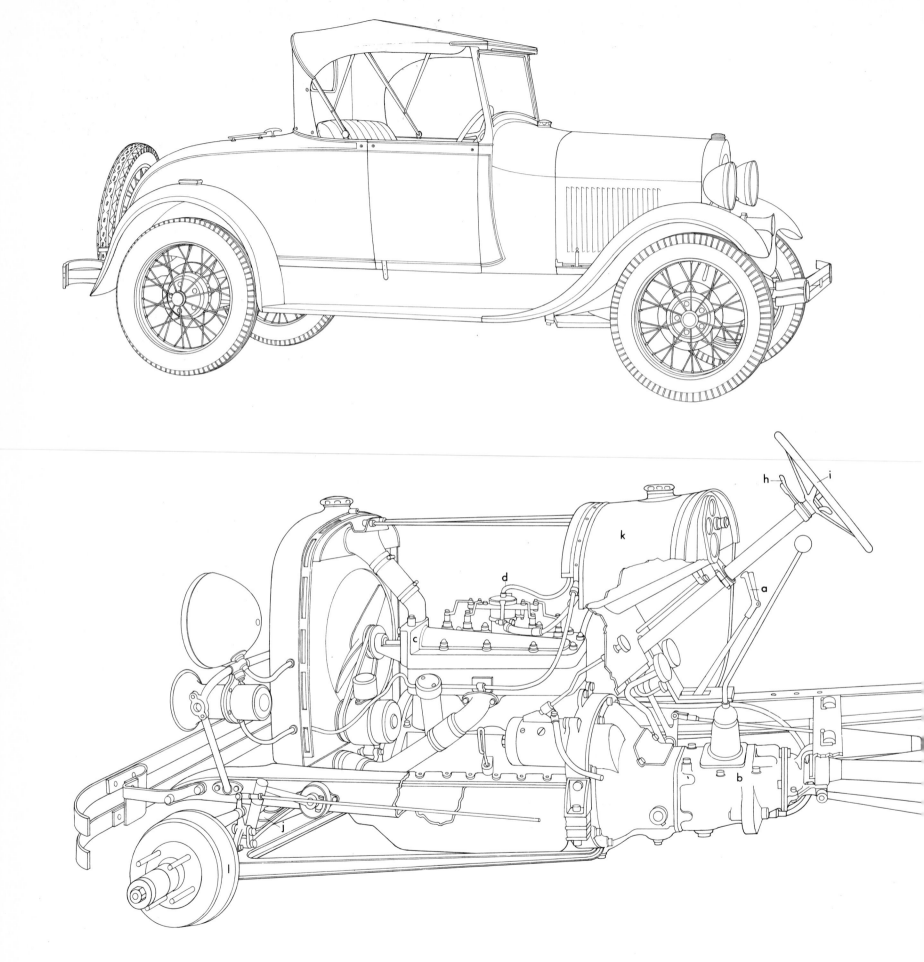

The Model A, Ford's second "Universal Car", shown (*top left*) in original 1928 roadster form and (*top right*) as a 1930 Fordor sedan. The difference between the two is essentially stylistic, though the observant will note that, on the drawing (*below*) showing one of the first chassis, the handbrake (*a*) is on the driver's side, whereas early in 1928, it was moved to the centre. The car was very much Everyman's Transport, its reliable, slow-turning, 3.3-litre four-cylinder engine giving 40 hp and propelling it at 60–65 mph (100–105 km/h). The delightfully simple three-speed transmission (*b*) marked a major departure from the T's pedal-controlled shift, but at long last, it enabled anyone who could drive a Ford to handle anything else and would eventually eliminate those special "planetary" drivers' licences issued by certain states to those whose experience did not extend beyond Lizzie. Most of the engineering was now copybook American: thermo-syphon cooling (*c*), coil ignition (*d*), hydraulic dampers (*e*), and a spiral bevel back axle (*f*). Ford, like Chevrolet, favoured torque tube drive (*g*), and it was still accepted practice to mount ignition and throttle controls (*h*) on the steering wheel. The wheel itself (*i*) had a diameter of 18 in (45.5 cm) – bus-size by the standards of our times. Primitive influences, of course, remained: Henry Ford was obstinately loyal to his transverse-leaf suspension (*j*) at both ends, giving excellent performance over farm tracks and bouncy rides on the highway. He also distrusted fuel pumps, retaining gravity feed from a dash tank (*k*). The mechanical four-wheel

brakes (*l*) were adequate only for a car of such modest performance. The Model A was manufactured or assembled, to the tune of over five million units in many countries, and as late as the mid-sixties over three hundred thousand were said still to be in daily use in the United States. What is also soon forgotten is that the model formed the entire basis for the Soviet automotive industry, going into production as the GAZ-A at Gorki in 1931. In the pre-Second World War period, it was virtually Russia's staple automobile, and truck editions (GAZ-AA) were still being made in 1948.

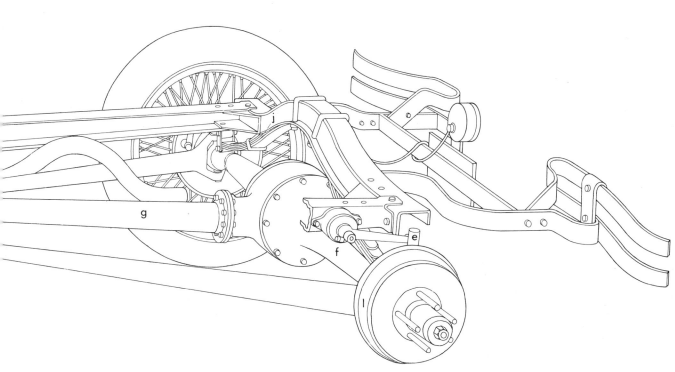

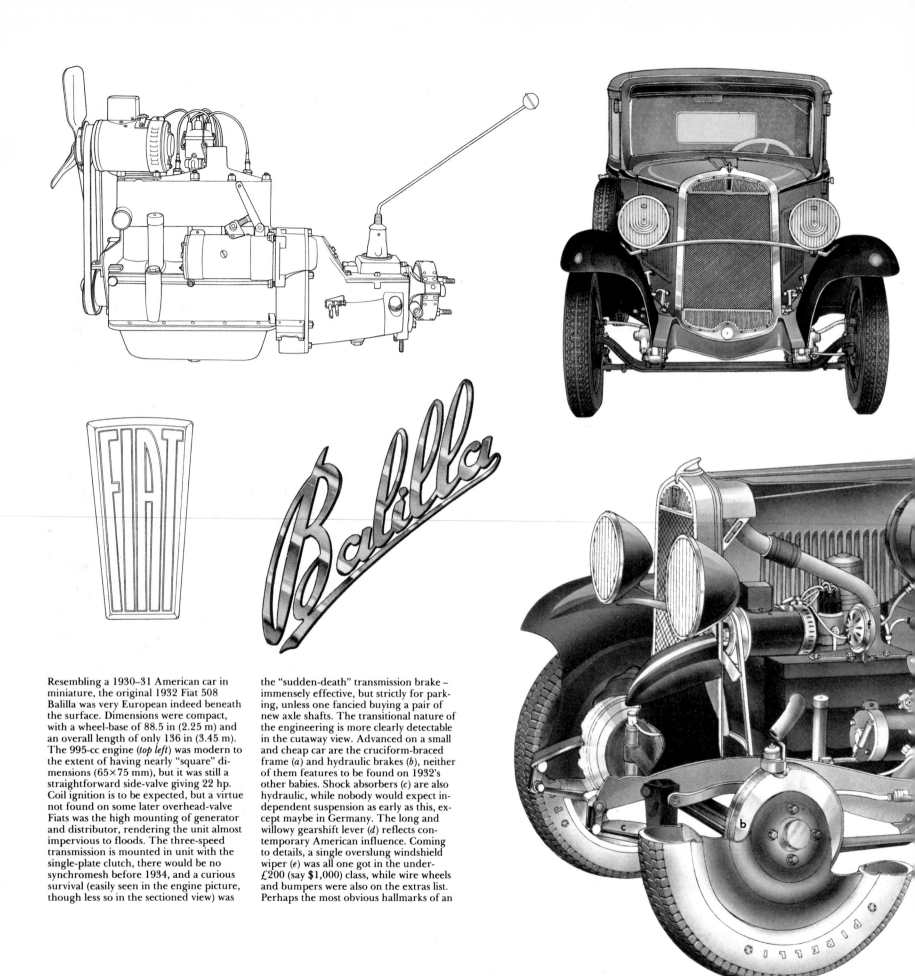

Resembling a 1930–31 American car in miniature, the original 1932 Fiat 508 Balilla was very European indeed beneath the surface. Dimensions were compact, with a wheel-base of 88.5 in (2.25 m) and an overall length of only 136 in (3.45 m). The 995-cc engine (*top left*) was modern to the extent of having nearly "square" dimensions (65×75 mm), but it was still a straightforward side-valve giving 22 hp. Coil ignition is to be expected, but a virtue not found on some later overhead-valve Fiats was the high mounting of generator and distributor, rendering the unit almost impervious to floods. The three-speed transmission is mounted in unit with the single-plate clutch, there would be no synchromesh before 1934, and a curious survival (easily seen in the engine picture, though less so in the sectioned view) was

the "sudden-death" transmission brake – immensely effective, but strictly for parking, unless one fancied buying a pair of new axle shafts. The transitional nature of the engineering is more clearly detectable in the cutaway view. Advanced on a small and cheap car are the cruciform-braced frame (*a*) and hydraulic brakes (*b*), neither of them features to be found on 1932's other babies. Shock absorbers (*c*) are also hydraulic, while nobody would expect independent suspension as early as this, except maybe in Germany. The long and willowy gearshift lever (*d*) reflects contemporary American influence. Coming to details, a single overslung windshield wiper (*e*) was all one got in the under-£200 (say $1,000) class, while wire wheels and bumpers were also on the extras list. Perhaps the most obvious hallmarks of an earlier age are up-draught carburation (*f*) and the fuel tank on the firewall (*g*). This latter was foolproof provided feed pipes did not clog, but it was hardly very safe. Not visible here are the hand throttle (still general practice but retained on Fiats long after it disappeared from other makes) and the curious plunger type ignition key (one rotated it to operate the lights). Curious things happened when the switch-wards began to wear, and it was not

proof against the attentions of ignorant car-park attendants! Launched in the depth of the Depression, the original three-speed Balilla sold over forty-one thousand units in two years, and the later four-speeders did even better, the side-valve line continuing until mid-1937. The model was built under licence in Czechoslovakia, Poland, Germany, and France. The French Balilla, rated at 6CV, became the world-famous Simca.

Also doomed were finishes which required more than a quick wipe-over. The new generation of motorists might not do their own maintenance – indeed, they were discouraged from so doing. Ford had long since instituted flat-rating practices throughout their dealer network, and the other American and European mass-producers would soon follow suit. The new motorists did, however, like something that was easy to clean – the Instant Car Wash did not exist, even in the United States – not to mention a coat of paint likely to outlive their own spell of ownership. DuPont's Duco cellulose had first been seen on the 1924 Oaklands, and by 1928, it was general practice outside the realm of the specialist coachbuilder, who would adopt it in the early 1930s. Hot on its heels came non-tarnishable chromium-plated brightwork. Considered vulgar and meretricious by many – Gabriel Voisin said he would adopt it "when Cartier sells artificial pearls" – it had crossed the Atlantic by 1929 and was probably the most important cosmetic change of the 1930 season.

All these were American innovations. One component, however, survived the 1920s without major change, and that was the gearbox.

Its concomitants, admittedly, did not. The cone clutch, fairly general practice in 1920 and still common in 1925, had been ousted by the single dry-plate type, though Morris and Hudson would keep their smooth wet-plate units right up to the end of the 1930s. "Fierce" has long been the accepted epithet for the old cones, and some of them were just that.

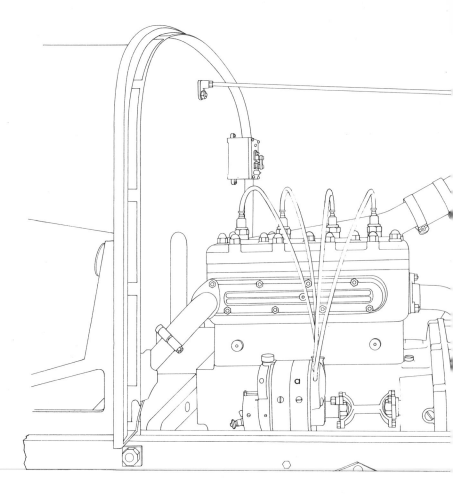

The type's one unpardonable sin was, however, that it required regular maintenance if it were to keep its good manners, and the new generation wanted no truck with dressings, let alone propping the pedal out overnight.

There had also been a change in shift levers, from the old visible gate to the simpler and less pleasing ball type, while more and more cars kept their "change-speed levers" in the centre.

Nobody will ever agree which came first – left-hand steering or centre shift – but both were logical in a country such as the United States, which had a right-hand rule-of-the-road; by 1916, a virtual uniformity prevailed throughout the American industry. Though Packard tried briefly to maintain the traditional image with a left-hand gear-shift as well, centrally-mounted levers (which meant the hand-brake, too) permitted entry and exit from either side, and therefore four doors on four-passenger car bodies. Early European converts to centre shift were Citroën (who made both left-hand and right-hand drive cars) and Morris (who would not bother with left hook until 1934), but Continental makers generally were slow to adopt the "American" driving position. In France and Germany, however, left-hand drive was in the majority by 1925, though in Italy only Fiat would take it up, from 1927 onwards. Upper-class makers, especially the French and Italian ones, preferred right-hand steering because it made sense on Alpine passes; the French *grandes routières* wore it obstinately to the bitter end, and left-hook Lancias were the direct result of an attack on the American market in 1956. In Britain, of course, right-hand floor shift had a long innings in front of it; the arrangement was *de rigueur* on upper-class machinery in 1930 (Sunbeam, for instance, supplied a central lever only to special order), while Rolls-Royce and Bentley fitted it to the final days of manual-transmission cars some twenty-seven years later.

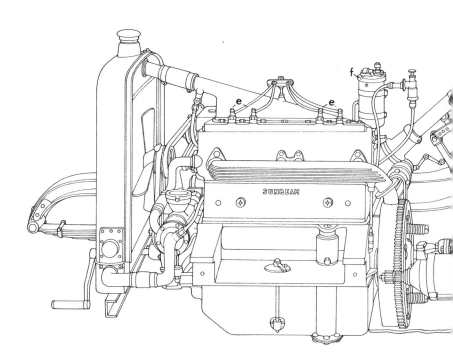

In other respects, this conservative approach to transmissions may seem curious. What Americans disliked, they tended to jettison, this going for the transmission brake, almost extinct in the United States at this stage, and restricted to an emergency role elsewhere since the advent of front-wheel brakes. They disliked shifting gears even more; so why, then, did synchromesh not make its appearance until 1929 (on Cadillacs and La Salles), while Europe's preselectors, already listed on

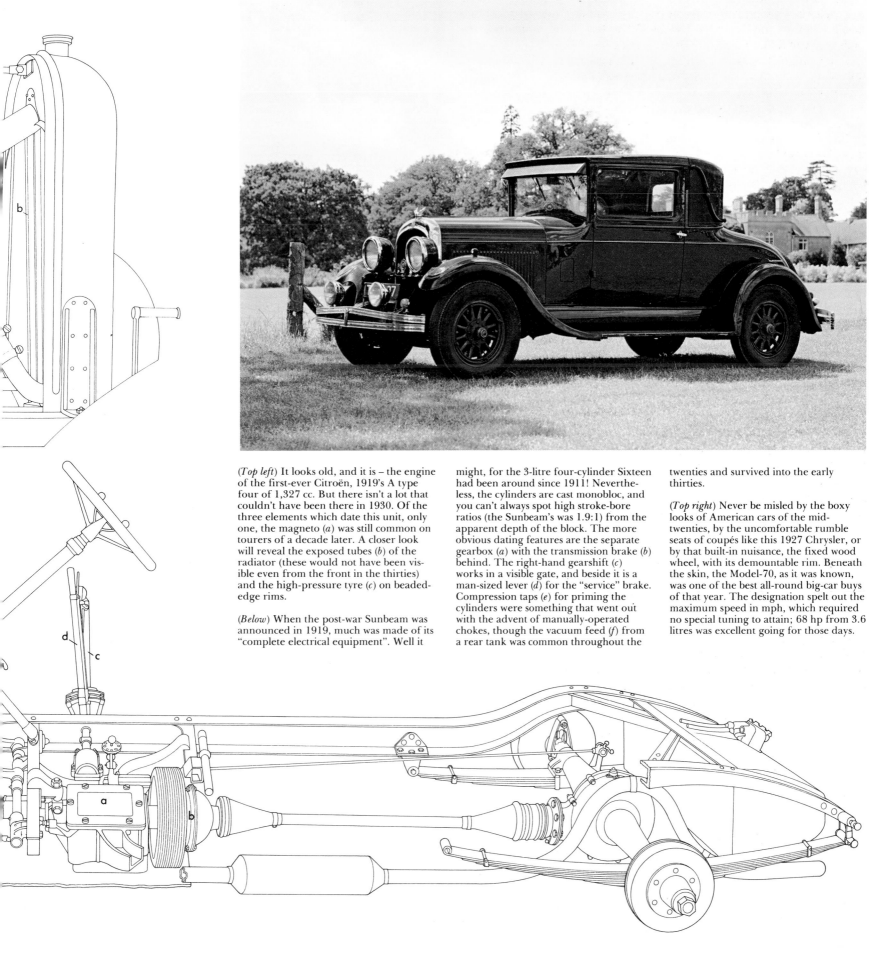

(*Top left*) It looks old, and it is – the engine of the first-ever Citroën, 1919's A type four of 1,327 cc. But there isn't a lot that couldn't have been there in 1930. Of the three elements which date this unit, only one, the magneto (*a*) was still common on tourers of a decade later. A closer look will reveal the exposed tubes (*b*) of the radiator (these would not have been visible even from the front in the thirties) and the high-pressure tyre (*c*) on beaded-edge rims.

(*Below*) When the post-war Sunbeam was announced in 1919, much was made of its "complete electrical equipment". Well it

might, for the 3-litre four-cylinder Sixteen had been around since 1911! Nevertheless, the cylinders are cast monobloc, and you can't always spot high stroke-bore ratios (the Sunbeam's was 1.9:1) from the apparent depth of the block. The more obvious dating features are the separate gearbox (*a*) with the transmission brake (*b*) behind. The right-hand gearshift (*c*) works in a visible gate, and beside it is a man-sized lever (*d*) for the "service" brake. Compression taps (*e*) for priming the cylinders were something that went out with the advent of manually-operated chokes, though the vacuum feed (*f*) from a rear tank was common throughout the

twenties and survived into the early thirties.

(*Top right*) Never be misled by the boxy looks of American cars of the mid-twenties, by the uncomfortable rumble seats of coupés like this 1927 Chrysler, or by that built-in nuisance, the fixed wood wheel, with its demountable rim. Beneath the skin, the Model-70, as it was known, was one of the best all-round big-car buys of that year. The designation spelt out the maximum speed in mph, which required no special tuning to attain; 68 hp from 3.6 litres was excellent going for those days.

Looking Ahead. The BMW Type 315/1 of 1934 is, of course, eclipsed by the legendary 328, surely the best all-rounder of the 1930s. People also tend to be unkind about the 315's ancestry: it was descended from the German Austin Seven via the 303, a pint-sized 1.2-litre six that performed little better than its British contemporaries. The 303 had a short life, but it left some useful legacies – a light twin-tube frame, transverse-leaf independent front suspension, a four-bearing pushrod engine, and a four-speed synchromesh transmission. The stock 315 with single carburettor and 34 hp was fairly uninspired, but the sports model's extra carburettor helped boost output of the 1,490-cc unit to 40 hp and speed to the middle 70s (120 km/h). The cars sold well in Central Europe and Scandinavia, as well as in Britain, where Frazer Nash took them up and were soon doing better with modern Germans than ever they had with their own strictly-bespoke chain-driven machinery. The BMW's brakes were mechanical (though hydraulics had been used on the 303), but by mid-1935, there was a companion 2-litre on the same chassis, sports versions of which were good for over 80 mph (130–135 km/h) on 55 hp. Sales in four seasons amounted to 9,765 315s and 6,646 of the bigger 319s, a creditable performance for the period.

the largest Armstrong Siddeleys, would never make any lasting impact at all?

The plain fact was that Americans chose to dispense with shifting altogether by devoting their efforts to big, slow-turning multi-cylinder engines that did all their work in high gear. Only the steepest hill or worst traffic snarls called for an indirect ratio: "0–70, and never a hand on the lever", was one of the safest and most persistent publicity themes. There was no substitute for cubic inches – or for more cylinders.

The first commercially viable six-cylinder car, of course, dates back to 1904, and the configuration had enjoyed a substantial vogue between 1906 and 1908, with some support from the young proprietary-engine industry. This craze was, however, short-lived; a brief world depression did not help, two extra "pots" meant two more of everything else, and Frederick Lanchester had yet to solve the problems of crankshaft balance. Long and whippy shafts led to tooth-shaking vibration periods. In 1907, Henry Ford might claim that he was the world's largest maker of six-cylinder automobiles, but within a couple of years, he (and almost everyone else) was back with fours. It was thus left to his compatriots to reinstate the type, which they had done by the outbreak of the First World War. By 1918, Cadillac's vee-eight and Packard's vee-twelve were established successes, even if in Europe multi-cylinderism was still the prerogative of the town carriage.

Multi-cylinderism spread down the American market from middle-class to cheap automobiles. In 1924, the four best-selling makes – Ford, Chevrolet, Dodge, and Willys-Overland – offered fours and fours alone, but five years later, Dodge and Chevrolet had added an extra pair of cylinders, John N. Willys backed his successful Whippet Four with a 3-litre six, and the only new four of any significance was Chrysler's Plymouth, a direct descendant of the once-popular Maxwell. And for those who considered a six inadequate, there was the straight-eight, not only smoother than the familiar vees, but blending well with a new stylistic idiom that called for lengthy hoods. The ultimate in multi-cylinderism would arrive, as we shall see, at the depth of the Depression, though it was undoubtedly conceived during the euphoric wave that preceded the stock market crash.

Smaller sixes were also on the way in Europe. In 1925, Renault's most modest six had run to 4.8 litres, while the comparable 510 Fiat was a 3.4-litre town carriage best suited to a paid driver. Opel were likewise toying with some hefty and expensive machinery, but only one British volume-producer (Singer) had a six-cylinder car on the market, and they sold precious few of these. At a higher level, Crossley of Manchester were boasting that four of their cylinders were as good as six of anyone else's, which did not, however, stop them launching their 2.7-litre 18/50 a year later – or selling it to members of the British Royal Family! The 1927 shows, however, would see an interesting race of scaled-down Americana. From Britain came Rover's 2-litre, the 2.2-litre Austin Sixteen, and the 2.5 litre JA-series Morris; Fiat countered with the Tipo 520; and Renault (already doing well with the 3.2-litre Vivasix announced a year previously) were exploring the ultimate in flexibility and gutlessness with the 1.4-litre Mona series. The pint-sized six, however, belongs properly to the 1930s; suffice it to say for the moment that, of the principal cheap European sedans in the 1,900- to 2,500-cc bracket listed in 1930, only such stalwarts as the Austin 12 and the KZ-type Renault remained faithful to four cylinders, and both these were listed alongside parallel sixes. Hillman's 14 had an even less felicitous stablemate in the shape of an unreliable straight-eight, while even the smaller national producers – Skoda of Czechoslovakia and Volvo of Sweden – fell into line. Further, though the Depression would decimate the ranks of the eights – of which there were some ten at peak in Germany alone – most of the sixes would see the lean years out.

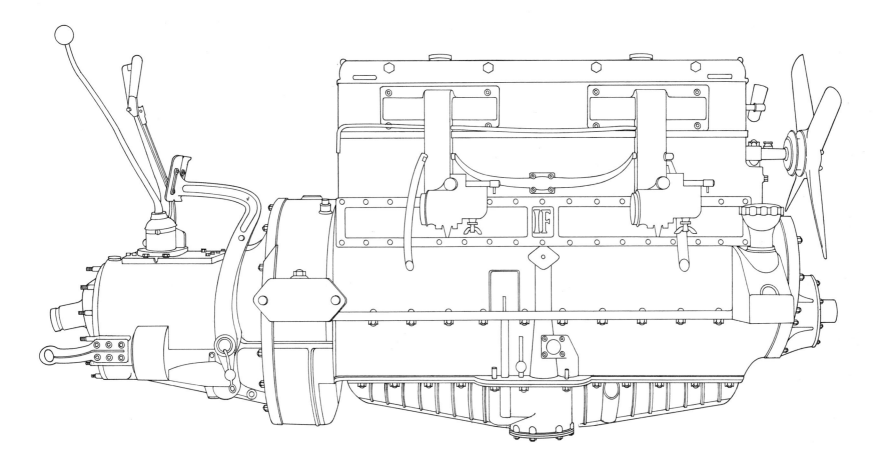

How many cylinders? For luxury and for cars to be driven in, the straight-eight was undoubtedly the smoothest unit in general use in the 1920s, and Isotta Fraschini (*top*) had made nothing else since 1919. This was one of their last, the 8B of 1931–34, with twin Zenith carburettors and an output of 160 hp from 7.4 litres. By the 1930s, a unit gearbox was no longer a heresy in the luxury class, though outside the United States few other makers still considered three speeds sufficient. Certainly they weren't on the 4½-litre Bentley (*below*), where the four forward ratios were high and close and selected on many open models by a right-hand lever mounted *outside* the body. The sixteen-valved overhead-camshaft engine ran to only four cylinders, and ignition was by dual magneto. The standard article, still being made in 1931, gave 110 hp and speeds of 90–95 mph (145–155 km/h), but with the optional supercharger, the main limitation was wind resistance, of which the Bentley had enough! The car was an anachronism, but a splendid one. No wonder some conservative clients preferred the four, with its "bloody thump", signally absent from the companion 6½-litre six.

(*Left*) Volvo in 1933, or a conventional shape covering conventional engineering. The "sit" of the wheels confirms beam axles at both ends, and nothing is streamlined in, least of all the spare wheels in those deep wells: hard work for the girls in the event of a flat, and lovely rain-water traps. The roof-line is more curved than it was in 1929, and the three-speed transmission incorporates a free wheel as well as synchromesh. This device rendered shifting entirely clutchless and improved fuel economy at the price of a loss of engine braking, which is why the more enthusiastic motorist tended to lock the device out and ignore it. As always, your Volvo Six came in a diversity of forms. Standard sedans like this one came on a 116-in (2.95 m) wheel-base, but there were two longer variants for the taxi trade, and an ultra-elongated type for "parade cabriolets", ambulances, and hearses. Such diversification was not peculiar to Volvo; Packard and Cadillac rang the changes on chassis length as well.

(*Below*) The price of an impressive hood and the purr of eight cylinders in line was wasted space, only too clear in this shot of a 1931 first-series CD-type Chrysler unit of 4 litres' capacity. The power unit is classically American – there's just more of it. The down-draught carburettor is not clearly visible, but its air cleaner is. The transmission is, of course, in unit with clutch and engine, but the shift lever has to "come easily to hand", and so it is long,

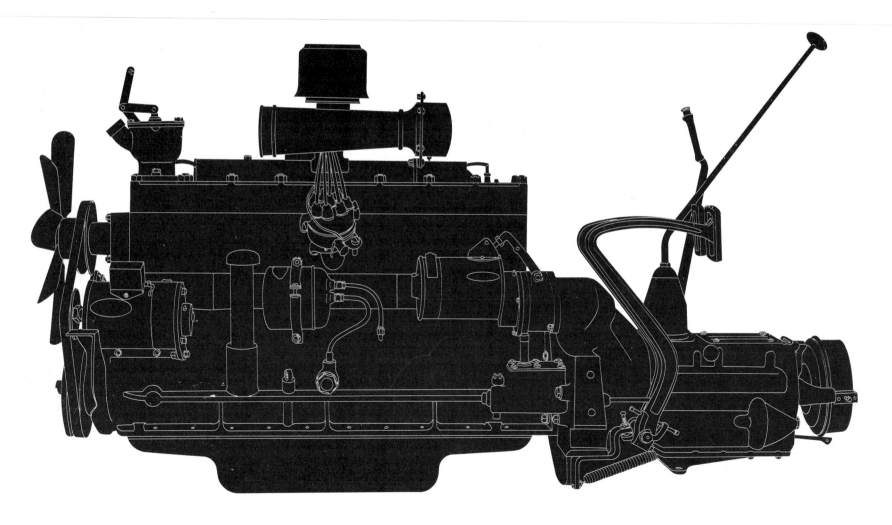

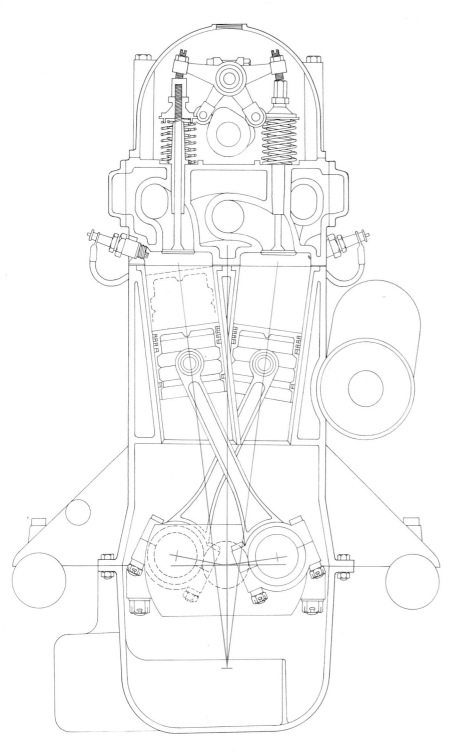

With mass-production came some interesting strides in overall performance. Contrast, for instance, that pioneer of the system, Citroën's 1919 Model A, with its 1929 successor, the AC4.

Engine capacity has gone up by twenty-three per cent – from 1,327 to 1,628 cc – and the 1929 engine is still a side-valve monobloc four. The increase in output – from 18 to 30 bhp – represents, however, a formidable sixty-six per cent, and the AC4 develops its maximum power at 3,000 rpm, not 2,000. Further, while three forward speeds still suffice, the new Citroën rides on a more robust frame with semi-elliptic instead of quarter-elliptic springs, and balloon tyres at 25–30 psi give a softer ride than the old beaded-edge type running at a pressure of 60 psi. There is a lot more car for the money, too: the A-type on its wheelbase of 111.5 in (2.835 m) was a cramped four-seater with only a single door, whereas the AC4 comes as a fully-enclosed, all-steel four-door sedan. Yet it occupies little more space; half an inch of wheelbase and four inches of overall length. The extra weight – 800 lbs (360 kg) odd – has been fully absorbed by the more powerful engine, as is discovered when one takes the wheel. The A-type was flat out at 40 mph (65 km/h), cruising gait being a leisured 37 mph; the 1929 car is good for 56 mph (90 km/h) and settles down comfortably at 47 mph (75 km/h). Fuel consumption, admittedly, is higher, but then fuel is cheaper, and the AC4 with its coil ignition is easier to service. With servo-assisted four-wheel brakes replacing the old rear-wheel and transmission layout, the car stops better. No detailed figures are available for the two Citroëns, but they are available for a brace of comparable Fiats, the 1919 501 and the 1,438-cc 514 introduced late in 1929. The former took a daunting 183 ft (86 m) to pull up from its normal cruising speed of 40 mph, but the latter managed it in 80 ft (24 m), a good year before the colossus of Turin switched to hydraulic actuation. Useless to observe, as vintage-minded diehards will, that the 501 had an engine of sewing-machine sweetness and a delicacy of control which the 514 signally lacked. The latter had all the modern conveniences; it also cost a lot less, being made in relatively larger numbers. Despite the Depression, 514s left the works at a rate of twelve thousand units a year as against eleven thousand for the earlier type. A more significant comment is that the new idiom called for more frequent model changes; the 501, launched at the time of the 1918 Armistice, was still around seven years later, whereas the 514 survived for precisely three model-years – from 1930 to 1932 inclusive.

This highlights one of the less happy aspects of the mass-production game. It could resemble a football league contest run on knockout rules. The choice lies between taking on the big battalions or facing relegation; there is no third division to assure at least a degree of survival for the failures. By 1930, the industry had crystallized into four main sectors: the big volume producers catering for the masses, the middle-class makers bidding in a higher price bracket, the manufacturers of luxury vehicles, and the specialists. A big combine of the type already operative in the United States needed to compete in at least three of these four categories. The same went for their European opposite numbers – in the 1930s, Nuffield in Britain and Auto Union in Germany. This latter empire sold DKWs to the masses, Wanderers to the middle class, and Horchs to the wealthy, success in these three fields compensating for the failure of the front-wheel drive Audi in the specialist sector. Since the latter's sole asset was elegance, one need not wonder that the division reverted to conventional drive on its 1939 models.

The specialists need not concern us at this stage. Their survival depends only on the whims of a tiny minority of the motoring public – and, therefore, on their ability to change direction at the right moment. Morgan's switch from three to four wheels in 1936 typifies such a timely

willowy, and not much more positive in action than the horrible column changes of 1938 onwards. Unusual on an American car is the drum-type transmission brake, strictly for parking. This device was never popular in the United States (when Fiat started to manufacture in New York State in the 'teens, they dropped it from their local variations), but Chrysler defended it on the grounds that it left the entire rear-wheel braking area free for the normal business of stopping!

(*Above*) *Multum in parvo* – or how to evolve a really compact engine without losing out on power. Your usual vee motor had a 60- or 90-degree angle, but during our period (and before), Lancia worked to angles which could be as narrow as 13 degrees and never exceeded 24. This is the original 1922 2.1-litre four-cylinder Lambda (still current in enlarged form as late as 1932), but the technique was applied to everything from the tiny 903-cc Ardea up to big vee-eights like the 4-litre Dilambda. Advantages were a short and rigid crankshaft, a square, box-shaped head with better water circulation, and a simpler valve gear – note the use of a single overhead camshaft where wider vees (the postwar Ferrari and Jaguar, for instance) required one per bank of cylinders. The Lambda block was only 15.5 in (39.4 cm) long, which meant not only more room for passengers, but also underhood access to transmission as well as engine.

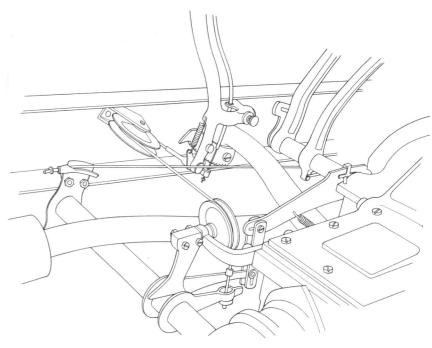

Looking at the 1930 Nash Eight (*above*) one wonders that it still used cable-operated brakes as seen in the drawing (*right*). Would not Americans have sought ways round the constant need of adjustment? The fact was that cables were trusted more than fluids and rubber piping. Of thirty American breeds with pretensions to volume production in 1930, only nine were addicted to hydraulics, these headed by the Chrysler Corporation stable (Chrysler, De Soto, Dodge, and Plymouth). Other significant supporters were Franklin and Graham-Paige: General Motors would not join in till 1934, nor Ford till 1939. The Nash Eight itself, though conventional enough in appearance, had two unusual features: overhead

salvation. Nor were the purveyors of true luxury doomed until after the Second World War – if Minerva and Isotta Fraschini failed to see the decade out, Rolls-Royce, Maybach, and Packard were still very much alive in 1939. But in the two lower echelons – from the Chevrolet–Citroën level to that of Buick and Humber – a savagely competitive element intrudes, with a knock-out battle of manufacturers spanning the inter-war years. The speed of such a battle is geared to the strength of an individual country's industry and of the market it serves, but the result is invariable – fewer manufacturers making more cars at more competitive prices. What started in the United States in 1923 would be reflected in the boom-ridden Japan of the mid-1960s.

In the United States, of course, the biggest combine – and in effect the only one in 1919 – was General Motors, which covered everything from the cut-price Chevrolet up to the Cadillac, by no means the leading luxury marque in those days. Ford had no volume-selling companion car until Lincoln added their cheap V12 Zephyr in 1936, while Walter Chrysler's big build-up occurred in 1928, when he absorbed the profitable Dodge concern and created two brand-new makes, the inexpensive Plymouth and the intermediate De Soto. Yet, in 1928, the Big Three commanded a sizable percentage of the national take – nearly fifty-five per cent of the 4.5 million new automobiles delivered that year.

Thus, a squeeze was inevitable. First to go were the smaller assemblers, whose function was often little more than adding a radiator with badge to an assortment of bought-out components. Typical of these was the Anderson Motor Company, based at Rock Hill, South Carolina, remote from the mainstream industry, despite the fact that it produced something more than a regional make. Advertising was organized on a national basis, and the annual sales potential was, perhaps, three thousand units, all in the capricious middle-class market. Such a set-up

was just viable in 1920, but hopeless in the accelerating tempo of ensuing years. The Anderson Motor Company had called it quits by 1926. Assembled breeds with some cachet – the Jordan, for instance, with its brilliant publicity campaigns – just made it into 1931.

Next on the list of victims were manufacturers proper in the twelve to twenty thousand-a-year bracket, which was not enough to cover more than two sectors of the market. These companies were only safe as long as they retained their key middle-class clientele. In this category fell Chandler-Cleveland, Paige, and Reo; Hupmobile, with a potential of perhaps forty thousand, were higher up the scale but still vulnerable. Alas! middle-class sales were the most capricious and suffered worst in the Depression years. The companies took longer to die, but it was all over by Pearl Harbor. Chandler sold out to Hupmobile in 1929, and seven years later, Reo switched to trucks for good. Paige won a new lease of life in 1927, with the advent of the dynamic Graham brothers, but the resultant Graham-Paige Corporation was in for a slow decline from their 1929 peak of seventy-seven thousand cars. They tried hard with new ideas: the "twin-top" four-speed gearbox in 1929, the revolutionary Blue Streak styling of 1932, and the centrifugally-blown straight-eights of 1934. In 1935, they offered a cheap six at near-Chevrolet price, but even a merger with the ailing Hupmobile empire could not save them. The 1941 Grahams were the last.

Even empires could fall. William C. Durant made his last bid in 1921, with a line-up that embraced (at peak) a challenger for Ford and Chevrolet in the Star, the Durant which "marked" Oakland and Oldsmobile, the Flint in opposition to Buick and the new Chrysler, and the luxurious and conservative Locomobile, more exclusive than any Cadillac or Lincoln. Within two years, the new group had worked its sales up to 172,000 units, but this still gave them only fifth place, and it was a flash in the pan. In 1925, the introduction of an inexpensive

valves and dual ignition. Flathead motors were reserved for their cheaper lines. The big valve-in-head six (if not the eight, which faded in 1942) would continue to power the top Nashes until they started on short-stroke vee-eights in 1955. Many Europeans would regard this Lincoln as the archetype of the American car in the early thirties, and its elegant lines and lengthy hood are typical. The rest isn't, even if one almost expects to see Herbert Hoover or Franklin Delano Roosevelt waving from the back seat – Lincolns were favourite White House wear in those days. The huge K-series was current in various forms from 1932 to 1940, but seldom seen. In 1933, nearly 475,000 Americans bought new Chevrolets and another 335,000 new Fords, but Lincoln's total production was only just over 2,000 cars, and in those sedan-oriented days precisely 88 were tourings of any kind. The open car with side curtains was nearly as dead as the dodo. The few lucky owners, however, were well supplied for their money, usually around $4,500 (£900) of it. The precision built vee-twelve motor gave 150 hp from 7.2 litres, enough to assure this 5,250-pounder (say 2,375 kg) a top speed in the middle 90s (150 km/h).

straight-eight Locomobile gave even better market coverage, but thereafter, the path lay downhill. Nineteen twenty-seven was the Flint's last year, the Star died in 1928, and even token production of Locomobiles had ceased a twelvemonth later. By 1930, Durant's sole passenger-car offering was a six with prices starting at $645 (£120) – just too far above Chevrolet, and sales of 20,900 against Ford's 1,155,162 told their own story. Durant struggled into 1931 with a companion four, but that was the end. Subsequent American and Canadian attempts at a revival came to naught.

Even greater was the fall of Willys-Overland, in the big league since 1910 and never out of the top ten thereafter, despite a financial crisis in 1921. Willys sold 315,000 units in 1929, when their market coverage almost rivalled that of General Motors's, with prices running from $525 to $5,800 (£105 to £1,160). The company had assembly plants in Belgium and Britain, and even a German subsidiary, but the Depression, coupled with a sudden abdication from four-cylinder models, brought the empire down. True, it survived a protracted receivership, but though passenger-car manufacture was not finally abandoned until 1955, Willys would always be an also-ran.

The moral was simple: relegation point was rising inexorably from the three thousand units a year of the early 1920s. By 1931, Hupmobile could still just about make ends meet on annual deliveries of seventeen thousand, but when the "little recession" struck in 1938, sales of thirty-five thousand a year represented desperation point. Of that season's tail-enders, Pierce-Arrow were already bankrupt; Willys, Hupmobile, and Graham were destined for the axe; and Cadillac and De Soto were rescued only by their membership of the Big Battalions, who seldom risked scrapping a major line. (The sole exceptions in our period were two General Motors breeds, Oakland and La Salle. The former was quietly overwhelmed by its cheaper companion-make, Pontiac, while

the La Salle was squeezed out by the bottom end of the Cadillac range and the more expensive Buicks). Nash alone rode out plummeting sales – and survived as an independent for another sixteen years. One may doubt if they would have achieved this but for the Second World War and the ensuing sellers' market.

This pattern of contraction would soon be reflected in Europe. Here small companies proliferated – and they went down like ninepins. In France conservatism and worn-out factories took their toll. So did pressure from the Big Three – Peugeot, Renault, and the upstart André Citroën. Clément-Bayard, Gobron-Brillié, and Mors barely survived the Armistice. The late 1920s would see the demise of such respected names as Charron, de Dion-Bouton, Hurtu, La Buire, Rolland-Pilain, and Turcat-Méry, while Léon Bollée and Rochet-Schneider quit in the early thirties. In Italy Itala never recovered from wartime mismanagement, though as late as 1934, attempts were made to keep things going. German casualties included Dürkopp, Loreley, Phänomen, Presto, and Protos, with NAG. following them into oblivion in 1934. The British story was much the same – as always, it was the middle-class producers who succumbed: Belsize in 1925, Arrol-Johnston in 1929, Star in 1931, in which year Lea-Francis suffered the first of several eclipses. Humber, Sunbeam, and Talbot were absorbed into the Rootes empire, Morris absorbed Wolseley, and Vauxhall became a subsidiary of General Motors, turning out cut-price cars and trucks. Lanchester, once the country's most individual luxury automobile, fell to Daimler and was transformed into an undistinguished middle-class sedan, and a badge-engineered one at that.

Even aspirants to the mass-production stakes suffered the fate of Durant. This was understandable – in a smaller market there was no room for any more contenders, and they picked medium-sized models when the public wanted something smaller. In such British hopefuls as

tended to boost Oldsmobile's then impressive sales by offering an up-market type of automobile listing around the $1,600 (£320) mark. Capacity was 4.2 litres, output 81 hp, and wheel-base 125 in (3.2 m) to the 1930 Oldsmobile's 113.5 in (2.88 m). The motor apart, mechanical elements were predictable, except that fuel was fed by mechanical pump to the Johnson dual-choke carburettor (*c* on the motor drawing below) instead of by the all-too-familiar vacuum system. One expected – and got – a three-speed unit transmission with central floor shift, a single-plate clutch, internal-expanding mechanical four-wheel brakes (the contracting type was on its way out, even in the United States), and semi-elliptic springing. The engine was ingenious, not least of all in its construction; it was the first volume-production vee-eight to feature both banks of cylinders cast monobloc with the upper crankcase, an innovation usually credited to Ford. The carburation apart, the most intriguing feature of the 90-degree Viking eight was its valve gear (*a*). Though of an L-head configuration, it featured horizontal

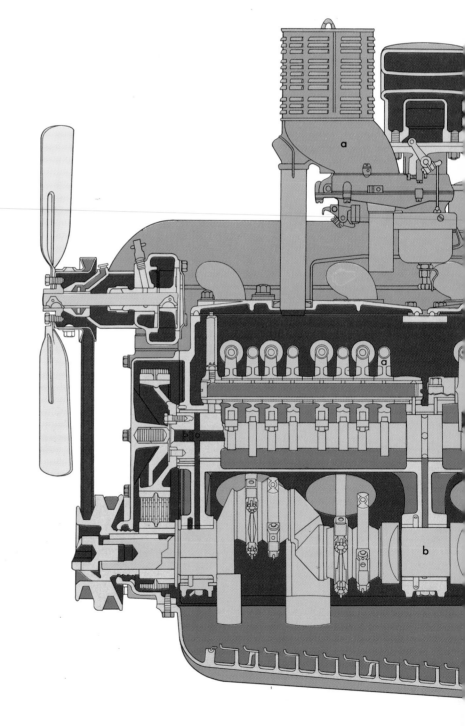

One might call the Oldsmobile Viking an unmitigated flop. It lasted only from April, 1929, until the autumn of 1930, few ventured outside its native United States, and only just over eight thousand attracted buyers. The Depression got there first. Views of the sedan (*left* and *right*) stamp it as unmistakably a late twenties design by General Motors, re-taining wood wheels. The front end treatment with its V-badge (signifying a vee-eight motor as well as the Viking name) is especially reminiscent of Harley Earl's legendary 1929 La Salle, and in convertible guise Oldsmobile's companion make looks very like Cadillac's. But while the La Salle was conceived as a cheaper and lighter Cadillac, the Viking was in-

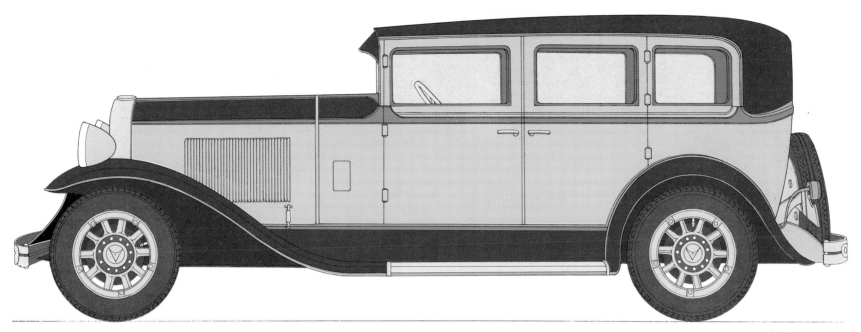

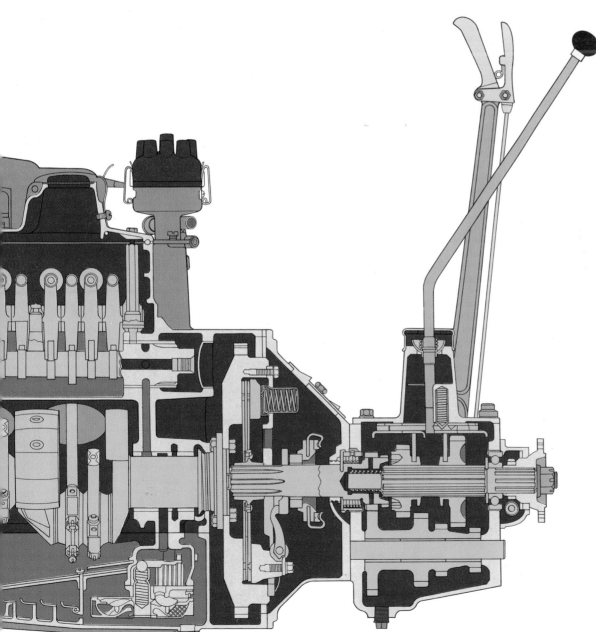

valves parallel with the ground, which gave a more efficient combustion chamber shape and were said to breathe as well as overhead valves. Where the system certainly scored was from the servicing standpoint, since valve adjustment called for no dismantling: the valves could be approached through cover plates within the vee. The three-main-bearing crankshaft (*b*) with 90-degree throws made for good balance. Nothing, alas, can save a fairly expensive middle-class car in a Depression, especially when it bears a new name. The Viking competed not only against the straight-eight Studebaker, the mid-range Chryslers, and the smaller Marmons, it also competed with the more expensive Buicks from the same parent firm. Buick, riding high at the nearly 200,000 units sold in 1929, tumbled to 119,000 in 1930. The Viking never got off the ground, and though General Motors's Oakland Division introduced a rather similar eight-cylinder engine design for 1931, this was Oakland's last year; the unit struggled on into 1932 as power for the more expensive of Pontiac's two lines, thereafter all General Motors's eights save the Cadillac's would preserve the inline configuration until 1949.

Angus-Sanderson, Bean, and Cubitt one can see the ancestors of 1948's Standard Vanguard, though they were killed off by the industrial unrest of 1920–21. By contrast, Clyno in England and Mathis in France were casualties of one and the same ambition – to beat the big battalions with insufficient capital. Clyno's Frank Smith consistently tried to match Morris's prices, and it killed his company in the end. The last straw was his bid for a £100 light car in 1928, something that even Morris would not achieve until three years later. In terms of sheer volume and survival, Emile Mathis fared rather better: his company was good for nearly twenty thousand units a year in 1927, and it kept going until 1935. It was, however, the same old story. Citroën's sales were a cool sixty thousand, and even he would run out of money when he tried to launch his new *traction* in 1934. Further, Citroën's exciting new experiment warranted a rescue bid from Michelin, whereas Mathis had nothing to offer save factory capacity. Thus, he suffered the same fate as a lesser rival, Jérome Donnet: he was bought up by foreign interests anxious to circumvent France's swingeing import duties. Donnet's plant made licence-built Fiats, and Mathis's Ford V8s. One cannot help adding an ironic postscript to show that the game of contraction never ends: Ford-France, hovering at the bottom of the first division in 1954, were snapped up by Simca, the erstwhile French Fiat operation. Ten years later, Simca, unable to fight unaided against the Big Three, were themselves absorbed by Chrysler International!

As for the assemblers, they fell by the wayside. At the 1923 London Show could be seen such native breeds as Airedale, Albatros, Autocrat, Bayliss-Thomas, Eric-Campbell, Eric-Longden, GWK, Hampton, Horstman, McKenzie, Marseal, Meteorite, NP, Seabrook, Turner, Waverley, Westcar, and Whitlock. Countless others could not even afford a stand. Most of them used such familiar components as Meadows or Coventry-Climax engines, and Moss gearboxes. Some had their engaging idiosyncracies – GWK's friction drive or Horstman's kick starter – but none of them were at Olympia in 1931, even if a handful preserved a token existence. The Whitlock, for instance, had transformed itself from an over-priced 1.5-litre challenger to Morris to a rival for the expensive Lagondas in the 3-litre category, but it profited the car not at all. Lagonda themselves were in trouble but were to survive a receivership in 1935.

In other respects the picture was the same as in the United States. Only the ante was lower. Of the less expensive runners-up, Singer of Coventry were just about a viable operation in 1939, with a potential of maybe nine thousand cars a year. Of middle-class makers, Riley and Triumph kept out of the receiver's hands until the eve of the Second World War, while rearmament saved one German contemporary, Stoewer, from trouble. In France, Berliet and Unic survived thanks to their heavy diesel trucks.

There remains one further legacy of the 1920s – better roads. If Australia's bitumen was a Second World War phenomenon, and if the first of the American freeways – the Pennsylvania Turnpike, following the route of a disused railroad – did not open until October, 1940, there were earlier influences at work. Not, be it said, in Britain, where primitive bypasses (we would now dismiss them as "inner ring roads") represented the limit to which cheeseparing governments would go. Nor yet in Germany: in 1930, Adolf Hitler's Thousand Year Reich lay three years in the future.

Italy's *autostrade* had, however, been authorized in 1925, in the shape of preliminary stretches linking Milan and Cremona, and Brescia and Verona. Subsequent plans embraced all the country's major cities, and by 1932, 387 miles (623 km) of *autostrade* were open. Longest of the continuous runs was the 136-mile (219 km) stretch – Turin–Milan–Brescia.

Not all assembled cars were small and cheap. The London-built Whitlock (*centre*) had started as a copybook 1.5-litre Eleven, but by the end of the decade (the breed lasted into 1930–31), it had become a luxury competitor for Invicta, Lagonda, and Sunbeam, using the 3.3-litre valve-in-head Meadows six. Promoted as "The Six that Satisfies", it was hardly ever seen, albeit Whitlock fitted a radiator which might have been mistaken for a product of their more illustrious neighbours, Bentley Motors, also building cars in Cricklewood at that time. The big brake drums heightened the resemblance, but only about thirty 20/70 Whitlocks were sold.

The baby car of a past decade. In 1930, the Austin Seven was beginning to be old hat. Outside the United States, the splash-lubricated engine was *démodé*, and un-coupled four-wheel brakes were unacceptable everywhere. Austin, indeed, were just about to link all four wheels to the pedal and remove some of the more hazardous pleasures from 7-hp motoring, albeit a clutch with a pedal travel that felt a fraction of an inch was still with us and would be until the end in 1939. Herbert Austin's Baby was, nevertheless, the effective prototype of the modern miniature car, and in 1930, it was being built under licence in three foreign countries – the American Austin Co. of Butler, Pennsylvania, were launching a left-hook edition, Dixi of Eisenach (recently taken over

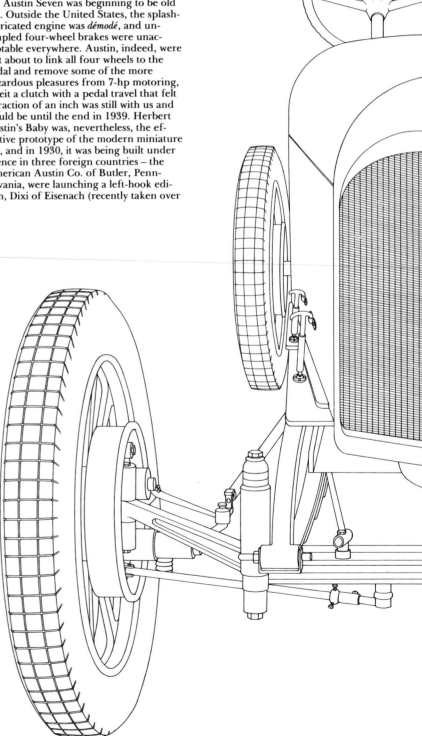

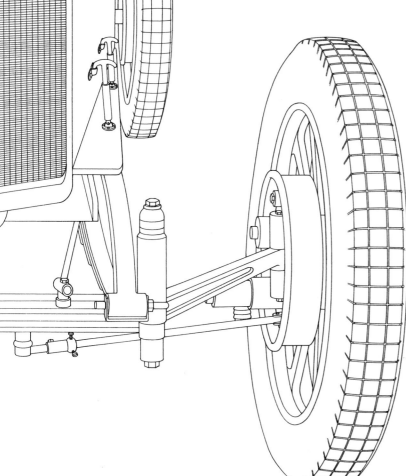

by BMW) handled German production, and Lucien Rosengart supplied the French market. Of these, the Rosengart was the least-publicized, yet stayed longest in the game, their 1952–53 Ariette retaining unmistakable traces of an Austin origin. Here is an early example from 1928–29: it's almost pure Baby Austin in a Rue de la Paix frock, even if the usual soup-plate wheel discs are missing from this roadster. The wide, ribbon-type radiator shell was very similar to that of the BMW-built Dixi, and the hood line is lower than a native Austin's. Prices paralleled those of the British prototype, at around the £110–120 ($550–600) mark, though despite a dealer chain in France said to be 2,500 strong, the little car never really caught on: Frenchmen wanted bigger cars like the 8CVs of Citroën and Renault. By 1931, the Rosengart was show-

ing a greater degree of sophistication, with semi-elliptic springs at the rear, and the last pre-war 4CVs were quite stylish, if a little too like Simca's version of the Fiat Balilla in appearance. The company even essayed something that Austin was wise enough to avoid: a species of Gallic Wolseley Hornet using a 1,097-cc six-cylinder motor in a lengthened (but not reinforced) frame. This one had the refinement of vacuum-servo brakes, while Rosengart would later try to challenge Citroën with a front-wheel drive car built under German Adler licence. This failed: and though the company fared somewhat better (around a thousand units sold) with a sporty 2-litre *Supertraction* using 11CV Citroën mechanical elements, they reverted in the end to gallicized Baby Austins.

Though fully lit at night, these were not, initially at any rate, dual carriageways in the modern sense. Mussolini, however, made them self-financing by the imposition of tolls. Curiously, the foreign press was not wholly appreciative. A contemporary report lamented not only the "deadly monotony", but also "the comparatively moderate speed at which drivers travel over them". Maximum speed was, of course, cruising speed, but this particular observer was surprised to find that neither was much in excess of 40 mph (65 km/h).

His explanation was, nevertheless, the correct one. "There appears", the report continues, "to be a critical speed at which all cars become noisy, tiring to handle, and uncomfortable to ride in." This certainly applied to the ill-damped suspensions, rigidly-mounted engines, and low rev limits of the middle 1920s – and in Italy roads had anticipated car design. Jano's brilliant new overhead-camshaft Alfa Romeos and Vincenzo Lancia's Lambda were too expensive for the average Italian, who had to make do with small Fiats and Bianchis and the more austere species of Ansaldo. Hence, the 1930s would see a new generation of short-stroke, high-revving engines in small family sedans. And if Germany's more dramatic *Autobahn* network would breed some in-teresting exercises in aerodynamics and high gearing, the 1932 Shows would introduce the world to two of the outstanding small cars of the era, the Lancia Augusta and the 508 Fiat, even though the latter would not reach its full flowering until the advent of the *millecento* version (Type 508C) in 1937.

To summarize the *autostradale* influence, let us take a look back to 1930 and the 514. In seven years, cylinder capacity had been substantially reduced – from 1,438 to 1,089 cc. Also down was weight – from just over 2,200 lb (1,000 kg) to a mere 1,874 lb (850 kg). The Millecento was more compact, measuring only 13 ft 3 in (4.05 m) from stem to stern. First-class hydraulic brakes and sophisticated suspension were only to be expected, but whereas a 514 would work laboriously up to 55 mph (90 km/h) and cruise at 45 mph (75 km/h), a good 508C would exceed 70 mph (115 km/h) and could be held at 65 mph (105 km/h) all day. Better still, its motorway-inspired aerodynamics, if not as spectacular as some of its German contemporaries, permitted a fuel consumption in the region of 35 mpg (8 lit/100).

Not all the concomitants of "pure transportation" were dull.

The extreme in the bespoke. Duesenberg made precisely 470 cars between 1929 and the end in 1937, and nothing cost less than $13,500 (£2,700) even in the United States. Though there were factory-approved bodies, a run of forty of any individual style was exceptional, while by 1935, when this SJ Airflow Coupé was built, fabric as a body rather than a top covering had been obsolete for four years.

A one-off by Bohman and Schwartz of Pasadena, this one reputedly set its owner back more than twenty grand (say £4,000). The rear seats had to be of opera type owing to the restricted headroom, and chromium plating was, exceptionally, limited to bumpers, hubcaps, and radiator shell. Even the side panels of the hood – usually cluttered up with assorted bright-work – are uncommonly restrained.

Chapter 2

PAINLESS SOPHISTICATION

The last ten years of peace were years of transition. At heart, this transition was sociological rather than technical. The automobile was at last emerging for good from its initial role as a rich man's plaything. Women drivers, hitherto a rarity outside the United States, were becoming more numerous in other countries; hence, engineering departments had to work still harder in the pain-killing department than they had done in the 1920s. Pressure lubrication, coils, cellulose, and chromium plate were not enough.

As we have seen, mass production was by no means unknown in Europe. By the end of the 1920s, Citroën, Peugeot, Renault, and Mathis in France, Opel in Germany, Fiat in Italy, and Austin, Morris, and Standard in England were capable of substantial annual outputs. Typical figures for 1929, the last pre-Depression season, were Morris, 63,522 units, Fiat, 42,780, and Opel, 34,578. These might be a drop in the bucket beside Ford's 1.5 million and Chevrolet's 950,000. They could not even match the 92,034 turned out by Chrysler, a strictly middle-class make – comparable European breeds in this price-class would have been content with a mere 10,000. There was no doubt, however, which way the wind was blowing. Even in 1932, Fiat, with one of Europe's weakest home markets behind them, managed to sell nearly 20,000 cars, of which over half stayed in Italy.

Labour might still be cheap, but capital was scarce. Therefore, to stay in the game, one had to turn out plenty of standardized vehicles in the cheapest possible way. The rat race had, however, not reached the alarming proportions to be encountered in the 1950s; a small maker with no particular *cachet* (Singer in England, for instance, or La Licorne in France) could get by on annual sales well below the ten thousand mark. Volvo of Sweden, who were on the way up, were as yet virtually unknown outside Scandinavia, yet with the aid of a healthy truck business they managed happily on a mere two or three thousand passenger cars a year. Economic stringency did, however, tend to produce too many restatements of warmed-over American themes, even if these showed themselves at their worst in the styling department. It also delayed the adoption of such progressive ideas as unitary construction and all-independent springing, which would have involved retooling on a formidable scale. It is worth remembering that, in 1932, it cost the Chrysler Corporation $9 million to convert the Plymouth engine plant from four- to six-cylinder types; hence, there was an alarming tendency to "change the colour of the upholstery and call it next year's model!". Despite the fiercely competitive tenor of the market, even the biggest firms worked on a two to three-year design cycle, ringing the changes on mechanical and styling improvements. The American Fords of 1933 and 1934 were virtually identical in both mechanical and styling departments, while Morris's major chassis and body changes announced during the summer of 1935 were not complemented by an engine redesign until the 1938 model year.

The world was edging gingerly into the motorway age. France's *routes nationales* might still be much as Napoleon I left them, and Britain might be wedded to perilous three-lane highways barely adequate to the 40 mph (65 km/h) cruising speeds to which her citizens were addicted, but the Italian *autostrade* were already a *fait accompli*, and the first German *Autobahnen* would be opened in 1935. Before the United States entered the Second World War, she would have her Pennsylvania Turnpike, herald of the coming freeway system. Thus, to the economic parameters that faced a designer in our period was added the need for a car capable of cruising at a sustained 60 mph (100 km/h) without either becoming airborne or showering reciprocating parts all over the road.

The state of the art in 1930 was not vastly different from that of 1920. The game had its rules, and the rules themselves were governed, as they had been for more than thirty years, by the *système* Panhard – a water-cooled engine with vertical cylinders mounted at the front of a chassis frame and driving the rear wheels through the medium of a friction clutch and a selective, sliding-type gearbox. Bevel-type rear axles predominated, and the suspension consisted of a leaf spring at each of the corners.

This covered almost every car on the market. Twin-cylinder power units, admittedly, were found in a few cyclecar hangovers and sub-utility models such as the British Jowett. Tatra in Czechoslovakia and Franklin in the United States preferred air cooling. Rear-engined cars cropped up from time to time – from the austere little Hanomag Kommissbrot recently retired from production in Germany to the aeroplane-fuselage shape of the costly straight-eight Burney Streamline (one of these latter had lately been commissioned by the heir to the British throne). Lancia of Italy built not only chassis-less cars but threw in independently-sprung front wheels as well, while the German Röhr boasted independent rear suspension into the bargain. On some British Alvises and American Cords and Ruxtons, the engine drove the front wheels. Peugeot followed the example of many a heavy-truck maker, preferring worm to bevel drive for their rear axles. These exceptions, nevertheless, served principally to prove the rule. "Putting the works up one end" still represented rank heresy, and any French designer would have been deeply shocked had he been informed that within less than half a century not a single model produced in the *système* Panhard's homeland would conform to the dictates of that system.

The Franklin Airman Sedan (*centre left*) of 1930. The heresies of the air-cooled Franklin were concealed beneath an orthodox exterior and had been since 1925, when Ralph Hamlin, the Los Angeles distributor, threatened to cancel his agency if the car wasn't given a "radiator" that looked like everyone else's. The result was elegant, especially when clothed with one of Franklin's exotic "factory customs", pleasing if hardly economic to offer once production fell below four thousand a year. The steering wheel spider (*bottom*) reflected Herbert Franklin's credo of "scientific light weight", being of aluminium. Bakelite was likewise replacing wood on rims. The six-cylinder Franklin engine (*opposite, bottom*) is immediately identifiable by its separate "pots" and by the huge sirocco fan keyed to the nose of the crankshaft. The shroud directed the air down a duct to the top of the cylinders, whence it passed downwards through the medium of steel or copper fins. The small oil tank alongside the fan supplies lubricant to the valve rockers. Clutch and transmission are the usual copybook American, though Franklin didn't adopt four-wheel brakes until 1928, and all their cars save the last vee-twelves and the cut-price Olympics featured wooden frames and full-elliptic springing.

True, there had been some significant advances. If full electrics had been *de rigueur* everywhere by 1922 at the latest, the need to cater for a broader, unmechanically-minded public had recently led to the abandonment of the magneto in favour of the coil and battery. Only sports and luxury models still clung to the older arrangement; on the latter, this tended to serve as a supplementary ignition. Four-wheel brakes, a sensation of the 1919 Shows, were now universal practice, even Ford and Chevrolet having surrendered to modernity on their 1928 models. With four-wheel brakes had come the balloon tyre, but the only other fundamental mechanical change had been the adoption of the silent, helical-bevel rear axle, which eliminated the endemic growlings of many an early-vintage machine. It was unkindly said that, on the cheaper axles of the 1930s, some warning of impending collapse was needed! (The old straight-bevel axles growled most of the time, whereas, on the later types, growls and whines were warnings of approaching trouble.)

In other respects, however, the period's major developments were aesthetic, cosmetic, and concerned with creature comforts.

Catering for the laity, who understood neither the Otto cycle nor the functions of a clutch, presented headaches in itself, even without the attentions of a cost accountant. Engines, admittedly, were now generally reliable and needed no drastic attention. It was not until the spread of motorways in the 1960s, for instance, that it became almost mandatory to endow an inline four-cylinder power unit with five robust main bearings instead of the three that were general practice in the 1930s –

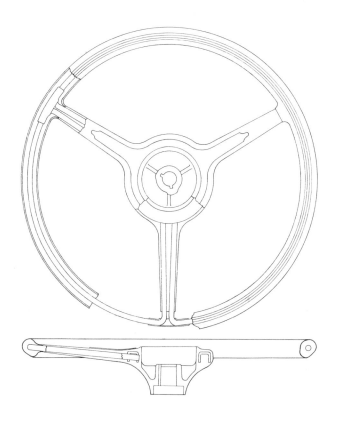

Two by General Motors – and one out-sider. The origins of the 1937 Chevrolet (*opposite, top right*) and 1931 Opel (*right*) are unmistakable, though six years sepa-rate them. Chevrolet were, of course, long-standing advocates of upstairs valves on their splash-lubricated motors. By 1937, we have such amenities as coil-spring independent front suspension, synchromesh, hydraulic brakes, and hypoid back axles, none of them to be en-countered on the German car. In any case, Europe's harsher fiscal climate and higher fuel prices called for a smaller and more frugal six than the Chevrolet, which ran to 3.2 litres even in 1931. The flat-head Opel disposed of 1.8 litres and 32 hp, and it was probably more automobile than the average German could afford to run. The company did well to sell over thirty thousand in three seasons. Finally, as a total contrast, the 1936 1½-litre Riley Adelphi sedan (*opposite, top left*). Here, the sole American influence is in the integral rear trunk with its external access. The rest of it is one hundred per cent British: handbuilt wood-framed coachwork, centre-lock wire wheels, a high-efficiency overhead-valve four-cylinder hemi-head engine, and a four-speed Wilson pre-selective transmission. In standard form, 70 mph (112 km/h) were about the limit, but its price of £350 ($1,750) matched the local figure for a Master Chevrolet fairly closely, and by buying British you saved £9 ($45) a year in circulation tax.

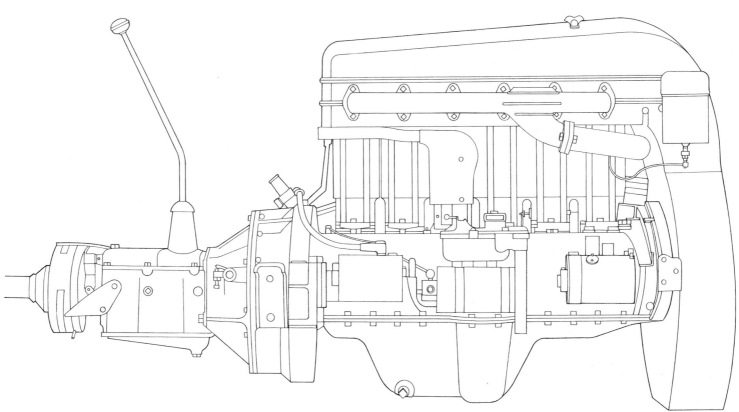

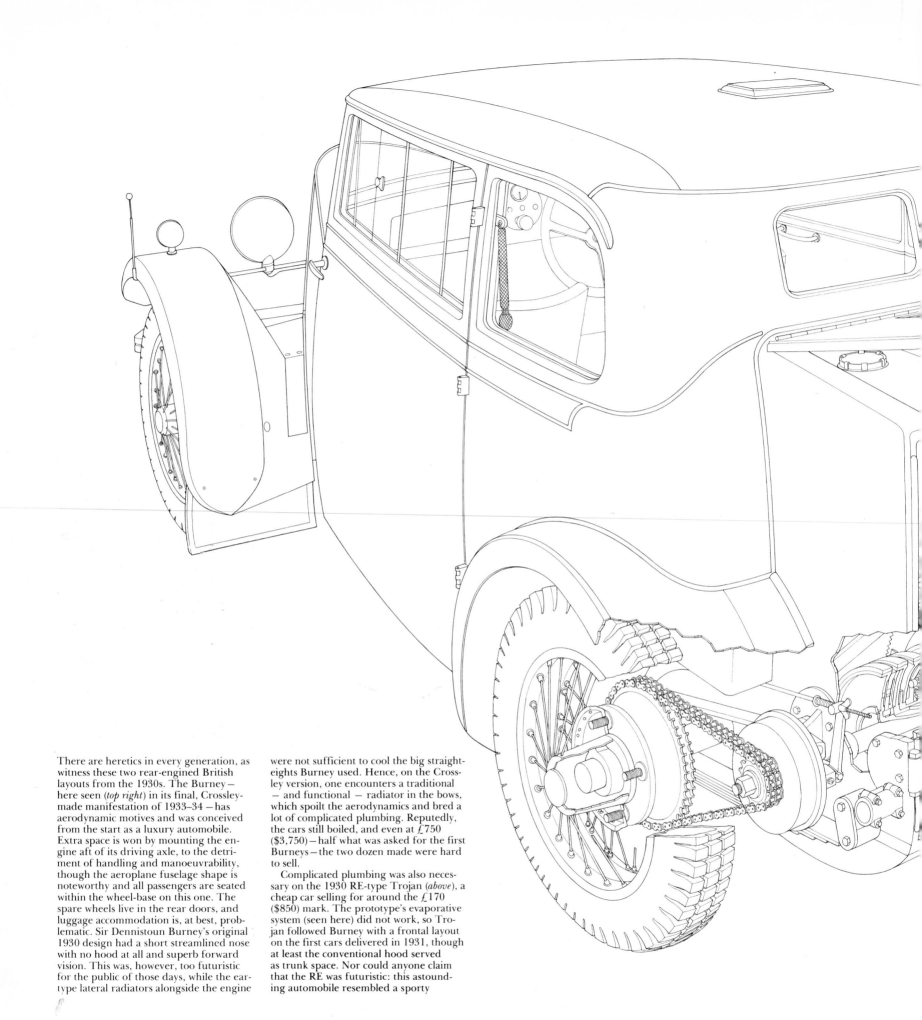

There are heretics in every generation, as witness these two rear-engined British layouts from the 1930s. The Burney — here seen (*top right*) in its final, Crossley-made manifestation of 1933–34 — has aerodynamic motives and was conceived from the start as a luxury automobile. Extra space is won by mounting the engine aft of its driving axle, to the detriment of handling and manoeuvrability, though the aeroplane fuselage shape is noteworthy and all passengers are seated within the wheel-base on this one. The spare wheels live in the rear doors, and luggage accommodation is, at best, problematic. Sir Dennistoun Burney's original 1930 design had a short streamlined nose with no hood at all and superb forward vision. This was, however, too futuristic for the public of those days, while the ear-type lateral radiators alongside the engine

were not sufficient to cool the big straight-eights Burney used. Hence, on the Crossley version, one encounters a traditional — and functional — radiator in the bows, which spoilt the aerodynamics and bred a lot of complicated plumbing. Reputedly, the cars still boiled, and even at £750 ($3,750) — half what was asked for the first Burneys — the two dozen made were hard to sell.

Complicated plumbing was also necessary on the 1930 RE-type Trojan (*above*), a cheap car selling for around the £170 ($850) mark. The prototype's evaporative system (seen here) did not work, so Trojan followed Burney with a frontal layout on the first cars delivered in 1931, though at least the conventional hood served as trunk space. Nor could anyone claim that the RE was futuristic: this astounding automobile resembled a sporty

fabric sedan of the period, with its semi-cycle fenders and rounded vee-radiator. Nothing was, however, the way it looked, as the drawing shows. The vertical four-cylinder two-cycle motor drove forward by roller chain to the axle via a three-speed epicyclic transmission, and (incredibly) there were no brakes on the front wheels, even in 1935, the RE's last season. Unlike the original Trojan, a rustic automobile which could climb anything on which the wheels could get a grip, the RE was nobody's favourite. It was overweight, underpowered, and tended to boil on hills. In any case, a cruising speed of 37 mph (60 km/h) and a maximum of 45 (72 km/h) were no longer adequate, even in Britain. Not much more than a hundred REs found buyers. Thereafter, Trojan, though still loyal to the two-cycle motor, confined their efforts to light trucks.

smaller Fiats and Singers, indeed, continued to manage with two. Rates of rotation, though going up, remained modest. The average 1930 American engine developed its maximum output at around 3,200 rpm, at which speed simple splash lubrication sufficed for Chevrolet, Ford, and Hudson, among others. Pressure systems had, however, long been general practice in Europe. Even in 1939, 4,000 rpm represented an acceptable limit on a touring car, albeit one important by-product of *Autobahn* influence was the narrowing of stroke-bore ratios. We have already encountered the small Fiats of the 1920s, but they remain classic examples of the way things were going. The company's standard small car of 1929, the 509A, had cylinder dimensions of 2.24×3.82 in $(57 \times 97$ mm$)$, and as the machine was overbodied and undergeared, it was revving its heart out at 50–55 mph (80–90 km/h). Its 1938 counterpart of only slightly greater capacity but shorter stroke – 2.68×2.95 in $(68 \times 75$ mm$)$ – developed half as many brake horses at 4,400 rpm and carried four people at an easy 70 mph (115 km/h). As for the 6,000 rpm commonplace in modern 1,100-cc sedans, this would have been acceptable only on the racing circuits, and beyond both the metallurgical and sound-damping capabilities of any maker. It is also fair to say that the necessary quality of tyres and fuel for the fulfilment of the ensuing performance would also have been unthinkable in 1939 – or in 1949, for that matter.

More power was certainly available: 20–22 bhp a litre was common-place at the beginning of our decade, but even "cooking" engines would be good for an honest 30 bhp by 1940. By this time, too, there was a marked swing from side valves to the greater efficiency of pushrod-operated overhead valves. This was, however, as far as the average volume producer would venture. Upstairs camshafts with their chain or gear drives were considered too noisy for family sedans and too expen-sive for the cost accountants. The sophisticated valve gears of Riley (pushrods, twin high-set camshafts, and hemispherical combustion chambers), Singer (single overhead camshaft), and Salmson (twin over-head camshafts) were not copied by rivals. Morris and Fiat tried over-head camshafts and then retreated in the face of costing and mainte-nance problems. Even in the rarefied realm of the luxury car, the

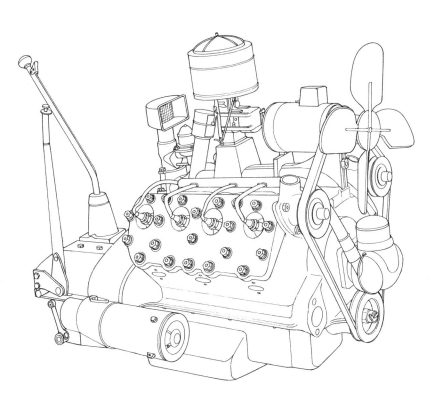

The rear-engined 150H Mercedes-Benz (*top*) is an oddity of 1934–35, and a forgotten one at that. Only 25 were made, though at least 6,500 of the touring 130H and 170H sedans and cabrio-limousines found buyers between 1934 and 1939. This odd creature resembled a long-tailed, notchback Volkswagen, though the engine was a water-cooled L-head four and hung over the rear "axle" at the end of a central backbone frame with all-independent suspension. Hatch space under the short hood (*bottom left*) was very limited, and a standard suitcase just would not fit, so the manufacturers offered a special fitted suitcase.

Ford's legendary 221-cu. in. (3,622 cc) flathead vee-eight engine (*bottom right*). V for voluminous body space and for less space wasted on the engine. This was used by Ford's overseas operations as well as by the parent factory, between 1932 and 1942, and after the Second World War as well. The vee-eight gave the power of eight cylinders from a unit that had the length of a four-cylinder engine, though on a wide-angle unit (90 degrees) like the

Ford, it was not really viable to use the same chassis as for a four-cylinder car, even if Ford did just that in 1932 and 1933.

Two essays in compactness, the 1930 Lancia Lambda with vee-four engine (*top*) and the 1935 German Ford with vee-eight engine (*centre*), and one car that demonstrates the straight-eight of the period — "an automobile of which at least half the length is hood" — the Horch 853A of 1938 (*bottom*).

Lancia's Lambda had the ultimate in compact power units, a vee-four with an angle of only 13 degrees between banks, and a block only 22 in (56 cm) long. Thus, despite the fact that the company did not use a unit gearbox, a very large proportion of the available wheel-base length (122 in or 3.23 m in the case of short-chassis cars) could be used for bodywork. This also made long-chassis cars very long indeed: even tourers could seat eight.

Once one had left the engine behind, Ford engineering was uninspiring. The three-speed synchromesh transmission was common to virtually every other American car, brakes were mechanical, and suspension was the classical Ford transverse-leaf type at both ends, admirable for assaults on muddy tracks and ploughed fields, but terribly bouncy elsewhere. The short wheel-base (112 in or 2.8 m) did not help either, though on the 1935 line they moved the engine over the front axle, thus sacrificing the elegance of the earlier Model-40 in favour of more body space and rear seats within the wheel-base. Differences between native and foreign strains of the Ford V8 (the car was also made in Britain, France, and Australia, as well as Germany) were mainly stylistic, rather than mechanical, though cars of entirely German or British origin retained mechanical brakes up to the outbreak of the Second World War. Only the practised eye can tell that this car comes from Cologne, rather than from Dearborn, Dagenham, Poissy, or Geelong.

Horch were wedded to eight-cylinder engines and made nothing else from 1926 to 1939, apart from a handful of prohibitively expensive vee-twelves. Significantly, though, they chose the more compact type of power unit for their middle-class line. During the same period, they turned out between three and four thousand straight-eights, the "sporting" 853 series (shown here) accounting for a round thousand of them. The 4.9-litre ten-bearing single overhead-camshaft engine, developed in 1930–31 by Fiedler and Schleicher to replace a less-than-satisfactory twin-camshaft unit, gave only 120 hp, and on a car like this, it was hardly reasonable to expect more than 80 mph (130 km/h). Nor did one get it. Most cars later than 1935 had the transverse-leaf independent front suspension, shown here (*bottom left*) on the smaller and relatively inexpensive 830B of 1937, and semi-elliptic leaf springs at the rear. However, up to the end, in 1939, some Horchs (usually long-chassis limousines) were still being delivered with beam axles at both ends.

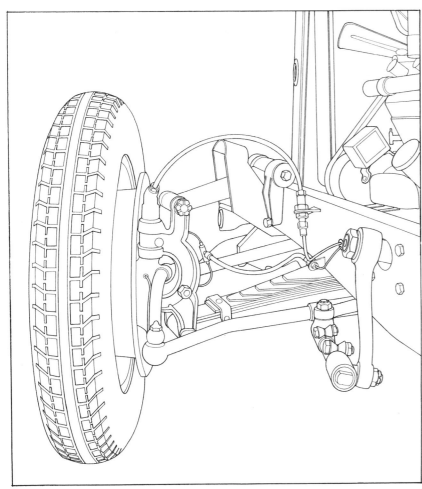

The 7.1-litre sleeve-valve Daimler engine (*right*) announced at the 1926 Shows served as the prototype for the company's twelve-cylinder units marketed up to 1935 and was truly a Double Six. Here, the twin water pumps (*a*), magnetos (*b*), and distributors (*c*) are visible, but the engine also had an individual four-jet carburettor for each block of cylinders. The engine gave 150 bhp at 2,480 rpm and needed to do so, since a chassis alone weighed over two tons, making limousines on the longest 163-in (4.1 m) wheel-base three-tonners. Incredibly, a sports chassis with underslung frame was marketed in 1930, but even on the 150-in (3.8 m) wheel-base, its appearance was almost a parody of classic themes, with 7 ft (2.1 m), no less, of hood. Five mpg (56 lit/100) on petrol and 350 mpg on lubricating oil meant that Double Sixes were for the wealthiest citizens only.

More cylinders mean flexibility, silence, and freedom from audible power impulses, but it is easy to see from this 1931 Maybach DS8 Zeppelin (*below* and *opposite*) why better sound-damping methods were

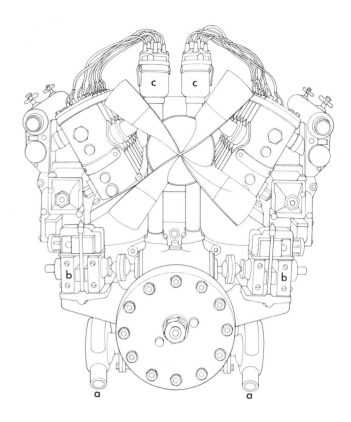

so welcome. Of 8 litres' capacity, the pushrod overhead-valve Maybach developed 200 bhp. Mounting the blocks at 60 degrees made for a fairly compact width, but length was another matter: a 4-litre six, after all, is quite long. The motor used every inch of space under a hood that was 7 ft (2.1 m) long, which explains why not a few Maybach hoods employed full-length lifting handles. Note the centrally mounted camshaft (*a*), the individual dual-choke carburettor (*b*) for each bank of cylinders, and the massive eight-bearing crankshaft (*c*). Even with liberal use of light alloys — the block was of silumin — the motor alone weighed 1,100 lb (just over 500 kg), or not much less than a Fiat 126 of our own times. A complete Zeppelin could turn the scales at close on 8,400 lb (3,800 kg). With prices that could run up as high as $40,000 (the equivalent of £8,000 then) in the United States, sales were understandably modest: probably not more than three hundred twelve-cylinder Maybachs of all types in ten years. Not shown here is perhaps the oddest aspect of the design — the transmission.

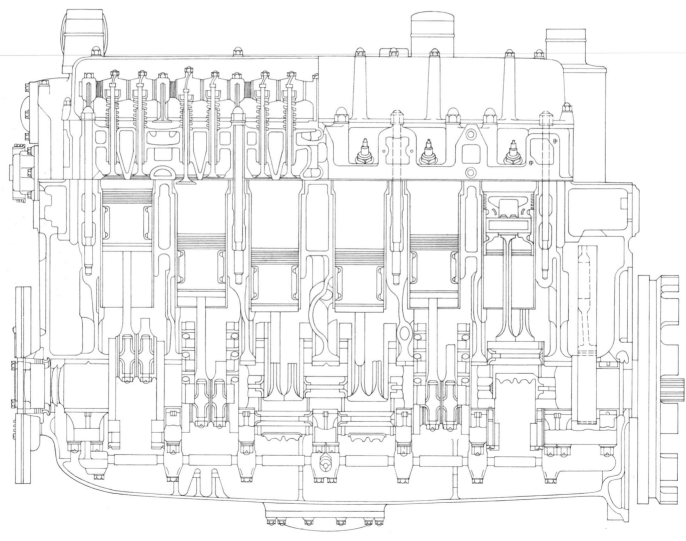

German Horch, which entered our period with a twin overhead-camshaft power unit, soon converted to the simpler single-camshaft layout. In any case, the development of high-octane fuels essential to greater mechanical sophistication was delayed by the Second World War. In Britain, the short-stroke unit was also delayed by the War, as well as by an unenlightened fiscal policy which took into consideration only the bore of the cylinders.

As to ancillaries, gravity feed still had its adherents, but the complexities of the vacuum system caused the simpler mechanical pump, by now universal in the United States, to gain ground fast elsewhere. Electric pumps, though favoured in mountainous countries owing to their relative freedom from air locks, were too complicated for the new generation of motorists, though the Nuffield Group in England adopted them successfully from 1932 onwards, and sold SU systems (made by one of their subsidiaries, Skinner Union) to a number of other British firms, notably Rover and SS. A captive source can be an excellent motivation, and the SU pump worked well, though over-electrification can present problems in the case of a flat battery.

Sheer power was, of course, secondary to smoothness and flexibility, and in this department the standardization of rubber engine mounts was perhaps the most important step. This improvement was not, however, universally accepted until 1933–34, and in the meantime, other aids to flexibility had to be explored.

The obvious aid – and one that had been prevalent on and off since 1904 – was more cylinders. Sixes and eights had been on the up-grade since 1926, and the trend continued well into the 1930s.

The compact vee-eight was never wholly acceptable. Its uneven firing characteristics led to an irritating "wuffle", large-scale manufacture called for costly tooling, and it took the almost unlimited resources of Ford to master the technique of mass monobloc casting. Europeans, fiscally discouraged from really big runs of anything larger than a 3-litre, left this type alone. Hence, its vogue in the 1930s was confined to two of the American giants: Ford and the Cadillac Division of General Motors.

The straight-eight proved more popular until the Depression really took hold; it appealed aesthetically as well as technically, as long hoods were all the rage in 1930. Further, firms with shaky budgets and anxious shareholders could purchase proprietary units of this type from Lycoming or Continental, a state of affairs which explains the formidable line-up of eights fielded by Weimar Germany at the peak of

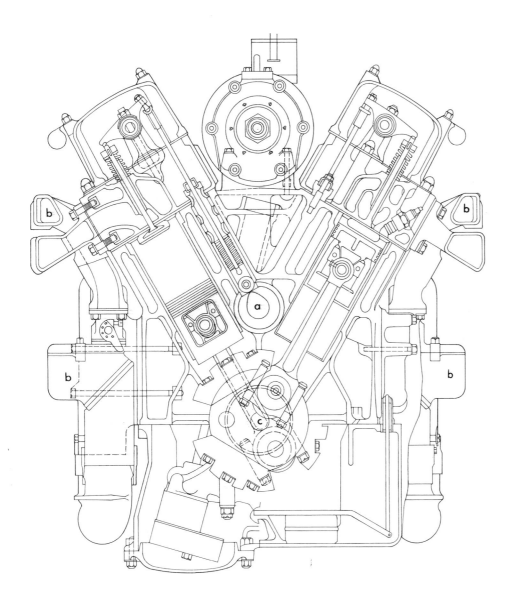

Outside the realm of the sports car it is an accepted axiom that the bigger an engine and the greater the number of cylinders, the fewer forward speeds are required. Not so Karl Maybach: though content with a two-speed-and-reverse affair on Model T Ford lines for his first, relatively modest 5.7-litre six way back in 1922, he had progressed by 1931 to the fearsome dual-range *Doppelschnellgang*, which offered eight forward and four reverse speeds at the cost, understandably, of some duplication of ratios. (*Above*) The attractive badge on the twelve-cylinder Maybach.

Sedans of the 1930s. The 1933 Vauxhall Light Six (*top left*) and 1934 Austin Light 12/4 Harley (*bottom*) are typical early thirties specimens with compound curves in evidence, especially around the forepeak. If the Austin's shape suggests other models, both British and German, then it is a direct consequence of Budd influence from the new presswork plants in Oxford and Berlin. The 1936 Renault Primaquatre (*centre left*) reflects American influences from a year or so before and utilizes the full width of the frame to make a six-seater out of a compact car. More interesting, though, is its famed flathead "85" motor of 2,383 cc, with four cylinders where one would still expect six. Rough it might be, but it was also tough and still fitted to light trucks seventeen years later. The 1939 Lagonda (*centre right*) and 1937 Lincoln Zephyr (*right*) represent two approaches to the twelve-cylinder automobile, though curiously, it is the expensive British car, at £1,600 or $8,000, that is the more sophisticated, with independently-sprung front wheels and hydraulic brakes. Fractionally bigger than the Lincoln – 4,480 cc as against 4,387 – it gave 158 hp to the American car's 113 – and needed to, since a sedan weighed over two tons and 100 mph (160 km/h) was already the norm for the *grande*

routière class. The semi-unitary Lincoln, as a Ford product, was still wedded to beam axles, transverse suspension, and mechanical brakes. The product-image called for the extra four cylinders, not the best thing from the maintenance standpoint, but between 1936 and 1948, the Zephyr family became what will probably be the best-selling twelve-cylinder line of all time. And for $1,190 (£238 at par), the combination of 90 mph (145 km/h) and 20 mpg (13.5 lit/100) couldn't be bad news.

Complication was the price of silence and smoothness in their ultimate form, though it is rather surprising to find Cadillac with a *new* sixteen-cylinder engine (*right*) as late as 1938. That it didn't sell (some five hundred were made in three seasons) was due as much to the "Little Recession" as to anything else, as it was a brilliant piece of work. With side-by-side valves for simplicity (and no worries on account of bulk) the engineers chose a wide 135-degree angle which allowed room for carburettors and manifolding within the vee. One distributor and one carburettor per bank of cylinders also made sense: treating it as two eights made it easier for mechanics. The result, though not much down on piston displacement, came out shorter and lighter than the original 1930 overhead-valve version, thus the theoretical loss of 15 hp mattered not at all. Unkind folk who dismissed the new flathead as "a lump of iron" had also forgotten that, in the era of alligator hoods, only those who worked on the engine got a clear view of it.

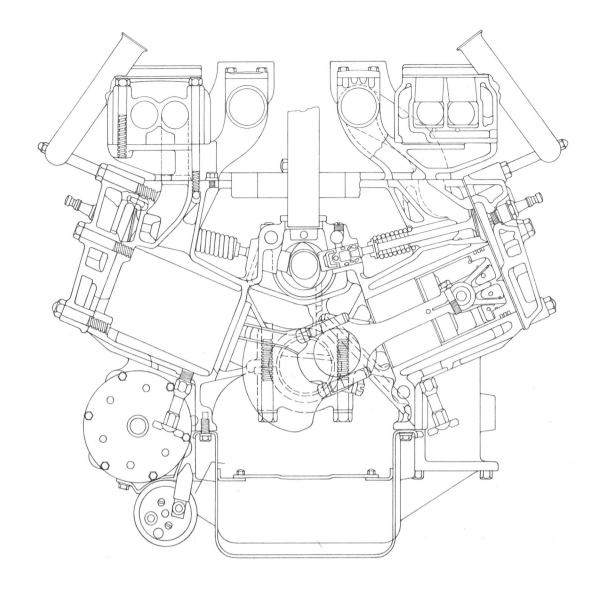

By contrast, this overhead-valve Cadillac Sixteen town car (*left*) of 1933, with Fleetwood coachwork, was cosmetic every inch of it, epitomizing the damn-the-cost Classicism which survived even into the years of *Brother, Can You Spare A Dime?* True, new stylistic evidences can be seen – the real radiator is hidden behind a vee-grille, the shell is painted, and even Cadillacs now had the fashionable fender skirts. The engine gave 165 hp from 7.4 litres, a three-speed synchromesh transmission was standard from the start in 1930, and with reasonably light bodywork, 95 mph (152 km/h) were possible. One didn't buy such a car for speed, though: the long wheel-base ran to 149 inches (3.8 m), even a simple sedan weighed over 5,000 lb (say 2,270 kg), and for 1933, Cadillac deliberately made their Sixteen exclusive, rationing the season's quota to 500 units. In those depressed times, however, they were lucky to sell 125.

the boom. Hansa and Simson – and probably several others – bought their units "off the peg" from Continental.

For those who insisted on the ultimate, there were vee-twelves and vee-sixteens; despite 1932's breadlines, American industry offered six distinct and different Twelves and two Sixteens (Marmon and Cadillac) that year. The price of undetectable power impulses and 0–100 mph in top gear was two of everything: on Daimler's Double Six each bank of cylinders had its own water pump, carburettor, and ignition arrangements. To this could be added prodigious thirsts: most of the big Americans averaged 9 mph (30 lit/100), and the Daimler was even worse. In any case, better sound-damping, independent wheel suspension, and, above all, aids to shifting would render such drastic measures superfluous by 1936, though Cadillac's Sixteen survived into 1940, along with the Twelves of Lincoln, Rolls-Royce, Lagonda, and Maybach. Mercedes-Benz had a new 6-litre vee-twelve on the stocks as well.

In passing, it can be mentioned that a major casualty of the new aids to silence was the sleeve-valve Knight engine, a sensation of 1909, and pursued energetically for several years in most of the major automobile-manufacturing countries of the world. Daimler led the British contingent and Willys was the American licencee, but other important firms in this field were Minerva of Belgium, Mercedes in Germany, and Panhard and Voisin in France. Silent it certainly was, and in early days, the fact that "it improved with use" cut down servicing costs in that it seldom required decarbonization. On the debit side were complexity, the expensive consequences of seizure, and a fearsome oil consumption which revealed itself in trailing plumes of blue smoke. By the beginning of our decade, Mercedes had already abdicated, Willys would quit in 1933, and Daimler two years later. The remaining loyalists – Minerva, Panhard, and Voisin – retained the Knight engine to the end simply because they could not afford to retool, albeit Voisin, in desperation, fitted their 1939 models with imported side-valve Graham units from the United States.

The trend towards the multi-cylinder engine reflected itself in the lower echelons of the market. By 1929, the 2-litre six was commonplace, and the 1930–35 period would see a brief craze (largely, though not exclusively, based in Britain) for real miniatures such as the 1.2-litre Triumph Scorpion and the 1.3-litre Wolseley Hornet. Such cars could accelerate smoothly away from 6 mph (10 km/h) in top, but on axle ratios of around 6:1, valve bounce was liable to set in well short of 60 mph (95–100 km/h). Their main interest to us is to reveal the cost accountancy school of engineering at its worst; such models were evolved by taking the frame of a small four and lengthening it without reinforcement to accommodate the two extra cylinders!

Just as better chassis engineering relegated the multi-barrelled giants to the super-luxury market, so also did it weed out the pint-sized sixes in favour of a new generation of fours. By the end of the 1930s, the big four was back again. In the United States, of course, the struggling Willys concern had long centred its energies on its 2.2-litre side-valve unit, known to every Allied serviceman of 1941 as the power behind the Jeep, but newcomers of 1936–37 were the 2,383-cc Renault 85, the 2,406-cc Stoewer Sedina, and Riley's classic Sixteen of very similar capacity. In 1939, sixes of less than 2 litres' capacity were once again in the minority.

The Wolseley Hornet and the sixteen-cylinder Cadillac, though poles apart in every other respect, were both attempts to solve the age-old headache of shifting gears. An enthusiast would use his box to capacity, extracting 15,000 miles (say 25,000 km) from even the primitive brake-lining material of the 1920s by keeping his foot off the brake pedal. The Smiths of the United States and Britain, the Duponts of France, and the

Schwartzes of Germany detested cog-swaps and never fully mastered the gentle art of the double-clutch. "Hanging on" to a high ratio was commonplace among elderly drivers even in the 1950s. The writer recalls a hair-raising run across Hampshire's Portsdown Hills in a Land-rover conducted by a retired chauffeur, who engaged third on leaving the city limits of Portsmouth and held it, restarts included, for the next thirty miles! Hence, much effort was devoted to alleviating the sufferings of such folk – and their cars.

The American philosophy, of course, centred round a big, lazy engine that did all its work in direct drive. The British, resigned to road conditions which demanded four forward speeds and liberal use of them all, were more concerned with painless shifting. Between them, however, the two English-speaking nations made the running in gearbox development between the years 1930 and 1940, just as France, Germany, and Italy introduced the everyday motorist to proper handling.

Synchromesh, first seen on 1929's Cadillacs and La Salles, offered truly clash-proof gears and freedom from the double-clutch technique. Initially confined to the two upper ratios (even where four speeds were specified), the system was all but universal in the United States by 1932, in which year it spread first to Britain and then to the rest of Europe. Few makers, of course, bothered to apply it to bottom gear (the Americans, indeed, would not do so until the middle sixties); this was an expensive luxury, especially at a time when this ratio tended to be suitable only for funeral processions. Alvis and the German ZF firm had effective all-synchromesh transmissions by 1934, but Hillman's version, a novelty of 1935, became a casualty of 1938's "little recession". Nobody noticed. Properly-spaced ratios were, sadly, reserved for the better sports cars. British four-speeders all too often suffered from "three bottoms and one top"; on Italian designs first gear was clearly intended for assaults on the vertical; and the short-lived four-speed transmissions tried in the United States between 1929 and 1933 featured two fairly high and close ratios (normal top and traffic top), a second which approximated to the normal first, and another example of the Italian-style crawler.

In the early 1930s, there was a short vogue for that economy device, the free wheel, which was often accompanied by an automatic clutch. The consequence was painless shifting at the price of loss of engine braking. Another refinement, though no novelty (Rolls-Royce had used it in 1907), was overdrive, in effect an auxiliary unit which furnished an extra cruising ratio for highway work, while holding the revs down. On early systems selection tended to be fully automatic; not a very desirable arrangement, since flooring the accelerator pedal automatically restored direct drive. On the majority of American cars so equipped the extra ratio was operative only in top, but at the other end of the spectrum was Maybach's fearsome *Doppelschnellgang* with its eight forward and four reverse ratios, hardly necessary on the elephantine automobiles produced by the Friedrichshafen concern. (This one, incidentally, was made available to other manufacturers and was actually taken up briefly by Lagonda in Britain and Walter in Czechoslovakia). By contrast, the American Auburn and the French Voisin favoured two-speed rear axles, already common practice in the truck world and used by Cadillac as early as 1914; these gave six or eight forward speeds, according to the type of main transmission.

Synchromesh was, of course, tailor-made for Britain's road conditions, and the majority of the country's major manufacturers had adopted it by 1934. A more peculiarly British answer to the shifting problem was, however, the Wilson preselective gearbox, first offered on 1929's larger Armstrong Siddeley models. It was, admittedly, a three-pedal affair, the clutch being replaced by a pedal which actually shifted

The Cotal transmission. On a 1936 Salmson S.4.D (*top left*), selection is via the tiny gate (*a*) under the steering wheel. On a Cotal, all the ratios can be used in either direction, which gave alarming possibilities to cars like the 3.5-litre Delahaye, capable of 110 mph (175 km/h). The engineer's drawing (*top right*) shows that the Cotal is an extension of the epicyclic system, in which planet wheels are spaced round a central sun wheel, meshing with it. Outside the planets, and meshing with them, is an annulus with teeth on its inner rim. On preselective boxes this annulus is held stationary by mechanically actuated band brakes, but on the Cotal, these latter are replaced by twin-plate clutches. The plates are held together by electromagnets, and this eliminates the whole physical effort of shifting gear, without in any way affecting driver control. A switch was enough to shift the gear, though the conventional clutch pedal had still to be used when moving away from rest, and throttle actions when moving up and down were similar to those made with a sliding-type transmission.

(*Centre*) The column-mounted selector of a preselective gearbox on a 1935 Armstrong Siddeley was labelled "low-medium-normal-high" rather than "1-2-3-4", a clear indication of how the factory thought the car should be driven. A safety stop was mounted on the quadrant between low and reverse, and the actual change was effected by depressing the gear-change pedal (which replaced the conventional clutch) after the gear had been selected. Electrical selection of gears was added in 1953. "It is possible," asserts the manual, "for the merest novice to drive in comfort and security, knowing that it is impossible to make a bad change of gear with its accompanying grinding noise, so distressing to the driver and passengers, to say nothing of the gearbox itself."

(*Bottom*) The workings of a simple synchromesh gearbox, with small cone clutches (*a*) interposed between sets of dogs (*b*). These cones make contact before the dogs begin to slide into mesh, the friction between the cones synchronizing the speed of the dogs. The drawings show the action on a downward shift from top to third. (*c*) Top. (*d*) Neutral. (*e*) Check. (*f*) Main shaft. (*g*) Third gear.

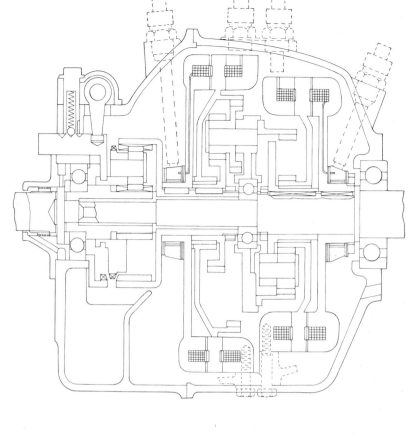

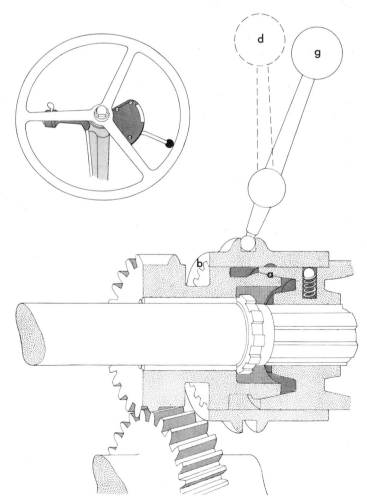

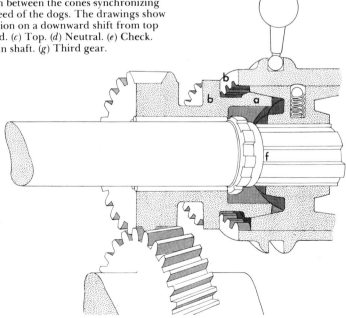

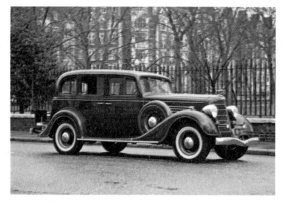

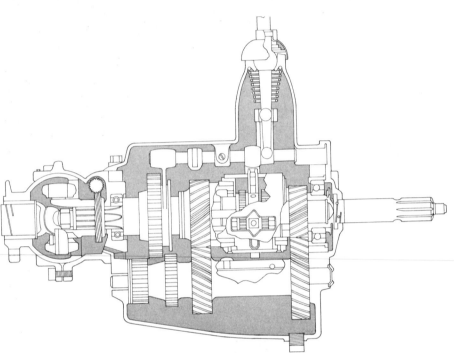

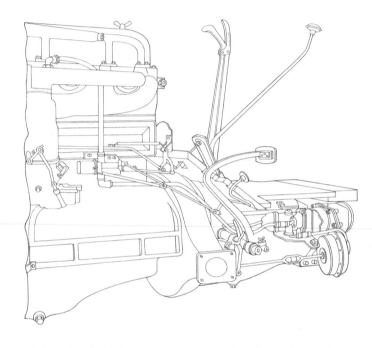

Cars and transmissions. (*Top left*) The 1932 60-series Buick convertible and (*top centre*) the 1935 50-series NA sedan of the same make, both overhead-valve straight-eights and both offering clash-proof, three-speed synchromesh transmissions. On the later example the radiator is becoming more of a grille, and one can detect the characteristic "sit" of the coil-spring independent front suspension adopted by Buick from 1934. The cross-section of a synchromesh transmission (*centre left*) forms an interesting contrast with the automatic on the opposite page, and illustrates the point that to make things simpler for the driver, one usually has to make them more complicated for the engineer and the maintenance man – even down to special transmission fluid for the automatic! Significantly, bottom gear was omitted from early synchromesh layouts, since few American drivers bothered with this ratio. In fact, the first mass-produced car to have an all-synchro arrangement was a most unlikely vehicle, the 1935 Hillman Minx (*bottom left*); it looks the uninspired family Ten it is, with a 30-hp 1.2-litre side-valve four-cylinder engine and indifferent cable-operated brakes. It was very flexible, and except in traffic or on hills, nothing much was gained from liberal use of the indirects – probably this is why Hillman decided to cut their costs and confine synchro to the top three gears after 1938. An intriguing halfway house (*centre right*) is the use of vacuum from the inlet manifold to give clutchless shifts, another novelty on 1932 Buicks. The selecting valve was actuated by the shifting bars of the transmission. Note, however, the retention of the clutch pedal: this was no case of belt-and-braces but was simply because the vacuum set-up functioned only between the two upper synchronized ratios. You did not get its assistance in low.

Painless shifting at last. The conservative 1935 17-hp Armstrong Siddeley (*right*), with custom cabrio-limousine coachwork by Salmons-Tickford, featured the Wilson preselective system. This still called for three pedals, the "clutch" actually shifting the gears already selected by a small quadrant on the steering-column. With a smallish engine and flywheel – the 17 ran to only 2.3 litres – physical effort was eliminated – and so were rude noises.

The 1940 Oldsmobile (*opposite, top right*) was the first car with two pedals and full automation: all one had to do was to select neutral, drive, or reverse, since the low range was strictly for emergencies like steep hills. The four base elements of the complex transmission (*below, main diagram*) were the fluid coupling with the flywheel (*a*), two planetary gear trains for the four forward ratios (*b*, *c*), and the reverse gear (*d*). The smaller picture shows the control system, located in the transmission sump. Actual power for the system was furnished by twin oil pumps at front and rear, the front unit providing immediate pressure starts, and the rear taking up its share once the car was in motion. Oil rather than spring pressure was used to actuate the majority of the elements, and a minor degree of manual control was exercised by the "kickdown", which ex-

erted extra force on the shifting valves when the accelerator was floored. It was, in fact, the only manual change-down viable in normal motoring, owing to the emergency nature of Low Range. Further, downshifts were impossible above 60 mph (100 km/h).

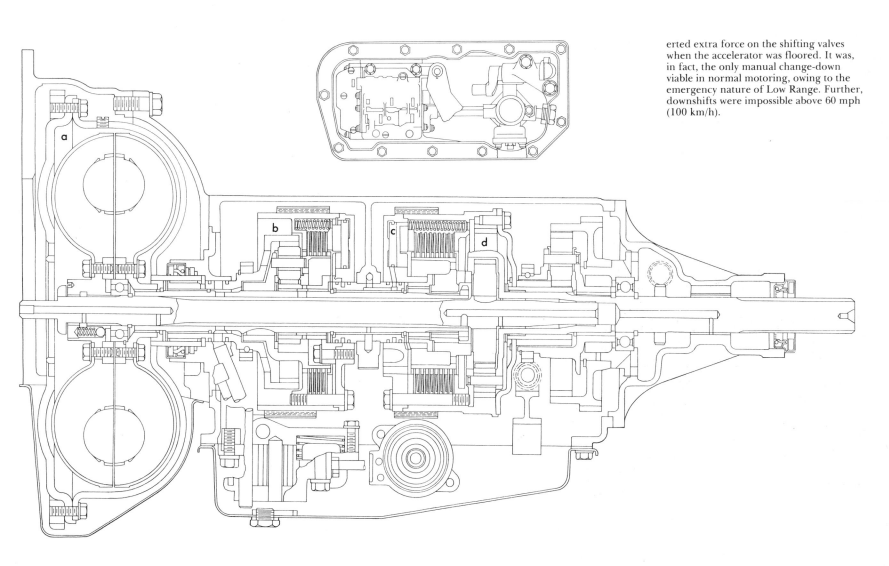

the gears after they had been preselected via a small lever on a column-mounted quadrant. (Some sports cars, notably MG and Lagonda, preferred a floor-mounted quadrant resembling today's "stick automatic"). Faults, complexity apart, were "clutch" slip, a plaintive syren-like wail, and a tendency, on big cars, for the flywheel to become argumentative if one forgot oneself and essayed an instant downshift. Daimler circumvented this last headache with their fluid flywheel, but preselection would become another casualty of the cost accountant, as the preselective gearbox was expensive both to make and to service. Fifteen British makers offered the system in 1934, but five years later, only Armstrong Siddeley, Daimler, and Lanchester remained loyal to "Wailing Wilson".

Wilson boxes were also tried by Isotta Fraschini in Italy and were standardized by some of the better French makers, notably Delahaye and Talbot, though the *système* Cotal was generally preferred on that side of the Channel, so much so that, by 1938, Delahaye were using up surplus Wilsons on less popular models. On this box the ratios were selected electromagnetically via a tiny column-mounted quadrant. Somewhat archaic was the use of a separate floor-mounted lever for forward and reverse, but the reward for unpredictable solenoids was the ability to utilize all four gears in either direction, which meant a theoretical 105 mph (170 km/h) maximum in reverse on a 3.5-litre Delahaye. This one, and Cord's rather similar electro-pneumatic shift of 1936, proved too delicate for the general public, though at least four British makers were experimenting with Cotals in 1939.

Now it was only one step forward to the true automatic. Georges Roesch of the English Talbot concern had already eliminated manual upward shifts (while maintaining a full manual override) on his 1934 version of the Wilson, and across the Atlantic Reo were offering a "self-shifter" in 1933. This was not a true automatic; it was, in effect, a two-speed dual-range box with automation confined within the individual ranges. Shifting from high to low range called for the use of the clutch; and, with only two forward speeds at the driver's immediate disposal, staying in high deprived the car of any noticeable acceleration. Much the same limitations applied to General Motors's first semi-automatic, offered on some 1938 Buicks and Oldsmobiles. The true torque converter, which required neither clutch nor an actual shift – beyond, of course, engagement of the emergency low range and of reverse – made its appearance on 1940 Oldsmobiles and was available on Cadillacs a year later. Its story properly belongs to the post-1945 era.

So, in effect, does that of column shift, magnified erroneously to the status of an automatic by American publicists. Its technical connotations are, in any case, peripheral, since the object was to clear the floor of obstructions and thus enable three people to share in comfort the bench seats of American cars. (In days when four doors were unnecessary, of course, the shift lever had been mounted on the right-hand side, still a U-feature on British cars until the general acceptance of automatic.) The best that could be said of the new arrangement was that it was superior to the strange dashboard linkages that accompanied the prentice years of front-wheel drive. Some of these assortments of cables are best not inspected, though they worked better than one might imagine.

By the mid-thirties, front-wheel drive, though a breach of the Panhard shibboleths, was no longer regarded as rank heresy. Though rear-wheel drive remained in the majority – in 1939, neither the United States nor Italy offered anything else – *traction avant* had been proven in use. In Germany, from 1931 on, DKW led the field; they had been joined by Adler a year later. Nor were these rare luxury items; the combined output of the two factories ran to around sixty thousand units in 1937 alone. Czechoslovakia's smaller, DKW-inspired two-stroke automobiles all used it, and since 1934, there had been an even more

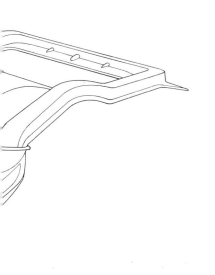

(*Far left*) The ingredients of the unitary body fitted to the 1939 Opel Kapitän. Here the pressed-steel floor unit incorporates what would normally be the chassis frame.

It is easy to see why the stylists went for the long, low look. They had to, when, as on the 1929 Cord, the entire drive unit was mounted ahead of 4.9 litres of straight-eight, seen here in side view (*below*). Of 205 inches (5.2 m) of automobile, 46 inches (1.2 m) were hood. The motor had to be turned round so that it would rotate anticlockwise, while the front brakes were inboard, and gearbox, clutch, and differential were all mounted in unit. The curious linkage running across the top of the motor, seen in the three-quarters view (*left*), past the high-tension leads, connects the gearbox to the dash-mounted gearshift, an arrangement also found on Adlers and Amilcar Compounds.

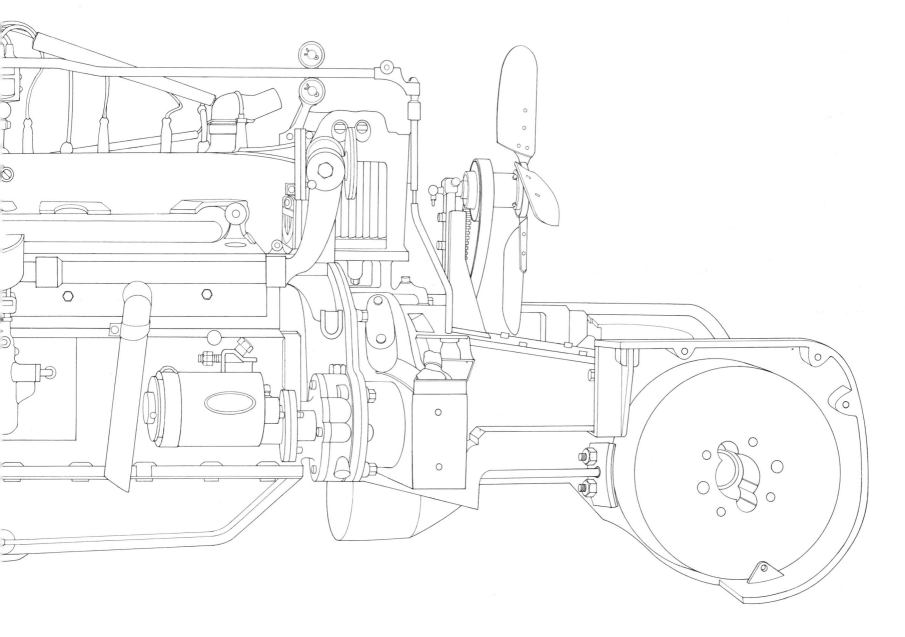

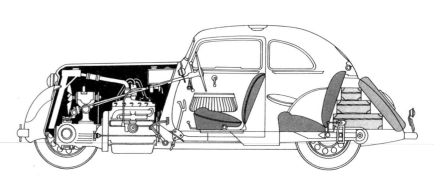

Front-wheel drive and rear engines. The 1934 Mercedes-Benz 130 H (*top left*) shows its formidable overhang from the rear, which made it something of a nightmare in crosswinds. A logical and far more manageable descendant is the Volkswagen (*opposite, top*), here seen in 1947 form, still without synchromesh or hydraulic brakes, but now with the definitive 1,131-cc 25-hp motor in place of 1939's 985-cc unit. This is one of the first cars to reach England, where the importers two-toned it to relieve the austerity of Wolfsburg's drab monochromes. DKW (*top right*), Adler (*centre*), and BSA (*bottom left*) all favoured front-wheel drive in the 1930s. The Adler cutaway drawing (*centre right*) highlights the extravagance of putting the gearbox out front, even if it does make for a length of hood more suggestive of three litres than the car's actual 995 cc. No wonder the artist made great play with the trunk space available! More frugal in this respect was the DKW (this is a 1939 model) on which the 684-cc two-cycle water-cooled twin engine was mounted transversely at the front of a simple backbone, but the chance to anticipate Alec Issigonis's Mini was frustrated by the make-image. The parent Auto Union firm liked their cheap baby car to resemble a scaled-down Horch, and this coach-built *luxus* cabriolet (lesser models had fabric

58

bodies) made an excellent job of it. It was, alas, expensive, overweight, and under-powered, being little more than the German equivalent of a Sunbeam-Talbot Ten. The BSA, Britain's sole volume-production *traction* in pre-war days, had a ten-year run in three- and four-wheeled forms, always with independent suspension by eight transverse springs (four each side) and with inboard front brakes. Ingenious it certainly was, but opinions were divided on its handling, and the 1,075-cc side-valve four-cylinder engine fitted to this Scout kept top speed down to a laboured 60 mph (95–100 km/h).

(*Centre left*) With heavy cars, some means

was needed to reduce braking effort without any loss of efficiency. Much favoured in the twenties and still used on European cars in the thirties was the Dewandre system, making use of inlet manifold suction. Release of the accelerator pedal causes manifold pressure to drop, and by connecting the manifold to a servo cylinder, it was possible to put this to work. The servo cylinder is exhausted of air, and atmospheric pressure drives a piston inwards, thus exerting force upon the braking system. Hispano-Suiza and Rolls-Royce used a different type of servo in the form of a friction clutch mounted on the side of the gearbox and rotated by the transmission.

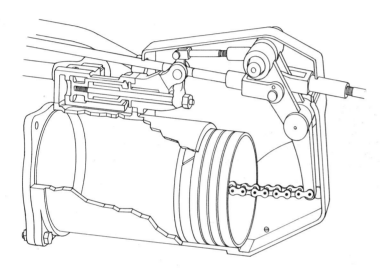

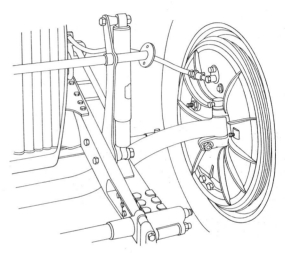

The ultimate for the grand tourist in the thirties was Bugatti's Type 57 (*left*), first seen at the 1933 Shows. After the franc slid three years later, it became a bargain at less than £1,000 ($5,000) in England. The lines of this regular, early-model *coach Ventoux* are spoilt by the exaggerated rake of the windshield, but the twin-cam straight-eight engine was tractable, and 95 mph (150–155 km/h) presented no problems. Bugatti had no truck with detachable cylinder heads, synchromesh, or independent suspension, but though early 57s retained mechanical brakes, hydraulic actuation (*centre right*) had been adopted by 1938. Note the generously ribbed drums and also the hydraulic piston-type dampers adopted at the same time. These replaced the complicated De Ram friction type, said to cost around £150 ($750) a set and to need "works" tuning. The Bugatti's 3,257-cc engine gave 135 hp, or 160 with the optional supercharger (Type 57C). In 1939, a stock 57C sedan put 112 miles (179 km) into a *standing-start* hour at Montlhéry Autodrome. The only real snag about such motoring in the grand manner was that there wasn't a friendly Bugatti dealer in every town, even in France, and the machinery was beyond the ministrations of the average mechanic.

important contender – Citroën, France's number one seller. The principle of "pull instead of push" made for vastly superior road-holding. Further, the absence of a drive shaft running the length of the car made not only for greater legroom, but also for a lower centre of gravity. What it did not yet achieve was the compactness associated with latter-day expositions of the formula of "putting all the works up one end". True, the DKW's vertical, twin two-stroke engine was transversely disposed, but nobody had devised any other means of fitting in anything bigger. Even when DKW themselves began tests of a three-cylinder engine in 1939, they had recourse to the longitudinal mounting still in general use. Add to this space-consuming arrangement a gearbox in front of the power unit, and the result was apt to be abnormal length, capitalized on the original straight-eight Cord of 1929 by some brilliant and much-imitated front-end styling. The practical disadvantages were heavier steering at low speeds, a poor lock (Citroën's 15/6 of 1939 required a 46-foot, or a 14-metre, turning circle), greater vulnerability in head-on collisions, and complicated gear linkages. A dashboard location was generally favoured, though the Alvis and early BSAs retained the old right-hand floor shift.

Where front-wheel drive was backed by adequate finances (as already mentioned, Citroën had to be rescued by Michelin) and a good service network, it succeeded. By the outbreak of the Second World War, Citroën's potential was some fifty thousand units a year, DKW's forty-five thousand, and Adler's perhaps twenty-five thousand. That such heresy was not for the small maker was demonstrated when Rosengart of France attempted to build – or, more strictly, assemble and trim – Adlers for the local market. The venture lasted less than eighteen months, after which the Parisian firm reverted to its original theme – gallicized editions of the Austin Seven. (They would later contrive an attractive sports sedan by fitting 11CV Citroën mechanical elements into their own platform frames and bodies.) Large front-wheel drive cars were beset with problems of weight transference. In the United States, E.L. Cord had two skirmishes with the system: the first, the L29, succumbed to the aforementioned weight-transference weakness, as well as to the problems caused by the Depression; the second, the better-engineered 810 of 1936, was altogether too complicated for Americans accustomed to a diet of the painless and insipid, not to mention flat-rate servicing and factory exchange units!

Rear engines played little part in the 1930s, for all the attractions of that perfect aerodynamic shape that was the prime chimera of 1934. One of John Tjaarda's styling prototypes for the Lincoln-Zephyr featured an engine at the back, but, though it reached the test stage, the end-product reverted to the *système* Panhard. Once again, linkages were a headache; a worse one was directional instability in crosswinds, which showed up only too well on Europe's new motorways. The big air-cooled Tatra V8, though quiet at speed and astonishingly efficient – 100 mph (160 km/h) on three-litres-odd and less than 80 bhp – was addicted to sudden and vicious rear-end breakaway. So was the little 130H Mercedes-Benz with its formidably overhung tail, though this under-powered creature disliked anything more than 50–55 mph (85 km/h). There was also the problem of combining a rear-mounted engine with rearward visibility, a commodity lacking not only on the Tatra, but also on Ferdinand Porsche's definitive Volkswagen, visible if not on sale by the latter half of 1938. The Volkswagen did, however, represent an intelligent approach to mass transportation in a sophisticated age and summarized much of the period's technical thinking. The recipe embraced a lightly stressed, frost-proof, air-cooled, flat-four engine of short-stroke type, capable of holding its appointed 3,200 rpm all day, allied to an aerodynamic shape offering the minimum of wind resistance. Here was the shape of things to come, and in more senses than

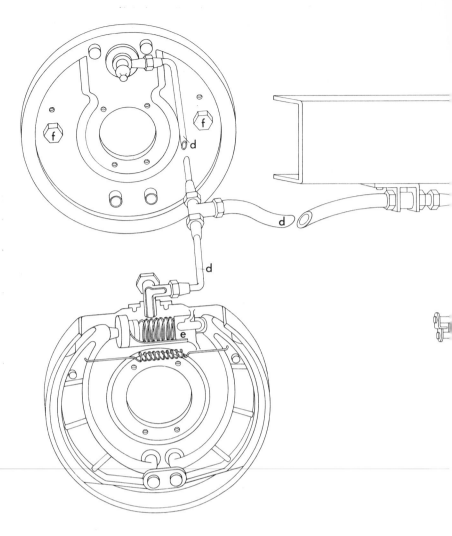

Popular on British cars – Austin, Daimler, Rover, and SS were among its users – was the Girling rod-operated system, on which almost the entire operating mechanism (*bottom*) is in tension, thus obviating one of the worst snags of cables. The brake shoes (*a*) are expanded by a cone (*b*).

On hydraulic brakes (*top*), pipe lines and pistons replace the rods or cables and levers of earlier brake systems. Depression of the pedal (*a*) displaces fluid in a master cylinder (*b*), through the movement of a piston (*c*). Pipes (*d*) connect the master cylinder to working cylinders (*e*), one in each wheel, and the fluid displaced from the master cylinder exerts pressure on opposed pistons in the working cylinder. Uniformity of pressure in an enclosed system gives perfect compensation. Though general practice in the United States by 1939, the system did not finally take over from mechanical arrangements until the end of our period. (*f*) Shoe adjusters. (*g*) To front brakes. (*h*) Supply tank.

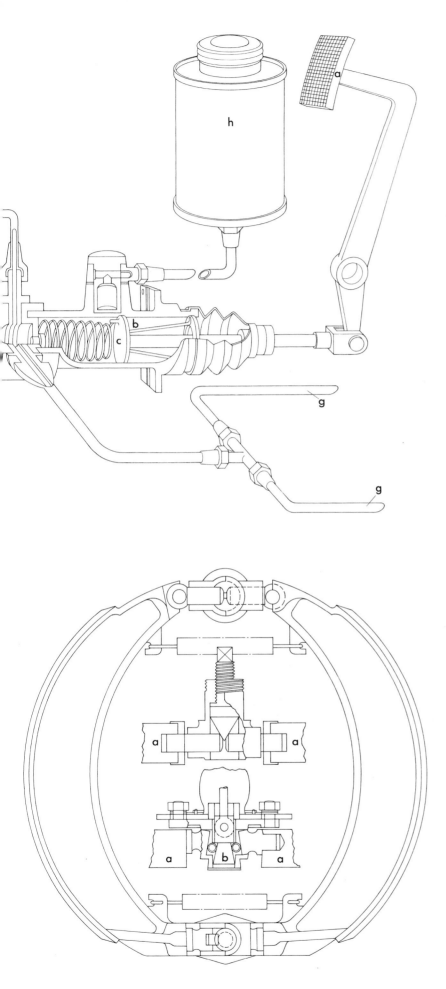

mere volume production. The Beetle's forty-year span would beat the Model T Ford by a substantial margin, even if total sales probably outran the Ford's by a mere eight or nine per cent.

In the braking department, of course, the Volkswagen was inadequate even by 1938's standards. The Third Reich housed the sternest of cost accountants; the car had, in theory, to be sold for RM990 (about £56, or $280!), and thus, the Beetle's anchors were old-fashioned cable-actuated mechanicals. They would continue to be just that for another twelve years.

Retardation had made considerable strides in the 1930s, albeit the picture is mainly one of a consolidation of ideas evolved in the previous decade. A better-class European or American sedan of the middle or later 1930s should cause no one any anxiety in the road conditions of half a century later, provided it be driven at the speeds for which it was designed – a steady 60 mph (100 km/h) in the case of bigger models, or 45–50 mph (75–80 km/h) in the under 1,500-cc class. It is only when one samples the period's *grandes routières* – such as the legendary V12 Lagonda – that one recognizes that even dual-circuit hydraulics working in adequately-cooled drums of generous diameter are not suited for 100 mph (160 km/h) on modern highways.

Brake cooling would, however, be a problem of the future. Spoked wheels of one kind and another would be regular equipment – apart from a preference in Continental Europe for the full disc – right up to 1937.

By the beginning of our period, the internal-expanding brake had won through; the earlier contracting type with its exposed and dirt-prone bands had been one of the casualties of 1929. Also a casualty was, thank goodness, the transmission brake. Long banished to the hand-operated emergency circuit, it had but two major adherents by 1935, Fiat and Chrysler. It was a snare to the unskilled, who sometimes forgot that its only safe function was parking and that habitual use at speeds above walking pace could have interesting effects on the drive line.

Mechanical systems saw the decade through, mainly because not everyone trusted fragile rubber pipes and potentially corrosive fluids, and because plastic was in its infancy. By 1939, however, hydraulics were virtually universal in the United States, while important European users were Morris, Vauxhall, and Rootes in Britain; Mercedes-Benz, BMW, Hansa, and Opel in Germany; Volvo in Sweden; Fiat and Lancia in Italy; and Citroën, though not Peugeot or Renault, in France.

Of the alternatives, cables had the merits of simplicity, cheapness, and of being a convenient means of linking the hand-brake to all four wheels. (This linkage was a regular concomitant of the much-used Bendix system.) Among the disadvantages was a tendency for the cables to stretch, giving crabwise stops unless they were frequently adjusted. Rod-operated types like the Girling, though less temperamental, called for heavy pedal pressure. Nonetheless, the hydraulic brake's even and progressive retardation won through. Servo systems, usually of vacuum type, were becoming popular at the end of the 1920s, when Hillman and Citroën had been among their devotees. In the depressed 1930s, they were reserved for large, vast, and expensive models such as the great American classics. Hispano-Suiza's gearbox servo was used by that company and by Rolls-Royce, though one of the defects of such assistance was a tendency to require a few seconds' thinking time when every second counted. Another common disease of the 1920s, a "loss of interest" below 15 mph, was, however, seldom encountered in later years.

As yet, power steering lay in the future, and few designers had adopted the precise rack-and-pinion gear almost universal today, albeit it was found on all front-wheel-drive Adlers, and on parallel Citroëns from 1936 onwards. The main concern of manufacturers, especially in

Car of the Decade: if there'd been international panels voting on such subjects in the 1930s, Citroën's *traction* must surely have taken the title. The skeleton view stands for the main structure as found on some three-quarter of a million four- and six-cylinder machines turned out between 1934 and 1957. Clearly visible are the main structural members and the front horns on which the power pack was mounted. Notice that though the shape has been tidied up (there are, for instance, no running boards), it reveals no exaggerated "streamline" tendencies of the type rampant at the time. Headroom is adequate and takes full advantage of the flat floor, the hood is side-opening, and the engine (if not the electrics or transmission) is more accessible than on many of the Citroën's later competitors. The dashboard (*top centre*) is typically austere, with the familiar single dial incorporating fuel and oil gauges, ammeter, speedometer, and odometer. Note the traditional

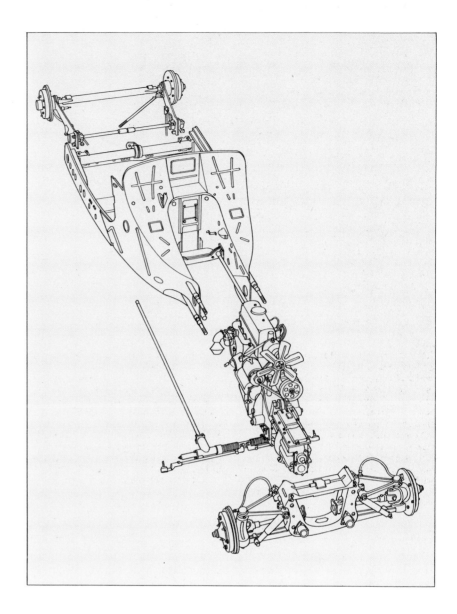

Citroën

opening windshield, though there are two discordant notes for 1934 – the pistol-grip handbrake under the dash, and the dashboard gear shift for the three-speed synchromesh transmission. Its action was very awkward, though BSA, DKW, and Adler used similar levers; the Adler's was, however, direct-coupled to the box and easier to handle.

(*Top right*) Citroën *traction* exploded and bared of body panels, showing the rack and pinion steering (*a*) adopted during 1936, the ingenious torsion-bar front suspension (*b*) which kept the front wheels permanently vertical and parallel, the engine-gearbox unit (*c*) and its mounting horns (*d*), and the base structure (*e*) com-

prising firewall and flat floor pressing. At the rear there is a simple tubular dead axle (*f*) with transverse torsion bar springing (*g*). Much was made of the wheel-out power pack, but Citroën maintenance was never that easy! The front and rear views show one of the first 15/6s of 1939 but reveal neither its impressive length of nearly 16 ft (4.9 m), which made for a turning circle of 46 ft (14 m). Definitely not a car for shopping in crowded city streets! Note the outward-opening trunk, an improvement on the first *tractions*, on which only the spare wheel was accessible without first shifting the rear seat.

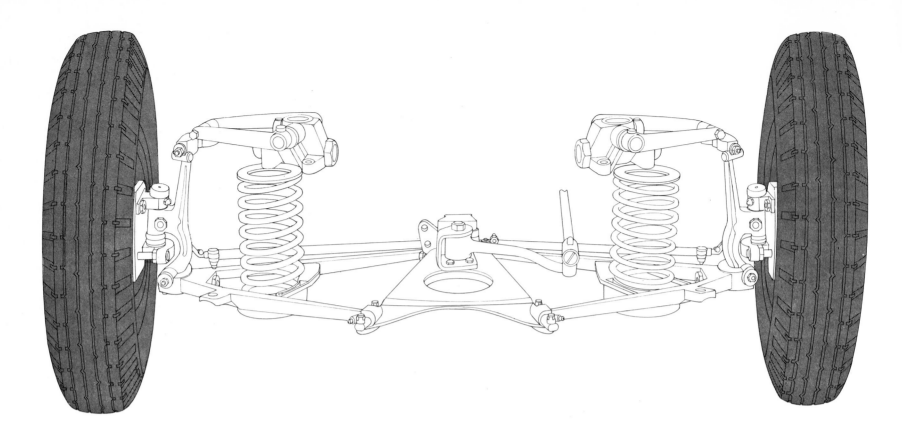

the United States, was not the best line through a corner, but how to reconcile the growing weight of the modern sedan with the faster-growing proportion of women drivers.

Hitherto, this had not been a major problem. The fair sex had preferred smaller cars, European favourites being the Austin Seven and the 5CV Peugeot. Open bodywork and an absence of frills and gimmickry had kept the weight of even a 1,500-cc family car down to one ton, and this went for the well-loved Model A Ford as well. Hence, two-and-a-half turns from lock to lock were viable without straining Madame's muscles. Manoeuvring some 1.8 tons of straight-eight Buick into a car park was, however, something quite different, and the only way out was a lower ratio: four-and-a-half or maybe five turns. Between 1932 and 1939, the Ford V8's steering ratio fell progressively year by year; while the original Model-18 had been "quick" on the hands, by the end of our period, keen rallyistes attached traction-engine-style handles to the steering wheels, the better to wind their cars through the wiggle-woggles of the Monte Carlo and similar events.

Perhaps the greatest advances – or at least the groundwork for them – came in the realm of suspension. Not that everyone agreed: more than one factory tried independent front springing, only to abandon it, in Rover's case too late for its deletion from the catalogue's first edition! As late as 1939, a leaf spring at each corner did the job for British mass-produced cars, with the exception of some Standards and the American-inspired Vauxhalls. Renault combined semi-elliptics at the front with a Ford-like transverse spring at the rear, while Ford themselves retained the bouncy, all-transverse arrangements that had been their hallmark for a good thirty years. Renault was, however, almost the sole conservative left in France, while in Germany, everything had gone over to the new order, with the exception of those cars built at Ford's Cologne factory and of a few older, luxury-car types. Italy's solitary cart-sprung contribution was the Bianchi, by now in token production only.

Thus the way of the world at the end of our period. In 1930, there were few heretics, of whom Lancia and Röhr were the most important. Shock absorbers were, however, universal, with hydraulic types replacing the primitive friction arrangements of earlier days. On luxury models (Rolls-Royce and Packard) they could be set to adjust the ride while the car was in motion.

Independent front suspension was, of course, motivated by different reasons on opposite sides of the Atlantic, as comparative drives in (say) a Lancia and a Buick will quickly reveal. In the United States, the objective was the so-called "boulevard ride", calculated to damp out the shocks to be expected on the poor surfaces of the backwoods, both at home and in such vital export markets as Argentina, Australia, and South Africa. General Motors's notorious "knee action" was publicized by photographs showing cars with conventional and modern suspensions each with one front wheel resting on a wood block some 6 in (15 cm) high. It was firmly pointed out that the "one with the knees" was the one also retaining a horizontal roof-line. This was true: bumps were smoothed out with commendable regularity. What the customer was left to discover for himself was that the cars rolled and pitched most disconcertingly in corners, while sudden braking caused the "knees" to curtsey frantically. (A switch to torsion bars on some later General Motors models was said to counteract this party piece, but it merely reversed it. The nose went up first!) Later coil-and-wishbone systems of the short-and-long-arm persuasion were much better, but Americans remained unconvinced. Chevrolet themselves would retain a beam-axle option in their catalogues right up to 1940.

Not that European designers were unconcerned with poor surfaces. The protagonists of sophisticated suspensions were Czechoslovakia and Germany – the former still with notoriously rough roads, and the latter desperately in need of foreign exchange. Germany's best export markets were Central and Eastern Europe, Scandinavia, and South Africa, all of them unkind to cars. European designers had also, however, a keen interest in handling, and the best torsion-bar systems, notably those of BMW and Citroën, were as sure-footed in the rough as in the

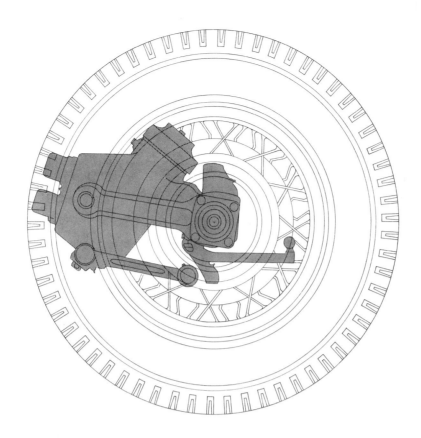

Suspension layouts. The short-and-long-arm coil system, here seen (*far left*) on a 1934 Oldsmobile, was effectively the prototype for later coil arrangements, whereas the Dubonnet "knees" (*left*) carried the front wheel on a single arm extending forward from the king pin. Hydraulic shock absorbers were incorporated into the system, which was oil-filled and, therefore, theoretically self-lubricating. Levels had, however, to be topped up at 25,000-mile (40,000 km) intervals, and owners did not always bother, so that heavy wear added to the Dubonnet's disconcerting habit of "curtseying" under hard braking. American ideas of suspension are, however, reflected in Vauxhall's 1935 publicity. Of the two sedans—the one in the upper centre a 1934 with semi-elliptics at the front—it was the car with knees that maintained the even roof-line. The Evenkeel independent front wheel suspension (*bottom*) on the 1936 – 47 Hillmans and Humbers was based on an equivalent construction on the 1935 Studebaker. Its characteristic was that the lateral springs doubled as the lower stub axle. The shock-absorber was mounted on the frame and was actuated by the upper stub axle via a linking rod. A shaped rubber cushion on the upper stub axle coped with excessive bumps.

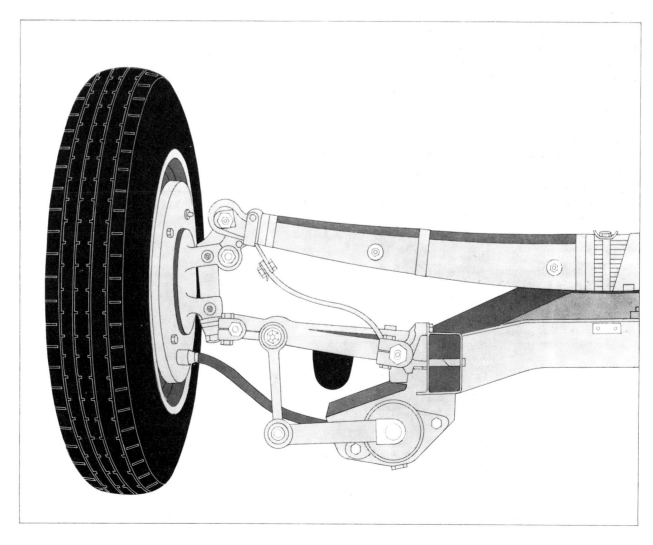

When one considers that it appeared in 1922, it's astonishing that the Austin Seven – 1930 (*top*) and 1935 (*opposite, top right*) – was still in production as late as the spring of 1939. More remarkably, its sales increased in the 1930s, peaking in 1935 (27,280 units). Main differences over a five-year period were coupled brakes and an extra forward gear, though this was added at the wrong end, giving an underdrive for assaults on the vertical. Weight went up faster than anything else – from 1,080 lb (490 kg) to 1,358 (615 kg), an increment which gave the more modern babies of Ford and Morris an even greater advantage.

In the 1,100-cc class, two late thirties offerings were the German Hansa of 1937 (*bottom*) and the 1938 Peugeot 202 from France (*opposite, centre right*). With its beetling hood and headlamps tucked away behind the grille (the battery lived there as well!), the Peugeot looks the more modern design. Its 30-hp overhead-valve four-cylinder engine had the near-square dimensions of 68×78 mm, and front wheels were independently sprung, but a three-speed transmission was deemed sufficient, and on pre-war versions brakes were mechanical. It was, however, an admirable workhorse and tided its makers over into 1949 and the advent of the unitary 203. Some 104,000 were made, as against perhaps 20,000 Hansas between 1934 and the war – but then Carl Borgward's empire was still young. This Hansa featured a typically German backbone frame with transverse-leaf independent front suspension and a swing-axle rear end, while brakes were hydraulic from the start; so were four forward speeds. It was as modestly rated (27.5 hp from 1,088 cc) as the Peugeot, but better looking. Oddly, the Hansa 1100 was scheduled for elimination under the Schell plan for rationalizing the German automobile industry, but its good export sales earned it a reprieve, and the model was still listed in Sweden in 1940.

Teutonic half-measures. By 1939, the six-cylinder Type 320 Mercedes-Benz cabriolet (*opposite, left*) had all-independent springing – indeed, its predecessors had been so endowed for six years – but the chassis was otherwise conventional and the engine a stolid and lethargic flathead. Eight years its senior is the Austro-Daimler Alpine Eight (*bottom*) from over the border in Vienna. The Austrian car is also of greater technical interest. True, the front axle rides on longitudinal half-elliptic springs, but clearly visible is the swing-axle rear end, tailor-made for twisty roads and poor surfaces, if sometimes a handful in the wet. The frame is a tubular backbone with outriggers for the body, fourth gear is an overdrive for fast cruising, and both cylinder block and barrels are of light alloy. Alas, all this weight-paring was exploited by Austrian coachbuilders, and most Alpine Eights weighed well over two tons, and sometimes nearly three. The engine's 115 hp weren't really enough, but then Österreichisches Daimler weren't after the sports-car market. If performance was what you wanted, you opted for the six-cylinder Bergmeister – a litre less of engine, more compact dimensions, and five extra hp.

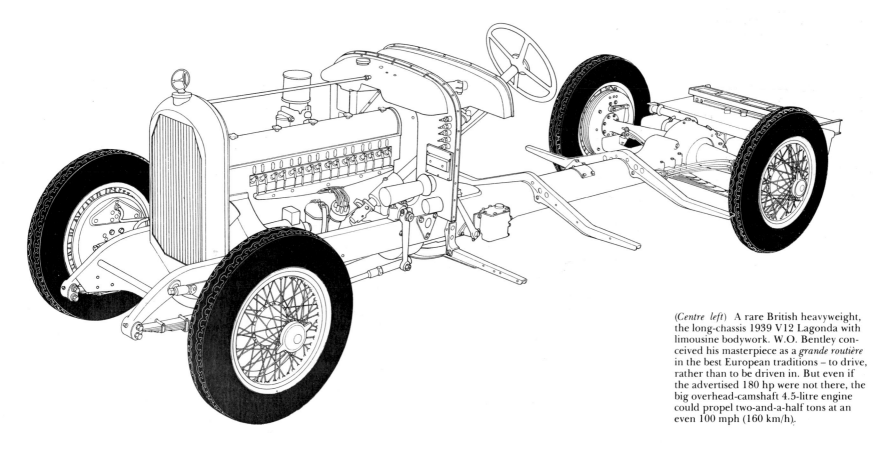

(*Centre left*) A rare British heavyweight, the long-chassis 1939 V12 Lagonda with limousine bodywork. W.O. Bentley conceived his masterpiece as a *grande routière* in the best European traditions – to drive, rather than to be driven in. But even if the advertised 180 hp were not there, the big overhead-camshaft 4.5-litre engine could propel two-and-a-half tons at an even 100 mph (160 km/h).

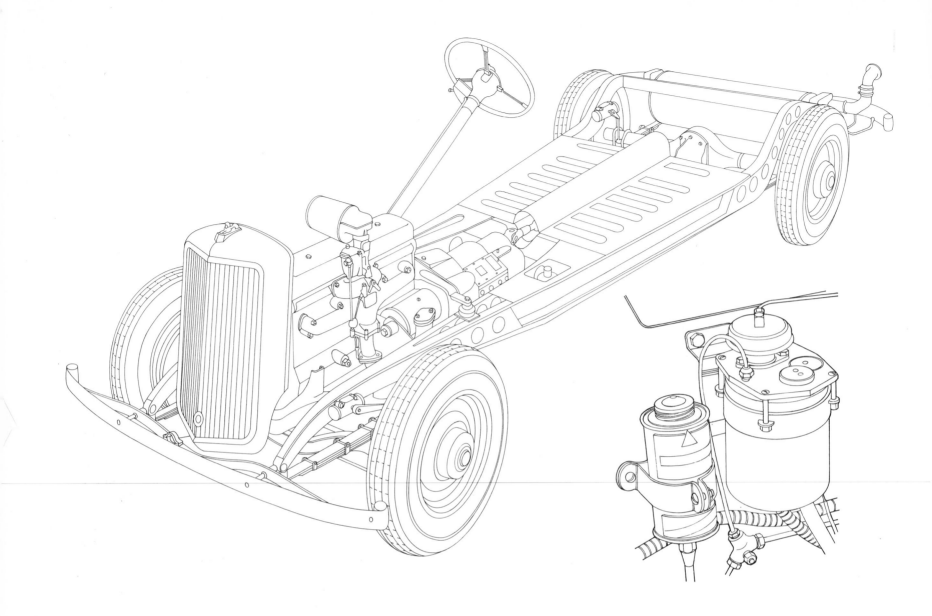

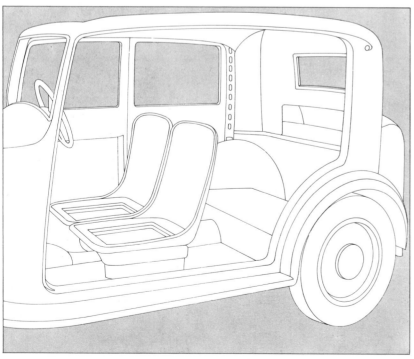

First steps to unitary construction. The 1939 16-hp Armstrong Siddeley (*above*) had a separate chassis, conventional suspension, and mechanical brakes, as well as the preselective gearbox standardized on the make since 1932. The "sealed floor fume-proof frame" was, however, rather more than that, since it gave the extra rigidity of a further box section, to which the body was bolted. Officially, it was the first Armstrong Siddeley not supplied as a chassis to special coachbuilders, and some cheapening is apparent in the stylizing of the sphinx mascot. Intended as a 70-mph (112 km/h) five-passenger sedan for "volume" production, it accounted for only some 950 units before war intervened.

The bare bones of an early unitary structure (*left*), the 1,196-cc Lancia Augusta of 1933, are interesting as they reveal great structural strength. Also interesting is another space and weight-saving device favoured by European small-car makers (among them, Triumph), the pillarless four-door configuration. It made for easy entry and exit but rattled fearsomely in old age, causing the doors to twist and lose their fit. Draughts were also a problem.

Built-in amenities. The Bijur system of automatic chassis lubrication (*above right*), here seen on a 1934 Rover, had reached Europe from the United States in the early 1930s. The reservoir was easily accessible, and the system was operated by that useful standby, inlet manifold depression. An elaborate system of metering jets was used, the grease gun being reserved for awkward places like the splines of the propeller shaft and the rear wheel hubs. Alas! tiny pipes became clogged with old age, and the cars of the 1930s had a long, enforced innings in front of them. Often the automatics were dispensed with in old age.

smooth. Lancia's coils and sliding pillars had proved their worth since 1922, while also excellent was Fiat's conventional coil-spring set up on the first 1100s, though this one was abnormally sensitive to tyre pressures. A significant factor of the better European designs was that they retained a wheel at each corner, thus attaining a superior weight distribution. Outside the realm of the big mock-Americans, one seldom encountered the monumental degree of overhang common to Detroit's efforts.

The all-independent system was largely confined to Germany, Austria, and Czechoslovakia; elsewhere conservatism and the cost accountant conspired to exclude it. It was not a system that could be grafted on to an existing chassis design. Even the pioneering Austro-Daimlers of the late 1920s, which combined independent rear springing with a beam front axle, used Karl Rabe's new tubular backbone frames (first pioneered by the Czech Ledvinka). Further, the then fashionable swing-axle arrangement had its limitations. Longitudinal corrugations often caught it unawares, and while it was admirably suited to cope with the stolid side-valve engines of the contemporary touring Mercedes-Benz, it could assume frightening attitudes when asked to transmit the 180 bhp of a supercharged straight-eight with blower engaged. Significantly, independent rear suspension promised to become one of the casualties of the inflationary 1970s.

Tubular backbone frames might have been the concomitants of Germany's new suspension units, but the conventional ladder-type chassis had plenty of life left in it. Design philosophy had, admittedly, changed from the whippy and inadequately braced structures of the 1920s, while one constructional feature hardly ever seen after 1930 was the use of a separate U-section sub-frame for engine and gearbox. Amidships cruciform bracing was perhaps the most important technical legacy of the first Cord, 1929's L29, and though there were still some horrors about (the Hornet and Scorpion were by no means the sole cases of haphazard up-engining in the Depression years), cruciforms of one kind and another had become accepted practice by 1935, assisted by rigid box-section side-members of generous depth. On bigger cars it was not uncommon to add further supplementary K-bracing aft of the gearbox, though the switch towards unit construction of motor and transmission tended to make this superfluous. The old disease of chassis flexing – which broke fuel pipes and helped bodies to disintegrate – was almost a thing of the past, except where the frame came out overweight and its side-members were too liberally drilled. Morris Eights of the 1935–38 period were notable offenders in this direction.

Curiously centralized "one-shot" systems of chassis lubrication, found on many a middle-class or luxury model of the 1930s, were not destined to survive long into the post-war years. Pressing a pedal on the floor every hundred miles or so might be a great deal more painless than a messy session with the grease gun (and cheaper than paying someone else to do it), but to be successful, pain-killers had to be foolproof as well as therapeutic, and one-shot systems were not. Hence, along with built-in jackets and self-adjusting tappets, they vanished from the scene, aided and abetted by horrible memories of "gummed up" vehicles retrieved from six years of storage in 1945! The Jackalls beloved of British makers could be restored to health with a medicinal dose of mineral oil, but the top end of a twelve-cylinder Rolls-Royce motor required more drastic remedies. Hence, the grease gun returned to favour, until such time as the industry came up with components "lubricated for life".

Unitary construction of chassis and body posed a large question mark throughout the latter half of the decade. The integration of the automobile was primarily the work of the stylists, who had intruded upon the American scene in the later 1920s. Indeed, their endeavours were all too often at variance with those of the engineers, especially in realms such as underhood accessibility (an alligator hood streamlines better, but the sides won't come off so that you can get at the fuel pump) and facia design (stylized instruments are all too often illegible). Nevertheless, however a car might look – and models like the Sixty Special Cadillac of 1938 contained no detectable appendages or afterthoughts – it was still essentially a chassis and running gear designed by engineers and wedded to a body created by artists. Even if the custom-coachwork industry had gone into a steady decline, many traditional chassis manufacturers (Rolls-Royce, Maybach, and Alvis, for instance) made no bodies themselves, and their measure of control over what went onto their chassis was limited to a right to withhold the warranty if the coachwork exceeded a statutory weight.

At less exalted levels, of course, a manufacturer had to budget for bodies as well as mechanical elements, and here the unitary system had its attractions. Foremost of these was structural strength: Chrysler and Citroën dropped cars off cliffs to demonstrate the advantages of the new idiom, and Morris staged a series of radio-controlled crashes to prove that 1939's integral Ten sedan was stronger than the separate-chassis type listed in 1938. On the debit side, a switch to unitary methods involved fearsome tooling bills, the amortization of which called for a long production run.

Worse still, the unitary system was inflexible: sedans and station wagons (the latter, as we shall see, as yet hardly a part of the motoring scene) represented the limit of stylistic diversity. When Vauxhall's Australian clients wanted a tourer on their new H-series Ten, a separate-chassis variant had to be offered, and Lancia made a practice of such a type to keep the specialist coachbuilders happy. Even more important were the economic limitations imposed on interim improvements. One could extract a few more brake horses from the engine by adding an extra carburettor. One could change the grille, lengthen the boot slightly, or maybe even alter the shape of the front fenders, provided that these latter remained separate entities, as they did on the original Citroën *traction*. Anything else – even suspension alterations on a major scale – would upset the even tenor of the road to amortization.

The owner had his worries, too. While he was more likely to survive a major crash, his car might suffer sufficient distortion in a minor one to make it an insurance write-off. Further more, body rust, already a problem with cheap pressed-steel coachwork, now meant structural rust as well.

The United States was logically the one country that could afford unitary methods. It was also the one that needed them not! Americans still demanded a choice of six or seven bodies per model, and going unitary spelt goodbye to convertibles. In any case, the same sheet metal was expected to last two or three years, and if a model failed to sell forty thousand a year during that period, it was no longer economically viable, chassis or no chassis. This, however, did not stop General Motors from trying out the new techniques, first on Opels in Germany, and then at the British Vauxhall factory. By 1940, all their European models had dispensed with a separate chassis, even if the home team would not take the plunge until 1959.

Semi-unitary methods were less expensive: once the car was put together, chassis and body were inseparable, but the two elements were constructed separately and then welded or bolted up. Typical of this technique were the Chrysler Airflow (1934) and the Lincoln Zephyr (1936). The Chrysler was, in fact, an interesting anticipation of the space-frame techniques which would emerge on specialist Italian sports cars in the late 1940s. The body was a "cage" to which the panels were welded. In Britain Austin typified a different and more gradual approach to the unitary ideal: on the company's last pre-war Eights and

Unitary structures. The Vauxhall (*bottom*) of 1938 is almost the copybook configuration and immensely strong. A heavy cross member is needed at the rear with rear-wheel drive, while additional strength was achieved by ribs on the underside, which also helped to cut out drumming. This drawing serves to explain the catastrophic effect of corrosion, especially in floor or wheel arches, but with long enough runs the system paid off. Vauxhall's H-type shape sat it out for ten years from 1938, and the L-type (1948–51) wasn't all that different. With front-wheel drive, of course, one doesn't need half as much bracing at the rear, and J.A. Grégoire's Amilcar-Compound (*opposite, top*), a sensation of the 1937 Shows, used light alloys to keep weight down still further. The short side members incorporated the sills and were tied at the front by a simple cross-member, while also part of the structure was the firewall, incorporated on this one with the windshield pillars. Alas! it was a case of too little, too late – less than seven hundred had been delivered before the Fall of France.

Unitaries clothed. Britain's 1939 Morris Ten (*top*), the 1300 Hanomag from Germany (*opposite, bottom left*), and the

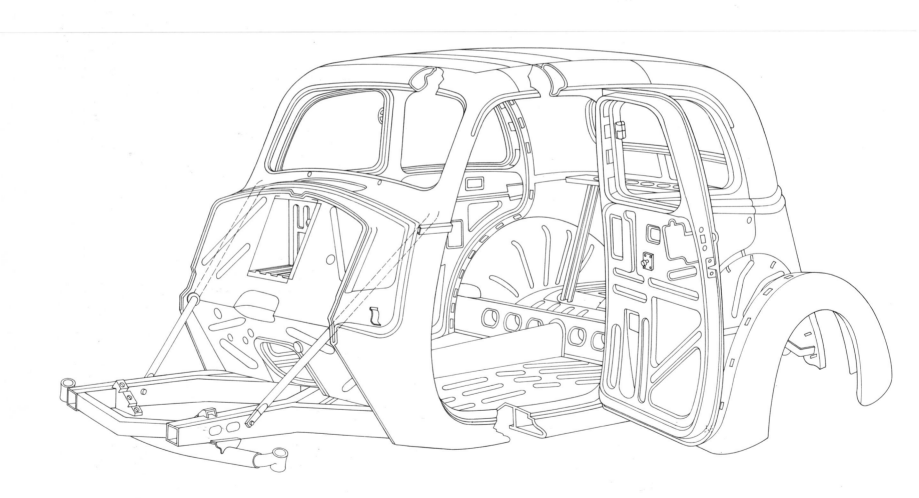

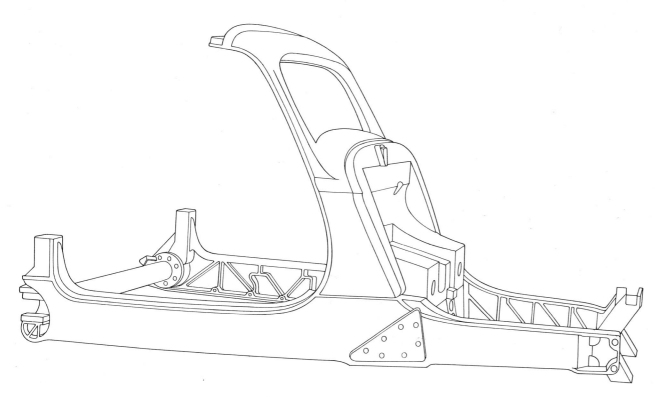

Nash 600 introduced in 1941 (*bottom right*) have conventional drive-lines, while on the 1938 Amilcar Compound (*centre left*) the drive is taken to the front wheels. For all its low build and absence of running boards, the Amilcar's looks are spoilt by the usual mock-American grille, while there's nothing in the appearance of the Morris or the Nash to suggest unorthodox methods of construction. The Hanomag's teardrop shape owes much to the high cruising speeds possible on Germany's new *Autobahnen*, though. The Nash is, by the way, the final 1948 manifestation of the original 60 series, though only the grille differs in substance from the first cars.

Odd man out is, of course, the 1938 57S Bugatti (*centre right*), the absolute antithesis of cheap unitary tinware, classical and bespoke to the Nth degree, and only just endowed with hydraulic brakes. It was also just about the fastest "street" machine one could buy in those days.

Tens the body was welded to a platform, the latter being integral with the chassis proper.

Perhaps the most advanced of all the pre-war unitaries was, however, J.A. Grégoire's Amilcar Compound, first seen at the 1937 Paris Salon. This showed what could be done by a combination of inspired metallurgy and the new idiom. The floor pan, firewall, windshield supports, door stills, and front cross-member were all of light alloy, the result being a four-seater sedan with a 1,185-cc engine, the whole thing weighing only 0.8 tons, where 1 ton was the norm for the class. Even more remarkable, the power unit itself was an obsolete side-valve four to which no lightening techniques had been applied. The Grégoire, alas, was to have a chequered career, and probably less than fifteen hundred cars of all types were made to the designer's own ideas. The post-war Dyna-Panhard, its best-known descendant, was heavily modified by Panhard's design staff.

The automobile of the 1930s looked rather as if it had been designed by parsimonious accountants for moronic owners. A surplus of chromium plate was no substitute for fine workmanship, and underhood finish was a thing of the past. Styling had ousted craftsmanship. With a few honourable exceptions, the vehicle was not fun to drive, and from a purely technical standpoint a 1939 model cannot be termed revolutionary in relation to what the same money would buy in 1930. What must stand to its credit, though, is that – used in the manner for which it was designed – it worked astonishingly well and would go on doing so for many years.

Semi-unitary construction on the De Soto Airflow, 1934. Here we have such considerations as a perfect aerodynamic shape – designer Carl Breer based his design on a study of bird and aeroplane flight – plus, once again, the need to accommodate all seats within the wheel-base. We have come a long way from 1929 in other respects. Moving the passengers forward involves shifting the engine over the front axle centre-line, and also fitting it into a sloping nose with high streamline fenders which necessitate an alligator hood. It also involved mounting the radiator laterally, an idea of more questionable merit. What is even more interesting is the all-steel girder framework, in effect a species of birdcage on which the body panels were hung. This took some of the strain off the "chassis", hence Chrysler were able to use side-frame rails which were much lighter and shallower than those on conventional cars. Even if the Chrysler and De Soto Airflows were not fully unitary in the Citroën or Lancia sense, they had one important advantage, and one which helped the Corporation to survive the less than enthusiastic reception accordes their "leap in the dark". Body panels were few in number; essentially, there were three: the top and the two sides. Further; they could be standardized throughout the full Airflow range. Future trends were anticipated by incorporating the main differences between Chrysler and De Soto – both dimensionally and in styling detail – into the front-end sheet-metal section from the windshield forward.

Chapter 3

BODIES – BEAUTIFUL AND OTHERWISE

At first sight, the story of coachwork in the 1930s is, once again, one of consolidation.

There were, outwardly, no new elements. Stylists – if not under that label – had existed long before Lawrence P. Fisher brought Harley Earl to work at General Motors in 1926. Unitary construction was as old as the automobile itself; many horse-drawn carriages had, indeed, no chassis in the accepted sense. What happened in the 1930s – and to a far greater extent in the first post-Second World War years – was that the work of chassis engineer and body designer coalesced to produce a new generation of automobile.

As we have seen, true unitaries were as yet uncommon. There is a tendency to swell their ranks by attaching a unitary label to the DKW, for instance, but this design featured a simple twin-rail backbone with outriggers. The major supporters of the new idiom in 1939 amounted to General Motors's two European houses (Vauxhall and Opel), Citroën in France, Lancia in Italy, and Hanomag in Germany. J.A. Grégoire's Amilcar was made in insignificant numbers only, while Morris and Renault were still hedging their bets (one unitary type apiece, with a wide range of conventionally-engineered cars as well). As for the latest Hillman Minx, announced on the eve of war, the principal beneficiaries of this, for some time to come, would be members of the Allied fighting services.

Stylistic integration had, however, come a long way since 1920 and was destined to make far more dramatic strides between 1930 and 1942. If we take General Motors's Cadillac Division as a leader (which it was in more senses than one), an intriguing comparison may be drawn between the 353-series Eight of 1930 and the Sixty Special of some nine years later. Hindsight and the collector mentality have ordained that the former is beautiful and the latter just another phase in the stylistic round of Detroit. That distinguished historian Maurice D. Hendry, however, puts it better, labelling the early-thirties cars as "cosmetic" and the later ones as "functional".

Say what one wishes, the 1930 car is still a combination, albeit a well-balanced one, of chassis and body. Integration is limited to the line of hood and belt, even if the fenders, with those almost mandatory wells for the dual sidemounts, complement the ensemble of, say, a "Madame-X" sedan by Fleetwood with the slant windshield. Radiator, bumpers, headlamps, running board, and spare wheels remain separate entities. The luggage accommodation is a shameless appendage; the primitive, unsightly, folding trunk rack, a stylist's despair. Only Packard ever managed to make a successful feature out of it.

Compare it with the Sixty Special shape. Gone is that uncompromis-ing radiator; it has been supplanted by a grille which blends into the front fender line, even if that complex pattern of chromium-plated bars has yet to spill over into the front apron. The headlamps are already receding into the fenders, and running boards have all but disappeared. Not only is there more room for baggage; it lives in an integral projection at the rear of the body, which forms a continuous line, apart from a notchback incorporated in the interests of rear-seat headroom. Bumpers may still pursue a fairly independent existence, but one feels that, at any moment, they may be sucked into the existing frontal ensemble. One is right: this will happen in 1942. As for the spare wheel – the customer can still specify sidemounts if he must, but why bother? There's plenty of room in that big trunk. Like it or not, the wire wheels have given way to plain discs, easier to clean and entirely viable now that improved sound-damping techniques have eliminated the characteristic clangour of those old Michelins on the 1919 Citroën and its contemporaries.

The separate chassis on both these Cadillacs are more rigid than those of many of the opposition. Yet the concept is far more unified than, say, the latest chassis-less Morris Ten with its separate headlamps and conventionally-shaped fenders. We have come a long way since 1914.

Initially, of course, an automobile manufacturer was a chassis maker. As likely as not, he had no interest in bodies. As late as 1910, Renault made few, if any, themselves, and Fiat tended to buy theirs out, even if their basic tourers were standardized. Mercedes owned their carriage shops at Sindelfingen, separate from the main works at Stuttgart. Austin were exceptional in that, even in 1908, "the whole of the carriage work is carried out in our own factory, where, with the aid of the latest and most efficient plant, we are able to fit any type of body the customer may prefer". They were also prepared to "send our carriage designer to confer with and advise anyone not able to visit the works" – surely a case of gilding the lily, when the catalogue already offered a choice of one roadster, seven phaetons, and all of five distinct varieties in the formal idiom.

In effect, Austin were running a custom body shop because they had the facilities. One cannot imagine Herbert Austin sanctioning a body on a rival chassis, though his neighbours, the Lanchester Motor Company, would so oblige customers on occasion. And this "separate" philosophy would outlive even the unifying influences of the stylist. The manufacturers of 1920 showed little interest in bodies, and their successors were content to farm out a surprising proportion of what appeared to be their own responsibility.

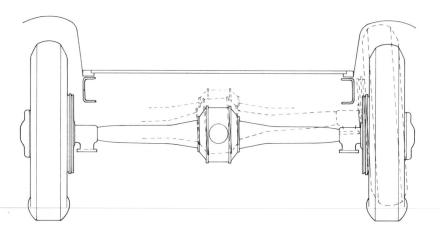

The 1934 Morris Ten (*top left*) and similarly rated 1938 Rover (*centre left*) are to a great extent look-alikes, thanks to bodies of the same make. Rover's cheapest sedans, like almost all Morris's, came from Pressed Steel at Oxford. A lot more handwork went into the Rover, a quality offering costing £248 ($1,240), some £70 ($350) more than was asked for the older Morris. It wasn't until 1938 that Morris would switch to the pushrod overhead valves found on every Rover since 1929. Oddly, though, it is Morris who offer hydraulic brakes: Rover would stay with rod-operated mechanicals until well after the war. The 3½-litre Jaguar (*bottom*) is actually a 1947 model, but the post-war improvements are minor and invisible in this picture; William Lyons's shapes were quite as ageless as Rover's contemporary sports sedans (which they made themselves) and even better proportioned.

It had a top speed of over 90 mph (145 km/h), a comfortable cruising speed of 80 (130 km/h), and an engine life in excess of 100,000 miles (160,000 km) at the price of a daunting thirst (16 mpg or 17.8 lit/100). That the 1938 Cadillac 75 limousine (*top right*) consumed even more fuel mattered little to the customers. Here were all the latest refinements, including coil-spring independent front suspension (all Jaguars made up to 1948 had beam axles) and the brand-new column shift. The 141-in (3.6 m) wheel-base made it an eight-seater.

Bentley under Rolls-Royce management, 1934. It isn't really fair to call the 3½-litre, here seen (*top*) with sedanca coupé body for four, a tuned 20/25 Rolls-Royce, though the engine is a twin-carburettor version of the Royce and the four-speed synchromesh transmission with its right-hand shift is authentic Derby, along with the famous mechanical servo brakes. The performance was in another class altogether: while the 20/25 was flat out at 70 mph (112 km/h), the 110-hp Bentley was good for 90 (145 km/h) and returned a surprising 20 mpg (14 lit/100). The manufacturer's drawing (*opposite, centre right*) is for the guidance of coachbuilders – in the best Rolls-Royce tradition there were no factory bodies – and shows the permitted clearances between axle and rear seat, and wheel arches and wheels. The rules were strict – an accompanying rider stated that if the car was intended for use with snow chains, an extra half-inch (1.25 cm) of clearance must be allowed over the arches. Also marked up for the body builder is the chassis plan view (*bottom*), of especial interest as illustrating the wastefulness of the old long-hooded classic layout. Wheel-base is 126 in (3.2 m, or 6 in/15.2 cm shorter than a 20/25 Rolls-Royce), but though the 96 in (2.4 m) reserved for the body is exclusive of trunk space, one has effectively to deduct 14 in (35.5 cm) for the firewall. The engine's position well back in the frame is also clearly visible.

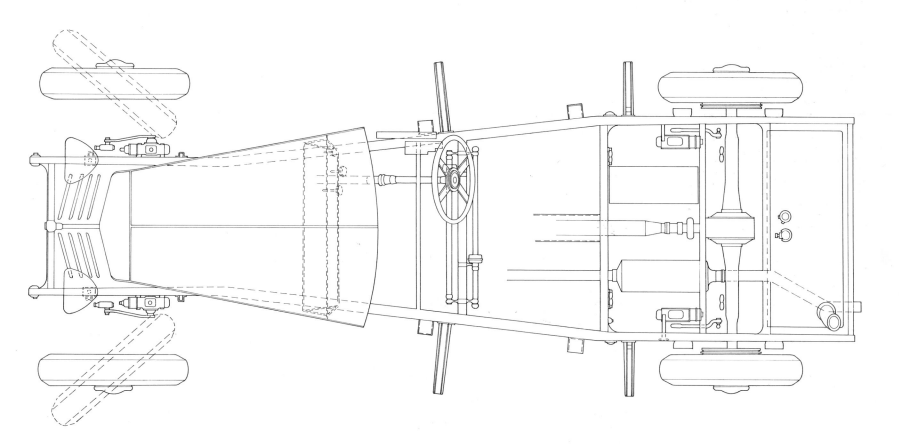

In the interim period before the introduction of their fully integral *traction avant* in 1934, Citroën switched to a "monoshell" form of body construction, here seen on their inexpensive 8CV 1.5-litre sedan of 1933. Since a separate chassis (*below*) was still used, other body types could be fitted, and small-volume production rendered monoshell methods unnecessary for these.

Here the various stages of Citroën's welded-up construction can be seen (*right*). First the two side panels, with sills but not as yet doors, are joined to the complete rear section. Then the top and the structural arch of the firewall are added, while the third phase embraces the dash and floor. Finally, the doors are fitted, though on some variants there was also an integral projecting trunk at the rear, not seen in this sequence. The structure was extremely rigid and could withstand major crashes. An interesting aspect of this form of construction was the metal overlap between the sections, used to strengthen the various welds. In addition to this 8CV body, also used on "light" editions of the 10CV and 15CV cars, there was also a three-window variation for 10s and 15s. Such expensive processes were, of course, only viable for long runs, and 1933 was not a time for such structural experiments, even in the case of a firm with a potential of maybe seventy thousand identical sedans a year. Probably less than twenty thousand of this two-window type were produced.

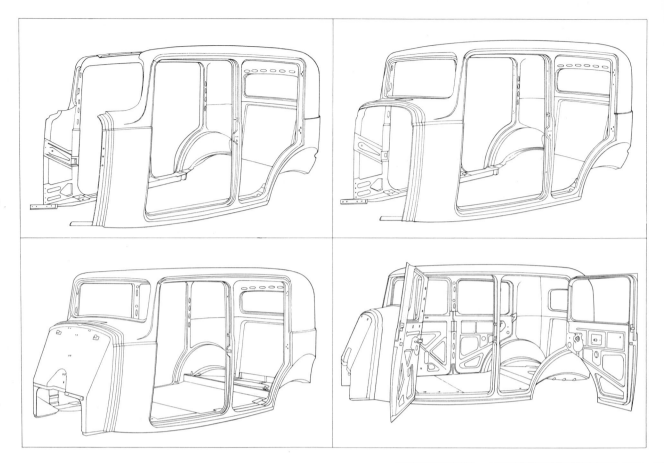

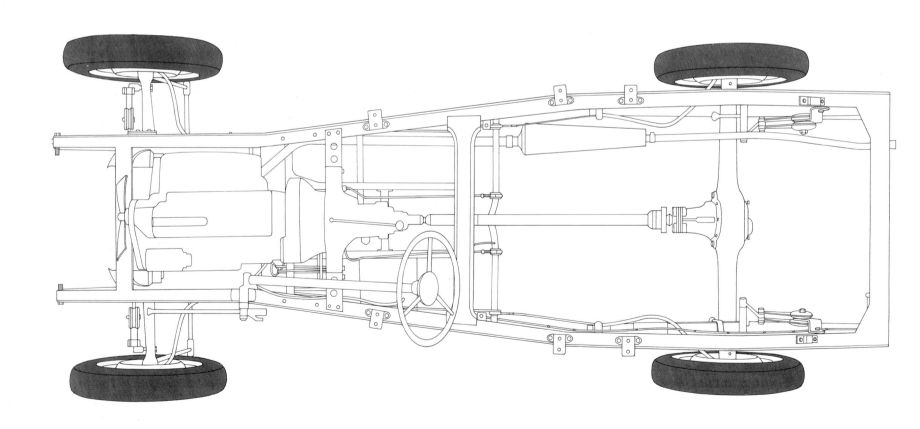

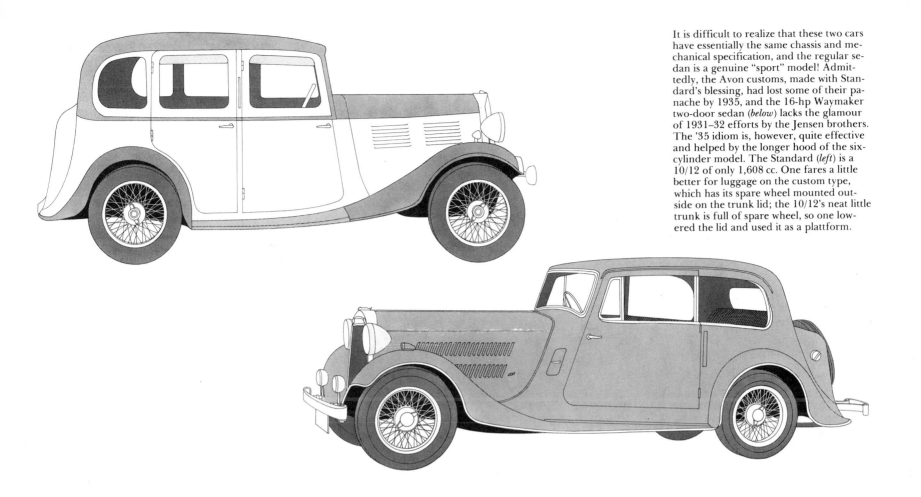

In the luxury sporting field, of course, bodies were of interest, whoever made them. W.O. Bentley, the Lyles of Invicta fame, and (especially) Gabriel Voisin were apt to tear up the official warranty if the end-product came out too heavy. Voisin denounced the American-style roadster in ringing terms and compared a car without luggage accommodation to "a weapon with no ammunition". But even in the 1930s, a "factory" body meant little more than a body built in series to a factory-approved specification, sold off the showroom floor with the chassis maker's guarantee. General Motors's cheaper coachwork was the physical responsibility of their Fisher Division, the specialized Fleetwood branch handling the costlier Cadillacs and La Salles. Ford drew heavily on such "trade" firms as Briggs and Murray; in 1936, it was estimated that the former company handled sixty-two per cent of Ford contracts, with twenty-two per cent going to Murray and most of the rest to Budd in Philadelphia. Other important Briggs customers were Chrysler (who would eventually absorb them), Graham, Hudson, and Packard. These American coachbuilders lived off the industry, just as did some of the major British houses – Charlesworth, for instance, and Carbodies. For the time being, coachbuilders would remain independent, though Nash had already solved their body problems by buying their main supplier, Seaman of Milwaukee.

The big trade coachbuilders were, of course, geared to longish runs. When Murray landed Ford's coupé contract in 1935, it may have seemed small pickings by contrast with Briggs's orders for sedans, but that year, Ford were good for close to a million units, and that meant a potential of one hundred coupés alone every working hour. Such a situation, inevitably, called for a two-way guarantee. The chassis maker had to be able to sell the cars as well. Hence, the ingredients of disaster were at hand, and disaster would supervene once the body specialists switched to unitary hulls.

For smaller runs, different arrangements were required. The chassis maker might be anxious to pad his catalogue, but how to do it when the additional style had a potential of, perhaps, one hundred units out of a model-year run of maybe twenty-five thousand? Setting up jigs in his own shops was hardly viable; far less so would it be to farm the job out to one of the giant press-work specialists. And in these days of all-steel construction and higher amortization levels, a run of at least ten thousand was called for, spread over three years at the maximum.

Thus, we encounter a new class of "tame" coachbuilder. German factories drew their cabriolets from Deutsch, Drauz, Gläser, and Karmann, with Salmons-Tickford as the British equivalent of this quartette. During the 1930s, this latter firm would build catalogued styles for BSA, Daimler, Hillman, Lanchester, MG, Rover, Standard, Triumph, Vauxhall, and Wolseley. In Italy, Fiat used Garavini and Viotti, among others.

Vauxhall, perhaps, show the body policy of the 1930s at its most typical. More interestingly still, they were one of the few firms which successfully effected the transformation from carriage-trade to big league. When General Motors took over in 1925, the factory was under-employed in relation to an annual potential of only fifteen hundred cars. In 1939, they were good for forty thousand, a figure they would surely have achieved but for the war. And before they went unitary, they prided themselves on their diversity of body styles.

Yet all they made themselves at Luton were the regular sedans. The four-passenger Light Six coupés, listed as factory bodies, were, in fact, made by Pressed Steel at Oxford. Two-door convertibles were usually

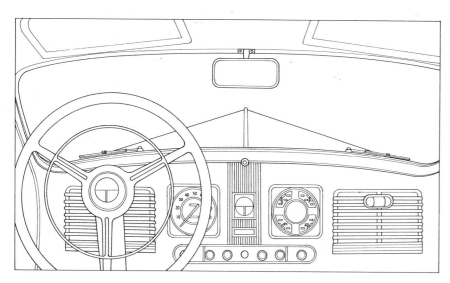

The 1938 Chrysler Imperial Eight marks the triumph of styling over most other considerations, though at least the facia (*top left*) contains instruments of recognizable shape. The sectioning of dials into four quarters (amps, fuel, oil pressure, water temperature) is a favourite space-saver of the period, and preferable to the later configuration (a fuel gauge, plus "idiot lights" for the other three!) The front end (*top right*) reflects the horizontal-bar motifs to which all American makers were addicted in 1937 and 1938. In Britain, of course, General Motors's local branch, Vauxhall, was the mainstay of the local custom-body industry. The 1933–34 AS-type Light Six Stratford sporting four-seater (*bottom*) by Whittingham and Mitchel of London had quite a lot of charm and cost only about £30 ($150) more than a stock sedan. The coachbuilder was not seduced by the snob appeal of sidemounts and managed to convey an illusion of greater length by extending the hood right back to windshield level.

The 1931 sixteen-cylinder Cadillac roadster (*opposite, top right*) looks every inch a thoroughbred, with its long hood (note the then-fashionable doors), scalloped fenders, sidemounts, and wire wheels. Proportions are near perfect, and only a dedicated utilitarian could complain that there is far too much car for two people. At the other end of the scale are two later American solutions for big families on vacation or in pursuit of heavy shopping. Ford's 1939 V8 Woody (*opposite, top left*) was probably the first station wagon to sell in big quantities. Bodies shared no panels with other styles and thus cost more to make: they also called for frequent revarnishing and were ill-suited for tropical climes. Some quiverful families preferred the seven-passenger sedan, a lengthened edition of the stock article, with jump seats. Unwieldy it certainly was: the 1939 P6 Plymouth (*bottom*) had its wheel-base extended from 112 in (2.8 m) to 132 in (3.4 m).

assigned to Salmons-Tickford, though earlier ones came from Martin Walter of Folkestone, plus a handful from Grose (Northampton), and Vauxhall's "tame" coachbuilder, the London-based Grosvenor. Sport sedans, by Holbrook of Coventry, Palmer of Dover, and even Bertelli of Aston Martin fame, figured in sundry catalogues, while all the four-door convertibles were Martin Walter's well-loved Winghams, also listed by Hillman and Daimler-Lanchester. Holbrook also produced a small number of sports tourers, though the majority of these came from Whittingham and Mitchel, a London house specializing in sportier styles. Those whose tastes ran to a traditional roadster or tourer could have it as late as 1935–36, from Duple, whose usual line of business was bus bodies, many of them for Vauxhall-built Bedford chassis. It is easy to understand why Martin Walter switched to commercial coachbuilding when Vauxhall elected to dispense with separate chassis.

"Tame" coachbuilders were an asset in those difficult days. Gordon of Birmingham built only on Austin chassis, Cunard on Morris, and until they were taken over by Standard after the Second World War, Mulliners of Birmingham worked mainly for Daimler. Standard themselves padded their range with attractive sporting bodies commissioned from New Avon of Warwick. It all helped make elegance and variety as painless as synchromesh – and still kept the cost accountants from complaining.

Some styles, of course, could not be fitted into the new idiom, however high their sales potential. Most important of these was the original woody-type station wagon, still regarded as a commercial vehicle, though usually fitted to a regular passenger chassis. Its social acceptance would be a wartime phenomenon. Hence, sales were low – the usual clients were ranches, hotels, and the Stately Homes of the Old World, where the woody doubled as transport for guns to the butts and servants to the village hop. Worse still, its constructional methods militated against every principle of press-work. At best, it shared cowl, windshield, and rear fenders with sedans or coupés.

Thus, woodies were farmed out. Ford, with the advantage of a factory-owned wood mill, made all the components but had Murray assemble them. When the Depression struck, a Kentucky firm took over the timberware. Chrysler bought from the Indiana-based US Body and Forging Company, while General Motors, for all the Fisher family's timber interests, were still using three outside suppliers in 1940. By this time, business had picked up – Ford alone disposed of thirteen thousand wagons that year, so they were able to reopen their mill and dispense with outside help. Chrysler, likewise, had switched to a fully-owned subsidiary, though even then the bits were sent to Detroit for assembly.

These complicated minor operations were necessitated by the spread of press-work: a good body shop accustomed to composite construction could easily have coped with the woodies in the 1920s, had there been a demand. But times had changed.

The big American operations – Briggs, Budd, Fisher, and Murray – were now matched by European ventures such as Pressed Steel in Britain, Chausson in France, and Ambi-Budd in Germany. These, like all the American companies save Fisher, were independent of the car makers; Pressed Steel, launched as a Morris exclusive in 1927, broadened its base after 1930, when Morris sold his share and let other firms cash in on the benefits of methods which eliminated screw joints and hand-work. Such plants cost money: £2 million ($10 million) of capital and £0.5 million worth of equipment (including a 245-ton press) went into the creation of Pressed Steel's Oxford works, but manufacture was simplified. A Budd-type body's side panels, from windshield post to rear quarter, were pressed out two at a time, and a set of door panels could be produced every twenty seconds. All sections were electrically welded and painted – though not trimmed – before despatch. By 1931, Pressed Steel were supplying Austin, Hillman, Rover, and Wolseley as well as Morris, while at pebk, they would be responsible for either complete bodies or panels for fourteen British factories. In Germany, Ambi-Budd's parallel operation in Berlin built for Adler, Audi, BMW, Ford, Hanomag, and even the up-market Horch.

Inevitably, the cost accountants had their look-in, and some cross-pollination resulted. This went beyond mere badge-engineering: a similarity between Morrises and Wolseleys was to be expected since both firms were part of the same group, but Rover's economy drive included the use of some Hillman Minx panels on their cheapest Tens, the same shape finding its way across the North Sea onto a few of Ambi-Budd's Adlers. By the same token, Berlin's Jupiter sedan, a more attractive shape, was common to four-cylinder Adlers and Hanomags – and also, curiously, to sports models of the Austin Light 12/6! The exotic front-wheel-drive Ruxton, an American ephemeral of 1930, actually used Morris-Wolseley coachwork, cut down to fit the American car's lower build: the rear quarter-lights, which wound down in Britain, had to hinge in transatlantic guise, since otherwise they would have fouled the wheel arches. Sometimes, this standardization would kill a make: Chenard-Walcker's promising 1935 front-wheel-drive sedan failed to win acceptance simply because, in the interests of economy, it used a Chausson-built body identical to that of the new French Ford V8s made in the old Mathis factory.

This system also made for complications in the styling department. Buying from Ambi-Budd or Chausson exonerated the manufacturer from investing in costly body plant. It could, if he wished, spare him the expense of paintwork as well, though many makers preferred to handle this aspect of the job along with the interior trim. At the same time, however, the system landed him with the old headache of amortization – a long run, or else. This was fine if the car sold; if it didn't, he had either to rework the mechanics round the old shape or face a substantial loss. Rootes had more progressive ideas than most of their British rivals, but the failure of their first Pressed Steel effort, the Hillman Wizard Six of 1931, is reflected in the continuance of essentially the same shape right up to 1935.

Unitary construction heightened these problems. Even where a basic body had to be retained for an extra year, a surprising amount could be done with the extremities, while work on engines and running gear was not wholly impeded. Hillman eked out the Wizard catastrophe with three grilles, two fender lines, and two different tail panels, while the suppliers of outside "semi-customs" helped. But once the chassis was built into the body, overall dimensions became constant, as did, for instance, the location of an engine bearer in relation to the firewall. One may suspect that even Citroën were saved by the war: otherwise, how could they have soldiered on into 1955 with no stylistic changes beyond 1952's projecting rear trunk?

The principles of unitary construction have already been discussed, as have the principal pros and cons. But from the standpoint of the body designer – and thus, ultimately, the customer – the big problem was the sheer inflexibility, though this would hit far harder in the post-war years. Further, a disaster could be a two-way one: one could be stuck at one and the same time with defective steering geometry and a shape that was no longer acceptable. The 1948 Step Down Hudsons had passed beyond redemption by chromium plate and minor fender alterations when they were finally scrapped at the end of 1954, while sometimes the public would give a car the thumbs-down before it had time to prove itself. Such a case was Grégoire's big R-type flat-four of 1949: while Hotchkiss, the licencees, certainly lacked the funds to get such an ambitious project off the ground, it is also true that the distaff

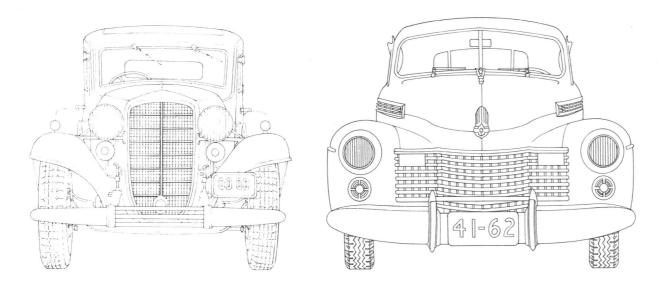

The march of styling, or how the cosmetic evolved into the functional entity. In the front view of the 1933 Cadillac (*left*), the fender skirts are not visible, and in any case, the frontal skirting would be the next stage. Cord influence is, however, detectable in the vee-grille, new on General Motors cars that year, and already, an attempt has been made to pretty-up the bumper. Everything else — headlamps, trumpet horns, and dual sidemounts — is out of doors, and the overslung wipers cannot park out of the driver's sight. On the 1941 Cadillac (*right*), however, there are very few excrescences: the pattern of heavy chromium-plated bars has spread from the grille into the fenders and is bidding fair to overwhelm the fully recessed headlamps. Likewise, the bumper is merging into the grille. All the other excrescences are out of sight, the spare wheel having been banished to the trunk.

The luggage problem (*bottom right*). The luggage grid (trunk rack) was an unsightly object at the best of times and tended to foul the spare wheel. On this 1932 Austin, a well for the spare wheel has been incorporated in the rear panel, but it was left to Packard (page 136, *bottom*) to make a distinctive feature of the excrescence.

Tidying up could destroy individuality, and Austin's 1935 grille was scarcely beautiful. One of the casualties of this clean-up was the radiator filler cap (*bottom left*), which went under the hood. This meant eventually that many a mascot was no longer functional, though there was some compensation in knowing that, when you opened the hood, you could top up radiator, sump, and battery at one sitting.

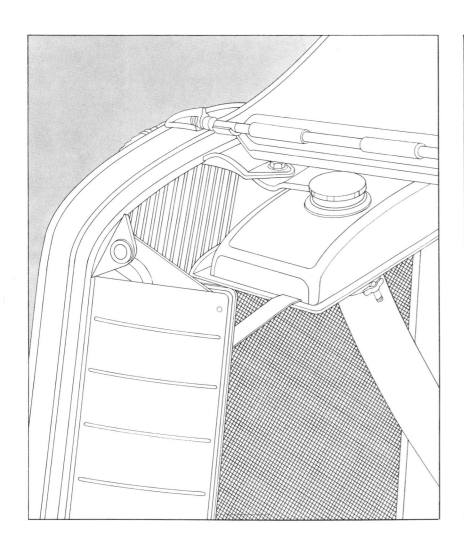

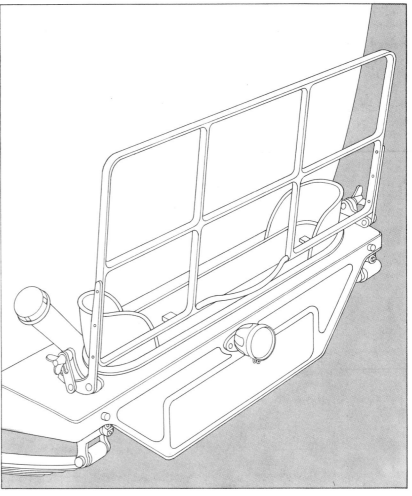

Diversity in coachwork. You really needed the long hood of a straight-eight to exploit the 1929 Cord idiom, and Chrysler's 1931 CD-type filled the bill admirably. The factory provided both the coupé (*opposite, top*) and the convertible (*top right*), though the fancy touches – dual sidemounts, tyre covers, and wire wheels – were extras. You could have a radio also on the closed models. On such styles, unfortunately, Americans still clung to the discriminatory rumble seat for extra passengers. Europeans didn't, so Chrysler's English branch offered a more sociable drophead four-some or convertible coupé (*opposite, bottom right*) by Carlton of London for local consumption. By 1939, the Americans had caught up with European thinking, and the result is seen here (*opposite, bottom left*) on Packard's 120 convertible. The firm's conservative styling rendered sidemounts more bearable than they were on Buicks and Cadillacs, though money had been saved by making the same chassis and sheet metal do for both the nine-bearing Super Eight and the less expensive five-bearing 120. The 1940 Nash (*top left*) is of interest as being a fastback at a time when other people were concentrating on trunkbacks – it is also apparent that styling was not taken too seriously at Kenosha.

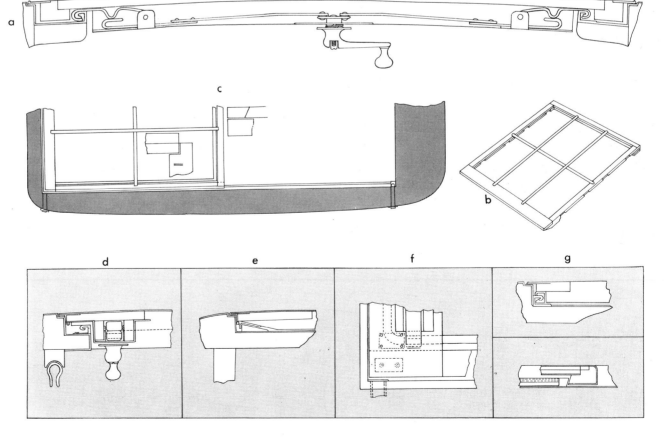

Typically British was the sliding roof (*bottom*); we show here the Saloonood system fitted on some British cars of the period. (*a*) Section through the sliding roof, showing the locking device. (*b*) Perspective view of the assembled sliding panel. (*c*) The roof and sliding panel seen from above. The sliding panel is seen on the left. Sections through various parts of the roof and panel (*d, e, f, g*) show the complicated construction. In a temperate climate it was remarkably leak-proof. One of the first users of a sliding roof were Standard, on the 1931 Big Nine (*centre left*), a lot of car for 1,287 cc, thanks to the British horsepower tax. Understandably, 55 mph (90 km/h) were hard work, but a bonus was the fuel consumption – only 36 mpg (8 lit/100). A safe if limited seller of the 1930s was the inexpensive limousine based on a big family sedan. This happened in most countries, though shown here (*centre right*) is a British example, the 1938 GL type Vauxhall 25 with 3.4-litre overhead-valve six-cylinder engine. Wheel-base was lengthened by 19 in (48 cm), and Grosvenor's custom body used a number of stock panels. If it sounds expensive at £630 ($3,150), remember that Daimler's least expensive formal carriage listed at close on £1,000 ($5,000).

All the same model, 1935 1.7-litre four-cylinder Peugeot 401s. Let's say the social equivalent of a Standard Twelve in England or a DU Dodge in the United States. Technical specifications are constant, though there is a choice of wheel-base lengths to allow the French to indulge their passion for *commerciales*, or seven-to-eight-passenger commercial sedans which came to be used to deliver goods during the working week. One from the bottom on the right is what we would now term a hatchback, with an upward-opening tailgate to give a good loading height at the price, maybe, of a knock on the head in passing. These long-chassis jobs, of course, called for lower axle ratios, also used in the very similar MK light truck family, which carried on into 1936 to use up surplus front-end sheet metal, a common habit in the industry.

Most intriguing of all the numerous variants is, however, the *decapotable électrique* (*bottom left*), an anticipation of Ford's legendary 1957 retractable on which the metal top was lowered electrically into a space behind the front seats. Peugeot persisted with this design for several years, but it was too complicated to meet with much success, especially since buyers had

a choice of three different types of orthodox soft-top convertible, including a traditional roadster with the refinement of wind-up windows. (Latterly, you could have a German-style cabrio-limousine as well, in the cheap 202 line made from 1938 onwards). American styling influences are much in evidence, especially in the fastback idiom used for all the sedans, though the low-set headlamps are still exposed and fender treatment remains orthodox. Note also that Detroit-style hood doors are still fashionable in France a good year after American stylists have gone over to speedstreaks. Peugeot also ring the changes on hood louvre design, with a more modern crib of American themes on the sportier bodies. Unlike those other devotees of body styles unlimited, Vauxhall, Peugeot made all their own coachwork. What is even more surprising is that the 401 had only a one-year run, accounting for less than fourteen thousand units, though some panels were common to the smaller 201 and 301 series, and a virtually identical line of bodies sufficed for the six-cylinder 601 at the top of the range. Here Peugeot took a leaf out of Chrysler's book by adding the extra length in the hood, where it did not affect other dimensions.

side objected to its drooping nose. Grégoire later wished he had hired Pininfarina to transform his ugly duckling, but such international cross-pollination was uncommon, even at the end of the forties.

Inflexibility of style was almost a worse handicap. With full unitary construction, the choice lay between two- and four-door sedans, and (in post-woody days) that admirable standby, the station wagon, though any attempt at bulk production of such a car in 1939 would have been financially disastrous. On a small and cheap model, one could sometimes eke out the tooling costs, as did Hillman and Renault, with a light panel delivery van; before the advent of Volkswagen's revolutionary Transporter in 1950, car-type vans were generally acceptable. Convertibles, however, presented a real headache. Without the necessary reinforcement of a steel roof, one was confronted with immediate firewall shake, followed by a speedy demise once rust, a unitary hull's worst enemy, set in. Hence the high mortality rate, and the subsequent astronomical collector-value, of Citroën's beautiful roadsters, discontinued after 1940. Vauxhall and Lancia circumvented the problem by offering chassis-ed versions; the former financing this extravagance by using the construction in their smaller Bedford vans, while the latter could hardly be called a mass-producer at any time and always worked to more modest parameters of output. The Germans – and later Ted Ulrich of Nash – had a more practical solution in the cabrio-limousine, a ragtop with rigid sides. It worked, though it had about as much aesthetic appeal as the *targhe* of the safety-conscious seventies.

The "desire to be different" occupied body departments as deeply as it did the engineers. As long as chassis remained separate entities, one could ring the changes indefinitely on engines, gearboxes, wheelbase lengths, and body styles. Austin's 1934 catalogue embraced over fifty different models, while in the same year, Peugeot's 1.5-litre 301 family came in fourteen styles, from a sporty roadster to a six-seater *familiale* for quiverful Frenchmen. The 1931 Renault catalogue listed seven variations of the pint-sized six-cylinder Mona, six of the indestructible KZ four, ten of the 3.2-litre Viva, and seven of the Nerva, the cheaper of the company's two straight-eights (the vast Reinastella ran to 7.1 litres and was strictly bespoke). In Germany Opel customers must have found life dull when the company went unitary. Five body styles, including a traditional roadster, were available on 1933's 1.2-litre, one of Germany's cheapest cars, but by 1937, the modern Kadett came as a two-door sedan or cabrio-limousine. Even a four-door model would not be added until 1938.

In the United States, of course, variations were almost limitless. Throughout our period, two- and four-door sedans invariably topped the best-seller lists, while roadsters and phaetons had virtually disappeared by 1935. Their successors were the convertible coupés, though oddly, these would retain the uncomfortable and discriminatory rumble seat into 1937–38, possibly because in the days of manually-operated tops, the shorter type was more manageable. Four-passenger "victoria" bodies, though they enjoyed a short vogue in 1932, were less popular, while even rarer was the four-door convertible sedan, a style much favoured by well-heeled Germans. Fixed-head coupés, like the ragtops, clung overlong to the rumble seat, though a favourite variation was the "business" model, on which the rear-deck space was reserved for baggage. Woodies remained rare; Ford's 1929 lead in this field was not immediately followed. Finally, there was a simple extension of the sedan theme – a long-chassis, seven-passenger job using many of the regular panels. If Ford ignored this type and Chevrolet confined its application to their taxicab range, Chrysler and Hudson made quite a few. So, incidentally, did Hillman, Vauxhall, and Austin in Britain, Opel in Germany, and all of France's Big Three. In the United States one could afford to drop an individual style for a season – neither Chevrolet nor

Dodge, for instance, listed a convertible in 1939 – but one dared not abdicate altogether. The Joneses of the automobile world, be they traders or actual owners, expect to be catered for all the time.

We shall discuss purely national trends in a later chapter, but if the decade had an "in" style, it was surely the convertible, call it a cabriolet or a drophead coupé. Never a big seller, for all the growing sex-absorption of press departments, it nonetheless occupied that "status" later to be usurped by the hardtop, the more luxurious station wagons, and the *targa*-type near-cabriolet. Germany was the convertible's stronghold, and undoubtedly some of the best workmanship and weather protection came from there. Internally lined tops were regular practice, though one paid for these in avoirdupois: Karmann's four-passenger body on the small Adler Trumpf Junior chassis – a standard sedan turned the scales at about 1,760 lb (800 kg) – boasted a top said to weigh nearly 110 lb (50 kg). All types of variation were available, as a study of contemporary Mercedes-Benz catalogues will attest. Of their offerings, the A was the sportiest, a two-passenger affair innocent of rumble, though occasionally a sideways- facing opera seat would be provided for a third crew member. The Mercedes-Benz B was a sobre two-door, four-window affair, while the C was the same thing, only more intimate, with blind rear quarters. The D had four doors, and the F – supplied only for real heavies such as the Nürburg straight-eight and the vast 7.7-litre Grosser – was a full formal, ideal for a trip to the opera. As this one was intended for chauffeur drive, unfurling of the massive top could safely be left to this unhappy hireling.

Elsewhere two-door four-passenger types predominated, offering intimacy and an individual line at the price of negligible rearward vision. (This may explain why contemporary British rallyistes preferred to run even unsporting models in the "open-car" category – conducting such a vehicle backwards was a nightmare, especially in the early 1930s, when long hoods and slit-type windshields were all the rage). Power tops, though tried by a few custom coachbuilders as early as 1936, did not become general practice even in the United States until 1940–41. They never spread across the Atlantic, though Peugeot would anticipate the ingenious metal retractables of a far later era with their *décapotable électrique,* a sensation of the 1934 Paris Salon. By contrast, the three-position top enjoyed considerable snob value, giving a sedanca effect in the intermediate position, and offering, as Standard asserted in a 1935 advertisement, "three cars in one".

Roadster-type bodies in the American idiom were rarer, though they had a following in France, always more susceptible to the ideas of Detroit. Citroën, Peugeot, and Renault all offered them in 1938–39; so, in a higher price bracket, did AC and Triumph on the other side of the Channel. The rumble seat, however, remained uncomfortable, even when Triumph sought to give it some added status on their post-war 1800. This curiosity featured windows in the deck lid, permitting the latter component to double as a second cowl, in the best Duesenberg tradition. The "foursome drophead", however, would remain popular until its ranks were decimated by post-war unitary influences. Nineteen British manufacturers listed such a style in 1935, and sixteen were still doing so three years later. The choice was wide: from the Standard 8 at £149 ($745), with rear seats suitable only for small children, up to £1,600 ($8,000) worth of V12 Lagonda. There was similar market coverage in France, while Germany fared even better, with everything from two-seaters to cabrio-limousines.

On its way out – and dead by 1933 – was one of the prime fads of the later 1920s, the Weymann system of flexible fabric construction. It reached its zenith in 1929, though Germans were not over-enthusiastic about it, and in the United States only Stutz saw fit to catalogue bodies of this type. Other surprising abstainers were Citroën (apposite, since

Fresh air and fun in the 1930s. A good halfway solution was the German cabrio-limousine, a stock sedan with a full-length roll-top but fixed sides. The 1938 Opel Kadett (*top left*) was one of the cheapest in Europe, at RM 2,150 or less than £150 ($750). Its main failing was that the lowered top impeded the driver's rearward view. The same went for contemporary full cabriolets like the 1935 Mercedes-Benz 290 (*top right*). This one was truly convertible, but the price paid for excellent Teutonic workmanship was excessive weight.

By comparison, three open British cars with demountable side curtains. The 1932 Morris Minor (*centre left*) (this is the rare early-1932 with fluted top to the radiator shell), had restricted vision with the top up, a failing also of the 1931 2-litre supercharged Lagonda (*centre right*). Its shallow windshield would have called for 'blind flying' techniques on a wet day. On a 120-inch (3 m) wheel-base there was plenty of room for four. Finally, pure traditional (*bottom*): only the painted radiator shell and rear trunk (dedicated wholly to the spare wheel!) mark this Austin Ten as a 1935–36. Aerodynamics meant nothing to Herbert Austin — eye-level vision was one of his obsessions.

(*Top*) The 1937 11 *légère* Citroën as an elegant roadster. Being unitary, it lost structural strength through the absence of a roof. It was also rust-prone and the mortality rate was formidable: Citroën quietly dropped the style after 1939

Also a structural headache was the lightweight Weymann fabric body, here seen (*bottom*) dissected. This angular example is an early 1924 effort by Rover, but the principle was still much in evidence in 1930–31. Upper left in the insert, the window frame. Below it, a door detail showing the window mechanism, and on the right, a cross-section of the complete door. *a* is the exterior covering in coloured fabric, *b* the cotton wadding used as insulation, *c* a waterproofed fabric lining on both sides, and *d* the interior trim. The window glass (*e*) dropped into cloth-covered rubber tubing (*f*). Initially, there was nothing to squeak or rattle, and nothing heavy either, but fabric did not take kindly to any extremes of climate, and as the wooden framing "worked", the whole elaborate structure came quietly apart. In England and France, Weymann strongholds, a common sight of the mid-thirties was a fabric sedan with cracks in the outer finish, through which soggy wadding was visible. The medium was, however, much favoured for big sporting sedans, not solely on grounds of weight: it eliminated the drumming from a large and noisy power unit. Many 4½-litre Bentleys were so bodied, but few survive in this form. The majority ended up as "replica" sport tourings "of the school of Vanden Plas", and who should blame the owners? All too many of the originals were ugly, with minimal vision in any direction.

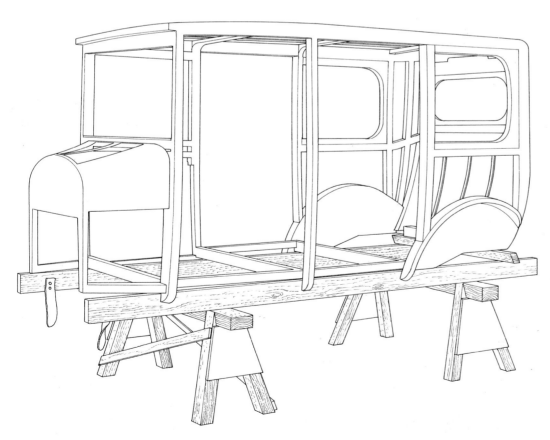

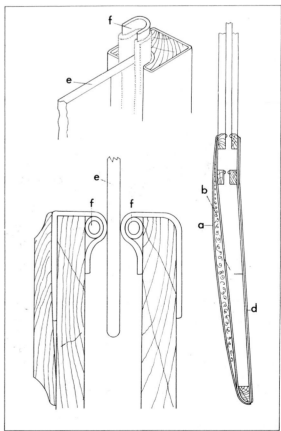

they were pioneers of all-steel construction), and Singer, who had tried it early on and found it wanting. For a while though, it was almost mandatory with other French makers. In England Jowett and Rover were perhaps its staunchest supporters. The *système* Weymann had its good points: it was appreciably lighter than a coach-built body, its leather covering was easier to clean and was fade-proof, and drumming (a bugbear of early closed coachwork) was entirely eliminated. A well-constructed specimen would withstand considerable abuse, but cheap, mass-produced copies were less solidly made and disintegrated rapidly, a familiar sign of decay being tufts of wadding projecting from torn fabric. With the demise of flexible fabric construction went the classic "in-style" of the final vintage years, the sportsman's coupé. The combination of a shallow windshield, a high waist-line, blind rear quarters, and (on more expensive specimens) non-functional plated landau irons lent the style a certain elegance. It was, however, of questionable use to the sportsman, since the impressive-looking rear trunk opened from the top – awkward in all conscience, but quite useless in conjunction with a rear-mounted spare wheel.

Fabric's only survival point was in Germany, where it lingered on as the outer skin of cut-price babies like the DKW-Front. On these it served to keep weight down, enabling four people to be carried at reasonable speeds on 684 cc and 16 bhp. A few Adlers and small German Fiats were also seen with fabric bodies, as was Ford-Cologne's attempt at a proto-Volkswagen in 1935. Despite a price as low as RM 1,850, *Der Wagen für Jedermann* never caught on. It was not, one suspects, the fabric: *Jedermann*, unlike John Smith or Marcel Dupont,

already expected independent front suspension, even in the bargain basement.

In any case, fabric interfered with another important aspect of the new desire to be different – bright colours. In these days of vivid and constantly-changing hues as an accepted means of eking out an obsolescent shape, one tends to forget that Ford was not the only early mass-producer wedded to a solitary shade of black. So was Dodge, even in 1925, when Hudsons, Essexes, most Hupmobiles, and all Studebaker sedans were blue. Buick essayed at least a degree of variety by assigning different colour schemes to individual models, and Citroën had injected a spark of brightness with the punning lemon-yellow of his 5CV runabouts. But generally, outside the realm of the sporty and the bespoke, dark shades and uninspired colour separations (in nine cases out of ten, the "second colour" was black) were the order of the day. Memorable in their time had been Rover's pseudo-sporting 9/20s: they were no balls of fire at any time, but their two-toning, in "strawberries and cream", made them more attractive than Austins, Morrises, or Singers. A further innovation of the 1920s was the "pen nib" colour separation, with a tapering flash of the second colour running down the top of the hood. Indelibly associated in British minds with William Lyons's Austin Swallow sedans, it was in fact the creation of American stylist Ralph Roberts from the famous Le Baron Studios. This led to better things and away from the primitive two-tone concepts of earlier years.

Alas! the best one could do with fabric was to finish fenders and wheels in bright shades – reds and greens were favourites – and add such touches as coloured steering wheels. Now, however, belt mould-

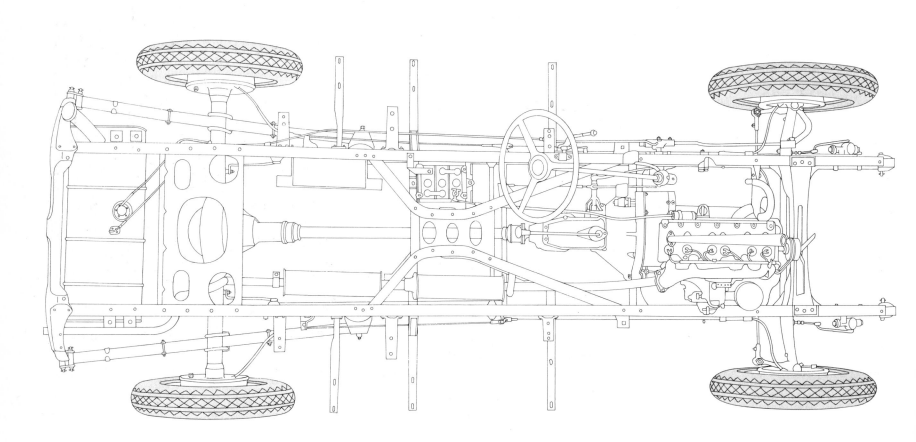

State of the art, 1932. The Essex chassis (*opposite*) is still a fairly simple affair. Americans did not need unitary construction, which was too inflexible for the wide choice of bodies and biennial styling changes characteristic of the period. In essence, we have the same set-up as on the 1930 Volvo 652 shown on page 21, but with one variation, the central cruciform bracing pioneered by Hotchkiss in 1921 and first seen on a production car (the Cord L29) eight years later. The Essex's frame is narrower than the Volvo's, hence the outriggers to serve as body mounts, regular practice on tubular backbone layouts. The battery is also still parked inside the frame, one of the irritants of the period, since a seat (the driver's, in this case) had to be slid back and a hatch raised to get at it. (Lifting the hood and topping up the battery has become a complete routine by this time, to be carried out every time one refuelled.) One might think the Essex's cable-operated brakes a retrograde step after the Volvo's hydraulics, but not everyone trusted the newfangled arrangements, and rubber piping was not as durable in 1932 as it is today. (It took the Second World War to teach the industry all about synthetics.) Note however that the brake drums are of fairly generous proportions, and these, allied to the wire wheels which were pretty general practice in the United States between 1932 and 1934, gave reasonable cooling and, therefore, freedom from fade. Not that the average motorist worried unduly about this prevailing 1950s problem in the days when 50 mph (80 km/h) was considered a high cruising velocity for the family sedan. The contemporary and brand-new Ford vee-eight was good for over 80 mph (130 km/h), but how many people who bought the model cared?

When six-cylinder cars were first marketed in the 1904–07 period, they were conceived as town carriages and sold on flexibility. Here two sixes from the beginning of our period—but from opposite sides of the Atlantic—show just how versatile the idiom had become. In fact, however, both the 1929 Essex (*bottom*)—very much the same car was still being offered in 1931, styling differences apart—and the 1933 Wolseley Hornet Special (*top*) had their roots in the laity's dislike of shifting. This had bred generation after generation of small and cheap sixes in the United States since 1915.

The Wolseley is merely the sporting development of Sir William Morris's archetype of the pint-sized six, launched in 1930 and combining small car proportions (and, in Britain, annual tax) with the ability to do almost everything in high gear.

One should not, therefore, be seduced by the Wolseley's obviously bespoke appearance into regarding it as anything more than a "sporty" automobile fabricated from mass-produced components, a formula pioneered in Britain by Cecil Kimber with the M-type MG Midget (1929) and one which has remained largely British ever since. The Essex, by contrast, was the parent Hudson firm's all-time best seller, 1929 being the season in which the group delivered over three hundred thousand cars, more than anyone else save Chevrolet and Ford.

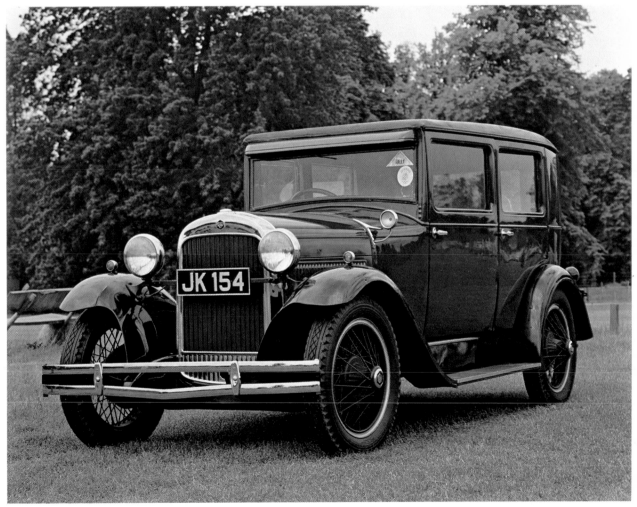

ings grew more ambitious. The modest "streamlining" of the Series II Morris and Wolseley sedans (1935–36) was accentuated by an ingenious belt treatment, especially on the more expensive Wolseleys, though nobody went as far as Renault in 1933, with their strip of darker cellulose running down the firewall from windshield level. It looked better than one might imagine. Such arrangements could, however, work only as long as fenders remained separate entities.

True pastel shades would be a post-war phenomenon. The colours of the 1930s tended to be darker and muddier, variations of a greyish fawn being used by Hillman, Renault, Opel, and Ford, though the last-mentioned firm called it "Cordoba tan". Metallics made their appearance in the United States in 1932. They succeeded, as they were a cheap means of reproducing something hitherto possible only by expensive admixtures of fish scales. On smaller cars, unfortunately, the effect was somewhat meretricious, though Fiat's British importers worked wonders with two-tone browns and greens on *topolino* coupés. Home-market versions, however, retained their sombre monochromes.

This general brightening up of the automobile had much to do with the integration of the stylist into design departments. Not that he was always welcomed. Styling was a dirty word where the elder Ford was concerned, and Herbert Austin was obsessed with eye-level vision – hence the perpendicular lines of his cars right up to 1936. Chrysler alternated between ambitious sallies (1931's Cord-like CD/CM family and 1934's legendary Airflow) and the stolidly dull, with the emphasis laid on engineering. Kaufman T. Keller, who guided the corporation's

destiny for many years, was certainly interested in styling, but his interest tended to be destructive. One of the less probable Keller credos was that all trunks should be able to house a milk churn standing upright, an eccentricity which explains why the outstanding mechanical virtues of the legendary hemi-head vee-eights of a later era were so depressingly cloaked.

Much of a stylist's work, of course, centred round the task of making an obsolescent shape look new. One has only to study the grilles of Hillmans, Renaults, or Standards of the later 1930s to realize that quick visual impact has been used to suggest more dramatic changes than are actually present. The individuality of Gordon Buehrig's much praised (and hastily created) 1935 Auburn front-end should not blind anyone to the truth: from the firewall aft, the car is virtually identical with Al Leamy's commercially unsuccessful 1934 effort! Pontiac's legendary silver streaks started in 1934 as plated fender trims, put there by Franklin Hershey to avoid an otherwise understandable confusion with the previous year's models. By contrast, La Salle's contemporary portholes, later to become a Buick hallmark, formed part of an "aeronautical" theme by Jules Agramonte, that would become a style leader.

Nor is it fair to say that styling was "invented" either by Harley Earl or by Edsel Ford, whose personal flair had already transformed that company's recently acquired Lincoln from a triumph of engineering over aesthetics into one of America's more handsome automobiles. One of the advantages of using trade coachbuilders was that their designers had a say in the appearance of the end-product – and both Murray and

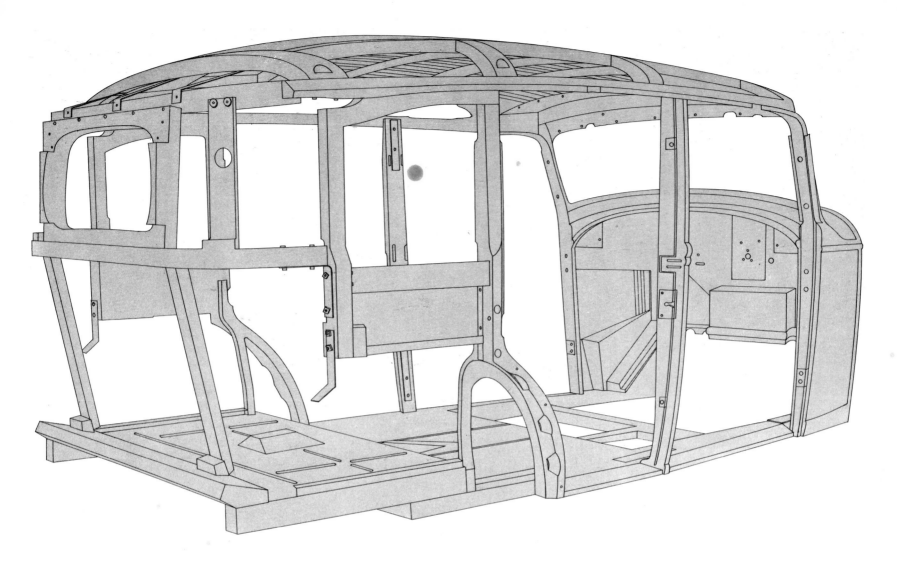

The first new stylistic theme of the thirties, the skirted-fender 1932 Graham Blue Streak (*left*). The compound curves of top and rear-quarters were not new, having been created by the Graham's designer, Amos Northup, for Reo's 1931 line. The vee-grille's rounded form, with a central bar, had first been seen on the 1929 Cord. The new fender skirts, however, were the vital touch. American manufacturers took a long, hard look at Northup's fender skirts and sloping vee-grille — and began to imitate them.

Shown (*right*) is a 1934 Ford V8, but Graham influence is also detectable on contemporary Chevrolets, Nashes, and Terraplanes, for instance. The Ford shape duplicates Graham's every way, though this three-quarter view of a Tudor Sedan shows the theme at its worst, thanks to an abbreviated wheel-base of 112 in (2.8 m) and the short hood resulting from the use of a compact vee-eight motor.

The structural picture (*top*) gives the lie to the oft-held assertion that all-metal sedan bodies were general practice in the United States throughout the 1930s. This is the framing of the 1932–33 Graham Blue Streak and is in wood, though a steel dash is used, and steel channel-selections in the forward doorposts give access to the wiring.

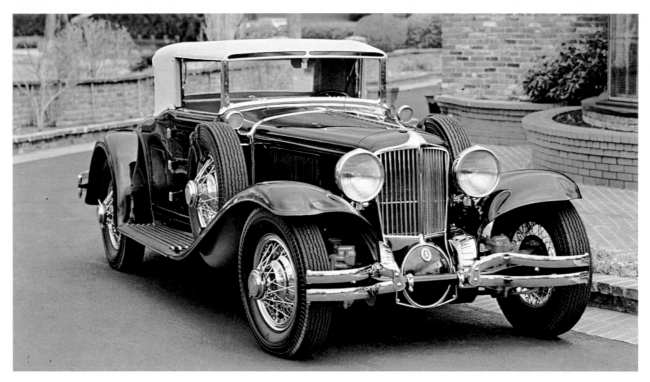

(*Left*) Classic shape of the early 1930s – as echoed by Chrysler, SS, and ultimately, Renault. Here is the prototype of these and many others – the L29 Cord convertible coupé as made from 1929 to 1932. Its long hood is crowned by a neat vee grille. Here a virtue was made of necessity, for the Cord's front-wheel drive called for a transmission set in front of an already lengthy straight-eight motor. This gave not only a longer hood, but also a handsome apron concealing the forward end of the drive unit. Beauty was won at the cost of indifferent forward vision. Worse, the new idiom didn't really blend with a smallish four- or six-cylinder motor, hence various stratagems had to be tried by copying makers to get proportions right. Chrysler added a vee-windshield on their 1932 line (their smaller CM of 1931 looked very stunted), while on William Lyons's SS the hood was also carried back almost as far as the windshield.

Theme and variation, or what the United States thinks today, Europe thinks tomorrow. The 1929 Chrysler line (*centre left*: this is a De Soto) popularized the ribbon radiator shell on inexpensive automobiles. The 1930 Swift from Britain (*centre right*) carefully aped it.

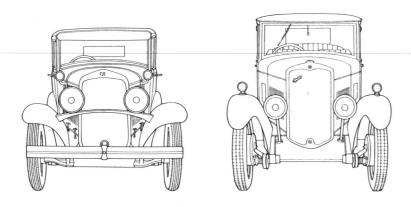

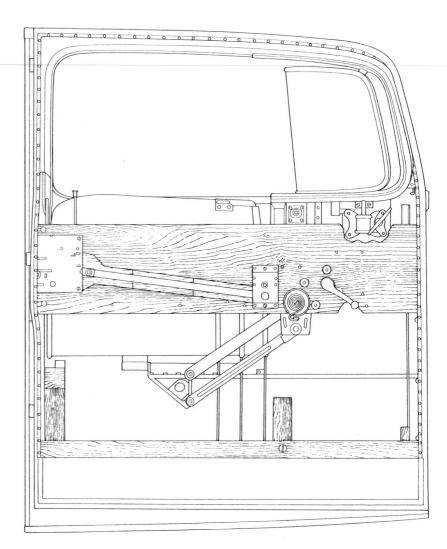

Briggs had carriage-trade connections, through their respective ownership of the Dietrich and Le Baron studios. Amos Northup, responsible for two landmarks of the 1930s, the Reo Royale and Graham's Blue Streak, was a Dietrich man. There was, however, always a good chance that a Board would turn its nose up at renderings submitted to it by mere body specialists. Nash's engineers complained that Alexis de Sakhnoffski's advanced ideas did not translate easily into sheet metal, while in order to sell his first major styling exercise to Hupmobile, the great Raymond Loewy had to buy one of their straight-eight chassis and translate it into reality at a cost to himself of $15,000 (£3,000). Nonetheless, General Motors had given the lead – and it was followed, albeit reluctantly.

In its original form, Earl's La Salle, prototype of the 1930 Cadillacs, was not a truly integrated design, though some of the Hispano-Suiza's elegance rubbed off, and it would set the fashion, in its later manifestations, for those hood doors which had become the rage in the United States by 1930; these, by the way, did not catch on wholesale in Europe, where their use was largely confined to French cars. More important, perhaps, was the narrow ribbon-type radiator shell, a more universal fad; among the shameless foreign cribs were the 1930 Fiats and Swifts.

Though La Salle influences would persist into 1931, the next phase was ushered in late in 1929 by the first Cord, largely the work of Al Leamy. Here necessity was the mother of invention: the combination of a big straight-eight motor and a frontal gearbox called for a hood of excessive length, and the whole affair was skilfully executed, with a vee grille, a shallow windshield, and a low roof-line. It is a matter of opinion whether vee windshields helped or not. Chrysler, the first of the big battalions to copy the Cord idiom, tried both configurations during the style's four-year run. Elegance was, however, won at the price of claustrophobia, and the Cord theme really needed a straight-eight to show it off to advantage. Studebaker circumvented the problem of an abbreviated six by coming up with a more aggressive vee on their 1933 and 1934 cars, but many of the smaller Chryslers looked stunted, and it is significant that the corporation never applied this style to their four-cylinder Plymouth. Everyone else, however, fell for it – even Packard, who used vee radiators from 1932 onwards. This would be just about their only concession to styling in the American sense.

The long, low look marked the first dramatic impact of American styling in Europe – La Salle themes, with their Hispano overtones, were, after all, only re-imports. The classic instance of the new idiom was, of course, William Lyons's first SS of 1932, which was pure Cord with the addition of the Old World's traditional cycle fenders, but vee radiators and long hoods also make their appearance on such conservative

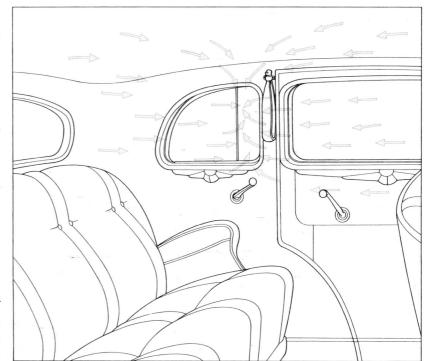

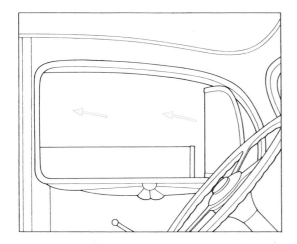

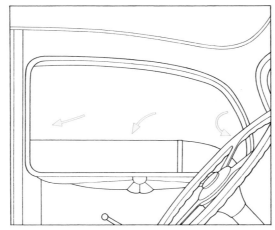

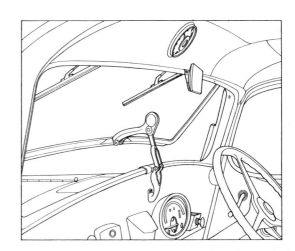

Draughtless ventilation. The Fisher system used by General Motors, showing its application to a front door (*opposite, right*), and to rear quarter-lights (*top right*). It served to complicate window-winding mechanisms more than somewhat. Further, General Motors held the patents, so other manufacturers had to figure out their own alternatives. Hudson devised an arrangement on which the ventipane at the front on the driver's side could either be wound out separately (*centre left*), or down with the main window (*centre middle*). Another Hudson feature (common to many cars on both sides of the Atlantic) was a full-opening windshield (*centre right*), a boon in fog, though presenting dust-sealing problems that would kill the idea in the end. Not that ventipanes and other sliding systems were devoid of headaches: some countries still made hand signals compulsory, and in such circumstances the arrangement was an in-fernal nuisance.

(*Bottom right*) The English gentleman's carriage made no concessions to styling. The Sunbeam Sixteen shape ran for six years with minimal change: one can only tell a 1931 or 1932 from a 1930 by the plated radiator shutters and hub caps, though by this time fabric bodies (Sunbeam had been prime addicts) were on their way out. Mechanically, the vehicle was refined rather than avant-garde: a pushrod six of 2.2 litres' capacity, coil ignition instead of the earlier magneto, semi-elliptic springs all round, and a four-speed transmission with right-hand shift (Sunbeam would supply a centre shift to order, but it wasn't the done thing). The accelerator pedal was, however, centrally located, and brakes were, surprisingly, hydraulic. Performance was unspectacular – about 65 mph (105 km/h) thanks to a weight of 1½ tons, but this mattered naught to the English gentleman. What did matter was his bank manager, less happy in those dark days about spending £700 ($3,500) on a mere automobile.

American shapes of the mid-thirties. The 1937 Hudson (*opposite, left*) and 1936 Studebaker (*top left*) show how others are following where General Motors led in 1934, with the compound curve. Neither is particularly successful, the Studebaker because it still uses the radiator-style grille of the Agramonte La Salle, and the Hudson because of its exaggerated waterfall arrangement out front, a mixture of Chrysler Airflow and 1935 Pontiac influences. It looked less bad with a trunkback, and Americans clearly thought so, too, though probably on grounds of the trunkback's extra baggage accommodation. (Chevrolet, who sold both shapes in 1937, unloaded over three thousand trunkbacks to every trunkless four-door sedan delivered.) The 1937 Pontiac (*top right*) is authentic General Motors, and one step further forward, mainly in the grille department, where a wide horizontal bar arrangement replaces 1936's narrow vertical band. While the make shared bodies with Oldsmobile, it was possible to distinguish the two breeds from the back as well as the front: Oldsmobile wore their tail-lamps streamlined into the body at belt level. Finally (*opposite, right*), we see a real advance, in 1938's Cadillac Sixty Special (this is actually the 1939 edition with a shorter, more attractive grille, but the rest of it is identical). Note the flowing line of the body from hood back to trunk, and the narrow European-style pillars which give an impression of light absent from the earlier turret tops. Fender treatment is tidier, too. But oh! those sidemounts! They weren't compulsory at home, but few export editions escaped the treatment.

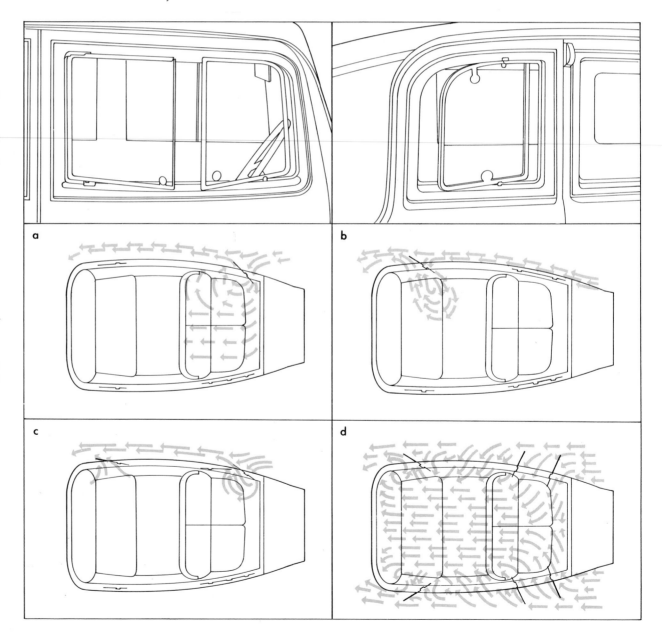

French makes as Berliet, Delaunay-Belleville, and Renault. Those who disliked the Teutonic overtones of the vee went halfway. Plated central bars sufficed on Hillmans and Standards; Citroën's 1933 models added a gentle curve, accentuated by some more chromium plating, already the stylist's best friend. The Germans and Czechs, already addicted to the vee motif, fell wholesale for long hoods, the ultimate, perhaps, being achieved on Busek's 1934 Aero, a 1-litre twin with, admittedly, front-wheel drive.

Having achieved a motif, the stylists now set to work to tidy the automobile up. The first major victim was the sedan's unsightly projecting forepeak. This was cured by a surfeit of compound curves; at the same time, fenders were given skirts. This fashion was ushered in on Northup's 1931 Reo Royale, though the celebrated skirts did not appear until a year later on the same designer's Graham, immortalized in the nurseries of the world by the Tootsie Toy company. The Graham also jettisoned hood doors in favour of inclined louvres, and everyone else followed suit, patterns of plated "speed streaks" being all the vogue. Graham influence was immediately detectable on the mid-1932 efforts of a desperate Willys-Overland Motors, on the 1933 Ford V8, and, as a clumsy parody, on Nash's 1934 line. Ford exported it to Europe on

their first true "foreign" car, the 933-cc Model Y made by Dagenham and Cologne alike, though they spoilt the effect by omitting fender skirts from the first series. These were hurriedly added towards the end of 1933.

Not that the excrescences had gone, by any means. Radiator filler caps might, and did, vanish underhood, even if such traditional European mascots as Mercedes' three-pointed star and Armstrong Siddeley's sphinx would remain functional for some years to come. But headlamps still lived out of doors, fenders stayed separate, and those handsome if not very practical sidemounts were still with us (try hauling a 19-inch wheel out of one of those rust traps on a wet day!). Trunks of any kind were confined to accessory catalogues. The big gimmick of 1933 from General Motors was Fisher No-Draft Ventilation: small ventipanes in the front windows which admitted air in controlled amounts. By 1935, the rest of the industry had similar ideas, but in the meantime, Harley Earl and Jules Agramonte had come up with the new straight-eight La Salle.

Here the designers were looking skywards, and aeronautical themes were predominant. Headlamps were now attached to the radiator grille (Rover had had a similar line in 1914). The compound curve had

Draughtless ventilation by numbers, or Packard's explanation of their new 1934 controlled system (*opposite*). It looks unnecessarily complicated, and it is – General Motor's Fisher No-Draft Ventilation was simpler, but it was also heavily patented, hence it was more important to avoid infringement suits than it was to be logical. Reading clockwise, the four lower diagrams show how air-flow is directed where passengers want it. (*a*) indicates front-seat ventilation regulated by the forward sections in the front windows. (*b*)

shows the way the rear quarter windows limit air supply to the back seats when used alone. In (*c*) all the quarter windows are open for the convenience of smokers on a wet day (cigarettes were not yet a dirty word), while (*d*) gives us air-flow unlimited on a stewing midwestern summer day. Not shown is an "impression of chaos" in which conventional windows are proved to direct all the air down the passengers' necks! The top two pictures show the actual mechanics of the system. Packard favoured a split arrangement, though

everything at least opened in the same plane if not in the same direction. In front (*left*) there was a vertical split, though whether this helped "quick signalling" is open to question: those who have driven 1960s Minis in countries where hand signals are still compulsory would doubtless confirm that there's no substitute for a traditional wind-down window. Nobody, fortunately, had patented the orthodox-opening rear quarter-light (*right*), which was definitely an improvement on a wind-down arrangement. Either type, though

common enough in the United States, was regarded as a luxury in Europe, and they were always a problem, the Packard type emitting a distasteful whistle at high speeds. One of the blessings we owe (indirectly) to the Cadillac Sixty Special and its stylists is the ultimate abandonment of the six-light (three-window, to Americans) principle in sedan bodies. Ventilation headaches apart, this meant fewer pillars and better vision once the wrap-round rear window had been achieved.

The straight-eight La Salle (*bottom*) was the style leader of its era, though by the time this 1935 example was made, the design was a year old, and its influence could be detected in Studebakers and Hudsons as well as in the rest of the General Motors range. Also it had lost its original biplane bumpers, too expensive even for the upper-middle-class market. Most significant, perhaps, were the "turret top" body with its compound curves, the pontoon fenders, and the retreat of the radiator. If this vogue for the tall and narrow didn't last long, grilles contracted in other directions. Other integrating touches were the attachment of the headlamps to the grille, and the disappearance underhood of the radiator filler cap. The "disc" wheels were, of course, only fancy covers concealing the steel-spoke type (as on English Talbots and Sunbeam-Talbots a few years later), while the portholes on the hood would reappear as a Buick hallmark in 1949, long after the La Salle's demise. On the mechanical side, the La Salle was General Motors's first car with hydraulic brakes, the coil-spring independent front suspension was found also on 1934 Cadillacs (and in a different form on lesser General Motors models as well), and the mechanics were basically Oldsmobile Eight, though owners soon discovered that there was little parts-interchange-

ability between the two breeds. At $1,650 (£330) for a sedan in 1934, however, the new car kept the wheels turning at Cadillac Division: of 13,014 cars delivered that season, more than half were the inexpensive straight-eights.

Integration taken a step further – on the 1941 Chevrolet sedan (*top right*). Mechanically, it is still the good old splash-lubricated 3.5-litre six-cylinder Cast Iron Wonder, but running boards have gone, headlamps have retreated into the fenders, and the new alligator hood permits shallower grilles which make up in width for what they've lost in height. Fenders and bumpers are gradually becoming part of a whole, if not necessarily a very harmonious one. The United States, of course, was not yet at war, and inflation had not bitten, so Chevrolet's cheapest four-door sedan cost only $795 (£159); "special de luxe" equipment added only another $56 (£10.20). Curiously, at the bottom of the market two-door sedans still outsold the four-door type (safer with young children?). What did one get on the world's best-selling automobile? Ninety hp, 80–85 mph (130–135 km/h), and cheap flat-rate servicing throughout the United States. Over 900,000 Americans thought the Chevrolet was a good buy in the last year of peace.

progressed a step further with the curvaceous metal Turret Top; it drummed infuriatingly, especially since Americans, unlike Britons, would have no truck with the sliding roof. The latest pontoon fenders were reminiscent of the then-fashionable aircraft-wheel spats, and even the bumpers were of "biplane" type. (The bumpers cost too much, so they were axed after one year.) Trunks were now integral and projected rearwards to give adequate baggage accommodation with external access. The radiator grille was tall and narrow, and once again, a spate of copies ensued. La Salle influences were detectable on the 1935 models of Hudson and Studebaker.

Alas! some untidying processes were also at work. After 1935, only Packard and the dying house of Pierce-Arrow sported grilles with any resemblance to the traditional radiator, while chromium plate came into its own. The prevailing theme of 1936 was the fencer's mask, seen at its worst on the Hudson, the Pontiac, and the curious Triumph Dolomite in England. This one was especially horrible, since the new masterpiece of die-casting was flanked by all the traditional British paraphernalia – separate fenders and headlamps, spotlamps, and twin wind-tone horns, another American import soon to be banished indoors by the march of integration. Horizontal bars replaced the fencing theme in 1937 and 1938, but in the meantime, Cadillac had taken a step forward with the Sixty Special.

The original grille of the Sixty Special was abominable, but the rest of it, if not wholly European in concept, achieved an excellent balance, with recessed running boards, a trunk which blended perfectly with the body lines and no longer resembled a gratuitous afterthought, and headlamps partially faired into the front fenders. The European four-window configuration with its thin pillars dispelled the claustrophobic air characteristic of American designs since the days of the L29 Cord. All General Motors makes had four-window notchbacks available by 1941. So had Studebaker, though Chrysler's Town Sedans remained fastbacks, and for several years, the industry hedged its bets between these two idioms.

Retreat into convention, or Chrysler's headline-making teardrop-shaped Airflow of 1934 (*lower*) was too much for Americans. This one was a straight-eight, though you could also have a 4-litre six with De Soto badges. The cars were tricky to maintain and pitched badly. The latter ailment was never fully cured, but by 1936, in an attempt to render looks more attractive, Chrysler had tacked on this curious widow's-peak grille. They also added a projecting trunk at the rear, which gave external luggage access at the price of inferior aerodynamics and a less balanced appearance. The last straw was the aggressive grille (very similar to that of regular Chryslers) used in 1937; less than 5,000 of the season's 108,000 new cars were Airflows, and they were to be the last. Henceforward, orthodoxy was the order of the day, as witness this 1939 C23 Imperial (*top*) using the same 5.3-litre engine as the old Airflow. Some Airflow influence survives in the fastback sedan body (favoured also by Ford, though General Motors preferred trunkbacks). In other respects, the car does not differ strongly from its rivals: alligator hood, receding grille and running boards, recessed headlamps, and column shift, plus the independent front suspension that the corporation had tried unsuccessfully in 1934, though never on Airflows.

Buick

The Doctor's Friend, 1936 style. In fact, the Buick Special's one cardinal feature, the overhead-valve straight-eight engine, is not shown at all. On the chassis (*bottom right*), one notes some characteristic 1936 items: the rigid cruciform bracing of the frame (*a*), the coil-spring independent front suspension of short- and long-arm type (*b*), the 16-in (40.6 cm) wheels and low-pressure tyres (*c*), and the hydraulic brakes (*d*), these last rapidly becoming the rule in the United States, though Ford would hold out with mechanicals for another three seasons. The complete car demonstrates to what extent the cult of the compound curve was carried. There is not a single sharp angle in sight. Vee windshields and large integral trunks were new on Buicks that year, though

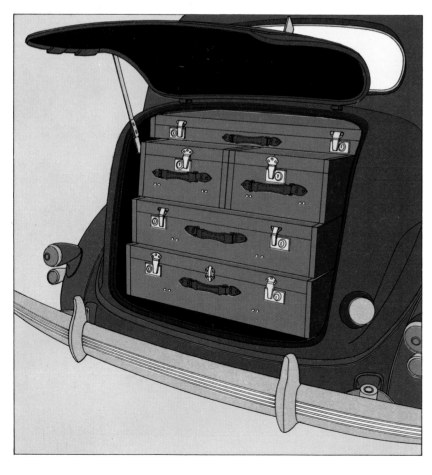

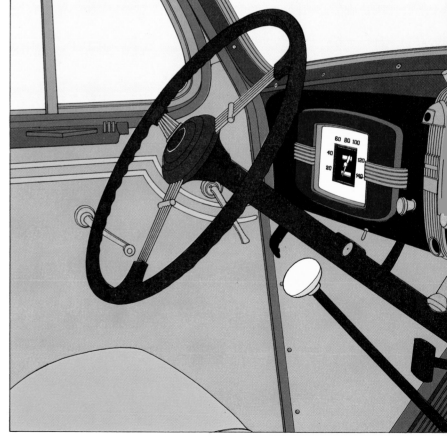

they'd already been seen on other General Motors cars in 1935. The steel-spoke wheels had only a year more to run: full discs would be in fashion by 1937. Headlamps and running boards are still exposed, and front fenders sufficiently unstreamlined to cope with the dual sidemounts. The trunk (*bottom left*) suggests that fitted suitcases were standard, which they were not, though when uncluttered by a spare wheel it could almost have accommodated the "two sturdy teenagers and a Great Dane" cited in Buick's catalogues. Within the "office" (*bottom centre*), styling triumphs over all other considerations. Even the clock on the glovebox lid matches the integrated but not very legible "information display" in front of the driver. The vee windshield was not an aid to forward vision, while the gearshift still sits firmly on the floor; note that as on most American cars of the period, it is cranked slightly forward to allow of three people on the front seat. And on the far left under the dash is yet another umbrella-handle handbrake.

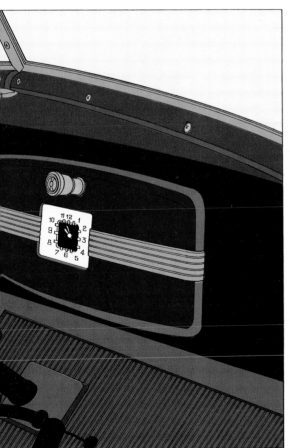

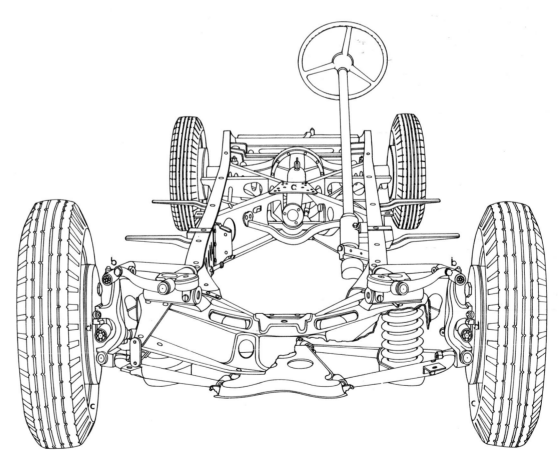

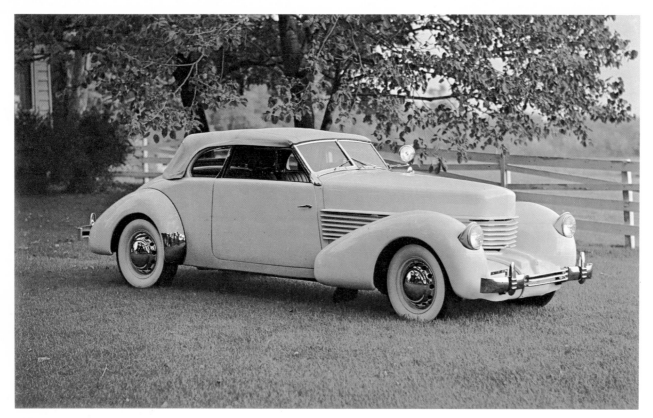

Facias various. Styled panels were not only American. A very odd one is found on the 1935 Singer Nine sports coupé (*bottom right*). In an attempt to avoid glare, the facia, otherwise conventional, is mounted at an acute angle.

The visual horror of the American idiom is detectable in the 1938 Lincoln Zephyr (*opposite, top left*), though the central dial is easy to read, adaptable to left- or right-hand steering, and allows plenty of room for radio and locker. By contrast, the 1938 British SS 100 shows a typical sports car layout, with big speedometer and rev counter in front of the driver. The other instruments are somewhat haphazardly disposed. The folding windshield is typical of the 1930s sports car, and on the SS there are also miniature aero screens to protect the crew when the main windshield is lowered. On the 1939 2.6-litre WA-type MG (*opposite, bottom*) the manufacturer's traditional octagon motif is perpetuated in the shape of the dials. Ergonomic influences are visible in the neatly grouped switches below the facia, though starter and ignition switches are separate.

Sheer glamour, a checkered production history, and technical problems connected with the front-wheel drive and electric gear shift tend to detract from the stylistic merits of the 1936 810 Cord, here seen (*left*) in its most sought-after form, the 1937 812-series supercharged phaeton

Further strides were made after Europe went to war. The glass industry, admittedly, had yet to master the single-panel curved screen, albeit Chrysler had used one on their biggest Airflows, and Hupmobile's Aerodynamic featured wrap-round inserts in the windshield posts. Gradually, however, grille, front fenders, and bumpers merged into dissonances of aggressive chromium plate, fuel fillers were flush-mounted, and rear fenders were integrated into the body. Cars grew steadily longer, Pontiacs gaining sixteen inches between 1936 and 1942.

Not all the clever ideas caught on. One that fortunately failed was the Chrysler Airflow, with its flush sides, spatted rear wheels, and waterfall grille. It found no native imitators, albeit direct cribs were perpetrated by Singer in Britain, Volvo in Sweden, and Toyota in Japan. But though stylists were becoming adept at selling their masterpieces to the public, the Airflow was altogether too much. Its alligator hood, with high, flush sides, made maintenance awkward, and early cars had no external luggage access. Neither Britons nor Swedes wanted it either: the Volvo Carioca sold poorly, while most of the 11-hp Singer chassis earmarked for the new idiom were completed with conventional bodies. Even when hurriedly reworked, first with a new widow's-peak grille and then with a bigger trunk, the Airflow proved a lemon. Another one that backfired was the 1932 Hupmobile with Loewy's cycle fenders: it coincided with the skirted Graham, and the dressier car appealed more.

Regrettably disregarded – or, more correctly, bowdlerized – was Gordon Buehrig's 810 Cord, the sensation of 1936. If the manually retractable headlamps were a gimmick and before their time, the low-mounted, wrap-round grille was an excellent idea. But where Buehrig's original was simple and unadorned, his would-be imitators laid the chromium on with a trowel. One has only to study the Chrysler Corporation's 1939 range to see what went wrong, though one cannot but admire the skill with which bar-patterns were cunningly shuffled to give four different front-end treatments for the four makes in the group.

(four-passenger convertible coupé). This one was good for over 100 mph (160 km/h) on 4.7 litres and 190 bhp. Gordon Buehrig's creation had an elegant simplicity of line, with the unadorned horizontal bars of the grille extending round on to the sides of the alligator-type hood. There was no superfluous chromium plate, and the radiator core was completely hidden. Also streamlined in was the fuel filler cap, while running boards were dispensed with, and the headlamps (here seen fully extended for use) were fully retractable, though they had to be wound in and out by hand. A curved front apron concealed the drive units: this

was, of course, a legacy from the original 1929 Cord.

Unsuccessful mimicry. Sweden's imitation of the 1934 Chrysler Airflow, the Volvo PV36 Carioca (*opposite, top right*). The fast back, rear fender skirts, divided windshield, and raised hood sides incorporating nacelles for the recessed headlamps are authentic Chrysler, though Volvo eschewed Chrysler's original 1934 waterfall grille in favour of their own version of the later "widow's peak". Unfortunately, the Swedes disliked the shape just as the Americans had, and precisely five hundred Cariocas found buyers.

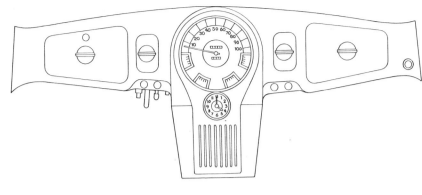

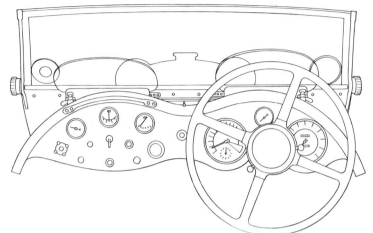

"What Detroit thinks today, Europe thinks tomorrow", though the Auto Union group in Saxony were pretty quick off the mark in this particular car. The front end of their Wanderer W24 reflects the 1937 General Motors idiom announced in the fall of 1936, and the German car was first seen at Berlin the following March. What one can see here (*centre*), however, shows that Auto Union had adopted the American idiom for the first time, though it was as yet limited to this Wanderer and the four-cylinder DKW with very similar chassis and sheet metal. The curved and skirted fenders, vestigial running boards, and ventipanes in the front windows are purest Detroit, as are the smooth flow of the roof-line and the fully integrated rear trunk, even if the spare wheel lives out of doors in the interests of *Lebensraum*, and luggage is accessible only from inside. Technically, of course, Germany is ahead of the United States. Though Wanderer are content with a stolid four-cylinder side-valve motor giving 42 bhp from 1.8 litres and propelling the car at an equally staid 65 mph (105 km/h), all four wheels are independently sprung and brakes are hydraulic, at a time when Ford, at any rate, were still wedded to mechanicals.

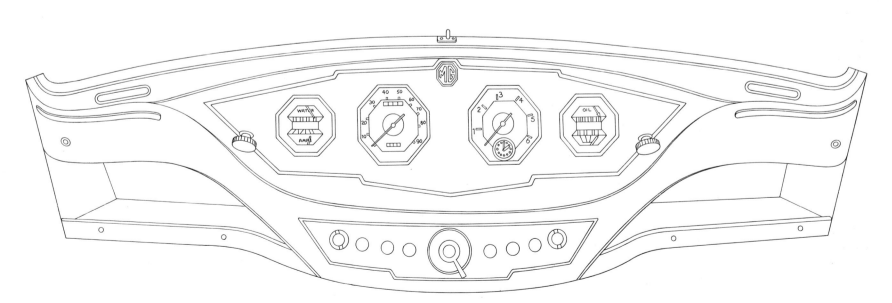

Second-hand American ideas. Only the fencer's mask grilles link the 1939 Rosengart LR4 (*bottom*) and the 1936 Riley Sprite (*opposite*). Motives were different, too. The French firm was trying to update its version of the Austin Seven, by this time blessed with conventional suspension and a more robust frame. The result was certainly chic, but rumour said that this cabriolet cost more than the imported British article, for all the swingeing tariffs, and sales of 5,650 cars in 1939 were hardly impressive. The Riley's grille was peculiar to this model and concealed the regular radiator. Power was provided by Riley's excellent twin-camshaft high-pushrod 1,496-cc four in twin-carburettor form, and the Sprite would do 85 mph (135–140 km/h). The works raced them (with light bodies and no fancy trimmings) and won both the 1935 and 1936 Tourist Trophies. With those big exposed headlamps and heavy fenders, one may doubt if the grille made much difference to the aerodynamics: many owners threw them away.

The stylist's brief, of course, did not end outside an automobile. He went to work on the inside, with interesting and sometimes curious consequences to the facia.

Dashboards themselves were a concomitant of the new streamlined facias of 1914–15. In the early 1920s, instruments were dotted haphazardly all over the place, though central groupings were becoming accepted practice by 1927, if not earlier. Further, they tended to be of postage-stamp size, while in the ascendant was one of the nastier American innovations, the drum-type speedometer on which only the actual speed of the moment was exposed to view. Such a device was standard even on the lordly Model-J Duesenberg, introduced in 1929.

Stylized panels soon appeared. The air-cooled Franklin featured vertical dials of unpleasing aspect, and those of the 1934 and 1935 SSs

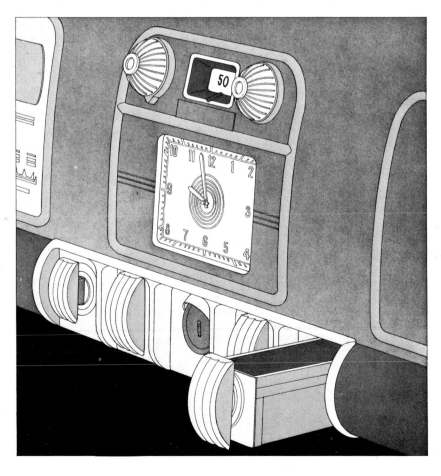

Pontiac facia (left), 1938. On this picture, the main dial can't be seen, but neatly styled into the secondary grouping are the radio (no push-button tuning as yet) and clock. Though Pontiac didn't follow some other makes in duplicating the radiator grille on the ashtray lid, the famous Silver Streaks are there for all to see!

were hexagonal, in answer to MG's well-established octagon, mercifully banished at almost all times from the facia. Thereafter, no holds were barred, horrors including Hudsons's curved panel of 1936 (to match the compound curves outdoors) and the unattractive rectangular display of 1939 Buicks. Sometimes, the nonsense was carried to extremes: the lids of Buick's 1936 ashtrays were miniature replicas of the radiator grille.

There were some compensations. In the main, instruments were now grouped where the driver could see them, and simplicity was the order of the day. The redeeming feature of the single oval dial on 1936 Hillmans was a huge ignition warning-light, the size of a bantam's egg, and tailor-made for the absent-minded housewife. Less commendable was an increasing tendency to replace instruments by warning lights, not always colour-coded in those days. Mercifully, nobody had yet anticipated Nash's 1949 brainstorm: on their Airflyte series all the instruments were grouped in a single binnacle attached to the steering column. Quite apart from problems of focussing, there was a miniature

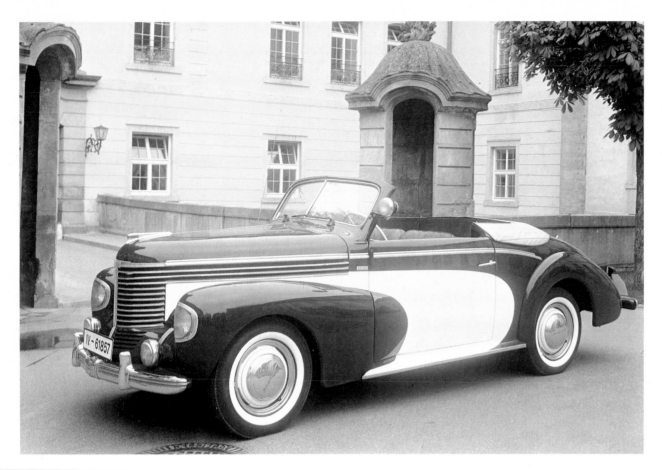

German themes, 1938–39. One expects some similarities between the 1939 Opel Kapitän (*top left*) and the 1938 Oldsmobiles on the opposite page – both makes come, after all, from General Motors. The newer Opel goes one step further, not so much with the grille but with the fully recessed headlamps. The cabriolet body and its flashy two-toning are the coachbuilder's doing; not so the fenders extending back into the doors, which are found also on the fully unitary sedan examples of this 2.4-litre overhead-valve six. Germans, of course, expected a full cabriolet in the range, which made it worth Opel's while to offer a separate chassis version even of a mass-produced car.

The aerodynamic 2.5-litre Adler (*bottom*) was a more expensive contemporary of the Opel, listing at a price some forty-five per cent higher in sedan form. Despite the suggestion of this drawing, it wasn't a unitary hull, being based on a punt-shaped chassis frame with heavy box-section side members, not unlike that found on Adler's smaller front-wheel-drive cars. The rest of the top-hamper, including fenders, was delivered from the Ambi-Budd bodyworks in Berlin and then mounted on the chassis. As befits an *Autobahn*-cruiser, spotlamps as well as headlamps were fully recessed, though legal requirements in some countries dictated that the parking lights stayed out of doors. One of the disadvantages of the perfect teardrop shape was a marked lack of rearward vision.

"We only export last year's styling themes", or this looks like a page of '38s from America. Actually, only the two Oldsmobiles (*opposite, bottom*) are from that model year; the Berliet Dauphine sedan (*opposite, top*) was the Lyonnais company's new model for 1939, this in spite of the more conservative, fully exposed headlamps. One may suspect that this may have been a deliberate attempt to conceal the origins of the Berliet's body, bought complete from Peugeot of Sochaux and common to that company's 2.1-litre 402. (Peugeot, of course, tucked *their* headlamps *inside* the radiator grille.) The

Oldsmobiles epitomize the themes of 1938: partly recessed illuminations, disappearing running boards, bumper overriders, and grilles composed of an assortment of horizontal bars. Oldsmobile's outer shell had a distinctive shape (it cropped up in unlikely places on motifs all over the car), while a neat trick was the use of a finer grille pattern to distinguish the more expensive straight-eight (*right*) from the six (*left*). This method of differentiation was on its way out: by the time the United States went to war, the big variation would be between trunkbacks and fastbacks (under sundry appellations), and one relied on hood length (or badging) to tell whether the car was a six or an eight.

forest of electrical spaghetti sharing the column with the gear-lever linkage!

Predictably, most of these American influences crossed the Atlantic, though styling was far more haphazard there, and too many popular models, especially French ones, resembled obsolete American sedans. Early examples of the integral trunk were far from practical. The French, who had long been addicted to *conduites intérieures avec malle*, kept their trunk, still opening from the top and seldom integrated into the body line. The British tendency was to add a nicely integrated excrescence at the rear and then fill it with the spare wheel, thus defeating the entire object. Fastbacks, too, were tried, though they had a short vogue, owing to limitations of rear-seat headroom. Morris and Standard were back with notchbacks by 1939, though Hillman's gentler slope was only sacrificed in favour of bigger trunks on the 1940 line. Fiat and Peugeot used the fencer's-mask idiom to good purpose: the short beetling hoods were unsightly but gave excellent forward vision, even if the French maker's trick of tucking the headlamps inside the grille was scarcely a bright idea. On the 1939 Morris 8, the headlamps vanished into the front fenders.

Even those big cars innocent of direct American antecedents looked curiously American. The Oldsmobile-like grille of the last pre-war Berliets was not improved by Marius Berliet's frugal practice of using Peugeot bodies; the Renault combined all the worst aspects of the Detroit idiom; and the 1940 Austins looked like scaled-down 1938 General Motors products – Austin would not catch up with the 1940 idiom for another seven years. In Sweden, Volvo tried a bit of everything: after the Airflow-inspired Carioca came the PV 51/52, a mixture of Chrysler and Chevrolet. Successive sixes spanning the war years incorporated the 1938 American Ford grille, the same breed's 1942 box fenders, and finally (in the post-war PV60), a Dodge-style body wedded to a 1939 Pontiac front end.

The styling revolution, of course, played its part in harassing the weaker brethren, already hard put to it to stay the course. In addition to keeping their product competitive, they had to make it look up-to-date. To mechanical gimmicks had to be added styling oddities. Graham, who had run out of cash and new ideas alike after exploring centrifugal blowers, tried an astonishing and shark-like concave nose in 1938, before joining forces with Hupmobile to exploit the body dies of the now-defunct Cord. It availed them not at all. In the same class fall Singer's curious "Airstream" experiments and Triumph's Hudson-*cum*-Pontiac front end.

The effect was felt worst in France, where the local Big Three were fast approaching the pre-eminence of General Motors, Ford, and Chrysler on the far shore of the Atlantic. Scissors and paste were now the order of the day. You either made your own chassis and bought bodies, or cloaked someone else's mechanics in a style that camouflaged their origins. Berliet bought bodies from Peugeot, and La Licorne from Citroën; cheaper Delahayes were seen with both Citroën and Renault sedan coachwork. Rosengart and Georges Irat created sporty (if not overly sporting) models from the proven mechanical elements of the 11CV Citroën *traction*. Chenard-Walcker, already humiliated by having to share bodies with Matford, were down by the outbreak of war to a choice between a Ford-bodied Citroën and a Ford-bodied Ford, though at least their suspensions came from the all-French source. Badge-engineering was upon us.

Not that this was new. A choice of radiator grille, sentiment, and customer ignorance could produce two identities out of one design. If Morris-Wolseley permutations were not as yet wholly rationalized, the goings-on at Coventry's respected Daimler factory were confusing in the extreme. At the height of their badge-engineering phase, in 1935, it

Contrasting coupés, 1938–39. The 2-litre Dolomite Roadster Coupé with six-cylinder pushrod motor (*top left*) was the flagship of the ailing Triumph company, and, unusually for a British convertible, featured a rumble seat at the rear. It looks a little naked without the accessory wheel discs usually fitted, and it's a matter of opinion whether that fancy die-cast grille in the 1936 Hudson or Pontiac idiom really blends with a traditional British shape. Still, it was good for 85–90 mph (135–145 km/h) and won rallies as well as *concours d'elégance*. By contrast, one expects a rumble seat on the 1938 Dodge (*bottom left*), though this style was also available as a Business Coupé with baggage space instead of extra seating. This British-assembled car has a plethora of extra illumination. There's a rumble seat again on the rare front-wheel-drive Citroën *faux cabriolet* (*bottom right*), offered only from 1934 to 1938, though the solid steel top and fixed rear window made the extra passengers feel "quarantined". This 1938 7CV is the British model with 12-volt electrics and leather trim. By contrast, the foursome drophead coupé (convertible victoria) was essentially a European type as late as 1938, when this semi-custom Vauxhall 14/6 (*top right*) by Salmons-Tickford was built, almost the last of its line, since 1939 Fourteens were unitary and available only as sedans. Sold through Vauxhall's own dealer chain, the car featured a three-position top, the usual claustrophobic rear quarters, and the never very satisfactory arrangement of a spare wheel mounted on the trunk lid.

was hard to sort out the various Tens and Light Sixes produced under the BSA and Lanchester banners, while only a name, a radiator, and £20 ($100), distinguished the Lanchester Eighteen from the Daimler Light Twenty. Both were 2.6-litre overhead-valve sixes rated at 20 hp under the British fiscal system.

Beneath even the most doleful 1930s shapes, however, could be discerned a new aspect of the automobile – a living room on wheels. This was, after all, only logical. The vehicle already offered dependable transportation, and the stylists had integrated its lines. Now, it was time to make it truly habitable.

The writer can recall long winter journeys in the 1930s, mainly in mass-produced British sedans. The entire crew dressed up in overcoats, and rear-seat passengers were armed with hot-water bottles. At least one window was open. Not, be it said, for hand signals – semaphore-type turn indicators had reached Germany by the late 1920s and the rest of Europe by 1934 – but to prevent the glass from frosting up. Wise motorists carried a raw potato to scrape frost from the windshield itself, since the accessory bar demisters of the period were less than efficient. Seats adjusted but did not recline, and though the average British car of 1935 was well equipped – the mandatory sliding roof, a remotely controlled rear blind, leather upholstery, arm-rests, an opening windshield, and even a clock – there was no heater.

By this time, such an amenity was a regular optional extra in the United States. Nash scored a bullseye in 1938 with their "air-conditioning", though in fact this was only a controlled heating and ventilation system. Real air-conditioning would not arrive until 1941, on the more expensive Packards. The windshield washer, essential if not compulsory in most countries today, was in its infancy. True, such a device was found on some 1935 Standards and Triumphs, but since it used radiator water, its early demise was predictable. More sophisticated versions were available in the United States by 1938. Bed-seats, pioneered by Durant in 1931, reappeared seven years later on Nash's extras list, while power assistance was being applied to the divider windows of limousines as well as to the tops of convertibles.

There was also the question of in-car entertainment. Car radio was one of the major amenities of 1930s motoring. Admittedly, reception was not up to modern standards, for all such eccentricities as "streetcar" settings on early American installations. Antennae were a constant problem, with whip-shaped circlets on the roof, and even an under-the-running-board type, recommended only for use on ragtops.

Progress was slow at first. Though several American manufacturers advertized their cars as "wired for radio" in 1931, factory installation was not part of the programme, since the work could take two competent technicians a good eight hours to complete. In spite of these early complications, Americans bought 145,000 car radios in 1932, and over a million in 1935. By this time, too, dashboards were being tailored to accept radio panels, which often meant scrapping a few automobile-oriented dials in favour of "idiot lights". Push-button tuning was a reality by 1939, and a vacuum-powered antenna was actually a catalogued option on 1940 Pontiacs.

The tempo was slower in Europe. Hillman's 1934 Melody Minx was one of the first cars offered with "factory radio", but on most conversions the control panel lived under the dash, where it barked the front-seat passenger's knees. The same improvisation went for heaters, where fitted; the fan on the writer's 1937 MG was positioned strategically within inches of his clutch foot, so that a fast downshift would produce sepulchral clanks from this unit. It was not until 1939 that the first built-in installations appeared on popular cars. By this time, music while one drove was quite cheap: SS Cars quoted a mere £20 ($100) inclusive of fitting, on their last pre-war models.

In the United States the drawing-room image went much further. Thanks to the Japanese, only fifteen thousand Pontiacs were sold in 1942, but the "personalization" available to customers went far beyond the nine single-tone and five two-tone colour choices. Far, indeed, beyond five different choices of cloth trim and the practical option of a booster for those inefficient vacuum wipers still beloved of Americans. Seat covers came in nine patterns, there was a "Kool Kushion" for long spells at the wheel, and the presence of an "in-car bed" showed that General Motors had no intention of losing out to Nash. "Vizor vanity mirrors" came with or without illumination, an extra ashtray could be attached to the front ventipane, and lights could be installed in the trunk and glove compartments. Entertainment was not limited to the in-car variety: Pontiac Division could sell you a portable radio for picnics. And if, in this aura of "thermostatic heat" and "controlled no-draft ventilation", you caught a cold, your friendly dealer was ready with a Kleenex dispenser to clip under the dash.

Chapter 4

CRYING ONE'S WARES

Automotive publicity went to town in the 1930s.
True, it was not as yet internationally oriented. Car exports still meant the United States first and foremost. Detroit's offerings might be gaining in bulk, sophistication, and ballyhoo, but they still enjoyed the widest distribution, just as they had in the 1920s, and, indeed, during most of the teens.

Unquestionably, Henry Ford's successful pursuit of mass production had been the main ingredient of this American dominance, but it was the First World War that opened the floodgates. All the other major car-making nations were now preoccupied with weightier matters. Even if a "business as usual" philosophy – plus a marked inefficiency in conversion to the weapons of war – allowed Britan's motor industry to turn out a fair number of passenger cars in 1915 and 1916, there were not enough to go round. Thus, American-built automobiles by the thousand suddenly invaded not only England, but also Britain's still-numerous dominions and colonies. Here their continuing hegemony was assured by low prices, ease of maintenance, and characteristics better suited to bush roads than anything offered by the rest of Europe.

Italy, of course, imported nothing, while German interest in American cars was a phenomenon of the later 1920s. France, however, proved fertile soil for Ford, if not for his up-market rivals; the government alone took eleven thousand new Ts and TT trucks in 1918, thus paving the way for the establishment of an assembly plant in Bordeaux soon after the Armistice.

Thenceforward, the United States moved in with a vengeance. During the 1930s, General Motors were assembling in Belgium, Germany, and Great Britain, not to mention in Australia and Japan. Ford operations were on a similar scale, while the youthful Chrysler Corporation were never far behind. The relaxation of Belgian tariff barriers in the 1920s not only administered the *coup de grâce* to that country's automobile industry, it opened the way for Antwerp's assembly plants.

Nor was this the limit. South America might be short on roads – even Argentina, her wealthiest republic, still had no all-weather system linking all her major cities – but this was no deterrent to Detroit. Ford, who began operations there in 1922, merely shipped carloads of Ts to the nearest convenient railhead. General Motors were assembling Chevrolets in the country by 1927, and Julio Fevre, the Chrysler concessionaire in Buenos Aires, was in the assembly business as well five years later.

The Great Depression was to take its toll. Even where prices were competitive – and they usually were – a Buick used more fuel than an Austin or Citroën. It also carried a higher annual tax. This, however, bit only where the impost was directly related to cylinder capacity or fuel consumption, as in Britain or France. In the former country American sales took a tumble in the 1930–32 period, and breeds as well-known and respected as Cadillac, Dodge, Nash, Studebaker, and even Chevrolet disappeared from the market. Nations with industries to protect protected them savagely; with the accession of Hitler, Germany, which had taken twenty-two thousand vehicles from General Motors alone in 1928, became virtually a closed shop. Czechoslovak duties inflated the list price of a Ford V8 – $500 (£100) at home and $1,300 (£260) in Britain – to an uneconomic $4,000 (£800). Even Switzerland adopted a protectionist policy, though she was locking the stable door after the horse had bolted. Martini, her sole passenger-car maker, was moribund in 1928 and dead by 1934.

Elsewhere Detroit ruled the roost. Even in 1933, the American automotive industry exported 63,754 cars – only four per cent of total production, but then the still-substantial demand for right-hand steering was filled from Canadian plants. Canada shipped twenty-nine per cent of her output abroad that year, the percentage reaching thirty-three in 1936, and again in 1938. We shall return to the realm of exports later on; suffice it to say for the moment that only American or American-owned concerns thought globally in their public relations.

This factor would govern the crying of wares. Only in specialist cases was advertising directed at a specific overseas market: in 1937, Chevrolet spent a lot of money promoting their new Cheetah model, with a taxable horsepower of only twenty-five, a good bet (or so they hoped) in Britain, where the regular G-series was rated as a thirty. Otherwise, export advertising consisted quite simply of fitting translated copy round a layout already tried out on the domestic market. (For right-hand drive one reversed the block!) Thus, we find Essex inflicting some truly American publicity on Swedes in 1930. "A Car for the Whole Family", proclaimed the copy-writer. "The Essex is not just a car for yourself, but for your whole family, because it is roomy – roomier than before, and roomier than other cars of the same size. You can easily get in and out through the extra-wide doors, you sit comfortably, and the car is comfortable and easy to drive." To make certain that Swedes (not to mention Brazilians and Britons) knew that it really was "roomier than before", a suitably distorted line block rather than a photograph accompanied this outburst. It made the boxy Essex look twenty feet long, and it got to Stockholm way ahead of the actual car.

Slogans, of course, didn't always translate. Hotchkiss's *le juste milieu* sounded fine in French, but "the golden mean" (not used in English-speaking countries) suggested too much compromise. Daimler, wisely,

109

...DÈS LES PREMIERS BEAUX JOURS PAR MONTS ET PAR VAUX AU VOLANT D'UNE

9$_{cv}$4$_{cyl}$4$_{vit}$ ou 11$_{cv}$4$_{cyl}$4$_{vit}$

BERLIET

SANS SOUCIS, AVEC UN MINIMUM DE SOINS VOUS AUREZ TOUJOURS LA PLUS GRANDE SATISFACTION. REMARQUÉS PAR VOTRE ÉLÉGANCE, ENVIÉS POUR VOTRE CONFORT, VOUS APPRÉCIEREZ **LES SOUPAPES EN TÊTE ET LES 4 VITESSES : DEUX FACTEURS D'ÉCONOMIE.**

USINES ET BUREAUX, VÉNISSIEUX (RHONE)

BOULEVARD DE VERDUN, COURBEVOIE (SEINE)

How to add charm to utility. If one had to pick two of the most mundane cars of the 1930s, the Model A Ford (here in English guise) and the 1934 four-cylinder Berliet from France would be "naturals". Actually, the Ford, with a gearshift compared to "slicing butter with a hot knife", was not without a certain charm, and anything would have been a welcome change after the idiosyncracies of Model T. Since, at £225 ($1,125) ex-works Manchester, the car was considerably more expensive than the native Morris-Cowley, Ford of Britain were stressing the up-market, miniature Lincoln image with real photographs, though they didn't mention Lincolns, hardly known in England in 1930. Styling had advanced somewhat by the time the Berliet arrived on the scene, so something had to be done to stress the warmed-over 1931 Cord-Chrysler hood and vee grille, rather than the boxy sedan body, with its mandatory, inelegant rear trunk. This particular idiom called for a long hood, which one didn't get with only 2 litres of four-cylinder engine. The copy precises and paraphrases Ford's interest in fuel taxes. Hence the adoption of valve-in-head motors by a firm who'd long been content with L-heads. The car offered nothing you couldn't get more cheaply on a Citroën or Renault – except, of course, rarity. Not that Berliet cared: they were already France's most successful makers of heavy trucks.

LINCOLN **Ford** Fordson

AIRCRAFT

NEW FORD DE LUXE FORDOR SALOON WITH SLIDING ROOF 24 H.P. £225 AT WORKS, MANCHESTER. *(14.9 h.p. £5 extra)*

Every riding and driving comfort you can desire

THE ENDURING beauty of the New Ford reflects the immense amount of trouble taken and money spent to build real and lasting value into this fine car. The lustre of elegant coachwork, built to give maximum safety, and rustless steel is matched by a degree of engineering skill and workmanship not to be found in any car at anything near the price.

It is one of the simplest cars ever built — easy to handle — responsive to the throttle — steady and safe at any speed. And it carries, as standard equipment, everything you need for your comfort.

Every detail of the New Ford has been designed to give you smooth, trouble-free and economical running during all the years of its long life.

Ask your nearest Ford dealer for a trial run.

NEW FORD PRICES				
Tudor Saloon, 24 h.p.	.	.	.	**£180**
Touring Car	..	.	.	**£185**
Standard Coupé	..	.	.	**£185**
Cabriolet	,,	.	.	**£210**
3-window Fordor Saloon, 24 h.p.	.	.	**£210**
De Luxe Touring Car	,,	.	.	**£225**

All prices at works, Manchester. 14.9 h.p. £5 extra.

FORD MOTOR COMPANY LIMITED : LONDON AND MANCHESTER

111

France's effort to promote the new Fords in 1932 stresses price – all the amenities one gets on the four-cylinder model for only 26,900 francs, though by this time one is saving only two taxable horsepower a year by opting for 105 km/h (65 mph) instead of the vee-eight's sizzling 130 km/h (80 mph). In those times of depression, the cheapest two-door sedans are shown rather than the more attractive – and more expensive – cabriolets. There is a careful, almost Bellochian, "mention of virtues": the dampers, which were hydraulic, duly rate a mention. The brakes, mechanical and destined to stay so for another six seasons, are dismissed as "powerful", which they were not.

112

reserved their 1934 effort ("Listen for the Silence") for the home market, while Morris's rhyming, jingoistic "British Made for Empire Trade" would hardly have gone down with Belgians, who had their own colonial empire and wanted it to buy FNs, much less with Germans clamouring for more *Lebensraum*. Advertising tended to be a local affair.

When attempts were made to produce something different for foreigners, the result could backfire. Leonard Lord, the then head of Austin, was shrewd enough to recognize that "You Buy a Car, but You Invest in an Austin" was not a catchphrase likely to appeal in America, the land of planned obsolescence and yearly trade-ins, but his American importers did him a grave disservice with that prime *double entendre*: "Let's Take the Austin: The Car that is Always At Home". Some British campaigns were double-edged too: MG's habit of painting SAFETY FAST on the more dangerous, angled railroad bridges around the London area would never have been tolerated in the accident-conscious atmosphere of a later era.

It is too easy to generalize on the early promotional techniques of the industry. A quick glance at automobile advertising up to the early 1920s suggests a division into four obvious categories – "nuts and bolts", testimonials, illustrious clients, and competition successes. Illustrations, where used, were bald line or half-tone blocks of typical vehicles, with an occasional fling with the whole range to demonstrate comprehensive market coverage. Yet, stylized, elongated vehicles, depicted in the *art nouveau* mode, with typefaces to match, were used by such pedestrian French makers as La Buire and Turcat-Méry around 1921, even if the English text of the former's effort was at a loss for *le mot juste*. "The La Buire", it observed, "is not a car for which the manufacturers put forward sweeping claims, but its makers can speak emphatically on the two features that make the strongest appeal to the experienced motorist – reliability and durability." On a more elevated level were Edward S. Jordan's prentice efforts. It should be remembered that while the legendary *Somewhere West of Laramie* didn't happen until 1921, Jordan was using comparable themes – and equally good artwork – when he launched his first cars way back in 1916.

Jordan's masterpieces were, however, exceptions in a sea of depressing prose. "Nuts and bolts" often expressed themselves in terms of vital statistics and prices, the dreariness of the content being accentuated by the determination of the press department to extract the last cent's worth from every precious column-inch. Singer's 1938 range announcement started off promisingly enough with: "The first 'luxury' car at a popular price", but soon degenerated into a lengthy catalogue of features such as "synchromesh 4-speed and reverse gearbox" (which it ought to have had, anyway, by that time). "Powerful Head Lamps" was even more platitudinous, and the unhappy reader who had ventured so far had then to endure a similar recital in support of the parallel Nine and Ten.

Variations on this theme included essays in the technological and statistical. Ford's well-remembered Vanadium Steel campaign of 1907–08 had its echo as late as 1920 in Maxwell's "steels made to order", and a lot could be done with sales figures. "Sixty-eight per cent more than last year" could, after all, merely mean a comparison between the first fine careless rapture of a new range and the last declining weeks of the old. Even in November, 1936, SS were not above claiming that in the past month they had commanded nearly ninety per cent of the 20-hp taxation class in Britain. This was admirable psychology: horsepower tax counted for a lot at the time, the company had but recently discontinued their tax-dodging 16-hp variant, and in any case there were few readers who stopped to figure out who made the competing Twenties.

Euphoria played no part in the nuts-and-bolts school of thought. Nor

did the latter change much; the only difference between 1935 and 1905 is that more was taken for granted. To head one's copy "No Broken Axles", as did an obscure British importer in the Dark Ages, would have been unthinkable. Dependability – if it had to be plugged – was best plugged by stressing high trade-in values. Armstrong Siddeley and Packard made much of their factory-guaranteed used cars; the latter, indeed, compared theirs to a Verdi opera seen from a cheap seat in the gods – "He sees the same program, hears the same music". Austin proclaimed a car "as ready for its second or third year of service as its first, ... whose innate quality commands the highest price when you care to dispose of it".

Along with nuts-and-bolts came the testimonials, though in a less snobbish and exclusive age, such observations (on the correct letterhead, of course!) as "The Car has now gone Ten Thousand Miles Without A Single Involuntary Stop" were superfluous. Instead, famous racing personalities, such as George Eyston and Malcolm Campbell in Britain and Barney Oldfield in the United States, were called upon to endorse a model in the best cigarette-promotion style. As many of these eminent drivers doubled as motoring correspondents, their views were valid, even if their paeans were not necessarily the result of actual ownership. As for "illustrious clients", these were on their way out. There were fewer monarchs around in 1930 than in 1910, so the old maxim, "When in doubt, list your maharajahs", no longer obtained. Dying purveyors of chauffeur-driven carriages (Isotta Fraschini, Minerva) still adopted such methods, the latter company in an attempt to defend good taste against the march of American vulgarity. ("Whilst everything is carried out with the best possible workmanship, it is quiet and dignified, a car of genteel luxury unsullied by any Sir George Midas ostentation.") Even in 1928, Fiat were not averse to long lists of notables who drove their humble 509A, but the object of parading these Balkan princelings and African emirs was to stress global rather than snob appeal.

Consumer-report techniques mentioning the opposition by name were rare and generally provoked by extravagant claims. Such a war broke out between Chevrolet and Ford in 1934, after the latter had done well in stock-car racing. It had been far commoner in the first decade of the century. "Look what our machine beat at the local hill-climb" was, if confined for obvious reasons to the specialist press, a permitted gambit in the United States; and not only were the defeated victims identified, but their list prices, always higher than the victor's, were given! With an established sporting *marque* such as Bentley, who commemorated their third Le Mans win with a handsome booklet succinctly titled *Again*, competition themes remained acceptable. They were less acceptable in the case of minor-league events nobody had heard of, and the method had its pitfalls, especially in the prentice or declining years of a manufacturer's career. Too many of SS's early successes were in static *concours d'élégance*, while Austro-Daimler, once a proud name in the tougher hill-climbs and rallies, were down to Ruritanian beauty parades by 1933. The *reductio ad absurdum* of typographic laurels came after the Second World War, by which time motor sport was an accepted topic in newspapers and radio. Thus, victory in an ill-supported sub-category of a major international rally could spur copy-writers to a frenzied FIRST! (96-point bold). The reader was supposed to – and usually did – ignore the six-point qualification underneath, referring to Modified Production Touring Cars, 1,501 to 1,600 cc. More knowledgeable students, of course, were undeceived; they knew who was still running 1,600s, and who had recently over-bored to 1,800 cc.

Factory-sponsored stunts were less common than of yore. There was less to prove. Top-gear marathons had still been popular in the 1920s,

BERLIN, JULI 1938
2. JAHRGANG HEFT 7

MotorSchau

PREIS RM 1.-

MOTORSCHAU VERLAG DR. GEORG ELSNER u. CO. BERLIN SW.68

The unattainable versus the only too at-
tainable, thanks to time payments! This
early Volkswagen advertisement (*left*) – off
the front cover of *Motorschau* magazine –
rates as state propaganda rather than
advertising in the Western sense of the
word. At the time it was published (July,
1938), the press had scarcely seen the car,
and one wonders if the artist had, either:
even allowing for poetic licence, both
front and rear look very like the last batch
of prototypes tried in 1937. The sedan's
rear-seat headroom has been exaggerated,
and the overhang at the tail is reminiscent
of the contemporary 170H Mercedes-
Benz. All the occupants of both cars look
healthy, dedicated, and earnest: note also
the "KdF" label (*Kraft durch Freude,*
"Strength through Joy", the motto of Dr.
Robert Ley's Nazi *Arbeitsfront*). *Volkswagen*
was still only a generic term in 1938:
everyone, including the foreign press, referred to the vehicle as a KdF-*Wagen*.
General Motors (*right*) are also a little
naughty, though 1935 Buicks really did
look that way; where they overreached
themselves was by showing the convertible
with dual sidemounts when ninety per
cent of the customers would buy the box-
ier sedan, anyway. American euphoria is
far more sybaritic than the German
species, and jargon is much in evidence.
"The gliding ride as only Buick gives it" is
only another way of saying coil-spring independent front suspension, and "automatic features" in those days of
synchromesh presumably refer to the
company's addiction to starters operated
by the gas pedal. The lady represents "the
vigor and exuberance of youth" with no
help from Buick, and if her father were
the parsimonious sort and figured that
she'd have to make do with a Chevrolet
convertible, he'd have to think again.
Chevrolet weren't making one in 1935.

Body by Fisher

It would greet you with a Smile · · ·

If your motoring has become a sort of hum-drum transportation, there is that in the Buick which will bring back the zest of driving your first car.

Just to see the Buick is to realize how vivacious and new it is in its smart beauty. To drive it and ride in it but once is to recognize that it brings to modern motoring something new and all its own.

For there is a difference that goes beyond the gliding ride as only Buick gives it, beyond the matchless ease of superb performance and the convenience of automatic features. There seems to be the vigor and exuberance of youth in all that Buick does; and it is not difficult to imagine that, if it were human, it would always greet you with a smile.

You can take that kind of car to your heart—which perhaps explains the undying loyalty of Buick owners, and the even more wide-spread favor which Buick is winning today among motorists of all classes.

· B U I C K ·

WHEN · BETTER · AUTOMOBILES · ARE · BUILT—BUICK · WILL · BUILD · THEM

HOTCHKISS
CHALLENGES ON PERFORMANCE

TIME SPEED ½ MILE	BRAKE TEST FROM 20 M.P.H.
95.74 M.P.H.	**21** FT. ● BEST FIGURE RECORD
'Autocar' Road Test, April 5, 1935	"'Autocar' Road Test of 1934 cars, December 14, 1934"

"AUTOCAR" says:
".... one of the highest performance cars at present on the market . . . Outstanding acceleration...round corners and curves in keeping with the ideals of sports car driving — with very little reduction of speed — the machine feeling rock-steady."

" Brakes have for some years been a very strong feature of this make."

ACCELERATION FIGURES
From rest to 50, 10.4/5 secs.
From   10 - 30, 3.2/5 secs.
From   20 - 40, 4.1/5 secs.
From   30 - 50, 5.3/5 secs.

"'Autocar' Road Test, April 5, 1935"

"COUNTRY LIFE" says:
". . . . holds the road in most remarkable manner, brakes are quite the best from point of view of power and smoothness I have tried this year."

"Capable of really high speeds and colossal acceleration, but, unlike certain other vehicles of this type which rely on their engine power alone, it is one of the safest vehicles that I have ever handled."

WINNERS of the MONTE CARLO RALLY 3 YEARS IN SUCCESSION —a feat no other Car has accomplished

HOTCHKISS THE CAR BUILT FOR THE CONNOISSEUR

EVEN CARS AT TWICE THE PRICE CANNOT GIVE SUCH PHENOMENAL PERFORMANCE AND HIGH SAFETY MARGIN

OLYMPIA : HOTCHKISS STAND No. 80. Also exclusive design bodies by the leading continental coachwork builders on STANDS No. 4, 5, 7, 13, 37.

A choice of coachwork on the 3½ litre chassis · · · **£675**

Super - Sports, 3½ litre, 100 m.p.h. Chassis with choice of coachwork **£795**

Showrooms : 27-28, Albemarle St., W.1., 'phone Regent 1038/9. Works : Great West Rd., Brentford, Middlesex, 'phone Chiswick 5591/2

British advertising for the 1935 French 3.5-litre Hotchkiss. Though well laid out, it is rather over-burdened with text: a hairy all-round performance counted for a lot when the Anglo-American Railton was plugging acceleration at the expense of contemporary railway publicity ("It's Quickest by Rail-ton" was a lovely riposte to "It's Quicker by Rail"). There was also a potential challenge to Bentley, which had been transformed, under Rolls-Royce ownership, into "The Silent Sports Car". And a Super-Sports at £795 ($3,980) cost little more than half the price of the Bentley. Elongation is carefully used to counterbalance the forward-mounted engine of the car; even with the illustrated Chapron cabriolet instead of the standard factory style, it was not quite as elegant as its picture.

the exploits of Violet Cordery and her various Invictas springing to mind. There were unofficial "saloon car hour" and "sports car hour" records to attack, and anyone who could put 100 miles or 160 km into sixty minutes on a stock model, using pump fuel, could rely on a few weeks of good publicity. Studebaker made capital out of their successes in the Gilmore-Yosemite Economy Run, and just before the war, Vauxhall sponsored a fuel consumption contest administered by their dealer-network, in which private owners were encouraged to compete. A brand-new feature could provoke a maker into something sensational. The slightly-tarnished image of Citroën's early *tractions* was undoubtedly rescued by the astonishing François Lecot, who set himself the task of driving one 400,000 km (248,560 miles) in twelve months, and won through, though nineteen hours a day must have been punishing for a fifty-eight-year-old. Less comprehensible was the exploit of the American Harry Hartz, who drove backwards around the United States in 1933 at the wheel of a specially adapted Plymouth. The theory behind this works-sponsored operation was that cars of the period had "better aerodynamics travelling backward than forward", whereas the forthcoming Airflow reversed the process. It all seems rather far-fetched.

The four advertising themes persisted – the maharajahs apart – throughout the 1930s and would, indeed, continue into the 1950s, leading one cynical observer to enquire why some advertisers consistently paid extra for colour when their copy was so totally uninspired. Jordan or no Jordan, Americans were so inured to nuts-and-bolts that Chrysler's first post-VJ campaign (plenty of colour, but not a car in sight) took them by surprise. Such a technique was, however, no novelty: Rolls-Royce had periodic spells of carlessness, and Duesenberg's best effort hit the roof in snobbery. A series run in the Depression years depicted a gentleman in his library (or Madame by her swimming-pool) with the simple caption: "He [or She] Drives a Duesenberg". Gladney Haig of Jowett, a past master of homespun, biblical prose, only bothered to show one of his company's stolid flat-twins when they had a new body style, which was seldom.

But new influences were at work – to stylize cars in picture, to emphasize the latest pain-killing techniques from every possible angle, and to inject an element of euphoria. This last would reach its zenith in such gems as Renault's *Ils S'Aimaient* brochure of the two lovers and their Floride (of course, it was a convertible), and Leyland's permissive "You Can Do It In An MG". The intent of Edward S. Jordan and his followers was, in effect, to tell the customer: "Buy This Car, and it'll be better than any dose of salts". Above all, they sought to blind him with science, using pure jargon (General Motors's Knee Action Suspension) or the camouflage of a routine improvement beneath a dramatic phrase. "Rhythmic Ride" was more euphonious than "Cushion Levelator", but they both added up to better shock absorbers than last year's.

Again, there was no real novelty. In pioneering days, automobile-oriented medicos of impeccable background could be persuaded to claim motoring as the panacea for everything – pure snake oil, in fact. Before 1914, Berliet and Hispano-Suiza had used very impressionistic colour-work to promote their luxury offerings, and in the immediate post-Armistice years, Delage scored a hit with a similar series: *Rapide et Silencieuse, Elle Passe*.

The motive in such cases was artistic. The cars were elegant, which is more than could be said for most cheap offerings of the 1920s. Thus, something had to be done to penetrate beneath that boxy skin and show that the new sedans had something euphoric to offer. A lay public neither knew nor comprehended the mysteries of overhead valves; and it could not be seduced by a dissertation on the relative merits of

THE MOST COMPLETELY EQUIPPED CARS AT OLYMPIA

Nuts and bolts at its most uninspired. Lots of facts – the gimmicks to cover up a lack of new ideas, or the money to finance them, and a leaf out of Rolls-Royce's book with the "two years' free periodical inspection". The illustration doesn't do justice to what was, in fact, a good-looking car, and not the Cord-and-cabbage-water idiom suggested. "Illustrated literature on application" hints at a shortage of dealers, whereas even in their declining years, Star had quite good agency coverage. Joseph Lisle, the founder, was violently opposed to volume production: "I would rather build one good car a day!" was one of his favourite sayings. In any case, in this specialist field advertising was really only a visual proof of survival, and when this plug for the 1931 range was published, the Star Motor Company had barely another eighteen months to go.

THE GLAMOROUS NEW 1939 PLYMOUTH! It is brilliantly new in styling, new in comfort, new in safety, new in economy. Experience the new smoothness of its improved Floating Power engine mountings, its easier-acting hydraulic brakes. Relax in the restful quiet of Plymouth's "radio studio" sound-proofing. This great new car is now on display at your nearby Plymouth dealer. See it today!

PLYMOUTH BUILDS GREAT CARS

PRICED WITH THE LOWEST

—

EASY TO BUY

The new Plymouth's low price and easy terms make it exceptionally easy to own. Your present car will probably represent a large proportion of Plymouth's low delivered price . . . the balance in surprisingly low monthly instalments. See your nearby Plymouth dealer today.

TUNE IN MAJOR BOWES' AMATEUR HOUR, C.B.S. NETWORK, THURSDAYS, 9 TO 10 P. M., E.S.T.

The United States versus Germany again – or fun versus duty. Both advertisements date from 1939, and the cars were both six-cylinder family sedans, though the 2.5-litre Adler was quite a lot more expensive, being in the Humber or Buick class, so to speak. The difference is one of outlook, between the automobile as everybody's friend, and the adjunct of a pan-Aryan superman commuting from one *Autobahn's* end to another. The Plymouth's background is Sunday-morning – drinks on the lawn, with the dogs in attendance. There's even a slight hint of poor relations calling, to judge from the Beverly Hills colonial residence behind. By contrast, the Adler's crew are heading into a symbolic nightmare worthy of Fritz Lang. Such advertisements as Plymouth used were generally accompanied by some quasi-technical drawings, and folksy jargon dressing up commonplace features as something special. Adler don't even mention that this is their prestige Six, with conventional rear axle where the familiar Trumpfs and Trumpf-Juniors (good for thirty thousand a year) featured front-wheel drive. It almost seems as if they were trying to frighten the *Herrenvolk* off. The 2.5-litre was one of the best aerodynamic shapes of its time, good for 85 mph (130–135 km/h), despite a modest flathead engine rated at 55 hp. Sales of a mere five thousand in three seasons reflected a highish price: RM 5,750 (£300 or $1,500) was quite a lot to pay for a car in Germany in 1939.

Adlerwagen sind Vorkämpfer des Fortschritts –

Abermals prägen die Adlerwerke einen neuen Begriff für Fahren –

Raumgröße – Wirtschaftlichkeit: **ADLER**
2,5 Liter 6 Zylinder 58 PS

expanding and contracting brakes. One has only to compare Maxwell's tedious 1920 discourse on steel with what Chrysler had to say of that marque's successor, the 1926 Model 70. "It spurts smoothly and easily ahead: it turns, it steers, it stops even as you think the thought. There's joy – new joy – in the lives of those who own and drive the new Chrysler Six."

The 70 might "respond to your will as if it were a part of you", but the accompanying photograph brought one back to earth. Hence, subsequent press campaigns used a stylized car shape which symbolized the Chrysler's undoubted virtues without showing such miseries as clumsy roof peaks and headlamps shaped like biscuit tins. Climbing ability was emphasized by tilting the printing block diagonally upwards. Others followed: Harry Ainsworth of Hotchkiss, only too aware that *le juste milieu's* appearance was mediocre, had artist Alexis Kow depict it in an elongated form, which sold a lot of cars and was cheaper than a restyle in the metal. Later on, Kow would perform the same service for the sleeve-valve Panhard, an individual machine but not always an elegant one. (His wife complemented his efforts by starting the fashion for parading with borzois at *concours d'élégance*.)

Artificially elongated hoods and speed streaks were complemented by the performing midgets, who were destined to outlive them. This family – which often included a dog – was truly international and consisted of approximately two-third scale humans, whose function was to stress the amount of room in any big sedan, be it American, French, or British. Their death was ultimately encompassed by the development of colour photography (real cars are always preferable) and by increasing emphasis on the station wagon, a vehicle dedicated to the indivisible load. Citroën's latter-day 2CV publicity was an outstanding example of this new realism.

Euphoria led inevitably to sex. Fairly antiseptic sex, be it said. Couples depicted in automobiles were usually married, or at any rate betrothed, and the object was to woo female drivers rather than to promote the sales of "bird traps". Not that the lady was often shown at the wheel; and hardly ever in Germany, where the sole concession to *Kinder, Kirche, Küche* was an austere housewife fetching her husband from the office in one of the tamer Mercedes Benz – never a 540K, which was a man's car. (The Germans were not averse to promoting the Luftwaffe, however: aircraft often featured in backgrounds.) As late as 1950, American makers tended to park Madame firmly in the passenger seat. Of that year's crop of sales literature, only Pontiac favoured women drivers. A few ladies were dotted about the catalogues of Buick, Nash, Oldsmobile, and Studebaker, but masculine domination was the order of the day. Oldsmobile's 1970 appeal to secretaries ("Wouldn't it be fun to have an escape machine") would have been unthinkable. As for allowing some of these ladies to be black …

Les girls were, nevertheless, firmly wooed. Austin added a dose of the old snake oil: "Many homes", proclaimed their catalogue, "are made healthy and happy because Mother and the youngsters are availing themselves of change of scene, fresh air, and sunshine." Lincoln carried the maternal instinct a step further with their 1937 Mother's Day advertisement. This was, of course, upper-class stuff; not many parents could afford to give Junior a $1,300 vee-twelve for his or her first car. Still, the mum who did "could wave goodbye to her children with a lighter heart – because they go in a Lincoln-Zephyr". At a more utilitarian level, Plymouths were said to appeal to housewives for their "immunity from squeaks and rattles, their freedom from frequent attention and adjustment, their sparing use of gasoline and oil … truly luxurious transportation at low cost". "Not a hair out of place" ran a choice piece of Buick copy showing a débutante stepping from her car, "thanks to Fisher's No-Draft Ventilation", though it wasn't specified

whether she drove herself to the ball. Nash went all out for feminine support in 1938, their "air conditioning" promoted by a glamorous blonde on the back seat in a fair degree of *déshabille* (for those times, that is). "Way below zero", ran the caption proudly, "and no wrap." Matrons were beguiled by a "life begins at 40" headline, but it meant 40 mph and went on to extol the virtues of the brand-new overdrive, one of a series of controls "literally made to order for flick-of-the-wrist driving".

Boy-meets-girl was an infrequent theme, though Dodge used an echo of *Laramie* ideas to promote one of their last roadsters. Snobbery, however, triumphed in this case. Our young couple were "individuals of standing whose personal belongings invariably are distinctive as well as correct".

If prestige counted most, value for money was an eminently permitted gambit. Noboby likes to spend money on fuel, and in 1938, Wolseley, as well as the modest Vauxhall and Standard, were talking in terms of low fuel consumption.

Standard presented their Eight as "the car built to beat the Budget", a reference to the recent tax increases and to their own preference for the long-stroke motor. In France the Simca-built Fiat 500 was credited with *l'appetit d'un oiseau* ("the appetite of a bird"), while during the Depression, Riley, with a sporting middle-class image, went even further: "Next Year will be a Year of Economy. It's Got To Be", though they made up for these Morris-like sentiments by reminding readers that their "car of economy" possessed "a standard of safety which no car lacking in experience of strenuous tests on road and track … can possibly offer you". Even Packard could ooze luxury now and then – what price "the rich luxury of genuine long wearing wool broadcloth smoothly contoured over deep hair cushions and oil tempered springs, tailored to the specifications of one of the world's leading orthopaedic surgeons"? Nevertheless, the main theme of the subsequent advertising campaign was a down-to-earth average annual repair bill of precisely $15.31.

Everything had, of course, to be *de luxe*. Stripped models sorted ill with euphoric techniques, and in any case, the public did not buy them. Morris's "hundred pound car" was the big sensation of 1931, but people still preferred to pay another £25 ($125) for chromium plate and a five-lamp lighting set. Auburn deliberately filled dealers' showrooms with "Salon" models loaded with extras; they sold better, and there was more profit on the deal. Much of the hyperbole in American advertising stemmed, in fact, from a determination to make the customer buy all the options which were never part of the package at the advertised price. Under the stripped-price system, almost everything was extra.

To illustrate the workings of the scheme, let us look at Nash's cheapest 1934 six-cylinder sedan at $695 (£139) ex-works Kenosha, Wisconsin. Assuming the customer lived near the factory and so was exempt from freight charges, the car he got for his money came with a single windshield wiper, no bumpers, and no spare wheel. Thus, "extras" essential to everyday motoring added a round $100 (£20) to the bill. Add such favourite gimmicks as radio, heater, dual sidemounts, clock, cigar lighter, and trumpet horns (most of them shown in the advertisement that had lured the prospect into the showroom), and the actual delivered price was pretty close to that quoted for the same factory's straight-eight. And while in theory you could drive away in a $695 Nash, "extras" were often compulsory. Every Studebaker President of the 1936 model run came complete with twin tail lamps, twin horns, and cigar lighters, but all these items were supplementary to the list price of $1,065 (£213). This policy would reach ludicrous proportions on Lincolns of the early 1950s, available only with "optional extra" automatic. This was a matter of prestige; as yet, the Ford Motor Com-

One that eluded the Holy See. Everyone knows the story of the 1934 Fiat Balilla advertisement featuring the lady whose skirt showed too much. Vatican pressure led to some minor but significant "fashion changes", though the uncensored original hangs in Fiat's factory museum to this day. Intriguingly, she was not the only Fast Lady to help promote the latest in baby Fiats. This delectable piece of publicity appears on the back cover of one of *Rivista*'s 1925 issues and is plugging the company's first true cheap miniature, the 990-cc overhead-camshaft 509, made until 1929. The thoughtful trick (confined, incidentally, to home-market cars) of recording the type designation in huge nickel-plated script on the radiator core saves the copy writer a lot of trouble, while the lady's anatomy helps to conceal the awful truth: the 509 was quite as boxy as any of the Chryslers later hymned — and camouflaged — by McKnight Kauffer. In any case, the birth of a new Fiat was (and is) a national event in Italy. To launch the 509, the company laid on a brand-new hire purchase (time payment) scheme. Why use a super model to promote something so utilitarian? One must remember that precious few Italians could afford cars (or glossy magazines, for that matter) in 1925, and probably not more than one in every two hundred citizens actually owned even a humble Fiat. Thus, "Song without Words" styles worthy of Rolls-Royce or Duesenberg in the thirties would not be impossibly out of place.

Reginetle

Artist's licence. The 1934 Panhard Six as it looked in the metal and as redrawn by that publicity-virtuoso Alexis Kow. Not even clever two-toning could make a beauty of this stolid sedan with its wood artillery wheels (you could have bolt-on wires, but not a lot of customers did), while the split-pillar *panoramique* wind-

shield merely highlighted the thickness of the stock 1931-type pillars and led to some curious reflections. The hood was long, even on the smaller six-cylinder models, but the Kow advertisement gives the impression of the rare 8DS straight-eight, a 5-litre affair made only in small numbers.

pany's own automatic was not ready, so to suggest dependence on General Motors's Hydramatic (which Lincoln used) would have involved loss of face. The time would eventually come when the customer paid extra for "low-cost" manual gearboxes, because demand for these was down to a trickle!

This may explain why utilitarian themes vanished from American advertising. Only Willys, in financial trouble and struggling to make ends meet with a 2.2-litre four at $495 (£99), could describe this dreary little creature as "the car that helps buy many things the family needs". After a brief, euphoric skirmish with "the spirit of youth", they were back on the economy trail in 1942, with "a straight-from-the-shoulder message to everyone who weighs the worth of a dollar" – not to mention a 25 mpg thirst on the eve of fuel rationing.

Blinding the customers with science was a safe gambit – especially if this suggested that in some way the manufacturer cared. The nasty umbrella-handle hand-brake was there to clear the floor of projections and accommodate three people in front, but it was promoted as a safety feature. So was Chrysler's unloved transmission brake, which was said to leave the drums on the wheels free for regular duties of retardation. Buick's radio was "specially designed for the acoustical properties of the Buick body". Nobody was averse to making a virtue out of necessity. The first post-war Crosley minicars were finished in "a light metallic gray-blue reminiscent of the wings of the mourning dove, reflected in the sunlight", but what the company did not add was that Powel Crosley was trying to save dimes by eliminating colour choices.

Fancy names concealed mundane features. Chrysler's "safety signal speedometers" of 1939 were what they purported to be, with different colour zones for different speed ranges. It was, however, naughty of Hudson to pass their warning lights off as "teleflash gauges". Press departments rediscovered – and murdered – classical Greek, while an assortment of euphemisms camouflaged the soggy independent suspensions of the period. Ford, of course, left these latter alone, preferring to defend their old transverse-leaf set-up as "long, slow action springs of multi-leaf design", but General Motors had "knee action", while Hudson boosted "Axle Flex".

Nor were such euphemisms fully explained. The 1939 Hudsons came with a choice of Handishift or Selective Automatic Shift. Also present were Automatically Controlled Wing Ventilation, Triple Seal Oil Cushioned Clutches, and Hydraulic Hill Hold, meaning, respectively, a new type of ventipane, the same old wet-plate clutch the company had been using for twenty years, and a sprag incorporated in the transmission to prevent the car running back on hills. Dodge, noted for a commonsense outlook, had "air styled headlamps" (attached to the radiator grille) in 1935. When their engine was enlarged and given a stiffer crankshaft in 1942, it acquired "Power Flow", while 1949's raised compression ratio promoted it to a "Getaway". Either way it was the indestructible old 230, which had roots going back to the beginning of our period, and which was destined to survive in light trucks until 1966. Hudson's "Miracle H-Power" (1951) had nothing to do with nuclear fission; they had merely thrown in an extra carburettor.

As for transmissions, no holds were barred. "Automatics" were not always automatic: Hudson's 1939 effort was an orthodox manual with clutchless change. Dog-Greek terms were used for the real thing: General Motors had Hydramatic and Dynaflow, Packard's contribution was Ultramatic, and Ford progressed from Liquimatic to Fordomatic. The streamline craze of 1934 taxed the vocabularies of press agents to the limit. Chrysler's Airflow was logical enough, and Hupmobile made "aerodynamic" a trademark. Pontiac called their 1935 turret top models Silver Streaks after a famous diesel train of the period; Nashes were "Speedstreams" or "Aeroforms". After all this, it is a little disappointing to discover that the limits of Hudson's "symphonic styling", a novelty of 1941, were some new ideas in two-toning.

Anything could be a virtue. In 1931, Chrysler offered "the driving pleasure of two distinctly different high gears," on their short-lived four-speed transmission, but two years later, the driver of a Reo had "nothing to do at all", since his car "automatically selects and engages the right gear for every road condition". Nowhere was it mentioned that on this "greatest invention since the self-starter" a range-change called for use of the clutch. By contrast, Vauxhall's "a perfect gear change every time" (synchromesh) sounds modest and unassuming. Ford, who were slow off the mark with hardtops in 1950, made up for it in deathless prose. The Lincoln Capri was "a brilliant gem in rich velvet, with wide, sweeping picturescape windows". "What a glorious experience," continued the catalogue, "it is to lounge in the abundant luxury of the Cosmopolitan Capri." And yet this car, unlike its General Motors and Chrysler rivals, was little more than a two-door sedan with a vinyl top.

The advertisers were making a determined onslaught on that most powerful of opponents, marque loyalty, which was certainly a force to be reckoned with.

The young SS firm, recording a banner year for their new Jaguars in 1936, claimed that one buyer in three was a repeat customer. If such a claim could not be made, the "experienced motorist" was a useful runner-up. Under Rootes control, Humber had changed their image substantially between 1929 and 1932, so a useful selling point was that "every third Humber owner you meet was a motorist before the War". Further, 87.5 per cent of such owners had had at least six previous cars; hardly surprising, when Humber prices started at £395 ($1,975), or what one paid for three Baby Austins in those days. The same year, the front-wheel-drive Cord, on its way out, claimed "extraordinary owner allegiance"; the advanced new transmission arrangements "spoiled them for other cars". Alas! Cord were doomed to disappointment; after a miserable performance (335 units sold), the company put the marque into mothballs for three years.

If advertising was used to woo new customers, the old ones were strengthened in their loyalty by a tightening up of dealer networks. Good agents meant good sales.

In early days, there were few garages, and responsible dealers were fewer still. Even in 1910, good dealer networks were confined to the United States and perhaps France. Elsewhere, except in the case of the most popular makes, the customer bought from the factory or from a distributing agent in the nearest big city. Exclusive agencies were not understood. "Any Make of Car Supplied" was a common catchphrase in Britain, and a situation from which neither trader nor client profited. The former received a lower discount, and the latter had to wait longer (and pay more) for replacement parts. Not that this latter service was necessarily inefficient; in 1910, Hotchkiss's London importers claimed that any part could be obtained from Paris within twenty-four hours. Ford apart, few manufacturers bothered much about the other agencies their outlets held. In the writer's small home town the Morris dealer not only ignored Wolseley (that franchise stayed where it had been in pre-Nuffield days), but also handled Talbot, already a Rootes subsidiary.

Dealer networks, of course, varied with the size of the company. In 1931, Chrysler had ten thousand dealers in the United States alone, irrespective of those who handled other makes in the group. In the same year, Fiat, for all their international ramifications, ran to a mere sixteen hundred, of whom some five hundred were in Italy. At the other end of the spectrum, Rolls Royce (who referred strictly to "retailers") had twenty-six in the United Kingdom, plus a small number of sub-retailers in more prosperous territories. Really small specialist makers – Frazer Nash in Britain, for instance – invariably sold direct.

Good dealers were imperative. They also tended to see the writing on the wall long before the public became aware of an impending bankruptcy. There were extensive defections during Hupmobile's declining years, and the demise of the Clyno in 1929 was undoubtedly accelerated by the withdrawal of Rootes support in the previous year.

Thus, young firms were often at a disadvantage, especially in the 1930s. If SS inherited some support through their previous connections (as the Swallow Coachbuilding Company) with Britain's important Henly chain, and Volkswagen inherited the Adler network after that company abdicated from cars, the American Austin firm was reduced to some very odd outlets, including at least one small-town grocer. Worse sufferers were foreign imports, since all too often the domestic opposition had snapped up the better garages.

To marque loyalty, then, had to be added dealer loyalty. A make could survive a technical or even an economic volte-face at the factory – more folk than would willingly admit it remained loyal to Vauxhall after the General Motors takeover, the cheap and nasty Cadet coinciding with a fall in their incomes after 1929. But what marque loyalty could not survive was poor service, and the record of the writer's family between 1916 and 1940 is an interesting illustration of the rewards a good dealer could expect. Of thirty-two cars and trucks owned during the period, all but eight were Morrises, and all but six were Nuffield products, the sons following the father's choice of make. At least two of these cars – one from the late 1920s and another bought in 1933 – were absolute shockers, and were rapidly passed on, but their failings were promptly dealt with by the dealer. It is also significant that, since leaving that neighbourhood, no member of the family has shown any great bias towards the Oxonian marque.

Servicing underwent one major change – the provision of factory exchange units. These had long been available in the United States but did not reach Europe until the middle thirties. Hitherto, a defective component – unless it could be replaced under warranty – had to be repaired, and often, it had to be sent away for repair to specialists. Such phrases as "recent rebore" are all too common in used-car advertisements of the 1930s and early 1940s. The new system was cheaper – and quicker.

Also a growing habit was the purchase of cars "on time". By 1928, fifty-eight per cent of all new models sold in the United States were the subject of hire-purchase agreements, even if Henry Ford disapproved, instructing his salesmen to stress the advantages to everyone of cash on the nail. By the 1930s, the official British figure was fifty per cent, but informed opinion suggested that seventy-five was nearer the truth; "putting it on the book" was still someting one didn't discuss in polite circles. Manufacturers often ran their own self-financed hire-purchase schemes; this went for all Britain's Big Six, for Fiat in Italy, and for Opel and DKW in Germany. Citroën even went so far as to assign separate chassis serials for cars so supplied, though this "security check" did not last long.

As war approached, euphoria was riding the crest of the wave. Americans knew what was coming, but one catches the spirit of a favourite post-war theme – "away from it all". In 1940, Lincoln invited their customers to take a trip into the hills of Vermont, "where many a road ... leaves the village abruptly and points towards the mountainside. It bends and twists, following the clear, stony brook beside it. Each turn brings its own little world of greenness, until an upland finds you in a whole swirl of intimate mountains". "If your car doesn't mind them", continued the travelogue, "roads like this bring their rewards." Needless to say, the Lincoln-Zephyr revelled in rural

MORE FUN PER GALLON

You can't measure it by slide-rule or calipers—but you'll know in your heart that the matchless thrill you get from a Lincoln-Zephyr is what you've always wanted in a motor car!

For you need only glimpse the breath-taking beauty of a Lincoln-Zephyr—feel the live horsepower of its 12 eager cylinders—relax in the cradled comfort of its magic *glider-ride*, to realize why owners everywhere get more fun per gallon in this "only-car-of-its-kind".

And that's just as true, whether you drive a Lincoln-Zephyr for business and social rounds, or to make the whole sports map of America, from Northern pine to Southern palm, your playground.

Created by Lincoln engineers and built to exacting standards in the renowned Lincoln precision plant, this new Lincoln-Zephyr is rugged, able, modern through and through, with he-car capacity to "take it." Different in design,

different in basic construction, different in engine—its operating-thrift is astonishing!

Unit body-and-frame construction in closed body types puts steel-welded safety around you. Sound insulation hushes road noise and traffic roar. Doors open by push-button. Tops on convertible models are electrically operated. The famous new *glider-ride* with scientific springing and larger shock absorbers fairly skims you over rough spots. Husky hydraulic brakes give you smooth, dependable, equalized stopping power.

Won't you visit your Lincoln dealer soon and arrange for a demonstration of the new 1941 Lincoln-Zephyr? Learn for yourself the pleasure of owning a car that gives you *more fun per gallon*—to look at, to ride in, to drive!

LINCOLN MOTOR CAR DIVISION, FORD MOTOR COMPANY
Builders also of the Lincoln-Continental, Cabriolet and Coupe; the Lincoln-Custom, Sedan and Limousine.

LINCOLN *Zephyr V-12*

Euphoria triumphant. By 1940–41, the rest of the world was at war, but the American car industry was enjoying a boom, and it no longer bothered with technical asides. The inserts in the 1940 Nash advertisement illustrated, in theory, an overhead-valve engine, independent front suspension (which curiously never went under that name), and their familiar "air conditioning", which wasn't quite what they said, though advanced enough for its time. In fact, they just showed cars in suitably escapist settings. The elongators have, as usual, been at work: the 1940 Nash was neither as long nor as wide as the artwork suggests, and the cheap flathead on the 117-inch (2.97 m) wheelbase was almost boxy, especially when fitted with the alternative trunkback style not usually depicted in Nash publicity. One must expect a plug for the company's by-now traditional bed-seats, but if you think "automatic overtake" means "automatic overdrive", you are wrong – it's the action of disengaging overdrive for maximum acceleration.

Lincoln were escapologists in the Busby Berkeley class: this 1941 Zephyr advertisement is almost brutally practical by their prevailing standards. "Glider ride" is somehow linked with twelve cylinders, something only Lincoln still offered; it was also an excellent cover-up for the hard fact that not even a long wheelbase and low build could really cancel out the weaknesses of Ford's all-transverse suspension. They were not afraid to assign a gender (masculine) to their car, hydraulic brakes get a heavy plug (people were so used to Ford's mechanicals that they'd forgotten this was the new system's third year). With war and rationing only a few months away, much was made of the Zephyr's modest fuel consumption, one of its few unassailable virtues. Oddly, the two-speed rear axle (an option by now peculiar to Ford Motor Company products) was ignored. Maybe they felt that the Lincoln's 20 mpg (14 lit/100) were good enough in their own right.

Night Flight

EXCLUSIVE with Nash ... manifold-sealed engine pick-up of 15 to 50 MPH in 12.9 seconds, high gear; also, an economy class-winner in the Gilmore-Yosemite Run (21.25 miles to the gallon).

BADLAND ROADS are smoothed by the Arrow-Flight combination of individual coil springs in front—super shock absorbers controlling long, synchronous springs in back.

*T*HERE'S MAGIC in the air tonight. Fleecy clouds sail high above ... and your road is a ribbon of glistening moonlight.

Keen and crisp is the whistling wind. But inside your Nash you're sitting snug and coatless, in the never-changing June of the "Weather Eye".

Far into the satiny night your Sealed Beam lights cut an arc of glareless day. Yawning bumps cast shadows ahead—but the line of your lights never wavers, so level is the Arrow-Flight ride.

You sit there ... fascinated by the ease you take turns, curves, hills, without slewing or slacking ... hands barely touching the wheel ... eyes never leaving the road.

And as you ghost through sleeping town after town, in the soft, soundless stride of the Fourth Speed Forward, only the speedometer shares your secret.

Then suddenly ahead, a tail-light blinks. But a gentle nudge of your toe, and the new Nash Automatic Overtake zooms you by in a terrific burst of sprinting power.

On and on you go, up starlit hill, down darkened dale ... your heart singing with excitement ... your Nash a silver phantom under the great white moon.

Sure, you can make up that convertible bed in back if you want to break the spell ... but chances are that when the sleepy world awakes, you'll be whistling over breakfast, three states away.

• • •

It's only fair to tell you this. You don't need the thrill of a moonlight night. In 60 minutes, anywhere, a 1940 Nash will make you unhappy 'til you own it.

Luckily, it costs so little you'll jump at the chance to trade in your old car. See your Nash dealer today and find out!

GREAT DAYS AHEAD with Nash's convertible bed, and automatic "Weather Eye" for conditioned-air comfort, cleanliness, on trips. Nation-wide service by 1800 Nash dealers.

Again... NASH
IT'S THAT NEW

mountaineering. One may hope that some jaded businessman, dreaming of his summer vacation, went out at this juncture and bought himself such a car.

They were still at it during the war years, promising "Someday, a rendezvous with the clouds". Euphoria had taken over.

Peculiar to the United States in our period – and indeed for many years to come – was radio advertising. The American technique has always centred around the sponsored programme rather than the interspersed commercial, and American citizens learnt to associate Major Bowes's Celebrity Hour with Chrysler, the André Kostelanetz orchestra with Pontiac, and old-time dancing with Ford (Old Henry was militant in his hatred of jazz). While such programmes were perhaps mildly educational, the commercials were frenetic. For Hudson, in 1934, there was no refined euphoria, no faint hint of "Getting One's Girl". The crescendo came in the best circus-barker style: "On the water, it's aqua-planing. In the air, it's aero-planing. But on land, Hot Diggety Dog, IT'S TERRAPLANING." How different from the ghost-story voice of the 1960s, adjuring one to enjoy "four-on-the floor", Posi-Traction, and the other delights of Pontiac's hairy GTO – "with care".

Political propaganda with the fresh air and fun of a 1939 Opel Cabrio-Limousine, or what can the *Herrenvolk* be looking at? Just to make sure that no official secrets percolate outside, the artist has used a stylized Junkers Ju.52 instead of the Ju.88 he could already have drawn. The doughty old 52 had, after all, been around since 1930 and was still employed by a number of European airlines.

Auf den Erfahrungen der in den letzten 3 Jahren zehntausend-fach bewährten Konstruktion aufbauend, sind dem OLYMPIA die neuesten Fortschritte der Technik dienstbar gemacht worden. Der neue Hochleistungsmotor, die beachtliche Vergrößerung des Innenraumes und der Spur, die bessere Sicht lassen ihn noch mehr als bisher die höchsten Anforderungen für Straßen und Autobahn, für Stadtverkehr und große Reisen spielend meistern . . . Altbewährtes und fortschrittlich Neues wurde so im OPEL OLYMPIA zu hoher Wirksamkeit vereint.

EIN NEUER OPEL OLYMPIA

Chapter 5

LUXURY IN TRANSITION

Irrespective of the cost accountants, the second inter-war decade was an exciting one for the luxury car. The difference from the first decade was, however, that the new generation of cars was aimed at the owner driver.

Of the Edwardian Delaunay-Belleville, round-radiatored favourite of Tsar Nicholas II, Fernand Charron had observed: "One doesn't *drive* such a car: it simply isn't done." The chauffeur-drive image continued strongly into the 1920s; if Vauxhall's 30/98 and Bentley's 4½-litre represented two similar, but far from identical, interpretations of the fast tourer theme, both companies worked hard at cars for those who preferred to leave the driving to others. Vauxhall were perhaps the more successful, with their D and OD types, though "W.O." 's 6½-litre six was a victim of the marque's sporting image rather than of any inherent defects of design. Both companies ran into trouble and came under new ownership, but the fate of those who stayed with pre-1914 ideas was a slow and lingering death. Delaunay-Belleville's luxury line had faded out by 1928. The company was destined to survive for another twenty-two years, but from making mock-Americans with Continental engines they degenerated to middle-class copies of Mercedes-Benz. The once-proud Minerva, still a sleeve-valve, was moribund by 1936. Isotta Fraschini abdicated quietly into aero-engines and diesel trucks, and Hispano-Suiza gratefully grasped the nettle of French rearmament. Twenty-seven manufacturers were exhibiting formal carriages at the 1928 London Show, but only thirteen of these were still in the game ten years later. Of the casualties, the United States's Franklin and Stearns, Belgium's Excelsior, and Britain's Star had vanished into limbo. Other makes, while still aimed at chauffeur drive, were by no means prestige offerings. In the late 1920s, the top of the Wolseley range had been the eight-cylinder 30/90 with a price-tag of some £1,600 ($8,000); its 1938 replacement was the Series III 25, a lengthened family sedan for half the money. Fiat's 2800 was a mock-American, large rather than luxurious, and in any case most of the 620 built went to the Italian army as staff cars. Renault's surviving eight-cylinder offering was the same kind of vehicle, only larger. Daimler, traditionally the purveyor of transport to elderly dowagers, survived by diversification. Their badge-engineered 1933 range covered everything from the 1,185-cc BSA Ten sedan up to the monstrous 40/50 Double Six as supplied to His Majesty King George V.

The demise of the old-school formals stemmed from sundry causes. To begin with, the new generation of plutocrats had grown up with the automobile, had mastered its mysteries, and enjoyed driving it, whereas their fathers and mothers had had no such inclinations. Why should they, when long-distance motor tours were strictly for the brave, when domestic labour was cheap and plentiful, and when coachmen could be trained into chauffeurs of a sort? To the pre-1914 generation, "motoring" meant being taken for a run in an automobile. One young society beauty of the early 1900s was described by the snobbish *Car Illustrated* as "devoted" to the pastime. In fact, she learnt to drive in 1931, on a Wolseley Hornet, because her husband could no longer afford a chauffeur!

By contrast, the middle-aged executive of 1931 might be hard enough hit by the Depression to opt for a Buick instead of a Cadillac, or an Armstrong Siddeley instead of a big sleeve-valve Daimler. The odds were, however, that he would have chosen the owner-drive species of either. In a world of coil ignition, quick-demountable wheels, cellulose, and chromium plate, his car required little sympathetic understanding and only a fraction of the maintenance that would have been essential in 1914, or even 1920.

The Depression played its part. Motor servants were not only a luxury, they were incongruous in an era of bread lines. Ostentation was something to avoid. Well-heeled Americans still bought Duesenbergs. Peak years for the Model J (minimum price $13,500 or £2,700 ex-works Indianapolis) were 1930 and 1931. But many of the well-heeled chose something less obtrusive. Chauffeur-driven Ford V8s were no uncommon sight in smart East Coast resorts in the 1933–34 period, so much so that the great coachbuilding house of Brewster offered special town-car variants. So did James Cunningham, most conservative and least publicized of the luxury-car makers. The Brewster version, with its flared front fenders and spectacular heart-shaped radiator grille, defeated its own object. Other shy millionaires opted for the anonymous limousines marketed by such specialist firms as Henney, Meteor, and S and S. These vehicles were mourning carriages based on their makers' assembled hearse chassis and were intended for morticians in quest of matching fleets.

Elsewhere, the trend was in the direction of cheaper seven-seaters. Though Daimler-Benz continued to market the ponderous Nürburg straight-eight, a near-Packard favoured by German ambassadors, they sold more examples of their long-chassis 2-litre, 2.9-litre, and 3.2-litre sixes. Renault dropped the enormous bespoke Reinastella in favour of cheap eights, while for slenderer pockets there were the *familiales* of the mass-producers. Nine people could be fitted into the 129-inch (3.25 m) version of Citroën's 11CV *traction*, and there were parallel offerings from Peugeot and Renault. Among less expensive British limousines were the Vauxhall and Wolseley 25s, the Austin 18 and 20, the 20/70

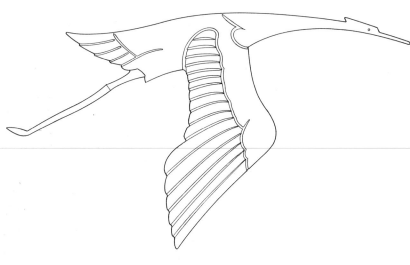

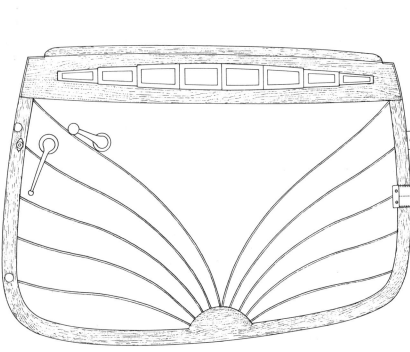

The cars depicted here represent a total of some 35 litres, for which an Englishman would have paid more than £15,000 ($75,000) new. Bodies are of course customs, or at worst semi-customs. Biggest of all is the 1934 Type-68 twelve-cylinder Hispano-Suiza (*top left*): below it can be seen the famous flying-stork mascot once worn by air ace Georges Guynemer, and the splendid tooled-leather door trim of Saoutchik's coachwork. The standard engine ran to 9.4 litres and a round 200 hp, though exceptionally, this actual car has the 11,310-cc, 250-hp, 68 *bis* unit normally reserved for railcars. A speed of 100 mph (160 km/h) presented no problems, though the three-speed transmission was a handicap: bottom was almost invariably too high. The car cost £3,750 ($18,750) in London. The 7.4-litre Isotta Fraschini 8A straight-eight of 1930 (*top right*), here seen as a formal cabriolet, was also afflicted with three forward speeds, but on a car primarily designed for chauffeur-drive, this didn't matter much. Top speed was around 85 mph (135 km/h), and this car was cheaper, at £3,000 ($15,000). Further down the scale (£1,700 or $8,500 should have bought it in 1936–37) is the Derby-built 4¼-litre Bentley (*opposite, top left*), here seen wearing concealed-top convertible bodywork by Vanden Plas. Cruising speed was 75–80 mph (120–130 km/h), but a welcome bonus was a modest thirst (18 mpg or 15 lit/100). (*Bottom right*) Rolls-Royce's contender, the 40–50-hp Phantom II, still in 1935 a pushrod six of 7.7 litres' capacity, with beam axles at either end. Its mechanical servo brakes were identical with the Hispano's (Rolls-Royce paid the Franco-Spanish firm a royalty), but the British car had synchromesh and four forward speeds. The 1935 Series I Railton (*opposite, top right*) doesn't look out of place in such company: it's even got Rolls-Royce-style rivets down the hood. But beneath that Terribly British exterior beats a 5.2-litre flathead eight-cylinder Hudson engine. Everything else you couldn't see was Hudson, too, which explains why you paid only £598 ($2,990) for this. Not that the Railton was a sheep in wolf's clothing: if 90 mph (145 km/h) was average for this class, there weren't many other cars around in 1935 that could waft four people in comfort up to 60 mph (100 km/h) in just over nine seconds.

Wholly bespoke. The Indian potentate who ordered this Napier (*bottom*) in 1908 got a big car to start off with, the engine running to six cylinders, 14.5 litres, and a reputed 90 bhp. He chose, however, to have it lengthened to a wheel-base of 15 ft (4.6 m), long enough for four rows of seats, just like a charabanc. The senior passengers in the second row had a duplicate set of instruments!

In the 1930s, anyone willing to spend £3,000 ($15,000) or more on a 40–50 hp Rolls-Royce could have the ultimate in appointments. This Phantom II (*opposite, top*) for one of Park Ward's customers was delivered in 1931. It is fairly restrained from without, only the spotlamps and the plated wheel discs distinguishing it from many other British formals of the period. Nor was the top-opening trunk an unusual feature. But we enter the realms of the exotic with the hinge-down tail-panel (*right*) housin a washbasin and all the essential toilet accessories. The cabinet work on the inside of the division conceals a full picnic set.

(*Opposite, bottom*) The central arm-rest in the rear seat of this Hooper-bodied Rolls-Royce sedanca houses a mirror and scent bottles for Madame.

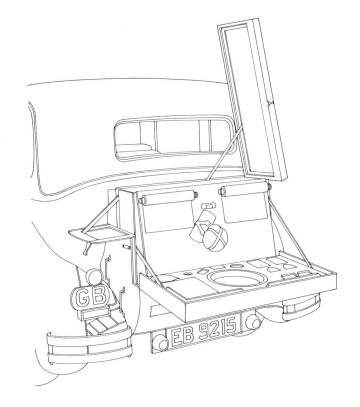

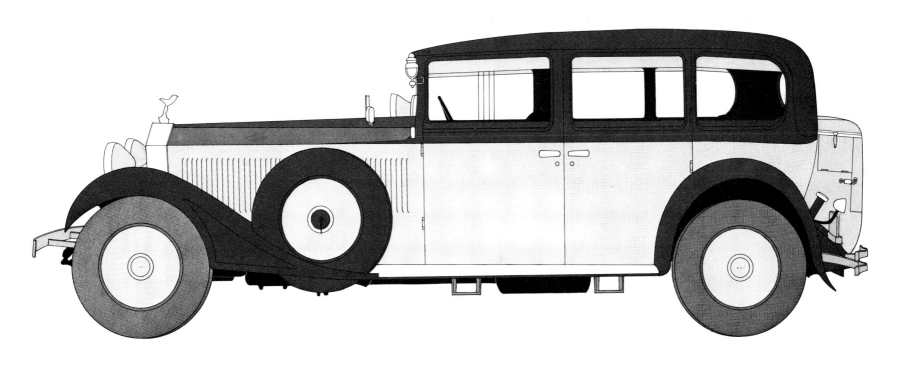

Elegant proportions at the price of non-ergonomics. The Mercedes-Benz 500K and 540K (1934–39) are almost the archetypes of what we term a classic, "an automobile of which at least half the length is hood". The photograph (*top left*) may reflect only the magnificence, but the cutaway view (*below*) shows what an awful lot of engineering is dedicated to the use of two people on the Grand Tour. A lengthy straight-eight engine is set well back in the frame, while further aft the body-builder has the agonizing choice between a pair of rear seats or enough trunk space for a longish vacation for our happy pair. (A bulky extended trunk would have spoilt the rear-end propor-

tions and perhaps only one sedan on this chassis, a 1939 effort by Freestone and Webb of London, really looked right.) The main influence of the 540K was nostalgic, as witness modern American replicars (sic) like the Clenet and (in latter years) the Excalibur, though this latter specimen started out as a modern edition of the older 38/250 SS.

By contrast, Brunn's formal cabriolet on the 1936 Lincoln K chassis (*top right*) is not unpractical. Here is a very large car intended primarily for chauffeur-drive, and there is no built-in space wastage – only that conferred by the European-style projecting trunk. The engine sits well forward in the frame, and headlamps are

receding into the front fenders. Emphasis here is on comfort and flexibility rather than on sheer speed, though in fact the Lincoln's 6.8-litre, 150-hp, flathead vee-twelve gave this 5,000-pounder a performance only slightly inferior to the 540K's – and one not dependent on a supercharger engaged by a second pressure on the loud pedal. Brakes were still mechanical, and Lincolns likewise lacked any kind of independent suspension, though what Henry Leland had designed with longitudinal semi-elliptics way back in 1920 was never subjected to the indignity of Ford's more primitive arrangements.

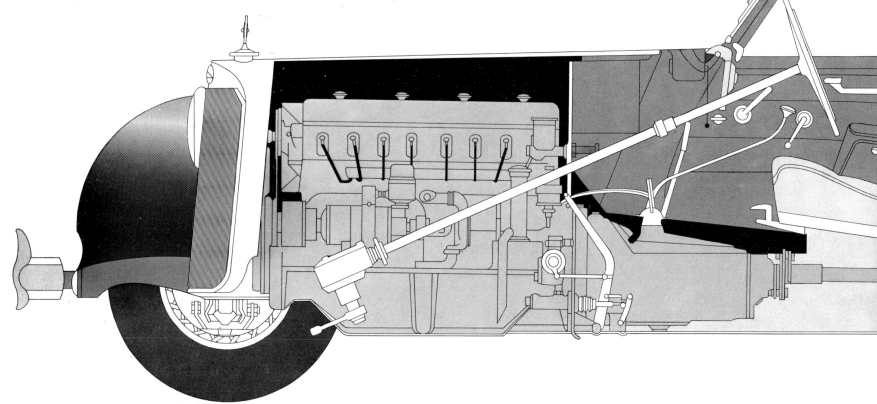

The decline of American classicism. The Model-J Duesenberg was ageless and one distinguishes a 1929 from a 1935–37 mainly by the body style. Remarkably little was done to the mechanics beyond 1932's optional supercharger. The dual-cowl phaeton (*top right*) is a 1929 effort by Derham with the later chromium-plated radiator shutters not found on the very first cars. The convertible victoria by Rollston (*centre right*) dates from 1933–34 and is one of their last traditional ones before they switched to fender skirts and smaller-diameter wheels (on the 1935 JN bodies). The 1948 Lincoln Continental (*top left*) was for many years the only post-Second World War model officially recognized as "classic". Mechanics are those of the cheap twelve-cylinder Zephyr, now up to 4.8 litres and 125 hp. E.T. Gregorie's delightfully-proportioned two-door coupé bodywork flew in the face of Detroit, and its exposed rear-mounted spare wheel (the "Continental kit") added a phrase to our automotive vocabulary.

and 80 Hillmans, and Humber's Pullman, the "Ambassador of Cars". The last-mentioned's 132-inch wheel-base would accommodate seven passengers in comfort, and appointments, the work of the Rootes-owned custom bodybuilders Thrupp and Maberly, were luxurious. However, it cost a mere £735 ($3,675) as against the £1,600 ($8,000) asked for a straight-eight Daimler or 25/30 Rolls-Royce, or even the £900 ($4,500) for a 90-series Buick imported from Canada. Better still, these Renaults or Humbers contained a goodly proportion of mass-produced parts (the Humber's engine was common not only to cheaper Snipe sedans but also to the 3-ton Commer truck) and so could be serviced by the local garage. During his short reign, Edward VIII of England bought not only the celebrated Buick, but a Humber Pullman as well. Gustav V of Sweden supported local industry by using a custom-built parade cabriolet on the Volvo six-cylinder taxi-cab chassis.

The great non-sporting classics, of course, survived in the United States, but even here there was a steady decline from 1930, when a formidable selection of custom-built carriages ranged from the 6.9-litre twin overhead-camshaft Duesenberg to the dignified vee-eight Cunningham. Other names of that period with price tags of over $3,000 (£600) included Cadillac, Chrysler's top of the line Imperial family, DuPont, Franklin, Jordan, Kissel, Lincoln, the biggest Marmon, Packard, Peerless, Pierce-Arrow, Ruxton, Stearns, and Stutz. Reo would explore this sector briefly in 1931–34, with their huge straight-eight Royale, while astonishingly, that coelacanth, the 9-litre T-head Locomobile (with roots going back to 1909!), had only just vanished from buyers' guides.

By contrast, this gallery of long-hooded elegance had gone with the proverbial whimper by 1939. Lesser Cadillacs now shared their sheet metal with Buick and Oldsmobile, and Packard's magnificent vee-twelve was in its final season. The traditional Model K Lincoln was barely in production at all, selling only 120 units, despite a choice of two wheel-base lengths and twenty-nine body styles. The multi-barrelled spree of

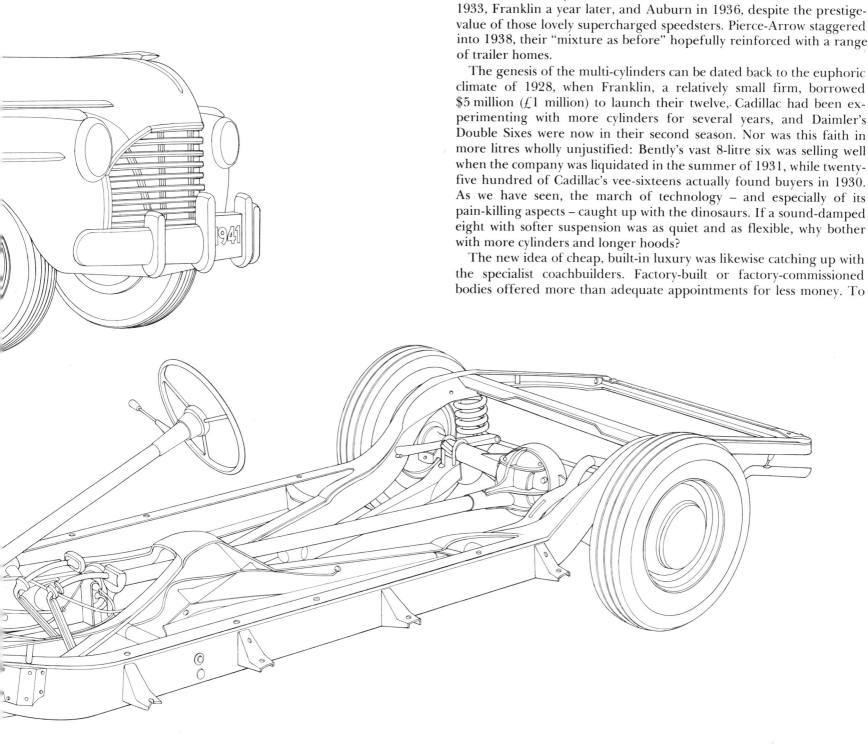

1932 was well and truly over, and of the purveyors of twelves and sixteens (Auburn, Cadillac, Franklin, Lincoln, Marmon, Packard, and Pierce-Arrow), only three makes survived. Marmon breathed its last in 1933, Franklin a year later, and Auburn in 1936, despite the prestige-value of those lovely supercharged speedsters. Pierce-Arrow staggered into 1938, their "mixture as before" hopefully reinforced with a range of trailer homes.

The genesis of the multi-cylinders can be dated back to the euphoric climate of 1928, when Franklin, a relatively small firm, borrowed $5 million (£1 million) to launch their twelve. Cadillac had been experimenting with more cylinders for several years, and Daimler's Double Sixes were now in their second season. Nor was this faith in more litres wholly unjustified: Bently's vast 8-litre six was selling well when the company was liquidated in the summer of 1931, while twenty-five hundred of Cadillac's vee-sixteens actually found buyers in 1930. As we have seen, the march of technology – and especially of its pain-killing aspects – caught up with the dinosaurs. If a sound-damped eight with softer suspension was as quiet and as flexible, why bother with more cylinders and longer hoods?

The new idea of cheap, built-in luxury was likewise catching up with the specialist coachbuilders. Factory-built or factory-commissioned bodies offered more than adequate appointments for less money. To

This landaulette (the coachbuilders called it a Custom Landau) is one of a series of styles planned by Brunn for the 1941 Buick Limited, their biggest eight on a 139-in (3.5 m) wheel-base. Significantly, the stock windshield and cowl were used, but though a variety of styles, including a convertible victoria and a town car, are illustrated in the catalogue, objections from the Cadillac division called a halt before any serious production could be undertaken. Buick, who had been making limousines with long wheel-bases since the early 1920s—and counted several European monarchs among their customers—discontinued this line after the Second World War, leaving the huge Cadillac 75 as the sole big eight-passenger sedan offered by General Motors. Edward VIII of England (later the Duke of Windsor) bought his first 90 in 1936, with repeat orders for similar cars in 1938 and 1939. The chassis was of sturdy design, with heavy X-bracing.

Throughout the 1930s, the Packard was probably the world's most widely distributed luxury make. The peculiar agelessness of its appearance is shown by these two Seniors, a 1933 sedan (*bottom*) and a 1936 phaeton (*top*). On the latter, a custom by Dietrich, the engine lies further forward in the frame, and the windshield has a pronounced slant, but there is still a family resemblance. Mechanical specifications are nearly identical: both have big nine-bearing side-valve straight-eight engines, three-speed synchromesh transmissions, mechanical servo brakes, and semi-elliptic springing. The view of the '33 shows a Packard hallmark, their own brand of trunk rack, fitted for some time even after integral trunks became regular equipment. They were certainly the only makers to turn this untidy excrescence into a distinctive styling feature.

(*Right*) In 1934, Packard hired G.T. Christopher from General Motors's Pontiac Division to mastermind their first essay in the low-price field, the 120. It was still a straight-eight and still distinctively a Packard, only its disc wheels indicating the lower price. This 1939 example shows

136

both concessions Packard would make to styling in the 1930s: 1931's vee radiator and the matching vee windshield adopted throughout the range for 1939. If this example looks very big for an inexpensive car, there is no optical illusion involved: this is an eight-passenger version of the 120, built on a 148-in (3.76 m) wheel-base and equipped with right-hand drive. The idea was to offer customers an inexpensive chauffeur-driven limousine, a rival to Buick's popular 90, and the American equivalent of the Humber Pullman and the Renault Vivastella. By 1939, of course, the same chassis and sheet metal were being used for Juniors and Seniors alike, which kept the price differential between the two lines down to less than $500 (£100). It features the column shift new that year, and the optional extra, overdrive.

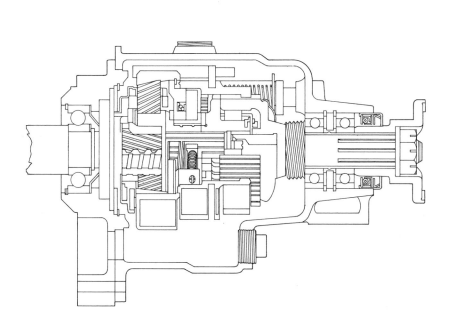

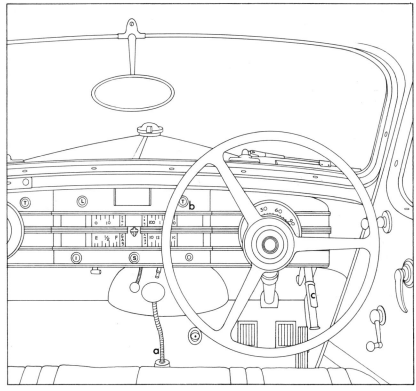

(*Centre*) Overdrive was no new idea. Many cars of the pre-1914 era had a "geared-up" top to enable high cruising speeds to be maintained without over-revving, and this (like fifth on modern European sporting cars, such as the Alfa Romeo) had the merit of simple selection via the normal shift lever. The snag (and one which caused Henry Royce to abandon the system after 1909) was an irritating high-pitched whine. What Packard did in 1939 with their "Econo-Drive" (*centre left*), which gave a high cruising ratio, was to

allow it to cut in on direct drive, if the accelerator were eased back; to return to direct drive, one merely floored the pedal and obtained maximum acceleration. A refinement on the more expensive cars, such as Packard, was a lock-out knob for driving conditions such as heavy traffic, where overdrive was not required. The normal American practice was to offer a choice of ratios only on high, though Chrysler usually had it on second as well. The extreme was reached in England in the mid-fifties on some cars which had

seven forward gears, including an overdrive second.

(*Right, below*) Facia on a Packard 120, 1938. Column shift lay a year in the future, most drivers still preferring a floor-mounted lever (*a*). There was still a hand throttle (*b*), and the hand brake (*c*) has assumed its classic "1940s" position under the dash.

137

the end of their days, Alvis never built a body, while in the 1933–39 period, Bentley, now of course under Rolls-Royce control, offered only "recommended" styles, which were sometimes made for "stock". Maybach, Hispano-Suiza, and Rolls-Royce remained wholly bespoke right up to 1939. But standardized cars were taking their toll on these.

At the 1923 London Show, the work of no fewer than eighty-four specialists was displayed, the traditional *haute couture* of the metropolis being matched by provincial specialists. These hailed not only from the big centres – Birmingham, Edinburgh, and Manchester, for instance – but from smaller towns such as Cirencester, Eastbourne, and Taunton. Only fifty-five firms showed in 1929, and by the middle thirties, the average had fallen below the forty mark. There were precious few new recruits, and these were mostly firms building bodies on such chassis as Wolseley and Vauxhall. There were no new names at all after 1936, while Barker would soon become a subsidiary of Daimler. Of the twenty-seven firms with stands at Earls Court in 1938, Pressed Steel catered only for the mass producers, while Salmons-Tickford and Carbodies earned their money by handling low-volume styles for the big battalions.

A similar decline was apparent everywhere else. If France's specialists gained a new lease of life by adapting their craft to the *grande routière* idiom, Germany, with some thirty-five coachbuilders in Weimar days, was down to nineteen by the outbreak of war. Many of these had a safe bread-and-butter line in semi-series cabriolets, albeit Erdmann und Rossi of Berlin combined a profitable line in one-off 540K Mercedes and Maybachs with the Rolls-Royce concession. In the United States, predictably, the decline had started earlier and continued at a spectacular rate: from thirty-one in 1925, to twenty-two in 1931, eleven in 1935, and three by Pearl Harbor. Of these, only Derham and Rollson (*née* Rollston) had any significance.

Important casualties of the late 1930s include Judkins and Willoughby, while Brunn expired in 1941 after Cadillac's management had vetoed a Buick scheme for the company to build small-production customs on their top-line 90 chassis.

In any case, integrated styling had sounded the specialists' death-knell. Suddenly, the coachbuilder found himself with a load of un-wanted and incongruous sheet metal. In the good old days – a term still valid in Europe as late as 1934 – his raw material consisted of a running chassis with dash and instruments. On cheaper models, usually beneath his dignity, the front fenders might be compulsory (in Britain they seldom were), but in general, the sheet metal was left to his discretion, though woe betide him if he monkeyed with a Rolls-Royce radiator. Pininfarina got away with a Maserati-style rake, but fulminations attended upon Henri Binder's Cord-like treatment unveiled at the 1936 Paris Salon. It mattered not that this outrage was perpetrated on a second-hand Phantom II chassis rather than on the latest Phantom III.

Now, however, anyone who chose an American chassis was presented with a *fait accompli* in the shape of a grille, cowl, and front fenders difficult to blend into an individual style. Swiss and German purveyors of cabriolets generally managed quite well – ponderous landau irons suited the American idiom – but by 1939, Buick's high-set sidemounts offered an almost insuperable challenge to Carlton and Maltby in England, while Thrupp and Maberly's attempts to construct a traditional top-hat limousine round an extended vee windshield were infelicitous in the extreme. Americans might have anticipated the "British" razor-edge treatment on their "panel broughams" (town cars or sedancas *de ville*) of the early 1930s, but in later years, these were viable only on the ageless Packard, which retained a vestige of the traditional as late as 1947. As an awful warning to meddlers, there were Flxible's "professional cars" on Buick chassis. Ambulances and hearses call for a higher waistline, so a few disastrous inches had to be added to hood and grille as well. It was a blessing that the customers were in no position to criticize...

With Duesenberg and Pierce-Arrow gone, Chrysler committed to the commonplace, and the real Lincolns on their last legs, it was Packard or nothing for the few surviving American coachbuilders. And while Howard Darrin's Victorias (sport tourers, in fact) and Rollson's sport sedans on the Packard chassis carried on the old tradition, Derham were down to customizations of existing mass-produced shapes. It was surprising how much could be done with an orthodox seven-passenger Chrysler Eight by the provision of blind rear-quarters and a fabric top. A mock-canework belt-moulding could redeem even a five-passenger Club Coupé from the commonplace. But customization was no kind of *haute couture*.

The new styling trends also affected the European coachbuilders. The slit-windshield and high-waistline fad reached its apogee in 1932, and hot on its heels came the streamline craze, with fastbacks and monumental rear overhang. Saoutchik's extravaganzas on the 3.5-litre Delahaye chassis, with their projecting tails, elaborate plated belt-mouldings, and full-spatted wheels were fine for a *concours d'élégance* at Le Touquet or the ceremonial processions of Indian princes, but for the man who wanted to travel fast and far, standard sedans or cabriolets (often by that maestro Henri Chapron) were more practical and less vulnerable. The few surviving plutocrats must have breathed a sigh of relief in 1936, when the razor-edge idiom was first applied to informal closed bodies. Along with the elimination of curves, the pillars were made thinner, giving better all-round vision. However, those painstakingly sculptured fenders were as expensive to repair as the bulboid.

Unitary construction, as we have seen, still lay largely in the future, and as long as the majority of cars retained separate chassis, the coachbuilders proved adept in applying their skills to humbler models. Gordon of Birmingham, who had started as beautifiers of the Model T Ford in the early 1920s, formed a long-lasting association with Austin. Wolseley's sporty Hornet Special was offered only as a chassis; hence, it kept some fifteen specialist firms happy between 1932 and 1935 – and there was always Vauxhall. Even Windovers, renowned till the end, in 1950, for their limousines and sedancas on Rolls-Royce and Daimler chassis, had a profitable line in semi-bespoke Terraplanes, marketed through Hudson's English dealer chain between 1932 and 1934.

But if the Americans were stultified by the new styling idioms, there were others, notably in Italy and Britain, who extended their ideas into chassis and mechanical improvement. Avon's Standards dispensed with Standard's sheet metal, even incorporating a mild degree of engine tune, while William Lyons's SS carried matters one step further: the car's underslung frame was made by Standard, but it was exclusive to his Swallow Coachbuilding Company. With the establishment of a design department under William M. Heynes in 1935, the divorce was complete, even if Standard continued to supply six-cylinder engines right up to 1939–40, and fours in the early post-war period. Also in this game were the Jensen brothers, who were producing their own Ford-engined cars by 1937, even if they, unlike Lyons, were still prepared to create coachwork for outside firms.

The Italian way was even more dramatic. True, as yet, coachbuilders and tuners were some way from fusing their efforts, and neither had achieved the status of individual marques, though in 1939, SIATA's Amica, a superbly proportioned miniature cabriolet on the Fiat *topolino* chassis, was unrecognizable as a Fiat. Nor had an Italian stylist been hired by a foreign manufacturer.

Italians, however, wanted no part of "compulsory" sheet metal. This was perhaps because the country's manufacturers were (and still are)

138

Continental custom coachwork might
have fitted the American chassis of the
early 1930s, but it was less felicitous on
the stylized front ends of 1936–39. Carlton were past masters of the art, specializing in English drophead foursome
coupés on American chassis. Here is their
four-door razor-edge sports sedan (top) on
the 1938 straight-eight Chrysler chassis,
with a straight, horizontal motif to grille
and hood louvres.

By contrast with the Carlton, the German-
Swiss idiom blended better. Here (centre)
is a 1937 Buick Special with four-door
convertible coachwork by Langenthal of
Switzerland.

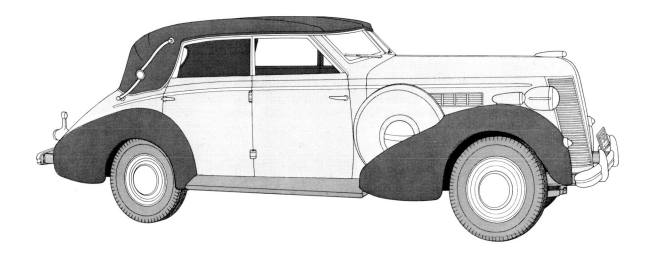

French eccentricities were not limited to
grande routière chassis: here (bottom) a 1934
effort based on Renault's straight-eight, a
Fernandez coupé-chauffeur sedanca. It suffered from outsize pontoon fenders of
vulnerable type, and the wheels look very
naked without their hub plates. The sedanca reached its zenith in the 1930s but
declined thereafter. Though town-car
types were strictly chauffeur-drive, some
of the European versions were less formal. However, the majority of chauffeur-
driven cars sold after the war went either
to government departments or to big cor-
porations, and thus the emphasis came to
be on comfort rather than on ostentation
and style.

Two super-cars, and one that isn't. One picks the 1937 Phantom III Rolls-Royce (*top right*) immediately: every inch of it looks bespoke, and the £3,000 ($15,000) one paid in those days was top whack for an automobile. Between 1936 and the outbreak of war, 710 were made. The 1936 Cadillac (*bottom right*), for all its Fleetwood labels, is semi-mass-produced: over 3,000 of these long-chassis eight-cylinder 75s were turned out in 1936 alone. An American could have five of them for the price of a Phantom III, and even a Briton could have a couple, inclusive of import duty on the car. Only the fender skirts on the Royce are concessions to streamlining. The Cadillac represents the 1936 General Motors turret-top styling in its largest size. The same body (albeit without the Fleetwood touch) would be found on the Buick Limited at just over $2,000 (£400). Interestingly, both British and American super cars

have some technical similarities – coil-spring suspension at the front and semi-elliptics at the rear, and vee engines, for instance. Both weigh around 5,000 lb (2,300 kg). Both use synchromesh transmissions and power brakes, though one expects three speeds in the United States and four in Britain, just as one might still expect Rolls-Royce to prefer their mechanical-servo anchors to the new-fangled hydraulics. Top speed in either case would be around 90 mph (145 km/h), but Cadillac's flathead vee-eight of 5.7 litres' capacity was a lot simpler and cheaper to service than the Royce's over-head-valve, 7.3-litre vee-twelve.

There are family resemblances between the Cadillac and the 1939 Buick Special (*bottom left*) plus three years' development of a stylistic theme by General Motors. The Buick convertible is, however, middle-class transportation costing $1,077 in its homeland and £535 in Britain.

Model (if not body style) production could run to five figures in a good year, and under the alligator hood was a well-tried 4.1-litre overhead-valve straight-eight giving 107 hp. Also present was coil-spring rear suspension which behaved peculiarly on corners; not that this mattered: Americans didn't corner fast. Here is a classic of 1939's transitional styling: the shallow three-piece grille, pontoon fenders, semi-recessed headlamps, and disappearing running boards. The sidemounts, however, look as if they had been thrown at the car by a dissident shop steward – the new fender shape prevented their being countersunk, but in not a few export markets they were almost mandatory. Their value was strictly snob: if they were omitted, some ignorant layman might confuse an upper-middle-class Buick with the lesser Oldsmobile!

afflicted with the deplorable habit of imitating each other. First, it was Fiat's pear-shaped radiator of 1911–12, then Isotta Fraschini came up with the mock-Rolls-Royce idiom in 1919, and Fiat led again at the end of the 1920s with a Chrysler-style ribbon shell. The 1934 Fiats looked horribly like Terraplanes from the front end; so did Bianchis, the last touring OMs, and even factory-bodied 6C-2300 Alfa Romeo sedans. The Fiat 1500's beetling hood, a 1935 innovation, was copied on 1936 Bianchis. By 1939, Fiat's front end was functional rather than elegant, the Alfa's a stylized restatement of earlier themes, and the Lancia's, as always, uncompromisingly angular. Thus, it was left to Pininfarina to create something different.

The maestro was no snob. He would exercise his art as happily on the lesser Fiats as he would on Isottas and Lancia Dilambdas. Further, grilles and front fenders were expendable. Some of his efforts were clever rather than felicitous: big Lancias did not take kindly to an Auburn-like boat-tail-speedster treatment, and the 1500 Fiat was too abbreviated to accept the mock-Cord idiom. But he did wonderful things with the Lancia Aprilia. This admirable little vehicle was characterized by a short hood, thanks to the compact dimensions of its 1,352-cc vee-four engine – a virtue on the standard article, since it allowed really roomy and well-proportioned sedan coachwork on a wheel-base of 108 in (2.75 m) without any noticeable overhang at either end. Short hoods, however, militate against true elegance, so Pininfarina combined an American-style vee grille and full-flow front

wings with a hood extending way back over the firewall, with a little dog-kennel of a coupé body at the rear. Eccentric this might be, but the car would pass for a short-chassis edition of Lancia's big 3-litre Astura at a casual glance.

Thus, by the late 1930s, Pininfarina – and Ghia as well – had attained American standards of integration, while retaining the individuality of the bespoke. No mechanical modifications were incorporated, but now only the hubcaps gave the game away. And just as Standard had adopted Lyons's original 1930 Swallow radiator for their own 1931 range, so Fiat took the Pininfarina vee grille for 1940 editions of their 1100 and 1500 models. The last vestiges of this theme would not disappear from Fiat's styling until 1953.

The latest idioms seldom translated well on formal carriages. A really large limousine means more of everything, and Chrysler's Airflow shape, for instance, was horribly inflexible. It looked its best as a standard eight-cylinder sedan: on De Soto's six-cylinder version the short hood had a stunted air, while the CW limousine on a 146-in (3.7 m) wheel-base was simply monstrous; no other word sufficed. In any case, the customers tended to have conservative ideas on automobiles and headgear alike, so Hooper's Daimlers and Mercedes-Benz's factory-built Grossers filled the bill better. In any case, such giants were strictly in the minority: by now, the *grande routière* concept was coming to the fore.

This phrase defies translation. "*Gran Turismo*", though already ap-

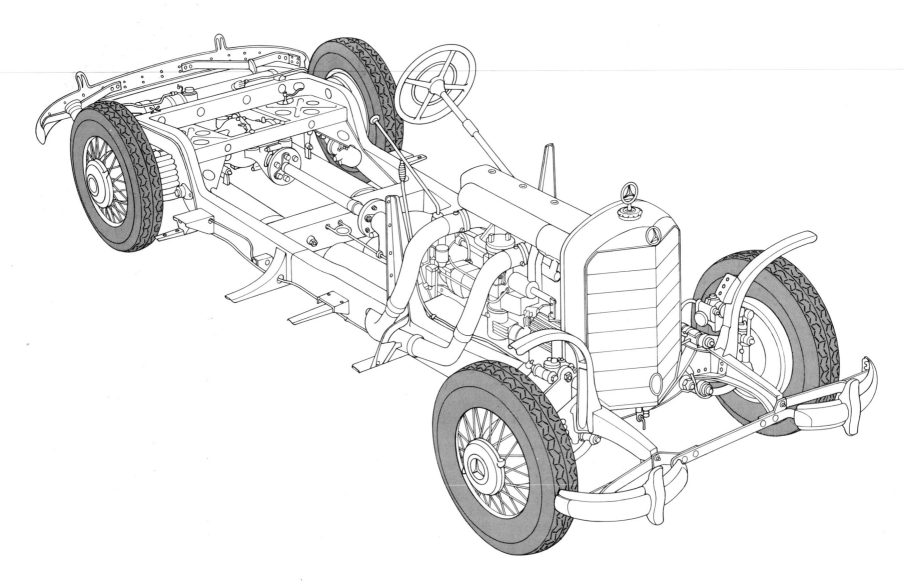

No better contrast between the old and new generation of fast tourers can be made than by these two, the Mercedes-Benz 500K of 1934–36 (*left*) and the Talbot-Lago of 1937 (*below*). In one respect the German car is more sophisticated, with its independent rear suspension, but everything is very massive, a complete car weighs 2¼ tons at least, and speeds of 100 mph (160 km/h) call for five litres of engine giving only 100 bhp without the benefit of a supercharger, and 160 for short bursts with a blower engaged.

The race-bred Talbot has a light and simple double drop frame and a compact wheel-base of 104 or 112 inches (2.6 or 2.8 m). Independent front suspension of transverse-leaf type is used, the mechanically actuated brakes work in drums of generous diameter and the unblown 4-litre twin-carburettor six-cylinder pushrod engine gives 140 bhp at 4,000 rpm. With reasonable bodywork, 100 mph (160 km/h) is available, and cruising speeds of 85–90 mph (140–145 km/h) present no problem.

plied to supercharged Alfa Romeos with closed coachwork as early as 1931, has later and confusing connotations. Suffice it to say that the idea of a *grande routière* was an automobile designed to be driven far and fast in comfort, and preferably with some degree of refinement, though the latter attribute might have shocked Ettore Bugatti and seldom applied to the bigger Hotchkisses as they approached their rev limit. The number of seats was not relevant, though most *grandes routières* had wheel-bases long enough to accept room for four people and their baggage.

Racing, again, was incidental, even if many of these cars made their mark on the circuits. The Type 57 Bugatti, the 3.5-litre Delahaye, and the 4½-litre Lagonda all won at Le Mans in their time, and the latter company's vee-twelve put up an excellent show on its only appearance at the Sarthe Circuit. The Hotchkiss company disapproved of racing, though this did not stop their Type-686 from winning several Monte Carlo Rallies, the last as late as 1950.

Essentially, the *grande routière* was an Anglo-French phenomenon. Italian fiscal policy discouraged large cars, so Lancia's 3-litre Astura was the country's only real contender in this category. The twin-supercharged 8C-2900 Alfa Romeo, probably the fastest off-the-peg automobile one could buy between 1937 and 1940, can best be described as a detuned racing model, marketed only as long as there were left-over Grand Prix engines on hand at the factory.

Germany, too long wedded to the brute-force policy of the big

supercharged Mercedes-Benz, produced little of merit. Though the last of the six-cylinder SS series was not delivered until 1935, the blown pushrod straight-eights that supplanted them were dauntingly heavy – a four-passenger cabriolet weighed over 2.5 tons and called for considerable steering effort at low speeds – and would attain 100 mph (160 km/h) only with the blower engaged, a practice recommended only for brief periods. The contemporary Horch, described by a keen owner as "wonderfully lazy and unsportive", was just as heavy but with less power. Its real métier was to amble along an *Autobahn* at 75 mph (120 km/h) in overdrive, and it was not really a car for Alpine passes or the narrow main roads of the British Isles.

In the United States the sports car was dead and buried. The twin overhead-camshaft Stutz lingered on into 1935, but the Duesenberg, though possessed of outstanding acceleration up to three-figure speeds (say 150–160 km/h) was a trifle unwieldy, as might be expected of something with a regular *short* wheel-base of 142.5 in (3.6 m). The supercharged Auburn's two-speed back axle gave it six forward speeds, but the chassis design was pure American, while complexity and protracted teething troubles killed the latter-day Cord, even if its handling, brakes, and gear ratios conformed to European norms, and its front-wheel drive enabled it to be driven into corners like a Citroën.

The Cord's performance, however, came close to the standards expected of a *grande routière*, especially when the optional supercharger was fitted – a top speed of 105 mph (165–170 km/h), with 88 mph

143

The faces of classicism – two from France, one from the United States, and one from Britain. The French term *grande routière* defies translation – it conjures up the idea of a long hood pointing southwards down some dead-straight *route nationale* of the 1930s, and two of the best hoods to sit behind were those of Hotchkiss (*below*) and Delahaye (*opposite, top right*). Both used simple 3.5-litre pushrod six-cylinder engines devoid of temperament or complexity, and output was anything from 100 to 130 hp according to tune, though Delahaye's competition engines (a Type 135 won at Le Mans in 1938) were good for as much as 160 hp and were still quite tractable. Maximum speed meant less to the average owner

than a steady cruising gait in the 80s (130–140 km/h), though this triple-carburettor 135MS Delahaye would exceed the "ton" (160 km/h) and the short-chassis Grand Sport Hotchkiss could attain it in favourable circumstances. Delahayes had independent front springing and (usually) Cotal electrically-selected transmissions; they also attracted some splendidly unpractical bodies from Figoni and Saoutchik, such as this roadster with full fender skirts. Somehow, the Hotchkiss roadster looks better, with its English coachwork by Lancefield. Britons, by contrast, thought big and heavy. Here is a splendidly original 8-litre Bentley (*opposite, bottom*) made in 1931. This magnificent *envoi* to a bygone age boasted

a 7,983-cc single overhead-camshaft six-cylinder engine with non-detachable head and dual ignition. The combination of 230 hp and high gearing allowed the vehicle to attain 100 mph (160 km/h) even with heavy sedan bodywork and a weight of over 2½ tons. There was no weight restriction on the maker's guarantee; the 8-litre could cope with anything a coachbuilder cared to fit. So, essentially, could the 1931 Pierce-Arrow Salon Eight (*opposite, top left*), though this was more a car to be driven in. The headlamps faired into the front fenders had been a hallmark of the breed since 1913 but were not compulsory. Engineering was typically American: a large nine-bearing side-valve straight-eight engine (6.3 litres, 132 hp),

servo brakes, a choice of three- or four-speed transmissions, and, interestingly, a hypoid rear axle to lower the vehicle. The Salon model was the biggest (wheel-base was 147 in or 3.7 m) and most expensive Pierce of the season. Regular prices ran from $4,275 (£855) to $6,250 (£1,250), but individual customs could cost as much as $10,000 (£2,000). Unfortunately, Pierce-Arrow could not stay the course; their alliance with Studebaker lasted only from 1929 to 1933, and with a regained independence, they had no second line of defence. They tried trailer homes, but these offered too much for the money. By April, 1938, the Buffalo (New York) factory had closed for good.

(140–145 km/h) available in third and an 0–50 mph (0–80 km/h) acceleration time of around ten seconds. The car would hold 70 mph (115 km/h) all day in the overdrive high gear, and the use of a 4.7-litre motor held fuel consumption down to a reasonable 15 mpg (18 lit/100), a great improvement on earlier giants, which relied on sheer brute force. The biggest six-cylinder Bentleys and Hispano-Suizas had run to 8 litres, and the SS Mercedes-Benz to just over 7. The only surviving dinosaur with *grande routière* aspirations was the last of Marc Birkigt's Hispano-Suizas, a 9.4-litre vee-twelve disposing of 220 bhp. Though available on a 135-in (3.4 m) wheel-base, there was little room for more than two people in this abbreviated form, and in any case, the three-speed gearbox was a handicap in really hilly country.

More typical of the new generation were the great French cars of the 1934–40 period – Bugatti's 57, Delahaye's 135, the 23CV Lago-Talbot, the D8-120 Delage, and the 686GS Hotchkiss. All save the 4.3-litre Delage (enlarged just before the war to 4,730 cc) had cylinder capacities between 3 and 4 litres, in spite of which the tamest of the bunch, the Hotchkiss, disposed of 125 bhp, sufficient to propel the short-chassis Grand Sports at around the 100-mph mark. If the Bugatti was, perhaps, a trifle too complicated for the layman, all were suitable for everyday use, the Delahaye's truck-based four-bearing pushrod six-cylinder unit having the least finicky of palates, allied to a modest thirst of 20 mpg (14 lit/100).

It also had a fairly modest rev limit, hence the competition fraternity preferred its short-stroke cousin, the D6-70 Delage. Alas, touring versions of this 2.8-litre machine tended to be overweight and thus less attractive, despite the undoubted advantage of the hydraulic brakes which Delahayes lacked. (So, incidentally, did all the local opposition except the Bugatti, which acquired these in 1938.)

Only Hotchkiss and Bugatti retained beam axles at either end, while Talbot used the Wilson preselective gearbox, and Delahaye and Delage the electrically-selected Cotal. Better still for export business, the *grandes routières* coincided not only with a period of surpassingly elegant coachwork, but also with the fall of the franc. Foreigners found that it paid to shop in France. Buyers from across the Channel could get change out of £1,000 ($5,000) on all save the straight-eight Delage, and a 686GS Hotchkiss at £675 ($3,375) in Britain cost £150 less than a Speed 25 Alvis, and less than half the price of a Derby-built Bentley.

English-speaking interpretations of the idiom tended to be heavier, more conservative in styling, and almost archaic in the suspension department, though Alvis had transverse-leaf, independent front suspension as early as 1934, and Lagondas acquired a torsion-bar set-up in 1938. Ideas had, however, been extensively refined. The *beau ideal* of English sportsmen in 1930 had been the supercharged 4½-litre Bentley, a traditional, almost Edwardian, four-cylinder with audible power impulses. The customers liked it that way, one of them complaining to "W.O." himself of the absence of "that bloody thump" on the first 6½-litre sixes. In rather the same idiom were the low-chassis 4½-litre Invicta of 1931 and the 1934 Lagonda of like capacity, both using Meadows's big pushrod six, and both strictly men's cars, though the Invicta was uncommonly flexible, a steady 60 mph (100 km/h) representing only 2,000 rpm. In a smaller class were the Alvis Speed 20 and the Talbot 105, both extracting some 90 mph (145 km/h) from power units of less than 3 litres' capacity. The high point of British *grande routière* thinking arrived in 1937–38, with the 4.3-litre Alvis and the 4.5-litre Lagonda V12. Both had a healthy fuel thirst, and the Lagonda's overhead-camshaft engine was a complicated piece of machinery, but even if the advertised 175 bhp never eventuated, the car was still good for over 100 mph (160 km/h) in sedan form, took the mandatory ten seconds to attain 50 mph, and rode extremely well. The

hydraulic brakes were entirely adequate for 1939 road conditions, though the price of traditional British appointments was a weight of 4,572 lb (2,078 kg). A Delahaye turned the scales at 3,136 lb (1,425 kg), and even the eight-cylinder Delage, a rather overblown creation which could have done with somewhat more than the 130 bhp it actually possessed, was lighter, at 4,210 lb (1,914 kg).

None the less, these Britons were eminently suitable for the Grand Tour and benefited from extensive workouts on Europe's new motorways. Early Derby Bentleys had suffered from run bearings on the *Autobahnen*, so from late 1938, an overdrive top was incorporated in the gearbox. A press Lagonda V12 held over 100 mph for 15.5 miles (25 km) of *Autobahn*!

More interestingly, the new generation of *grandes routières* on either side of the Channel usually carried sedan or convertible bodywork, though tourers had been traditional on Bentleys, Invictas, and the earlier Lagondas. In France, open coachwork was essentially reserved for the circuits, though the advent of the new idiom coincided with the tail-end of the craze for American-style roadsters, quite often seen on the big Hotchkiss in the 1934–36 period. Alvis and Bentley always catalogued tourers, even in 1939, by which time Lagonda's sportiest style was the rare Rapide 2/3-seater convertible, confined to the short chassis. Such coachwork was, however, fading out of the picture; grand tourists could not be bothered with side-curtains. Out of 1,177 3½-litre Bentleys delivered between 1933 and 1937, only 65 came with "tourer" bodywork, some of these, in all probability, being convertibles with wind-up windows.

Grandes routières were, of course, for the few. Seven hundred pounds ($3,500) was a lot of money in 1936, and its equivalent would have bought a "Senior" Packard, if not a Model K Lincoln, in the United States. Thus, inevitably, there were attempts to achieve comparable

performance at lower cost: hence the first wave of sporting Euro-Americans, or, more strictly, Anglo-Americans.

The combination of European chassis and styling with a big, lazy American engine had already been tried in France and Germany in the late twenties, and representatives of this crossbred strain would persist into 1933. The motive was not, however, performance; it was the need to find the cheapest way of extending the range to include a straight-eight model without reducing anxious shareholders to apoplexy. In France, Delaunay-Belleville headed the list of Continental users, the short-lived Lucien Bollack favoured the Lycoming, and the Sizaire Frères broke new ground with a sleeve-valve Willys-Knight Six. In Germany, Hansa bought from Continental, Stoewer copied similar designs, and Audi's Eights were based on the recently-defunct Rickenbacker. Even the exotic *Double-Huit* Bucciali, for all its fantastic appearance and huge plated storks on the hood sides, used a sixteen-cylinder power unit made up of two Continental blocks.

By contrast, the *fast* Euro-American was a British invention. The theme would go international only some twenty years later, when France's Jean Daninos sought to re-establish the *grande routière*. His Facel Vegas was to use the Chrysler vee-eight because there was no suitable European – let alone French – engine giving the right performance at a viable price. The Facel was to cause major repercussions in Italy as well as Britain, but that is another story.

The 1933 Railton looked a British sports car, every inch of it, even down to the Invicta-like radiator and badge, and the same classic rivets down the hood. It was "made" in the old Invicta shops at Cobham. The machine was as fast as a 4½-litre Invicta, accelerated better – a staggering 7.3 seconds to 50 mph (80 km/h) – and cost about half the money. But everything not immediately apparent to the beholder was pure unadulterated Hudson, from Jefferson Avenue, Detroit.

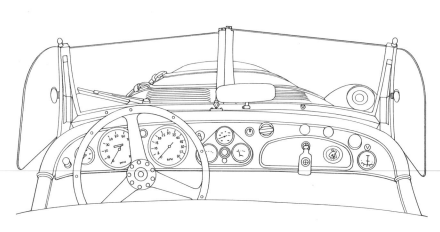

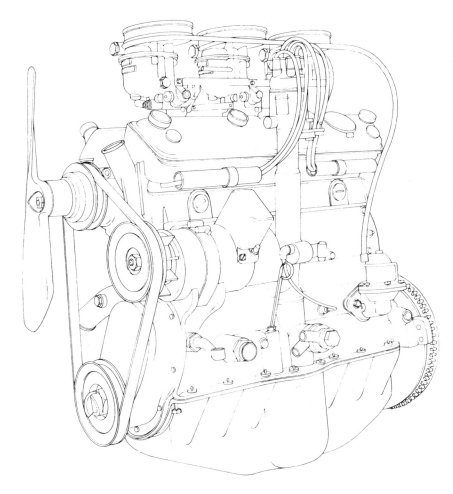

Sports Cars of the 1930s. Best all-rounder of later days was the BMW 328 (*opposite, top* and *centre left*) of 1936–39, even if the instrument panel was too functional for Britons. With 80 hp from a triple-carburettor 2-litre pushrod six (*left*), a light tubular frame, transverse-leaf independent front suspension, and hydraulic brakes, it weighed in at low 1,700 lb (770 kg) and was good for 100 mph (160 km/h). Production was modest, at 464 units, but for those who wanted more luxury and the same performance, the 80-hp engine was available as an alternative to the standard 55-hp type in the 327 cabriolet (*opposite, top right*).

Out of nearly 2,000 customers, 569 preferred the performance option, though even a basic 327 was more expensive than a 328. Italy's 1750GS Alfa Romeo (*opposite, bottom left*) of 1930–33 was a vintage hangover based on Vittorio Jano's single-camshaft 6C-1500 announced in 1925. In its final form, however, the blown twin overhead-camshaft 1,754-cc engine pushed out 85 hp, and it would do an honest 95 mph (150–155 km/h). An English price of £1,150 ($5,750) explains sales of only 219 of all series. The classical lines of Zagato's spyder body were, however, cribbed by other makers, notably Riley for their 9-hp Imp (*bottom centre*) of 1934–35.

The excellent twin-carburettor 1,089-cc four-cylinder engine went into an abbreviated 90-in (2.3 m) wheel-base but weight was 1,904 lb (863 kg), an interesting comparison with the more powerful Alfa's 980 kg. The Riley's beam axles and mechanical brakes, if not its Wilson preselective transmission, featured on two other fine specimens of British traditional, the 1936 1½-litre HRG (*opposite, centre right*) and William Lyons's immortal SS100 (*bottom right*) of 1936–40. The SS managed over 90 mph (145 km/h) on 2,664 cc and 102 hp, while the 3½-litre edition would comfortably achieve the ton (160 km/h). Handling was hoppity, but the seven-bearing sixes were very tough, and owners included one crowned head. Only 309 of the 13,610 SS Jaguars made in the last four years of peace were, however, 100s. The HRG was even rarer – only 26 of the original Meadows-engined type were built between 1936 and 1939. "Yesterday's car today" featured a long-stroke 69×100 mm four with magneto ignition, cable-operated brakes, crash transmission, and quarter-elliptic front springs. It was still being made in very similar guise in 1952. A complete absence of streamlining didn't prevent a top speed of around 85 mph (135 km/h) and an 0–30 mph (0–50 km/h) acceleration time of 4 seconds.

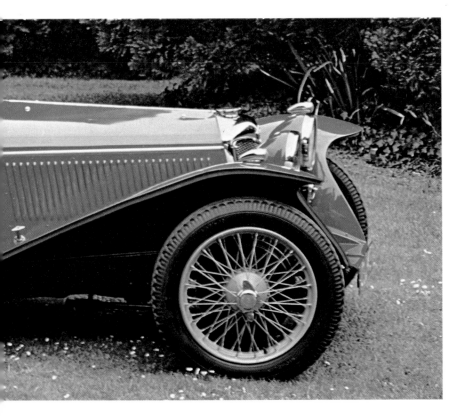

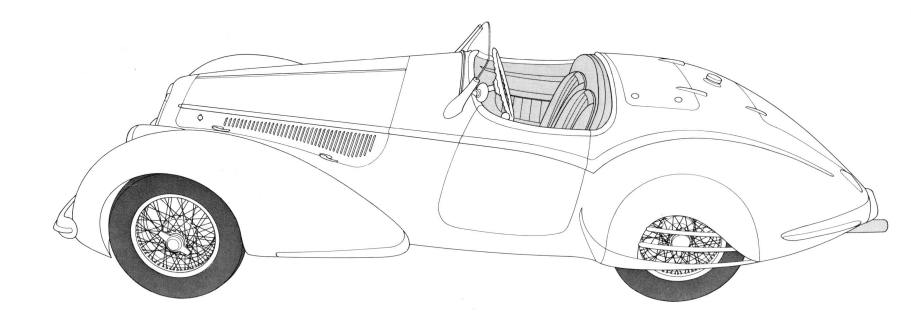

The basis of the first cars was the short-lived 4-litre Terraplane Eight, replaced by the 4.2-litre 254 Hudson early in 1934. Remarkably little was done to the chassis. The frame was lowered by two inches, the suspension reinforced by telescopic dampers, and British electrical equipment, though not initially of 12-volt type, was fitted. At 2,260 lb (1,027 kg), the sports tourer was 400 lb (182 kg) lighter than even a low-chassis Invicta. The price of £499 sounds expensive when translated into dollars at $2,495, but it was a bargain in terms of an Alvis at £695 ($3,480), or an M45 Lagonda at £795 ($4,000). And in England even an unmodified Terraplane Eight sedan cost £385 ($1,925).

Further, the Railton did its job well. The three forward ratios furnished by Hudson were entirely adequate, since high gear sufficed for everything: only a second was saved by using the intermediate ratio between 30 and 50 mph (50 and 80 km/h). If properly maintained, the Bendix brakes sufficed, and the splash-lubricated motor would sustain many more revs than were usually asked of it.

The Railton sold some fourteen hundred units pre-war, more than any of its imitators, of which the Brough Superior from the famed Nottingham motorcycle firm was also Hudson-based, but the Lammas used the blown Graham Six, while Atalanta and Jensen imported only motors and transmissions, Lincoln-Zephyr in the former case, and Ford or Nash in the latter. The specialized Allard – as yet aimed solely at the English type of reliability trial – featured modified Ford components with a choice of Ford or Lincoln power.

The Ford V8 was, of course, also produced in Britain, but generally speaking, the makers of hybrids suffered from two handicaps. The first of these was the British horsepower tax: the Hudson was a 29 and the Lincoln-Zephyr a 37. At the beginning, this mattered little, since the Invicta and Lagonda were rated at 30 hp. A worse worry was technical dependence on Detroit, as yet uncommitted to any horsepower race.

True, Hudson managed to extract quite a lot of power, unasked, from their straight-eight. What started with 113 bhp was good for 132

by 1938–39. Hydraulic brakes were standardized from 1936 onward, so the Railton got these as well. Alas! these improvements were not sufficient to counter the endemic English disease – better coachwork appointments and more weight. Railton sedans put on 300 lb (136 kg) in three years.

In any case, by 1938, there was a cheaper and more patriotic way of acquiring all the Railton virtues save sheer standing-start acceleration. The cash saving was a cool thirty per cent, and better still, the new menace was taxed as a 25, less than any of the engines favoured by the Anglo-American specialists. The 3½-litre SS Jaguar had arrived.

Henceforward, the Jaguar would be the yardstick by hich any fast luxury tourer had to be assessed. As yet, it was not a major force in export markets, though the French makers would have been well advised to watch Swiss sales earlier than they did. But once the French embarked upon their fiscal massacre in 1947, the British car was destined to overwhelm Delahaye and Hotchkiss. Jaguar was a profitable venture: its foreign rivals were not.

Lyons and his chief engineer, W.M. Heynes, broke no technical shibboleths. The engine was a straightforward and untemperamental pushrod six with seven mains, which matched the Hotchkiss's 125 bhp from the same capacity (3,485 cc). The frame rode on orthodox semielliptic springs at either end, and the brakes were rod-operated Girlings. At 3,668 lb (1,667 kg), the sedan was heavier than a Railton – and all the better Continentals. Top speed was an unspectacular 90 mph (145 km/h), and acceleration was about par for four-door sedans in this class.

On the credit side was the traditional British styling. The radiator was set well back behind the headlamps, and the wood-and-leather interior was executed with a dignity and elegance the world would soon come to associate with William Lyons. Gone was the flashy look of the original SS, and a layman would associate the car with a price tag of £1,000 ($5,000 in those days). In actual fact, the 3½-litre cost £445 ($2,225), and

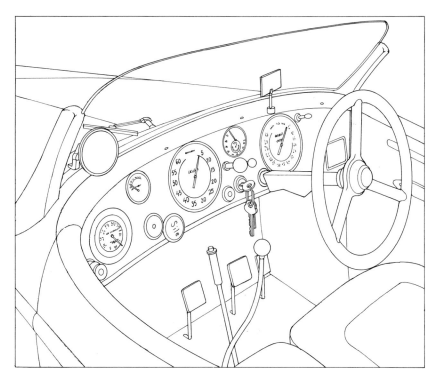

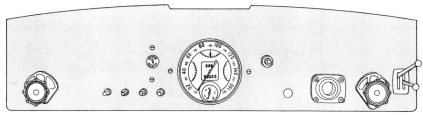

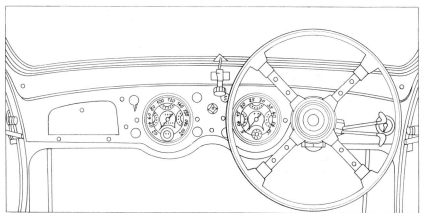

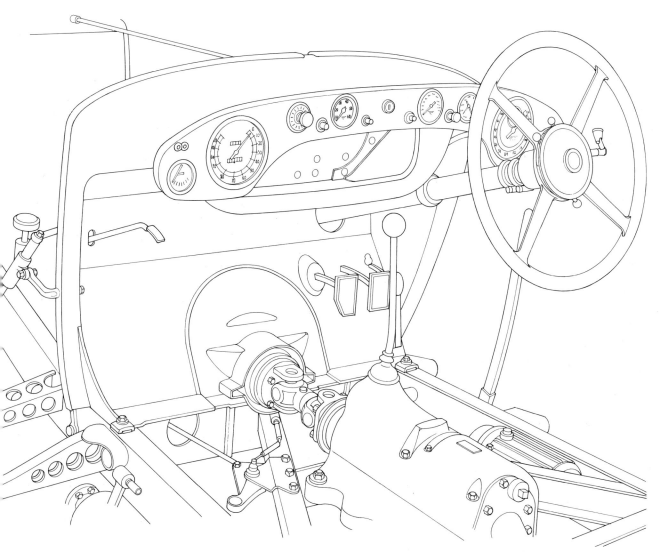

(*Far right*) The Alfa Romeo 8C 2900B. By
1938, Alfa Romeo had progressed to a
new all-independently sprung chassis in
which they mounted a twin overhead-
camshaft, twin supercharged straight-
eight engine straight out of their 1935
Grand Prix cars. It was probably the fastest tourer one could buy at the outbreak
of war, with a top speed of 125–130 mph
(200–210 km/h). Production was, however, limited by the stock of engines
available, and a price of over £2,000
($10,000) proved a further deterrent. The
Alfa's instrument panel (*top left*) is fitted
with a large speedometer and a tachome-
ter. There is a shock-absorber control on
the dashboard, and this can be adjusted
for hard or soft ride.

Grande routière instrument panels. The
Type 57 Bugatti had a very austere panel
(*top right*), with a central dial; the aircraft-
type ignition and throttle levers on the
right are of interest. The Delahaye 135
(*centre right*) has a grouped panel and a
comprehensive supply of instruments,
even if it lacks the ornate layout of earlier
days. The 4.3-litre Alvis (*left*) shows an
untidy distribution of instruments right
across a wide facia, with the rev counter in
front of the driver and the speedometer
in front of the passenger.

All the cars here have right-hand drive,
which was favoured on mountain passes
and in crowded streets: one was nearer,
respectively, to precipices and suicidal
pedestrians!

What the ordinary Italian bought, and what his *carrossiers* made their name on. The good old 1100B Fiat in 1947 form (*top*) was the same as it had been ten years before, apart from a vee-grille cribbed from specialist coachbuilders such as Ghia and Pininfarina, who used it indiscriminately on Alfa Romeo, Fiat, and Lancia to give their wares their own hallmark. However, a Fiat was a Fiat, and factory bodies were pedestrian. So were Alfa Romeo's sedans on the standard chassis: the 1947 6C-2500 Sport (*bottom*) was, however, rather more exciting. Like the cooking model, it featured a twin overhead-camshaft 2.4-litre six-cylinder engine, all-independent suspension, hydraulic brakes, and (regrettably) column shift, but on 110 hp it was good for the "ton" (160 km/h). It was a natural for the body specialists: here is Pininfarina's cabriolet. This usually went out with the regular Alfa grille: one wonders if the one on the car, with its late fifties Jaguar overtones, is a piece of inspired anticipation or a later gloss.

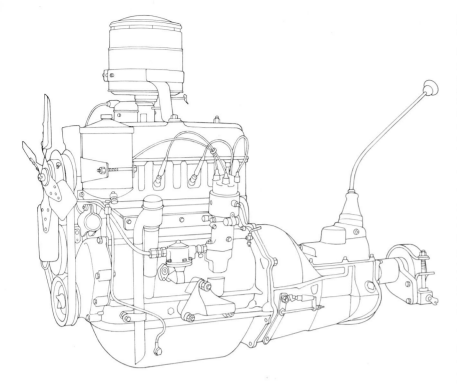

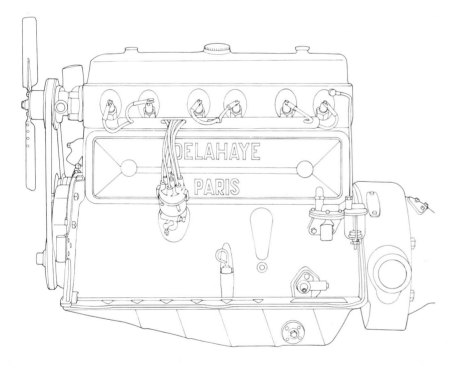

Pushrod overhead valves for simplicity. Both the Fiat 1100 (*top*) and Delahaye six (*bottom*) had humble origins, and both ended up by propelling sports and competition vehicles at indecent speeds. The Fiat started life in 1932 as the 995-cc side-valve Balilla on 20–22 hp; in its later (1937–52) form, it was enlarged to 1,089 cc with upstairs valves and gave 32–36 hp. Note the air cleaner dominating the scenery, and the low-mounted distributor which "drowned" rather easily in wet weather. The instruction manual discouraged one from exceeding 4,400 rpm, but special engines evolved by firms like Cisitalia ran up to 6,000 and more, with outputs the right side of 60 hp. The four-bearing Delahaye six, here seen as the touring 18CV of 1934, was originally intended for use in three-ton trucks but went racing to even greater purpose. In its most familiar Type-135 MS form, with triple carburettors and a capacity of 3.6 litres, it gave 120 hp, but the version which won Le Mans in 1938 was developing something like 160, and still wasn't fussy about lower-octane fuels. When Delahaye finally merged with Hotchkiss in 1954, the engine was still going into cars – and some quite big trucks as well.

the factory would go on to make 5,424 of the series, not to mention over 7,000 of the smaller 2½-litre, hardly a *grande routière* but capable of 85 mph (135–140 km/h). (By comparison, some 2,000 Delahaye 135s were made between 1936 and 1954.) For those in quest of ultimate, hairy performance there was the short-chassis 100 roadster, perilous in the handling department but possessed of the same simple mechanics. This one was a rally winner; barely 300 were made all told (including 2½-litre versions), and among the customers was a monarch, King Michael of Rumania.

The SS100, of course, belonged to the "rough and tough" school. There were no concessions to creature comforts, and the bodywork, with cutaway doors, primitive top, and exposed, "Le Mans"-style slab fuel tank, conformed to the same English school as had bred the small MGs, Morgans, and Singers. This type was, in fact, so British that we shall deal with it later on as a "national" speciality. Virtually no other small sports cars of any interest were made anywhere else in the 1930s. France's traditional Amilcars, Salmsons, and BNCs had breathed their last by 1930, and their successors, the front-wheel-drive Georges Irats, Lamberts, and Rémi-Danvignes, were produced only in small numbers. The same went for Stewart Sandford's four-wheelers, by 1939 no more than Morgan 4/4s with French Ruby engines. In Germany, Adler's stock sporting Trumpf-Juniors (as distinct from the cars raced by the works) were underpowered. As for Fiat's delightful little 508S Balilla of 1934, higher geared and better braked than most of the British opposition, it was much rarer than its competition record throughout Europe (and the exploits of such campaigners as the Franco-Italian Gordini and the German Brendel) would suggest. Total production was probably around fourteen hundred units, a drop in the ocean beside the twelve-thousand-odd overhead-camshaft MGs produced between 1928 and 1936.

The Fiat, admittedly, featured a short-stroke 65 x 75-mm engine and hydraulic brakes, but chassis and suspension were traditional, and so was the styling, cribbed directly from Zagato's magnificent Alfa Romeo *spyder* first seen in 1929. The 508S Balilla must stand as the last flowering of an older generation, although it was constructed of mass-produced parts.

Bespoke sports cars of the early 1930s, be they Jano's six- and eight-cylinder twin overhead-camshaft Alfa Romeos or the expensive Aston Martins, Frazer Nashes, and Squires from Britain, combined vintage engineering and classical styling. These ideas died hard, being perpetuated right into the 1950s by the small HRG concern in the southern suburbs of London, on stark, efficient two-seaters, initially Meadows-powered, but latterly using overhead-camshaft Singer units. Most new thinking came from the *grandes routières*, though, from 1935 onwards, roadgoing Alfa Romeos were seen with hydraulic brakes and all-independent suspension. The next real breakthrough was, however, German, as visitors to the Nürburgring meeting in June, 1936, would discover.

Up to now, there had been super-sports cars, usually Italian, which meant Alfa Romeo – Maserati's "street" offerings had always been few and far between. Small sports cars, a French preserve in the 1920s, were now essentially British, while the initiative in the "heavy" class was shared between Britain and France. What the Germans offered was a middleweight contender of great promise, the 328 BMW.

From humble beginnings as Austin's German licencees, BMW – already renowned for motor cycles and aero motors – had come a long way. Their first true sports car had been the 315/1 of 1934, a 1.5-litre six disposing of a mere 40 bhp but blessed with excellent steering, independently sprung front wheels, and a light twin-tube frame. It had better aerodynamics than the British opposition, and in subsequent

The Known Way. There is nothing very remarkable about the 1939 3½-litre SS Jaguar convertible beyond an exciting combination of looks, performance, and price. Most people unfamiliar with the work of William Lyons guessed this last at around £800 ($4,000); in fact, it retailed in England for £445 ($2,225). For this money one got a top speed of 90 mph (145 km/h) with a little to spare in favourable conditions, a cruising speed in the low 80s (say 130 km/h), and a fuel consumption of 16 mpg (17.8 lit/100), which was not excessive for this class of car. Engineering was solid and conventional – X-braced frame, rod-operated brakes, semi-elliptic springs damped by hydraulic shock absorbers, a four-speed synchromesh transmission, and a Standard-built overhead-valve pushrod engine which gave 125 hp at 4,250 rpm

from 3,485 cc. Unkind things were said of the dural connecting-rods tending to wilt at high revs, but such untoward incidents seldom happened except after some 100,000 miles (160,000 km); a worse fault of elderly Jaguars, obvious from the close fit of the engine under the hood, was the escape of fumes through the firewall. The car was not particularly light at 3,668 lb (about 1,660 kg), and by the standards of our times, a 0–70 (112 km/h) acceleration time of around 20 seconds would set no rivers on fire. The satisfaction of driving a Jaguar was "feeling rich", surrounded by plenty of wood and leather, and behind an untemperamental engine that was almost invariably a first-touch starter. The cutaway view, of course, cannot conceal the almost total lack of rearward vision on an English drophead coupé with the top up. SS Cars, as the

Jaguar's makers were still known, were still a long way from the big league production-wise, even if the make was represented in most European countries, and as far afield as the Baltic states. Their best year so far, 1939, saw deliveries of a little over 5,000 units. The beam-axle pushrod Jaguars, now with hypoid rear axles, went back into production in 1945 and were continued until they gave way to the Mk V, with torsion-bar front suspension and hydraulic brakes, at the end of 1948. It would be easy to blame the relatively small number of 3½-litres built – 5,424 as against 7,222 with the smaller 2½-litre motor – on British horsepower tax, were it not for the fact that the 2½ had two years' head start (it came out in 1936) over its bigger sister.

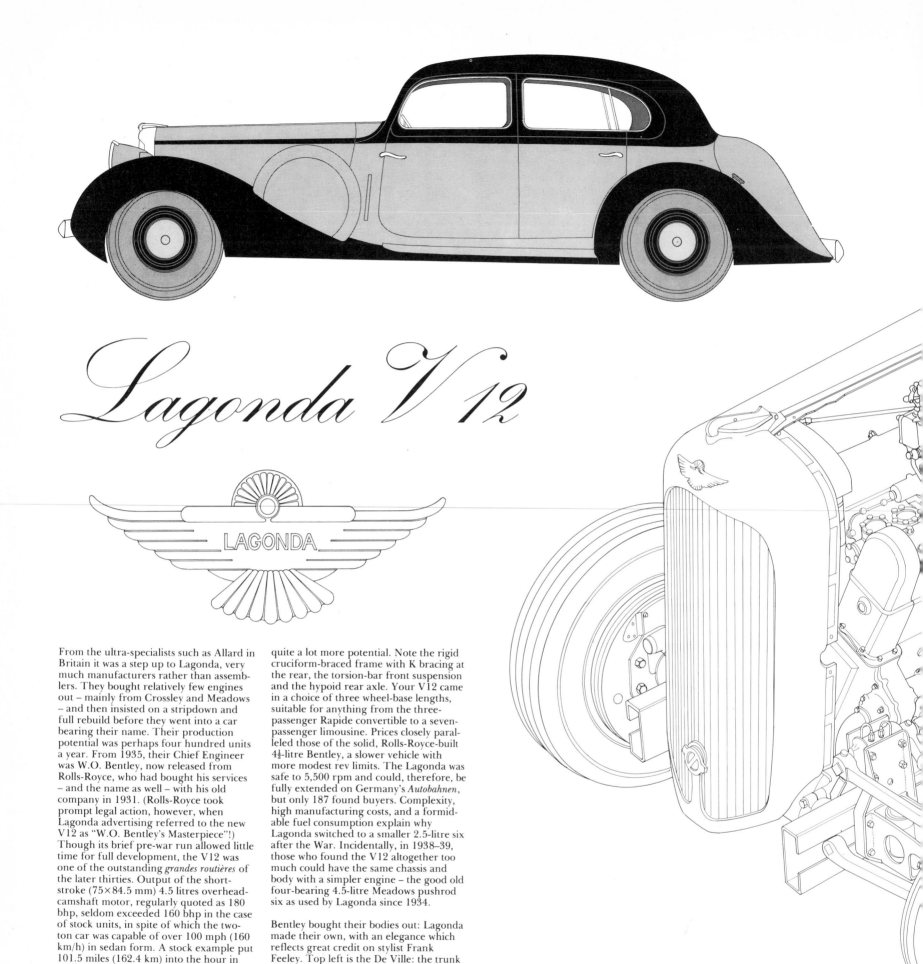

Lagonda V12

From the ultra-specialists such as Allard in Britain it was a step up to Lagonda, very much manufacturers rather than assemblers. They bought relatively few engines out – mainly from Crossley and Meadows – and then insisted on a stripdown and full rebuild before they went into a car bearing their name. Their production potential was perhaps four hundred units a year. From 1935, their Chief Engineer was W.O. Bentley, now released from Rolls-Royce, who had bought his services – and the name as well – with his old company in 1931. (Rolls-Royce took prompt legal action, however, when Lagonda advertising referred to the new V12 as "W.O. Bentley's Masterpiece"!) Though its brief pre-war run allowed little time for full development, the V12 was one of the outstanding *grandes routières* of the later thirties. Output of the short-stroke (75×84.5 mm) 4.5 litres overhead-camshaft motor, regularly quoted as 180 bhp, seldom exceeded 160 bhp in the case of stock units, in spite of which the two-ton car was capable of over 100 mph (160 km/h) in sedan form. A stock example put 101.5 miles (162.4 km) into the hour in 1938. With the four-carburettor unit used at Le Mans in 1939, the Lagonda had

quite a lot more potential. Note the rigid cruciform-braced frame with K bracing at the rear, the torsion-bar front suspension and the hypoid rear axle. Your V12 came in a choice of three wheel-base lengths, suitable for anything from the three-passenger Rapide convertible to a seven-passenger limousine. Prices closely paralleled those of the solid, Rolls-Royce-built 4½-litre Bentley, a slower vehicle with more modest rev limits. The Lagonda was safe to 5,500 rpm and could, therefore, be fully extended on Germany's *Autobahnen*, but only 187 found buyers. Complexity, high manufacturing costs, and a formidable fuel consumption explain why Lagonda switched to a smaller 2.5-litre six after the War. Incidentally, in 1938–39, those who found the V12 altogether too much could have the same chassis and body with a simpler engine – the good old four-bearing 4.5-litre Meadows pushrod six as used by Lagonda since 1934.

Bentley bought their bodies out: Lagonda made their own, with an elegance which reflects great credit on stylist Frank Feeley. Top left is the De Ville: the trunk space on the regular sedan is depicted bottom right. The De Ville was Lagonda's idea of a combination owner-chauffeur sedan, usually called a Touring Limousine in Britain. It featured a divider and a higher roof-line but was generally sporting in appearance. A hallmark of Bentley's pre-war Lagondas was the provision of dual sidemounts in metal covers painted to match the body colour. These were not what they seemed: there was only one spare wheel, the other sidemount carrying the tools. Nor was the idea original. Volvo had used it way back in 1929. Some people felt they looked clumsy, and one eminent American ordered his V12 convertible with a conventional trunk-mounted spare.

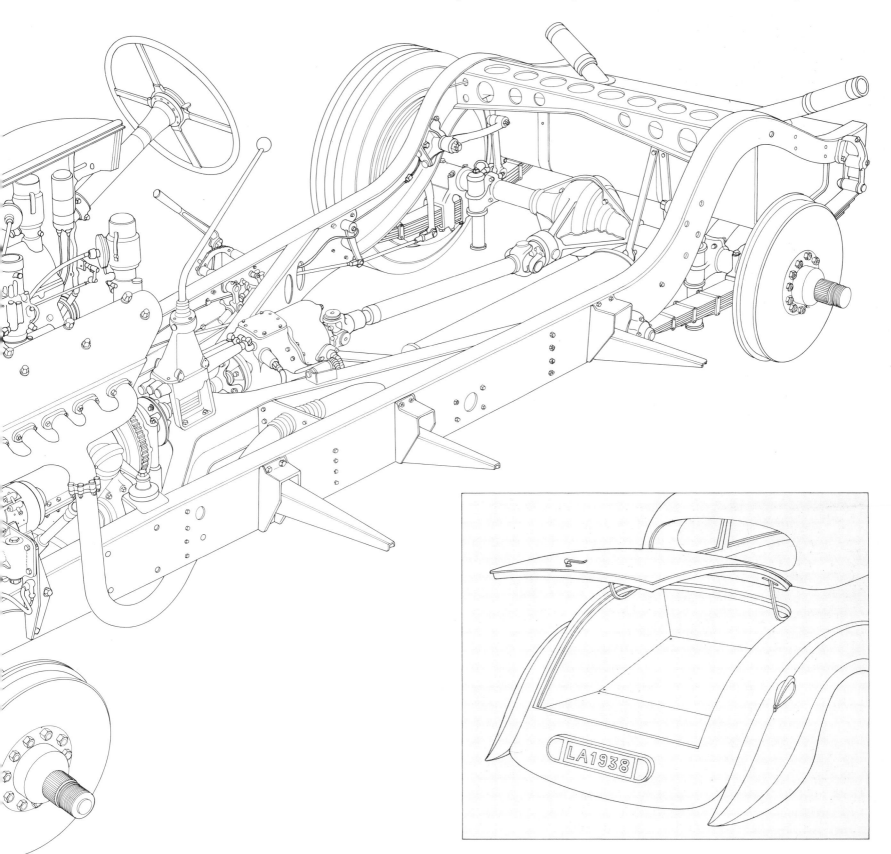

1.9-litre (Type 319) form speed went up to 80 mph (130 km/h).

The 328 pursued the same theme, but capacity was increased to 1,971 cc, and a new head with hemispherical combustion chambers boosted output to 80 bhp in three-carburettor form. Further, the mechanical brakes of early BMWs had given way to hydraulics, and the car combined a low weight of 1,826 lb (830 kg) with a habitable aerodynamic two-seater body. Cars bought off the showroom floor were capable of 95 mph (150–155 km/h) and 100 miles (160 km) could be put into the hour under track conditions. The 328 was a superb all-rounder. It dominated the 2-litre sports racing class; it also distinguished itself in rallies, sprints, hillclimbs, and even British-style trials. A 328 would be Stirling Moss's first competition mount. For those in quest of more comfort, the triple-carburettor motor was available in the touring 327 chassis, supplied as a coupé or convertible. The closed sports car – as opposed to the true *grande routière* – was about to take its bow.

We were still some way from the *gran turismo*, a creation of the 1950s. But even in 1938 and 1939, more and more closed cars were to be seen in such sports-car marathons as Le Mans and the Mille Miglia. Pioneers of this idiom had been Adler, with their 1.7-litre front-wheel-drive *Rennlimousinen*, perfect aerodynamic shapes which went indecently fast despite their lightly stressed and tuned side-valve four-cylinder engines with a potential of 45 bhp at best. They were also frugal of fuel. Soon to follow their lead were Alfa Romeo, Lago-Talbot, and BMW, while streamlined Fiat and Lancia coupés were raced only in Italy. By contrast, Fiat's 508CMM of 1938 was something which Italians, at any rate, could buy. This sports Balilla replacement was hailed by *The Motor* as "a 1950 model come to town". At 1,792 lb (814 kg), it was not particularly light for an 1100. Nor was it very powerful, only 42 bhp being claimed, no more than Riley had been extracting from engines of similar capacity, for street use, in the early 1930s. Savio's two-passenger aerodynamic coupé coachwork gave indifferent vision (none at all to the rear), but the value of minimal drag was remarkable. The little Fiat attained 95 mph (150–155 km/h), cruised at over 80 (130–135 km/h), and used fuel sparingly – consumption was 40 mpg (7 lit/100) at cruising speeds. Though exports had not yet begun when war broke out, the writing was on the wall.

Others followed suit. The 1939 season saw tests of aerodynamic sports sedans by Bentley and Lagonda, the former attaining 120 mph (190 km/h) on a 2.87:1 overdrive top gear and putting 114.63 miles (184.47 km) into an hour. Both were full four-seaters – the Lagonda, indeed, was timed at 124 mph (200 km/h) on Montlhéry autodrome with three passengers aboard. Though neither car was destined to reach the public in 1939 form, the way was open for models like the Lancia Aurelia GT and Jaguar's XK family.

A good solid bottom end – or no need to be frightened of revs. Only Packard actually made publicity capital out of crankshafts, quoting their weight in their catalogues. It's exceedingly unlikely that the average motorist of 1937 knew what went on underhood, and in pre-*Autobahn* days, people didn't drive fast enough to run big-ends in the normal course of events. The 4.3-litre Alvis, however, was solidly built, and there is something reassuring about this massive seven-bearing affair with its hefty flywheel. There needed to be: the fastest and most powerful of the immediate pre-war range developed 137 hp and was one of the few catalogued four-door sedans genuinely capable of 100 mph (160 km/h). The rare short-chassis tourings were quite a lot faster.

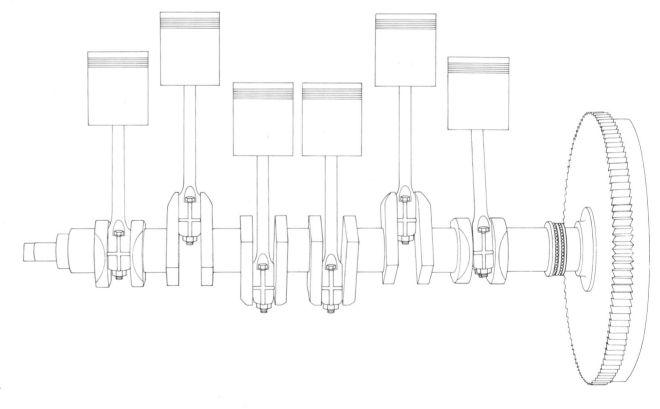

Chapter 6

CHACUN A SON GOUT

As we have seen, cars designed for the world remained an American preserve in the 1930s.

There has always been a leading nation in the automobile-export game. For all Germany's role as the nursery of the art, and for all the plodding reliability of the early belt-driven Benz, there was no world market to exploit in the nineteenth century. Thus, when the boom came, France could move in with everything from the simple one-lungers of Darracq, de Dion-Bouton, and Peugeot to the formidable chain-driven de Dietrichs and Panhards. Though Wilhelm Maybach's Mercédès had regained the technical lead by 1901, the French (and others) simply copied his design and cashed in on foreign sales, long before the United States had emerged from the chrysalid, gas-buggy phase.

Sheer weight of mass production had given the United States the lead by 1912, if not earlier, and this dominance continued throughout the 1920s. If the Model T was outmoded by 1924, others took over – the Chevrolet, the Dodge Four, and John N. Willys's Whippet, and, in a higher price class, Buick, Hudson, and Studebaker. European fiscal policies did not have any major effect on the quantity of American exports. A world dollar shortage, however, did, and after 1945, we would see a series of new hegemonies: first Britain, then Germany, France, and ultimately, from 1969 onwards, the rising sun of Japan.

"Designing for the world" was thus not part of a European maker's credo, and national characteristics stayed uppermost. There were, it is true, a few long-term exceptions: André Citroën's dreams of a universal car were turned into reality, in Europe at any rate, by his cheap and simple offerings of the 1920s. Outside the Americas, the immortal 5CV of 1922–26 is one of the commonest vintage species encountered today. Citroëns were assembled at various times between the wars in Austria, Britain, Germany, and even Mussolini's Italy, though they had been expelled therefrom for good by 1932. Alas! the price of the *traction's* sophisticated design and handling was the loss of trade in less sophisticated countries, and thus its sales were confined to Britain, Scandinavia, the Low Countries, and Portugal. Fiat tried even harder, if only because the home market could easily be supplied without working a second's overtime – in 1934, the last "good" year before *Il Duce's* costly Ethiopian adventure, Italians registered 30,150 new cars, or a mere 1,500 fewer than were turned out by Fiat's domestic plants. The colossus of Lingotto had to export to stay in business.

Mussolini's idea of an export target was ninety per cent. This would never be realized. Italy's average showing in our period never approached the fifty to fifty-five per cent norm of 1911–14, much less the seventy per cent attained in the first years of the 1920s, the golden age of the 501 Fiat and the first Lancia Lambdas. Fiat, Lancia, and Alfa Romeo were, however, respected wherever enthusiasts foregathered, and the principal market for the magnificent eight-cylinder Isotta Fraschinis was always the United States. In the 1930s alone, Fiat manufactured or assembled (not necessarily throughout the whole period) in Britain, Czechoslovakia, France, Germany, Poland, and Spain, the legendary *Millecento* almost assuming, by 1939, the role of a "family sedan for Europe".

Unfortunately, what Europe wanted did not necessarily conform with the requirements of countries further afield. The frugal, taut-handling little *topolino* was easier to service than a *traction,* but the combination of toy-like proportions, low gearing, and a 13-bhp output (plus the uncompromising two-seater bodywork) rendered it useless in Australia. In the 1920s, the Commonwealth had been one of Fiat's best export markets, since Australians had been prepared to pay over the odds for superior workmanship, as in the case of the 501 and 505. Subsequent offerings told a sadder tale: the fussy little 509 was ill-suited to bush motoring, the crypto-American sizes of the 1927–33 period offered nothing that a Buick or Nash did not, except a higher list price and more expensive spare parts, and the 500 competed against cheaper British Eights and Tens, thanks to Imperial Preference, by which goods produced within the Commonwealth paid lower duty in Commonwealth countries.

Another serious challenge came in the later 1930s from Nazi Germany. Its cars were sophisticated and heavily subsidized. In 1937, an Opel Kadett was actually cheaper in Britain than at home, thanks to a forty-three per cent government subsidy. This explains how Opel's exports climbed from 13,900 for the whole of the 1920s to a formidable 184,045 between 1931 and 1940, a figure uncomfortably close to Britain's total overseas sales in 1937 and 1938 alone. Nor were the bargain-basement Opels on their own; the front-wheel-drive Adlers, the 170V Mercedes-Benz, and the 2-litre BMW enjoyed considerable popularity abroad. In 1938, the two-cycle DKW was a Swedish best seller; it also enjoyed a brief vogue in South Africa, though the fabric bodywork tended to shake itself to pieces on the washboard roads of the up-country. But once again, vehicles designed for the relatively good road conditions of a tax-conscious Europe fared less well in Australia, India, or South America. There were high freight costs and constant servicing problems.

In any case, only Buick could build a Buick – at any rate in quantities sufficient to hold prices down to a level that would absorb freight and duty. The Germans never got around to establishing assembly plants, which could have circumvented some of these problems. Try as the European makers might, their big cars were too heavily taxed to sell in sizable numbers at home, and so the cost per unit went up. Morris's Series II Big Six must rate as a commercial success, but total sales were a mere 18,000-odd between July, 1935, and the summer of 1937, during which time Dodge turned out well over half a million units in the United States alone. Their Canadian plant, which supplied those British Empire markets in which Morris sought to compete, produced 10,029 units in the calendar year of 1936.

The Americans were geared to world markets. General Motors controlled Vauxhall in Britain and Opel in Germany, producing cars from locally-manufactured materials and thus circumventing any possible appeal to local patriotism. From 1932 on, Ford offered independent foreign models; even the French Matford, closest of the European types to American specification, had a local content amounting to over ninety per cent.

Even where wholesale manufacture was not essayed, there were local versions to suit fiscal conditions and national tastes. German-style cabriolets featured in Ford's Cologne range, while parallel Matfords followed the Gallic idiom from the firewall aft. To meet rapacious taxmen, the Ford Company offered their Model A with a 2-litre engine option, though this was sold mainly in Britain and France – it was superfluous in Germany. Other purveyors of tax-dodging power units in Britain were Chrysler and Hudson, while Packard toyed briefly with wider stroke-bore ratios on the first 120s they sold in the Old World. Europeans liked inexpensive seven-passenger sedans, so General Motors's Antwerp factory listed a long-chassis Chevrolet, offered only as a taxi with a General Motors Cab label in the United States. Britons demanded leather upholstery, sliding roofs, and, if possible, 12-volt electrics. Chrysler gave them all three from 1934 onwards, while Hudson imported cars "in the white", painting and trimming them to United Kingdom standards in their Chiswick shops.

Local body variants were extensive. In Argentina and Australia standard roadsters and phaetons outlived their domestic counterparts, with, in Australia, Holden-built roadsters available on 1939 J-series Chevrolets, albeit the style had been extinct in the United States since the end of 1935. Semi-customs by local coachbuilders were found in importers' catalogues. In 1936, almost any American chassis could be had "off the peg" in Britain as a "foursome drophead coupé" (convertible victoria). Carlton fulfilled the requirements of Chrysler and Buick, Dodges came from REAL, and Hudsons and Studebakers from Salmons-Tickford. Until the Hitler ban on imports, a similar policy obtained in Germany, where Buicks wore bodies by Bühne or Gläser. Nordbergs of Stockholm did the Swedish "specials", and Langenthal took care of Swiss requirements. Complicated name-swaps were entirely permissible in order to improve an image. To a Briton "Plymouth" spelt gin and Sir Francis Drake, so all Plymouths sold in the United Kingdom between 1933 and 1939 (and there were plenty of them) went out as "Chryslers".

Even on a falling post-Second World War market, the Americans stayed in the game, with 2.4-litre Opel-engined Chevrolets for Swiss cabbies, and Plymouths with Perkins diesel motors for their Belgian counterparts. But elsewhere a foreign customer had to reconcile his requirements with the domestic output of the country whose wares he fancied. The era of six-cylinder Ford Cortinas in Australia, Brazilian Fords of Renault ancestry made in a former Willys factory, and South African Hillmans with Peugeot diesel engines lay far ahead. Isolationism was the order of the day.

The reasons for isolationist attitudes could be fiscal. Britain was wedded to horsepower tax calculated on the number and bore of the cylinders only, which explains why a 1,488-cc Opel Olympia and a 2,996-cc 3-litre Bentley of the 1920s paid the same annual tax – £12 in 1938, and £20 ($100) in 1939. The Italian system was harsher – the *Millecento* Fiat, an 8CV in France and a 12-hp in Britain, was a 13 at home. The tax also rose progressively as capacity increased, which explains why Isotta Fraschini had to sell their "50-hp" abroad, and also why none of the three major manufacturers offered anything bigger than a 3-litre after 1937. Though, in the later thirties, France preferred a fuel tax, taxable horsepower was never very far away. The Japanese were beset with a complicated network of automobile control laws which barred virtually anything of over one litre's capacity.

Road conditions likewise played their part. Czechoslovakia's highways were still generally poor, hence sophisticated suspensions and rigid backbone frames were the order of the day. A beam axle at either end was a rarity by 1938. Sweden, with long distances and poor out-of-town roads, favoured the American type of vehicle, Volvo's staple throughout the 1930s. Japan's narrow and tortuous lanes had their effect not only on length and width, but on axle ratios as well. In Germany and Italy, the advent of the motorway age gave us the opposite picture: good aerodynamic shapes, high gearing, and relatively modest outputs. As for Britain, a combination of first-class surfaces, more steep hills than many a mountainous country, and a total absence of a coherent road policy produced the inevitable results: good brakes, plenty of easy-change transmissions, and old-fashioned suspensions.

The British, in fact, looked no further than their captive export markets and tried only half-heartedly in these. "Big cars for the colonies" appeared from time to time – the larger Series II Morrises, the Chevrolet-inspired B- and G-series Vauxhalls, and, best of them all, the Humber Super Snipe, just emerging in numbers when war intervened. This compact was evolved by installing the big 4.1-litre flathead six in the 114-in (2.9 m) wheel-base chassis designed for the 3.2-litre home-market type. Alas! its home-market price was approximately double what an American paid for his Buick, and this rubbed off on the citizens of Bombay and Brisbane, who did not want wood and leather and were still less willing to pay for them.

British exports were not very significant in the 1930s. In 1938, only two European countries – Sweden (1,587) and Denmark (3,224) took more than a thousand units. Thanks to Imperial Preference, Australia took 23,611 and New Zealand 13,590, but between them the United States and Canada sold 36,977 cars to the Commonwealth and over 10,000 to the Dominion, despite the latter's stronger sentimental ties and more "English" road conditions. Africa was an American preserve. Britain's sales of 5,573 units to the Dark Continent may have delighted the boardrooms of Coventry and Birmingham, but their wares were outnumbered 7 to 1 by those of the New World, and nearly 10 to 1 in the Union of South Africa, most motorized of all the African states.

Thus, the only British cars that sold well abroad were the specialities – the luxurious and bespoke (one Packard, after all, looked very much like the next one, however well it was made), and the small sports car. In these two fields they had little competition, and with a strong home market, exports were not of vital importance. Even in 1932, at the depth of the Depression, the country had registered 156,030 new cars, and this had risen to an impressive 274,355 by 1938.

The small sports car was a curiosity. In this class there was no need for synchromesh, though MG had it by 1936, and both this company and Riley had espoused the *système* Wilson in its golden years. The BSA Scout, admittedly, was blessed with front-wheel drive, but it was never a big seller, and Morgan's independent front suspension dated back to the company's first tricar in 1910. Bodies were stark and engineering

It could only have been made in Britain. Perhaps too sweeping a comment, since in 1934, Salmson and Amilcar were making small sporting sedans of some refinement in France, and their cars generally performed better than the regular mass-produced tinware. A comparison between this Riley 9 and (say) the contemporary Hillman Minx would appear loaded in the former's favour. The Riley's sophisticated valve-in-head 1,098-cc motor with its hemispherical combustion chambers gave 35–40 hp against the 30 extracted from Hillman's flathead of almost 100-cc greater displacement. Hillman used a conventional transmission: Riley offered the option of a Wilson preselector giving painless shifts. Hillman bodywork was of pressed steel: Riley favoured the traditional composite wood-and-metal technique. The Hillman looked the cheap sedan it was: Riley's sporting Monaco style, a débutante of 1927, had been updated sufficiently to keep it a style-leader, set off by such individual touches as a fabric top (some were metal) and centre-lock wire wheels. Production-wise, Hillmans would have outnumbered Rileys at least 4½-to-1. However, the latter make not only had a magnificent competition record but was still adding to it. Had not a Nine won the 1932 Tourist Trophy outright, while 1934's successes included second and third overall at Le Mans? In England the Riley paid £1 ($5) less annual tax than the Hillman.

Prestige and character were not, alas, all. Hillmans rusted, and Riley body frames were rot-prone in old age. At £325 ($1,625) this Monaco cost nearly double the asking price of a *de luxe* Minx. Both cars relied on cable-operated brakes that needed frequent adjustment, and the Riley's far superior handling was not matched by a markedly superior performance. True, it was about four seconds quicker to 50 mph (80 km/h), but it weighed 280 lb (130 kg) more than a Minx and was perhaps 3 mph (5 km/h) faster in a straight line. If you wanted "sports-car performance" – say 70 mph or 112 km/h – you paid extra for the twin-carburettor "special series" engine. The Nine, indeed, was a classic case of the "British disease" – more refinement, too much weight, and not enough extra horsepower to balance the equation. A 9-hp Sedan tested by the motoring press in 1931 weighed 2,016 lb (916 kg): its 1937 equivalent, with twin carburettors as standard, turned the scales at 2,464 (1,120 kg) and would barely exceed 62 mph (100 km/h). It also took over half a minute to reach 50 mph.

Rival three-wheeler philosophies, 1933. The Morgan (*top*) is a sociable motor cycle on three wheels for the sporting fraternity; the BSA (*bottom*) is a car with one less wheel to exploit a loophole in the then British tax laws. On Morgans, the single rear wheel was driven by chain; on the BSA, power was transmitted to the two front wheels by spur gear. The Morgan was a somewhat crude if rapid fun-car which lacked either a foot accelerator or coupled brakes, while the standard electric starter couldn't really cope with the 40-hp 1,096-cc vee-twin JAP engine, available with air or water cooling to choice. Like the Morgan – and unlike conventional British four-wheelers of the period – the BSA had independently sprung front wheels, though designer F. W. Hulse chose a transverse arrangement rather than the Morgan's traditional coils. From 1930 to 1932, it used the company's own smooth if not very powerful 1,021-cc overhead-valve air-cooled vee twin, a smooth and flexible water-cooled four being an option thereafter. Note the inboard front brake drums: the BSA's anchors, like the Morgan's, were coupled. The Birmingham-built three-wheeler, however, did not long survive the withdrawal of the tax concessions in 1935, albeit BSA continued their Scout line of front-wheel drive four-wheeled models. Morgan survived, even if sales dropped dramatically from 659 in 1934 to 137 in 1936. The reason for their survival was, of

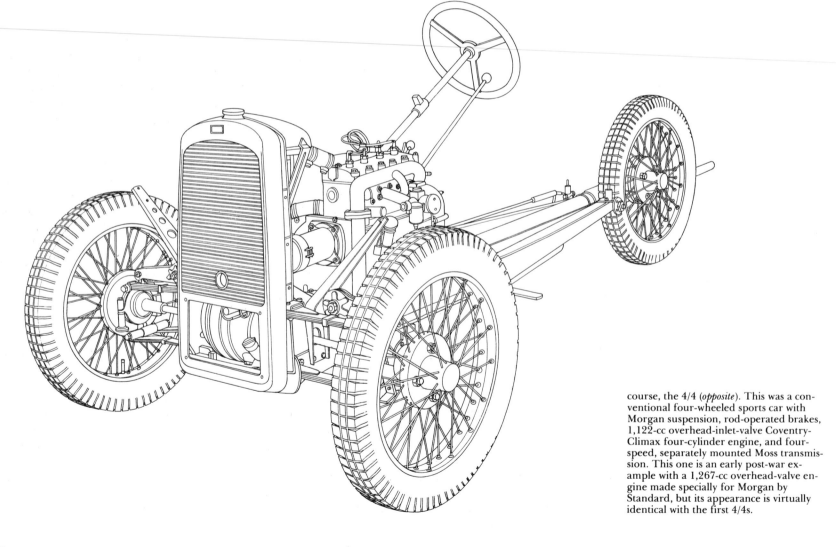

course, the 4/4 (*opposite*). This was a conventional four-wheeled sports car with Morgan suspension, rod-operated brakes, 1,122-cc overhead-inlet-valve Coventry-Climax four-cylinder engine, and four-speed, separately mounted Moss transmission. This one is an early post-war example with a 1,267-cc overhead-valve engine made specially for Morgan by Standard, but its appearance is virtually identical with the first 4/4s.

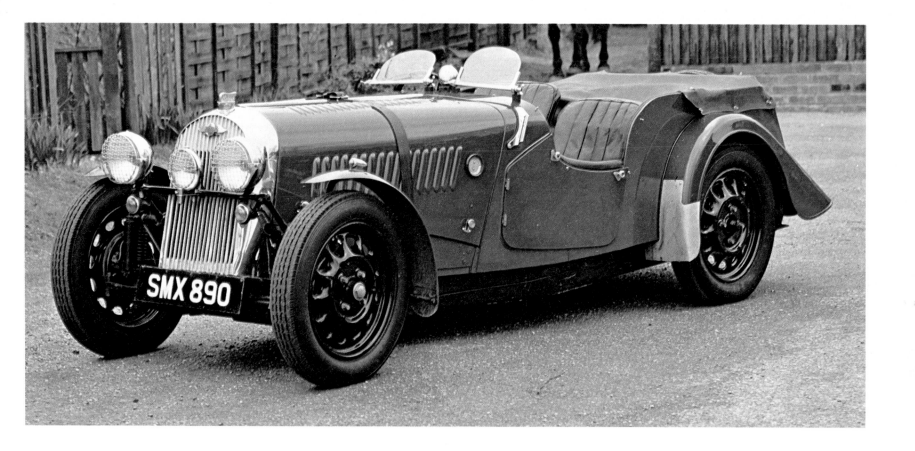

simple. Above all, the product was "trials oriented", and "trials" meant assaults on the narrow, muddy, and near vertical. Oddly, this did not make for high ground clearances; what it did add up to was an assortment of depressingly low axle ratios. The product, however, furnished cheap fun: in the middle 1930s, £220 ($1,100) would buy an overhead-camshaft MG or Singer which could be driven to work during the week and used for mild competitions at the weekend. After MG switched to three-main-bearing crankshafts in 1934, the events did not have to be quite so mild, either, while the later pushrod T series were a great deal more civilized. Of the pseudo-sports fringe (Morris 10/6 Special, Hillman Aero Minx, Talbot Ten), perhaps the less said the better, though they looked the part, especially when cluttered up with stoneguards, quickfiller fuel caps, grab handles on the dash, and leather bonnet straps.

By contrast, the three-wheeler, once a national favourite, was on its way out. Tax concessions in its favour were withdrawn in 1935, and within two years, the number of manufacturers in this sector had fallen from five to one. The one, inevitably, was Morgan, and even they could never have kept going but for the introduction of their four-wheeled 4/4 at the beginning of 1936.

The semi-luxury specialists, by contrast, had no real equivalents anywhere else. There were some parallels with Delahaye, La Licorne, Salmson, and Ariès in France, while Hansa, BMW, and Hanomag in Germany, and Lancia in Italy catered for the same sort of clientele. Their cars, however, were wholly different.

The annual potential of the factories in this sector could be anything from three hundred to six thousand units. Chassis tended to be unsophisticated; of 1938's major challengers – Armstrong Siddeley, Daimler-Lanchester, Riley, Rover, SS, Talbot, and Triumph – only the bigger Humber-based Talbot and the smaller Daimler products offered

independent front suspension. Triumph alone considered hydraulic brakes worth the candle. Separate chassis and traditional composite-construction bodies were the order of the day, and fancy aerodynamics were confined to Triumph's mock-Pontiac grille. Outside Daimler's carriage-trade contributions, cylinder capacities ranged from the 1,185 cc of the Talbot Ten (shared with the cheap Hillman Minx) to the 3,670 cc of the biggest Armstrong Siddeley. What one did get – and for prices well within reach of Britain's prosperous middle class – was wood and leather, proper facias with circular dials, windtone horns, sliding roofs (very British indeed!), and built-in jacks. The 1½-litre SS Jaguar sedan offered 70 mph (112 km/h) and 26 mpg (11 lit/100) for £298 ($1,490).

True, the squeeze was on, and God was, as always, on the side of the Big Battalions. This meant SS (working up to five thousand units a year), Rover (with a potential double this), and the subsidized cars such as Rootes's Talbot and the touring MGs from the Nuffield Group. Riley and Triumph already hovered on the verge of receivership, and Armstrong Siddeley were sustained by a devoted clientele and a healthy aero-engine business. The British Salmson company, whose limited-production S4C and S4D had competed in the same class, were about to abdicate into precision engineering. SS and MG enjoyed modest export sales in countries like Switzerland and Portugal, but the others were for strictly British and Empire consumption.

Britain offered the widest choice of any country. Fifty-two different makes were quoted in 1930, from Morris (fifty-two thousand cars that year) to Beverley, who made perhaps fifteen expensive straight-eights in eight years and regarded automobiles as a hedge against a possible decline in their general engineering business. In 1939, admittedly, only forty-one marques survived, but variety was still limitless. At the bottom end of the spectrum was the comic Rytecraft Scootacar, a road-going dodgem which no one took seriously; at the other end was the twelve-

Yes, the Singer (*opposite* and *bottom*) is British. It couldn't have been made anywhere else, this 1934 Le Mans Nine sports two-seater. Though they'd been the third biggest British manufacturer (after Morris and Austin), Singer never recovered their form thereafter, struggling on with small outputs, diminishing profits, and (latterly) outmoded shapes they couldn't afford to scrap. There were usually too many models (the 1932 catalogue included side-valve, pushrod overhead-valve, and overhead-camshaft engines), while their successful small sports cars suffered a mortal blow in 1935 when the entire works team was eliminated from the Tourist Trophy with spectacular steering failures. This, as well as low overall gearing aimed at the trials fraternity, gave the Singer an unhappy image with the traditionalists which it didn't deserve. The company's adherence to two-bearing crankshafts after MG had gone over to three in 1934, didn't help, either. On the credit side, Singer were among the pioneers of overhead-camshafts on cheap, mass-produced cars. Their utilitarian Junior (1927–32) was so equipped, as was its successor, the 972-cc Nine, on which this twin-carburettor sports model was based. By 1935, all Singers had overhead-camshaft power units, while even the small ones had hydraulic brakes, not to be found on any MG before 1936.

With one foot always in the "bread and butter" camp – there were seven basic models in 1934, from the Nine sedan to a seldom-seen 2.2-litre pushrod Silent Six – and no outside backing, Singer could never really compete against MG, who made sports cars and nothing else, and had the support of the parent Nuffield organization. Something like 2,500 Sports Nines – tourers, coupés, and two-door sedans as well as this Le Mans speedster with its exposed slab-shaped fuel tank – were made in 1934. The model was good for 75 mph (120 km/h), could be worked up to 56 mph (89 km/h) in the lowish third gear, and could manage 30 mpg (9.3 lit/100). The make was exported to Sweden and France as well as to Commonwealth countries. The pictures show the fold-flat windshield, aero screens, humped cowl, spring steering wheel, and quick-filler fuel cap. This example has suffered some modifications: side lamps were originally fender-mounted, and fenders are of the full cycle type favoured for trials rather than the longer "street" version: those at the rear have been shortened. The 1948 Fiat 1100B (*top*) was in some ways a more modern answer to the Singer formula: in other words, a four-door sedan of little greater capacity (1,089 cc) or overall size, which was quite as fast, rode better, used less fuel, and handled like a sports model. And by the time this one was built, the 1100 family had been in production for eleven years. Fiat, however, were careful when it came to running a parallel line of sports models. Such things did exist, but they were expensive and made in very small numbers: more impecunious Italians made do with home-tuned sedans.

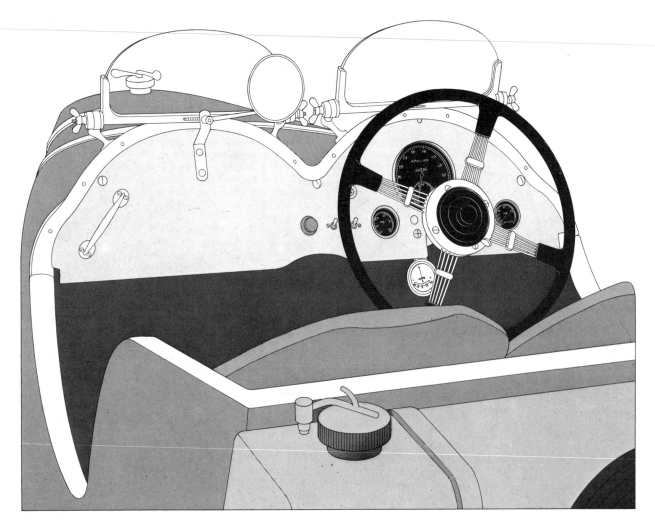

KV 5669

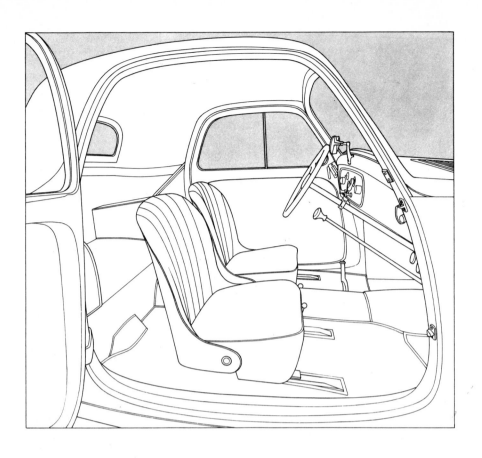

Franco Fessia's masterpiece was the 1936 Fiat 500 (*opposite*). Italians called it *la topolino* (Mickey Mouse is feminine in their language!), Britons the mouse, and Danes the *mariehøne* ("maybug"). This is Simca's French-built version, though only the badge tells one so. Note the lift-off hood (in front of the radiator), the hatch in the firewall giving access to the dash-mounted fuel tank, the sliding windows (extra body width!), and the recessed door handles. The interior would take two six-footers easily, but the back space was strictly for luggage (or, in emergency, small children). Adults were apt to dislodge the battery hatch and receive either current or acid on their hindquarters. It was, however, worth it for the superb handling and a negligible thirst – 51 mpg (5.5 lit/ 100).

French convention and advanced thinking from Germany. Neither the 1938 Hotchkiss 686 (*top left*) nor the contemporary Renault Celtaquatre (*centre left*) boasts either independent front suspension or hydraulic brakes, though Hotchkiss had tried the latter and found them wanting. The Renault's 1,463-cc two-bearing flat-head four-cylinder engine has roots going back to the mid-twenties, and the styling of this cabriolet is very American indeed. The Hotchkiss isn't styled at all, but boasts an indestructible 3.5-litre pushrod six giving 100 hp in touring form and up to 130 as a *Grand Sport* – a true *grande routière* for those who didn't fancy the complexities of a Bugatti or the exotic coachwork all too often inflicted on Delages, Delahayes, and Lago-Talbots.

German engines weren't always inspired: side valves sufficed for both the 1935–36 Mercedes-Benz 200 (*top right*) and the 1,074-cc unitary Opel Kadett (*centre right*). The Mercedes, with a laboured 60 mph (95–100 km/h) from two litres and 40 hp, would have been less happy on an *Autobahn* than the Hotchkiss, but all four wheels are independently sprung and brakes are hydraulic. The Opel, of course, was both transport for the people and a fertile source of foreign exchange for the Treasury: export prices were subsidized down to the point where Britons paid less (£135, in fact, or $675) than Germans. For this money one got only the basics: Dubonnet knee-action suspension (and all this implies) at the front, no synchromesh, and the most austere of interiors. Nonetheless, 75,060 Opels were sold abroad in the last three years of peace.

Different approaches in different lands. (*Above* and *opposite, bottom*) two of Vittorio Jano's classic Alfa Romeos, the 8C-2300 straight-eight and the 1,900-cc twin overhead-camshaft six of 1933 which was the final flowering of the original 1750 line. The six, for all its late twenties engineering, actually ran to synchromesh – though never left-hand steering. Note the proper visible 'gate' and positive reverse stop of the ventral gearshift, and the liberal drilling of the chassis to save weight. The 2.3 was just about the fastest "street" machine one could buy between 1931 and 1934, with as much as 165 hp available from the supercharged twin-camshaft straight-eight engine, lots of noise, and in-

credibly direct and sensitive steering. At some time, it has been updated with a characteristic 1937-style Alfa grille. Even more individual, if less sporting, was the 1937 T87 Tatra from Czechoslovakia (*opposite, top*) featuring an air-cooled vee-eight engine at the rear of a backbone frame. Ride was excellent, and 95–100 mph (150–160 km/h) was good going on an unblown 3-litre sedan. In pre-Second World War days, it was not as yet reserved for the political elite, hence over 2,300 were sold up to 1939, plus another 1,721 in the early post-VE years. Too small for Americans in 1936 was the Willys 77 (*opposite, top right*), with 2.2 litres, 48 hp, and only four cylinders, long after Ford

and Chevrolet had abdicated into multi-cylindered units. Wheel-base was 100 in (2.5 m), and home-market customers paid only $415 (£83). Willys were, however, going through a period of receivership, so the end-product was what it looked to be – warmed-over 1933 with mechanical brakes, a beam front axle, and no synchromesh. Its modest sales should have warned Standard, Fiat and Renault that their early post-Second World War 2-litre sedans weren't the answer to the people's car question, ... and yet, not a few Australians replaced their fifteen-year-old Willys 77s with Standard Vanguards.

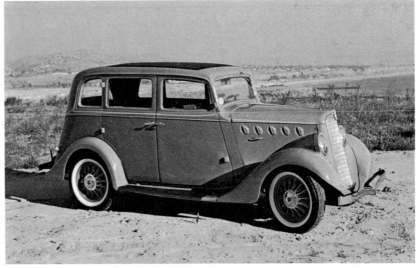

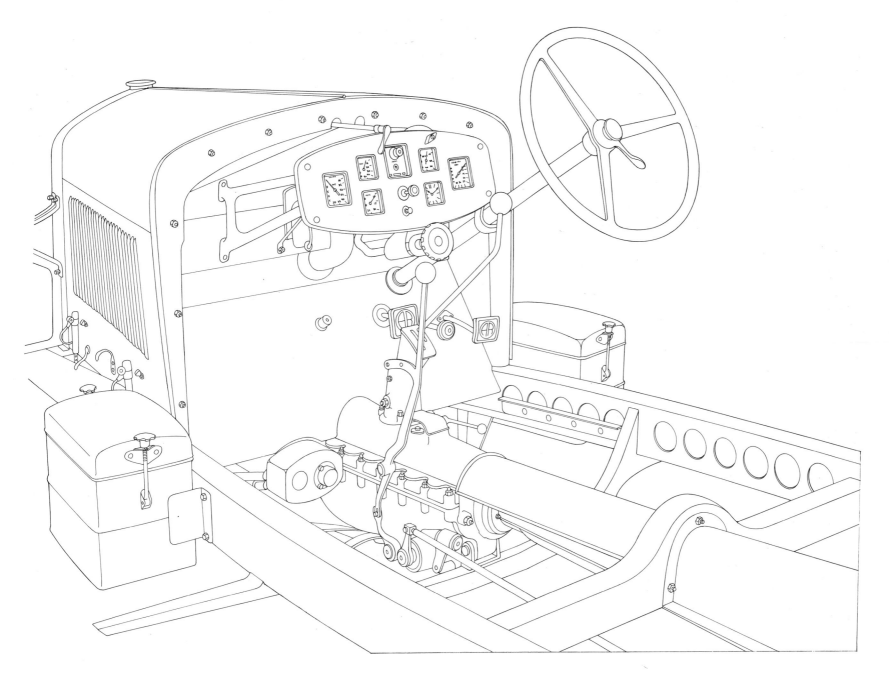

cylinder Phantom III Rolls-Royce, priced from £2,800 ($14,000) upwards. Specialist machinery included the Anglo-Americans of Atalanta, Jensen, and Railton, and even a chain-driven sports model, the Frazer Nash, of which one (the last) was completed that year. Ranges were complicated: Morris offered five models, from the 918-cc Eight up to the 3.5-litre 25, and his group (by now embracing Riley as well as MG and Wolseley) could ring the changes on twelve distinct and different engines and thirteen basic chassis types. Standard, whose biggest car was a six of a mere 2.7 litres, had five other models, a policy which spelt rationalization only by comparison with their 1936 programme – three distinct and separate ranges adding up to a total of ten models. One wonders how they made it all pay.

We have met most of the other British characteristics already. There were no cheap cars with independent front suspension before 1935, and even in 1939, no Nuffield, Austin, or Dagenham Ford product was so equipped. Hydraulic brakes were coming into the picture, with Rootes gradually making the switch in 1939–40, albeit Standard, Austin, and Ford stayed with mechanicals. Every de luxe sedan – and some with a "standard" tag – had a sliding roof, and only Fords used cloth trim unashamedly, though in the under-£200 ($1,000) class all that shone was not necessarily leather. Wood could well be appliqué over metal, too. Efficient synchromesh was, however, mandatory; a car like Italy's Lancia Aprilia with a really fast traditional change would have been unthinkable. Equally unthinkable in Britain would have been its short-stroke engine – 1,352 cc from a British drawing-board would probably have come out at 11 hp, possibly 12, but never at 13, as was the case of the Aprilia in Britain.

Britain was, perhaps, the extreme case, not because her export-to-production ratio was the lowest, but because the distribution of her exports was so narrow. Other countries had their national characteristics; if a typical British offering was a Ten of 1,100–1,300 cc, the Frenchman tended to go for something larger, say 11CV and two litres.

Such a formula reflected a bigger country and longer distances, but while France was the home of the *grandes routières*, her touring machinery was stolid and dull, with the emphasis on toughness rather than on delicacy of handling or luxurious appointments. Few cattle were sacrificed to furnish the interiors of Citroëns or Renaults. Brakes were not a strong point; of the Big Three, only Citroën offered hydraulics, even in 1939, and the *traction* itself was an oasis in a dreary desert of mediocrity – the Renault Monas and Celtas, indestructible Peugeots with their worm-drive back axles, sedate Berliets and Unics. Really small cars had little appeal; cyclecars were dead by 1925, and a year later, Citroën dropped their 5CV. It was much mourned, but nobody came up with a viable replacement. Rosengart's gallicized Austin Seven never sold as well as it might. In the Depression year of 1933, Mathis offered a miniature of under one litre's capacity, but the smallest of the big sellers were the 201 Peugeot (1.2 litres), the Renault Monaquatre (1.4 litres), and the 8CV Citroën (1.5 litres). Just before the war, Renault made a bid for sales with their Opel-inspired 1-litre Juvaquatre. If there was a copy-book French type, it was the *familiale*, called a *commerciale* when the addition of a fifth door at the rear made it possible to carry goods in it as well. This station-wagon ancestor (the term is still applied to "stripped" wagons) was a catalogue staple, often afflicted with abysmal ratios: top on long-chassis Peugeot 201s of the 1931–32 period was 7.76:1. While usually found in the 10/11CV taxation class (Citroën even retained rear-wheel drive for their 11UA series as late as 1938), *familiales* and *commerciales* were offered on the 747-cc Rosengart chassis. The success of Citroën's post-war 2CV, a rationalization of this theme, shows that the demand was, and is, genuine.

Autostradale influences spelt "square" engine dimensions and high top

(*Bottom left*) Fiat's Ardita of 1934 was one attempt to combine easy access with doors of moderate width. Other addicts of the pillarless system included Triumph and MG in Britain and Licorne in France, though in the United States Chrysler dropped it like a hot potato after showing one prototype in 1933. The reasons were not hard to find: eliminating the centre pillar might permit the fitting of four-door sedan bodywork on the abbreviated 88.5-in (2.25 m) wheel-base of Fiat's original Balilla, and arthritic aunts might still get in and out painlessly. However, aged passengers would be less appreciative after the car had received a few years of hard usage. Doors "worked" and warped, with some unpleasing rattles and draughts. Reliable latches were also a problem, though Fiat persisted with the arrangement until the end of 1952 on their 1100.

(*Bottom right*) Conduite intérieure avec malle (trunk sedan) was a frequent term in French catalogues of the early thirties, though the trunk was either an optional extra or reserved for de luxe models, such as this 1932 CGL Citroën at the top of the company's range. Stylistically, the concept was primitive: the trunk looked the afterthought it was, and since bodies were often made shorter to accommodate it, they tended to seem naked when it was not specified. Many trunks opened only at the top, limiting their usefulness. On the Citroën version, however, the back also came down, and the spare wheel with it, adding to the weight of the lid and to the strain on the hinges.

(*Top right*) Hatchbacks in 1953? Yes, but we didn't call them that. In fact, the idea goes a long way further back, to the "commercial sedans" by American (Willys) and British (Jowett, Morris) manufacturers in the late twenties and early thirties. Such an idiom had an even greater following in France, where just about every maker of inexpensive cars offered a *commerciale*, usually a long-chassis edition of their four-cylinder model with room for seven or eight, detachable rear seating, and a fifth door at the rear. Citroën's 10CV (and later 11CV, as seen here) had sufficient power to cope with the extra load, but cars like the Austin Seven-based Rosengart also received the treatment, resulting in abysmal gear ratios and negligible performance. Ordinary, hearse-style side-opening doors were commoner in the 1930s, but when Citroën reintroduced their *commerciale* for 1953, the entire tailgate (including the *traction*'s new projecting trunk) swung upwards to give maximum loading width as well as height.

Hanomag

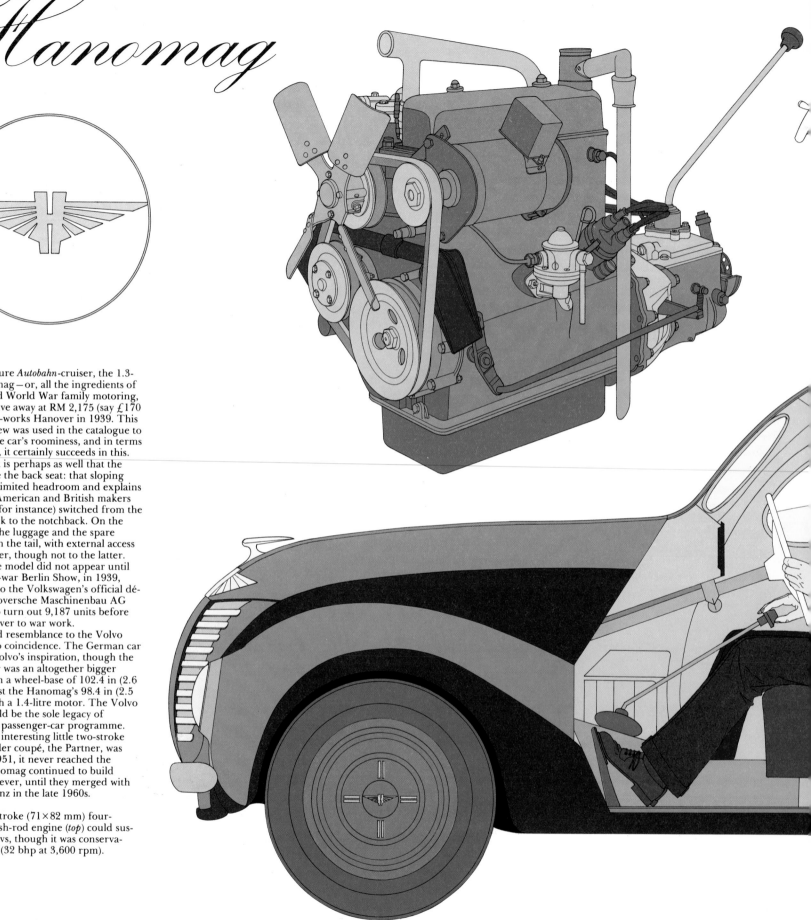

The miniature *Autobahn*-cruiser, the 1.3-litre Hanomag—or, all the ingredients of post-Second World War family motoring, ready to drive away at RM 2,175 (say £170 or $850) ex-works Hanover in 1939. This sectional view was used in the catalogue to illustrate the car's roominess, and in terms of legroom, it certainly succeeds in this. However, it is perhaps as well that the ladies chose the back seat: that sloping roof spells limited headroom and explains why some American and British makers (Standard, for instance) switched from the true fastback to the notchback. On the Hanomag the luggage and the spare wheel live in the tail, with external access to the former, though not to the latter. Though the model did not appear until the last pre-war Berlin Show, in 1939, (this was also the Volkswagen's official début), Hannoversche Maschinenbau AG managed to turn out 9,187 units before they went over to war work.

A marked resemblance to the Volvo PV444 is no coincidence. The German car served as Volvo's inspiration, though the Swedish car was an altogether bigger vehicle, with a wheel-base of 102.4 in (2.6 m) as against the Hanomag's 98.4 in (2.5 m), and with a 1.4-litre motor. The Volvo PV444 would be the sole legacy of Hanomag's passenger-car programme. Though an interesting little two-stroke three-cylinder coupé, the Partner, was shown in 1951, it never reached the public. Hanomag continued to build trucks, however, until they merged with Daimler-Benz in the late 1960s.

The short-stroke (71×82 mm) four-cylinder push-rod engine (*top*) could sustain high revs, though it was conservatively rated (32 bhp at 3,600 rpm).

172

(*Top left*) A full alligator hood gives plenty of room round the engine. Characteristically German was the all-independent suspension, and brakes were hydraulic; synchromesh was absent, being reserved for the company's bigger cars.

(*Top right*) There are two simple dials on the facia, but no wood, real or simulated, within. Or leather upholstery, for that matter. The windshield pillars are rather thicker than would be tolerated today, and rearward vision is not the Hanomag's strong suit, either.

gears in Italy, but the proximity of the mountains could produce some very peculiar intermediate ratios. A wide gap between second and third was little better than the old British formula of "three bottoms and one top". Brakes and handling, however, were generally good, and one had to over-rev an Italian engine well beyond its limit before expensive noises supervened. Of the Fiat *Millecento* it was said that the manual specified 4,400 rpm, it throve on 4,800, and could *occasionally* attain 5,200 with impunity. Much the same parameters governed German thinking, only the German was a less exuberant driver, addicted to the massive and willing to accept poor low-range acceleration in return for sustained *Autobahn* cruising speeds. Long experience with motor cycles had also inured him to the two-stroke, and proper mixing pumps were available at most garages.

Of the other isolationists, an odd case was Czechoslovakia. Alone of 1919's new Treaty Republics, she had inherited a ready-made automobile industry. In Habsburg times, Praga, Skoda (Laurin-Klement), and Tatra (Nesselsdorf) had been respected names, albeit their products seldom ventured far outside Franz Josef's domains. The country was self-sufficient and stayed that way, thanks to savage protectionism.

Exports, it is true, were limited to neighbouring Central European countries; it was not until 1937 that Czechoslovakia's Big Three began to look westwards. The industry, however, had its own problems. Its average annual output in the 1930s was a fraction under ten thousand passenger cars, divided among four major and three minor concerns, and no factory ever broke five thousand units in a single season. Yet Praga, Skoda, and Tatra, at any rate, had to be general providers in the sense of Renault or Fiat, with potentials of over fifty thousand a year and extensive outside interests. Not that the Czechs were lacking in this latter respect, Skoda (and the Ceskoslovenska Zbrojovka, makers of the Z automobile) were major arms firms, and Praga and Aero had extensive aircraft interests. But to make everything from utility runabouts to luxury limousines was really beyond their compass, and whatever the country's post-war ideology, some rationalization would have been imperative. In 1937–38, there were twenty-four distinct and separate native models on the market, Skoda alone contributing seven. This diversity becomes even more startling when one reflects that Britain's Big Six offered less than thirty basic types in the same period. None the less, bad roads and an engineering tradition led to some interesting results: the big Tatras wore their air-cooled engines at the rear; Aero, Z, and Jawa featured front-wheel drive, and there was not a single beam front axle in sight.

The Czechs were isolationists with export aspirations, but Japan remained a closed shop. By 1939, a few Datsuns had found their way into neighbouring Far Eastern countries, and there had even been an abortive trial batch sent to Australia in 1934, but Japanese cars were treated with the same derision as Japanese aircraft. And with some genuine justification in this case – there was nothing of the quality of the Zero aircraft in the automobile industry's locker.

Japan, in fact, laboured under almost every imaginable deterrent. True, her swingeing import duties had been successfully circumvented by the United States's Big Three and their assembly plants – so much so that the government had to clamp down on such activities in 1938. But nothing could be done about the brutal tax structure, worse than Britain's or Italy's. Cyclecars, admittedly, paid only £11 ($55) a year, but the annual rate on a 20-hp model (say 3 litres' capacity) was £62.50 ($312.50). Further, a complicated structure of automobile control laws laid down exactly what an "authorized vehicle" was. These laws covered not only the cylinder capacity, length, width, and useful load, but also the price and even the number of forward speeds! Up to 1933, a top limit of 750 cc was imposed on domestically produced models, and even

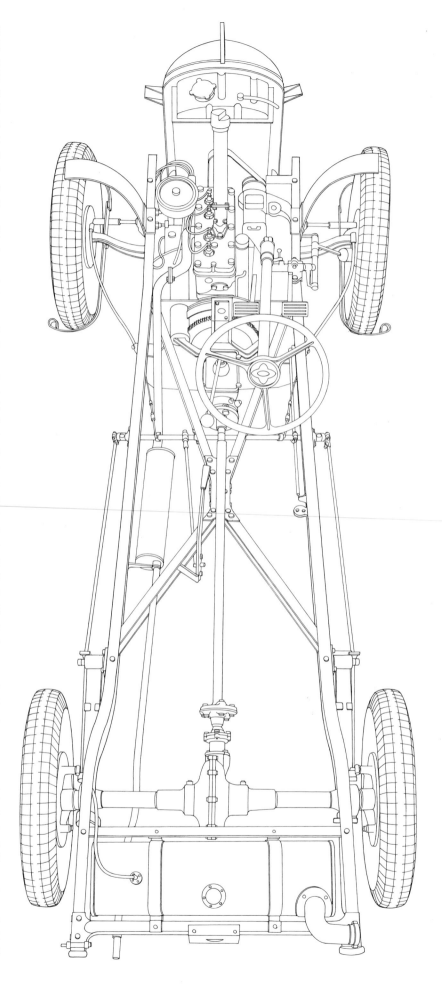

Very typical of Japanese design in the 1930s and clearly conceived round restrictions of size was the Ohta. A short and simple chassis frame (*opposite*) has some rather fragile-looking cruciform bracing, while brakes are cable-operated, and the engine is a small side-valve four of 736 cc. Bodies (*top right*) are not unattractive, though an inch or two of extra wheel-base would have improved their proportions. Big cars were mainly for the armed services, and the 1937 Nissan Six was effectively the cheaper species of Graham Six with a 3.7-litre engine in 1935 form. Graham provided both the body dies and technical assistance.

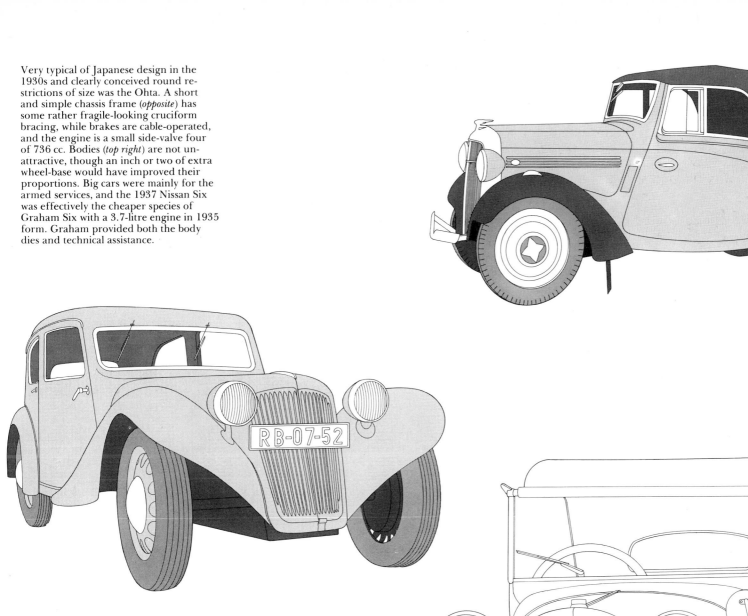

Czechoslovakia's Aero evolved from a primitive minicar (*bottom right*) into a modern front-wheel drive two-stroke (*centre*). Novotny's original model was built up around a punt-type frame riding on quarter-elliptic springs, with no front-wheel brakes and no differential. Incredibly, a string-type starter of the outboard type was fitted. The original 500-cc water-cooled single-cylinder engine soon gave way to a 662-cc twin. By contrast, the 1937 Type 30 had all-independent springing and a 1-litre two-cylinder power unit giving 32 bhp. Like many front-wheel drive cars, Aeros kept their gear levers on the dashboard. A handful of A30s were produced after the war, but the Aero Minor of 1946–52, though also a front-drive two-stroke and partly built in the Aero works, was in fact a Jawa descendant with plenty of DKW in its ancestry.

Which of the two upper cars is the conservative? Logically, one would suspect the Mercedes Benz Type 320 from 1938 (*top right*), as it has the styling that characterized most of that company's cars for some twenty years from 1934 onwards. In its pre-war form, the Type 320 had a flathead six-cylinder engine which had either 2 litres' or 2.3 litres' capacity producing 40 and 50 hp respectively. It is difficult, in fact, to distinguish between the 1935 Type 200 and the Type 230 of immediate pre-war vintage, as the middle-class car buyers of Central Europe were at that time more interested in solid construction and reliability than in styling. The 1948 Holden sedan (*top left*) belongs to a different generation, though what one cannot see is actually more conservative: the Holden had semi-elliptic springs at the rear, while Mercedes Benz had long been advocates of swing axles.

One must remember that the basic 1948 Holden shape (see also pages 186–87) was still around in 1956, with only a new grille to distinguish the FJ of 1953 from the original model. By this time, the 1938 Cadillac Sixty Special theme was almost antediluvian. Not that this mattered too much in Australia, of course. Once you got away from the main centres of population, roads were still bad, so a high ground clearance and a soft suspension were highly appreciated. Furthermore, many Australians considered simple mechanics and good dealer service to be more important than keeping up with the Joneses of the United States. (Anyway, if one wanted current American styling, there were always the locally assembled Fords.)

Two generations of baby cars, the one unwanted, the other well-loved. The

American Austin roadster of 1932 (*centre left*) was an attempt to sell Britain's favourite Baby (*opposite, centre*) to Americans who only thought they wanted it. They liked the cartoon jokes and the posed publicity pictures showing Hollywood starlets with the car, but the shrewd journalist who pointed out that the Austin cost 41 cents per lb, or roughly double of what one had to pay for a Model A Ford, had hit the nail on the head. It had a mirror-image 747-cc engine to accommodate left-hand drive, disc wheels and demountable rims instead of the spidery wire wheels of the British edition of the car, and front-end styling aped Chevrolet.

The first year's sales amounted to 3,633 units. During the eleven years of its life, the American Austin (later Bantam) was never far from receivership – and often in it.

The Fiat 500 of 1936 (*centre right*) was the logical successor to the British Austin. It was a big car in miniature, with independently-sprung front wheels, hydraulic brakes, and a four-speed synchromesh transmission. Its handling was viceless up to its maximum speed of 53 mph (85 km/ h). Fuel consumption was staggeringly low and the roll-top convertible body just about the cheapest example of the style on the market. In nineteen years, nearly half a million units were produced by Fiat themselves, while licence production was carried on in France and Germany. Its designer, Dante Giacosa, wisely kept it a strictly two-passenger job until the more powerful valve-in-head 500B engine was developed in 1948.

(*Opposite, top*) The Buick of Central Europe. This sectioned view of the 1939 Type 230 Mercedes-Benz Six reveals its

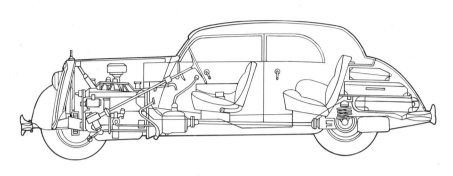

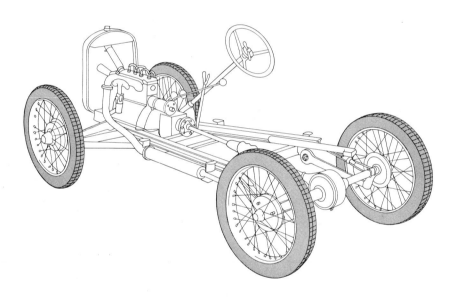

twenty-five years later, nothing over 1,500 cc was permitted. Such bigger cars as did reach the market – in 1937, the Toyota had a 3.2-litre motor and Nissan-Datsun's near-Graham was a six of 3.7-litres' capacity – went mainly into government service. Indeed, makes such as Chiyoda and Sumida were about as available to the average Japanese as was the ZIS to Russians.

Dimensional rules, of course, bred miniatures. The mid-thirties Datsun, with an Austin-like 722-cc four-cylinder engine, was a mere 123 in (3.1 m) long and 46 in (1.2 m) wide, appreciably shorter and narrower than even a Fiat 500, though slightly bigger than Herbert Austin's original Seven of 1922. These miniatures were necessary, for the country's roads were narrow, and the streets of her cities narrower still. Here the need was for a motorized substitute for rickshaw or handcart, in the form of odd little three-wheelers with two driven rear wheels. Though Daihatsu would later cram a sedan body onto such a chassis, this Japanese speciality was almost invariably a commercial vehicle. The strain survived into 1972.

The government's main objectives were trucks for the armed forces and the expulsion of American commercial interests. They were uncomfortably aware that less than 2,800 of 1934's 35,000 new registrations were of purely native origin. Slowly, General Motors and Ford were squeezed out, but though Nissan-Datsun's 1937 passenger-car potential was said to be 15,000 units, the authorities had no intention of letting them make that quantity. Trucks were wanted – and trucks had to be made. Toyota's output between 1936 and 1942 was revealing: 20,000 commercial vehicles, but only 1,404 of their Chevrolet-based sedans and phaetons. Production and sales controls were tightened in 1939, and from 1940, distribution was controlled as well. And while Japan was incapable of satisfying domestic demands, she was unlikely to become a force in foreign markets. In any case, nobody wanted a 1929-type baby car with 1933 styling and a 6.5:1 top gear.

The third great bastion of isolationism would, ironically, be the United States, though this was by no means apparent in 1939, when cars were still being shipped abroad at an impressive rate. Even 1940 was quite a good export year. The Buick, as a relatively expensive automobile, was likely to suffer worse from the events of September, 1939, than Chevrolet or Ford, but the season's foreign shipments were still a creditable 9,872 units.

Alas! the war cut the United States off from many of her safe markets. The loss of the European belligerents was not a disaster, but Nazi expansionism had overrun many of the profitable "neutrals" and isolated the others. Even Australian sales had begun to taper off long before Pearl Harbor – Ford's deliveries were down from the pre-war peak of 14,584 units to a mere 3,479 in 1941. This effectively left South America, where requirements did not differ vastly from those at home, apart from a need for fewer frills and tougher suspensions. Thus, Detroit's 1941–42 models were clearly designed for Americans, presaging 1946 form. Also hovering in the background was an increasing domestic trend towards overall speed limits. Cars were being designed to be safe to 70 mph (110–115 km/h) and no more, and to the established deficiencies (in European eyes, that is) were to be added brake fade. We shall see what happened in the post-war era.

In smaller countries, the concept of a "national car" never bulked as large as one might expect. There were no dramatic balance-of-payments problems in the 1930s; thus, it was cheaper to import than to set up an industry from scratch. Or, for that matter, to prop up one that was dying on its feet, as in the classic case of Belgium. There never was such a thing as a typical Belgian car – from the standpoint of King Albert's subjects, that is.

Here was a country rich in minerals and technical *savoir faire*, and

independent rear suspension by swing axles and coils. It also shows its conservative proportions, with the engine set well back in the frame. One did not expect an exciting performance, even with an overdrive top gear, on 55 hp in a vehicle with a weight of 3,150 lb (1,430 kg), but, like the Buick, it was solidly built, it was backed by a good dealer network, and it came with a goodly variety of bodies, from a roadster to a limousine. This is the Cabriolet "B" – standard Mercedes-Benz label for a full convertible with two doors, four seats, and four windows. The two-passenger "A" was, of course, more elegant and destined to become an international collectors' piece in the 1970s.

Basic Baby of the 1920s – and of the early 1930s, too – with copies, licensed or otherwise, emanating from Butler (Pennsylvania), Paris, Eisenach, and Tokyo.

This Austin Seven chassis (*centre*) is a 1929, but the crude A-shape with minimal rear bracing was still around at the end, ten years later. So was the primitive suspension inherited from Peugeot's 1919 Quadrilette – a single transverse spring at the front and longitudinal quarter-elliptics at the rear. The 747-cc flathead four-cylinder engine was progressively worked up from 10 to 16 hp, but the car put on too much weight too fast – from 784 lb (365 kg) in 1923 to 1,456 lb (660 kg) in 1937. The four-speed transmission adopted in 1932 didn't help much, since the extra ratio came in at the bottom, and with its 23.3:1 ratio, it was very much an underdrive. In 1929, of course, the four-wheel brakes were still uncoupled, which meant the use of both pedal and lever in a crash stop.

Putting The Works Up One End. The Czechoslovakian Tatra 77 of 1935 was 212 in (5.4 m) long and, though the ingenious wrap-round windshield, shown in the head-on view, made for excellent forward vision in conjunction with a vestigial hood, the sloping tail reduced the driver's rearward view to virtually nil. The sectioned view shows how the hood (a) was utilized to house the spare wheels (two were usually carried) and the reservoir for the centralized chassis lubrication, though there was generous luggage accommodation (b) over the fuel tank, behind the rear seat. Early 77s had a central driving position, but on production models left- or right-hand drive was available, the latter being the rule in Czechoslovakia until 1938. The tube of the central backbone (c) can be seen behind the front seat: this forked out at the rear to carry the engine. Independent front suspension was by a transverse-leaf arrangement; at the rear longitudinal cantilever springs (d) were used in conjunction with an oscillating axle. The engine, an air-cooled vee-eight developing 60 hp, drove forward via a single-plate clutch four-speed synchromesh transmission. Note the provision for a starting handle (e), which could produce the comic, if occasional, sight of an embarrassed chauffeur cranking his limousine from the "wrong end". The entire power pack could be removed for servicing.

backed by one of the richest and most heavily exploited African colonies, the Congo. But in the pioneering years, Belgian automobile manufacturers were mesmerized by the proximity of the snobbish British market, where both Métallurgique and Minerva were firmly established in 1914. The latter company, indeed, retained their foothold there into the early 1930s. They also had useful connections in France, Scandinavia, the United States, and even in Germany. Unfortunately, as we have seen, Minerva's speciality was the first victim of the Great Depression, as the company was wedded to the obsolescent Knight sleeve-valve engine, and their idea of a cheap car, 1934's 2-litre M4, was the sort of thing the French made cheaper. Even a belated fusion with Imperia, the country's no. 2 maker and already an empire through the absorption of several lesser companies, achieved little, since Imperias, though more modest than Minervas, were also competing against French imports in the 9–11CV category. The Liège arms firm of FN did, admittedly, try to offer something more suitable for the man in the street, but once a relaxation of tariffs added the challenge of Renault and Citroën to that of the Americans, they abdicated. No passenger cars were made at the Herstal works after 1935. By the time the Germans invaded the country in 1940, the only Belgian automobiles in production were Imperia's local editions of the front-wheel-drive Adler from Frankfurt. *Achetez Belge* – a slogan plastered over FN's last catalogues – was now a dead letter.

The Austrians tried rather harder. In 1919, having lost three of their more successful factories to Czechoslovakia, they were left with only Ferdinand Porsche's sporting Austro-Daimlers, Puch (always more interested in two-wheelers, into which field they would abdicate in 1925), the Steyr arms firm, and Gräf und Stift of Vienna, whose wares matched the Rolls-Royce in quality and price alike. Of these, only the Steyr had any widespread appeal, the firm operating as a one-man band

from the late 1920s right up to 1938's *Anschluss*. By this time, they had merged with Austro-Daimler and Puch, phasing the former's luxury cars out of production by 1935. Thanks to ordnance and truck interests, they remained commercially viable on sales which averaged four thousand units a year during our period and on modest exports, comparable to Czechoslovakia's. In principle, however, Austria was linguistically, economically, and technically too close to Germany to support a domestic automobile industry, and it is significant that, after the Second World War, Steyr-Daimler-Puch AG restricted themselves to local variations on themes by Fiat.

Chacun à son goût is scarcely a term applicable to Soviet Russia, where there were no shareholders and precious few paying customers, even during the more capitalistic phase of Stalin's New Economic Policy. Lenin and his successors had to rebuild an economy devastated by external and civil wars. Roads were never the country's strong suit, and in the dark winter of 1919–20, many bridges had been cut up for firewood. In any case, Tsarist Russia, for all Nicholas II's Delaunay-Bellevilles and profitable agencies for makes like the German NAG, the Italian Fiat, and the British Vauxhall, had never registered many cars. There were only some six thousand all told in 1912, of which perhaps one-third were based in St Petersburg (Leningrad).

Thus, the passenger automobile played a minuscule part in the scheme of things. Imports were minimal; latterly, they consisted of big Packards and Lincolns intended for VIP transport. Serious manufacture, likewise, did not begin until 1932, with the construction of the huge Gorki factory (GAZ). Gorki's staple was the Model A Ford in 1930 form. Remarkably, in view of the harsh climate, these were invariably open touring cars in the early days. The GAZ-A and its more sophisticated descendants – they looked like 1934 Ford V8s but used four- and six-cylinder engines – represented the only personal transport any

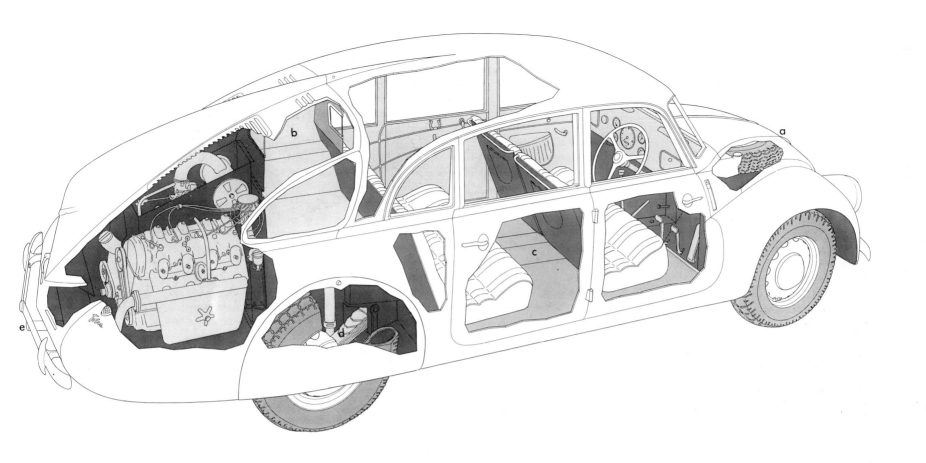

citizen could hope to acquire. The Buick-based ZIS of 1936 was strictly a badge of rank and made in quantities so small that the cost per unit was reputedly $75,000 (£15,000). Ironically, Old Henry's Model A would end up as more of a national automobile in Russia than ever it was in its homeland. Russia's version of the Jeep was authentic Model A underhood, and commercial editions were still being made in 1948. Total production has been conservatively estimated at 1.5 million units.

Russian thinking, in fact, centred on obsolescent foreign designs that were simple to produce and could be operated with minimal maintenance. American themes would be supplemented after the war by German, when Opel's Kadett tooling was seized as reparations. This policy would pay off in the end, though not until the early 1960s, when the 2.4-litre Volga sedan, an updated amalgam of 1930 Ford and Willys ideas, began to find buyers in more backward countries on the strength of an adequate ground clearance, simple engineering, and a comprehensive tool kit. State-subsidized export prices, of course, played their part. But even in 1950, there was no such thing as a typically Russian automobile.

To find "national" cars, we shall have to turn to Sweden and Australia, and only the former country had anything concrete to offer before 1948.

Like Belgium, Sweden was a highly developed country, but geographically she was very different. Distances were long, the winter climate harsh in the extreme, and the railroad system hampered by the terrain. Something more flexible was wanted, though initially Swedish industry concentrated on trucks. Tidaholm built little else, while Sweden's two major pioneer makers, Scania of Malmö and Vanis of Södertälje, celebrated their 1912 merger by gently phasing out their passenger-car lines. The process was complete by 1924. For the time being, Swedes were content with American automobiles and their high ground clear-

ances, though as a neutral, the country never barred German machinery, as did the victorious Allies. Quite a few German cars found Swedish buyers in the 1920s.

Motorization, however, spread apace. By 1927, Sweden's 127,000 passenger cars compared interestingly with Italy's 172,000, and the far-sighted Assar Gabrielsson was recognizing the need for a native product to compete against the wares of Detroit.

Belgium had built cars for foreign plutocrats who ran out of money. The British built cars for themselves, and the Japanese built them in spite of themselves. Gabrielsson and his partner Gustaf Larson, however, set out to build something tailor-made for Swedish roads and Swedish motorists; in other words, a commonsense affair based on American designs and created by men with first-hand experience of the American industry. Better still, the Volvo was designed from the start to incorporate components suitable for adaptation into light trucks of up to 2 tons' payload. Their famous side-valve six of 1929 may have had close affinities with the Continental from Muskegon, Michigan, but it had a long run in private and commercial applications. Nothing was ever wasted; even in the late 1950s, an American-style vee-eight intended for the abortive "Philip" sedan (it looked like a 1951 Kaiser!) was made to pay for itself in the group's last petrol-powered four-tonners.

True, the Volvo looked like last year's efforts from Detroit, and styling tended to be a strange mixture of opposing American strains. The idea almost foundered at birth because its creators elected to market the original ÖV4 as an open tourer, in a country with arctic winters! Fortunately, sedans (type PV4) were on the market by mid-1928. Since trucks were as yet Volvo's mainstay, the operation could survive on modest annual sales. The 1,000-a-year mark was not passed until 1937, and the best pre-war performance was 2,034 units in 1938. Further, by British, French, or German standards, Volvos were

By the end of our period, there were only 168,262 post-war civilian examples in circulation, which meant well over another eighteen million to go, but only a Venusian would fail to recognize this as the Volkswagen Beetle, albeit in original 1938–39 form. From the side, the only obvious differences from a VW of the 1970s are the absence of chromium-plated brightwork and energy-absorbing bumpers, though once behind the wheel one would notice the difference: some 20 mph (32 km/h) less in maximum speed, a corresponding lack of acceleration, the need to double declutch when shifting gears (no synchromesh in '39), and rather uncertain cable-operated brakes. What you do have is the low wind resistance, sufficient to assure *Autobahn* cruising speeds of 55–60 mph (say 95 km/h) on a car that won't go much faster except downhill. Ferdinand Porsche also struck the perfect compromise between a long hood (space consuming on a rear-engined car) and the "cab over engine" effect one gets on light commercials such as VW's own Transporter and the modern American Chevyvan. Sitting ahead of the front wheels can have a disorienting effect on those without a truck-driving background.

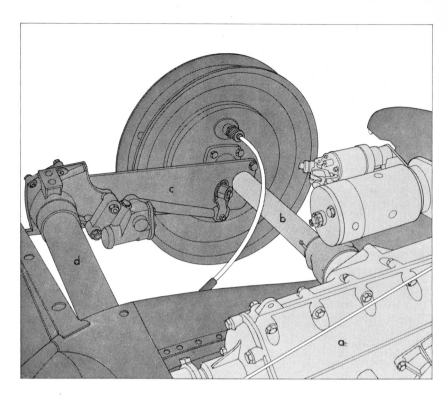

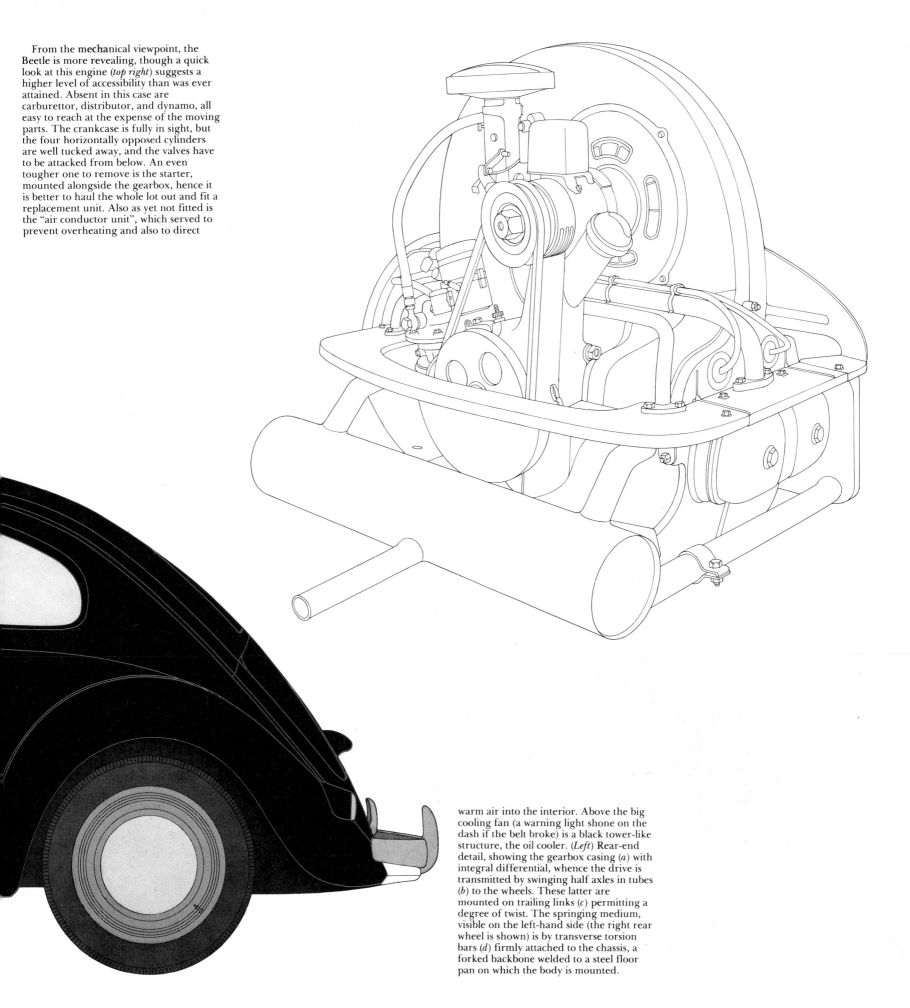

From the **mechanical** viewpoint, the **Beetle** is more revealing, though a quick look at this engine (*top right*) suggests a higher level of accessibility than was ever attained. Absent in this case are carburettor, distributor, and dynamo, all easy to reach at the expense of the moving parts. The crankcase is fully in sight, but the four horizontally opposed cylinders are well tucked away, and the valves have to be attacked from below. An even tougher one to remove is the starter, mounted alongside the gearbox, hence it is better to haul the whole lot out and fit a replacement unit. Also as yet not fitted is the "air conductor unit", which served to prevent overheating and also to direct

warm air into the interior. Above the big cooling fan (a warning light shone on the dash if the belt broke) is a black tower-like structure, the oil cooler. (*Left*) Rear-end detail, showing the gearbox casing (*a*) with integral differential, whence the drive is transmitted by swinging half axles in tubes (*b*) to the wheels. These latter are mounted on trailing links (*c*) permitting a degree of twist. The springing medium, visible on the left-hand side (the right rear wheel is shown) is by transverse torsion bars (*d*) firmly attached to the chassis, a forked backbone welded to a steel floor pan on which the body is mounted.

181

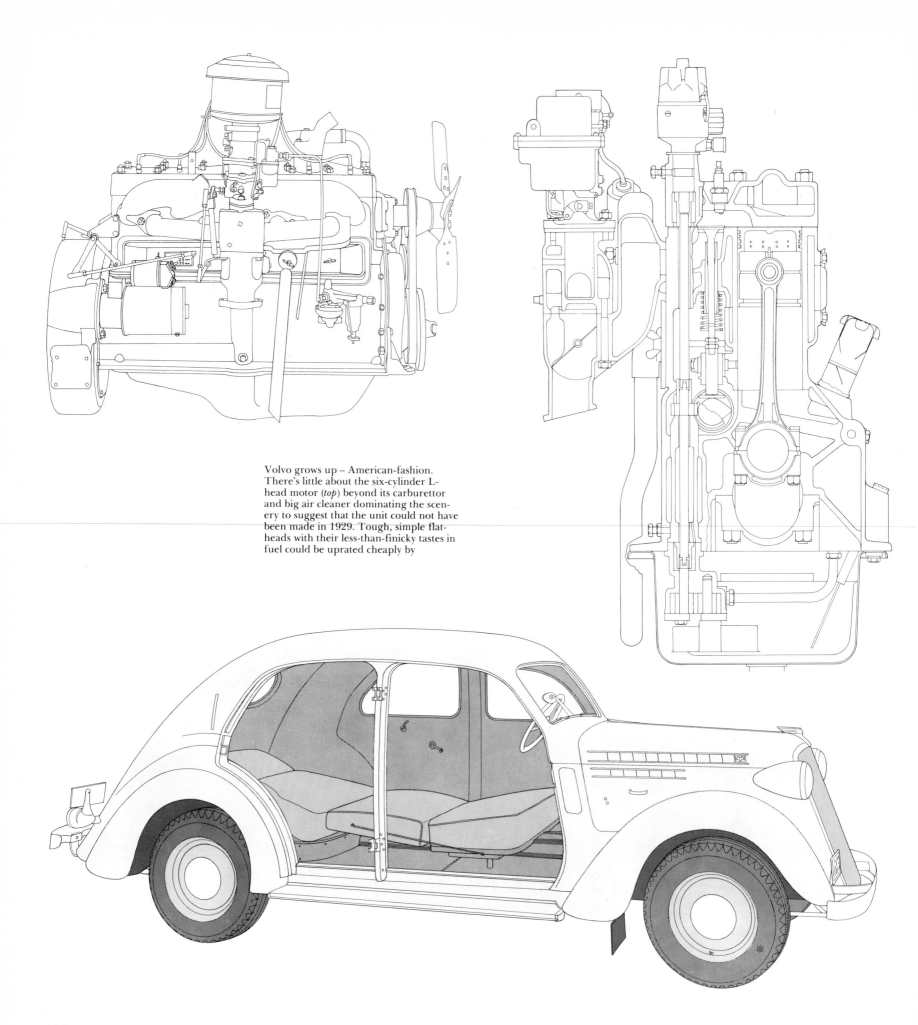

Volvo grows up – American-fashion.
There's little about the six-cylinder L-
head motor (*top*) beyond its carburettor
and big air cleaner dominating the scenery to suggest that the unit could not have
been made in 1929. Tough, simple flat-
heads with their less-than-finicky tastes in
fuel could be uprated cheaply by

On the post-war PV60 we get the same American themes slightly warmed-over to resemble the new Detroit line of 1940–42. The upper view does not show either of the two major mechanical changes: coil-spring independent front suspension once more and a steering-column gear shift. The transatlantic heritages visible are an upward-opening alligator hood, a Dodge-style fastback sedan body with a gentle slope to allow for adequate headroom, and a generously-dimensioned trunk of external-access type. Running-boards have virtually vanished: not so the headlamps, which Volvo preferred to keep out of doors in the interests of cheaper repair bills – and manufacturing costs, for that matter. From the side, the car could easily be mistaken for a 1940 Dodge or Plymouth, but the front end (bottom) was pure 1939 Pontiac.

lengthening bore or stroke (always the latter in countries with tiresome tax formulae!). The Volvo was no exception: it gained some 700 cc and 35 hp in a decade and had a thirty-year run. Volvo, like some American makers (Chrysler, Hudson) even tried independent front suspension, only to drop it again for a while. This happened on the PV51/52 of 1936 (bottom), promoted as "Sweden's

Ideal Car". This picture shows one of the principal differences between the PV52 and the cheaper PV51 – seats which fold down to form a bed. In 1938, Nash would make great play with this aspect of the "living room on wheels" image (later they would even offer accessory window curtains for hard-up honeymooners) but Sweden seems to have pipped the United States in this case.

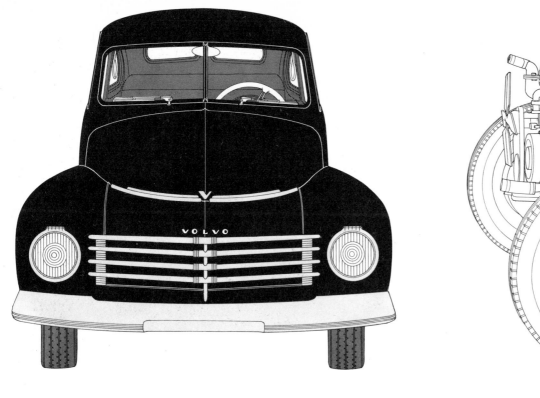

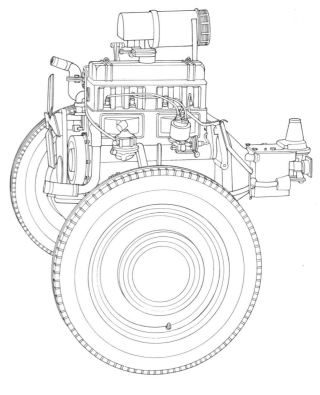

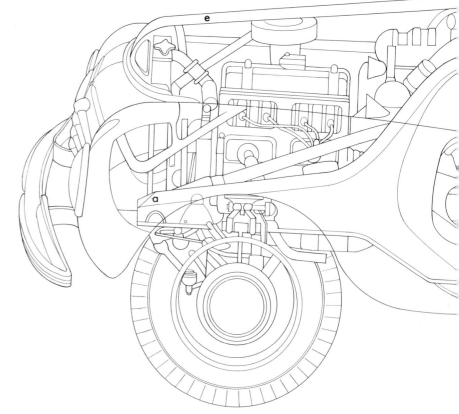

Even if the Saab board – and their clientele – might not agree, the Volvo PV444 had virtually become Sweden's national car by the end of our period. It was certainly the only Swedish model one was likely to encounter outside the homeland, albeit export sales were limited and ventured no further afield than the Low Countries. The shape was American: the box front fenders (*top left*) reflect the 1942 Ford, and the fastback (*opposite, right*) was clearly inspired by General Motors's 1941 two-door styles. Even more aggressively Detroit is the facia (*opposite, left*), notably the plastic horn rim and the arcuate speedometer later cribbed by Rootes of Britain for their Humber Hawk and Sunbeam-Talbot 90. The use of three forward speeds rather than four likewise reflects American thinking, while on early PV444s there were such American-built components as Carter down-draught carburettors, Autolite coil ignition, and Wagner hydraulic brakes. Volvo, however, preferred a floor shift in the willowy 1930s idiom. Basing their design on the German Hanomag 1300, Volvo's engineers, like Holden's in Australia, opted for unitary construction, an act of faith in view of their modest production potential in the 1940s. Their faith was justified – the 100,000th car of the type left Gothen-burg in January, 1955, and even then the shape had ten years of life in front of it. Front-end styling changed – so did the underhood scene – capacity went up from 1.4 to 1.8 litres, and output from just over 40 to some 80 hp, which meant speeds in excess of 90 mph (145 km/h) instead of the 73 mph (117 km/h) of the original version. The structure, of course, stayed the same way all along the line. Power pack and front suspension (*top right*) were mounted on the front horns of the base structure, Citroën-fashion (*a*), and the floor pan (*b*) was integral as well. A low drive line was assured by a hypoid rear axle (*c*). Streamlining is more than skin-deep, with a recessed fuel filler (*d*) in the rear quarter panel, while the hood, as on the contemporary six-cylinder PV60, is of alligator type (*e*). The use of rigid axles and coils (*f*) echoed Buick practice since 1938, though the Volvo handled well. Despite the limitations of three forward speeds, the car would accelerate to 50 mph (80 km/h) in just under 18 seconds. If, in early days, it was not truly competitive – even on the home market in 1947 it cost £3 ($8) more than an imported Hillman Minx – it was faster, more powerful, and better sprung than the British car, and the spares situation, obviously, was easier.

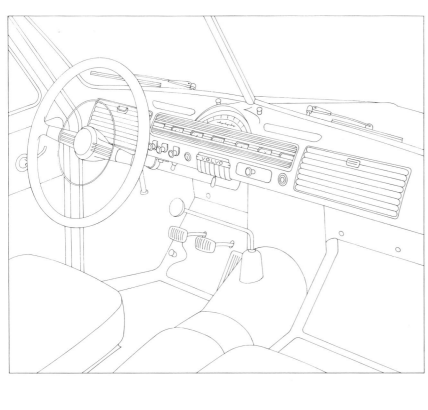

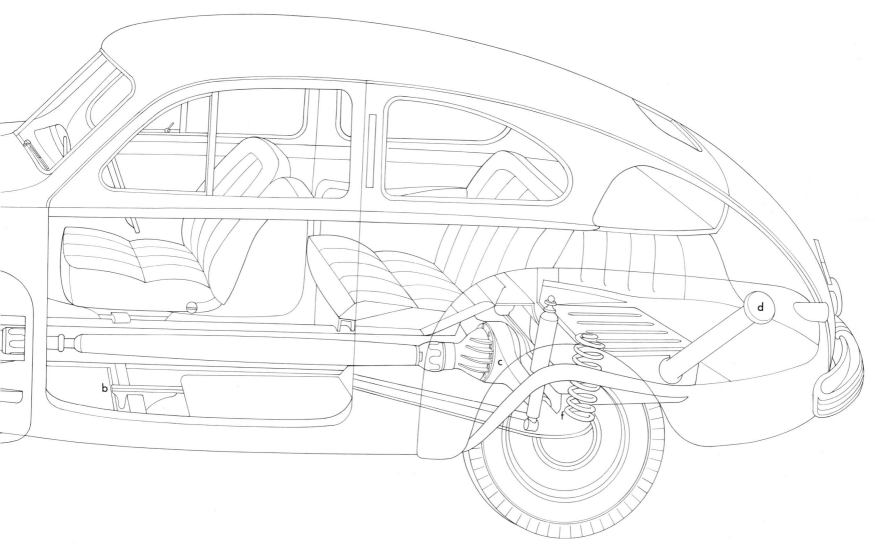

At first sight this appears to be an American "compact" about twelve years ahead of its time. This impression extends far beyond the 1946–48 stylistic idiom – integral headlamps, three-piece grille, heavy bumpers with overriders, vee windshield, and a sedan configuration obviously inspired by 1938's Cadillac Sixty Special. Beneath the skin, the resemblance continues: at the front we find a classic coil-spring arrangement and a straightforward overhead-pushrod six-cylinder engine of Chevrolet-like appearance complete with valve down-draught carburettor and big air cleaner. The gearshift lever is on the steering-column, and the drive is transmitted via an open propeller-shaft (Chevrolet, admittedly, preferred a torque tube) to a hypoid bevel rear axle. Brakes

are, of course, hydraulic: mechanicals had effectively vanished from the American automotive scene by 1940. If the rear springs seem unduly long, they are the semi-elliptics long beloved of Detroit. The right-hand steering, of course, might puzzle slightly at a time when the United States was cut off by the dollar crisis from many a British Commonwealth market, and the car sits somewhat high – in fact, ground clearance is 9½ in (24 cm). What gives the game away on so typical a General Motors layout is the use of full unitary construction in the Vauxhall or Opel idiom, something as yet confined in the United States to smaller makers like Nash and Hudson. Here is "Australia's Own Car", the 2.2-litre Holden in its original 1948 form, often incorrectly termed the

186

bespoke: though side-valve engines alone were cited in catalogues, the overhead-valve versions used in later trucks could, and did, find their way into passenger cars on a special-order basis. The PV656 family of 1935 was available in eight distinct variants – sedans, limousines, taxis, and specialist light commercial chassis. When the war interfered with fuel supplies, Volvo not only marketed their own wood-gas generators, but threw in a well-engineered trailer to carry the latter unit. Exports were of no significance; other European countries had, in any case, little interest in expensive mock-American sedans when they could buy the real thing more cheaply. Volvo, however, were quietly building up their foreign truck connections. By 1939, they had outlets in South America and South Africa as well as agencies in Belgium, Finland, and Holland. These exploratory efforts were to stand them in good stead when they switched to smaller and more individual sedans in 1945.

If Gabrielsson and Larson drew their financial support from the SKF ball-bearing company, Australia's Holden had the advantage of an even bigger head start, as a product of a wholly owned General Motors subsidiary in Melbourne. Though its story properly belongs to the late 1940s, it merits inclusion at this juncture as a copybook national-car scheme.

Not that it was the first such attempt. F.H. Gordon's Australian Six of 1919 very nearly succeeded. It foundered – as had the Anderson and the Jordan on the other side of the Pacific – because it was built up from an assortment of assembled bits. Worse still, they were American bits, and there was no such thing as air freight in the early 1920s. No degree of quality control could be exercised over something that Gordon's team could not make themselves, and a flood of complaints and "warranty replacements" had put his company out of business by 1925. Subsequent essays in the American-Australian and Anglo-Australian idioms – right up to 1935's Auburn-like Egan Six – went the same way. The American article was cheaper and had a name behind it. In any case, Australian dealers were reluctant to take on anything with a history of service troubles.

A sizable saving on duties could, in any case, be effected by importing cars "completely knocked down" (CKD) and using local labour to assemble them. Major American and British manufacturers followed this policy in the 1930s, many of them saving the washing still further by fitting Australian-built coachwork. In 1930 alone, Holden's Woodville plant – still independent of General Motors – built bodies for Austin, Chrysler, De Soto, Morris, Hillman, Humber, Hupmobile, and Willys-Overland as well as for all the General Motors breeds then marketed in the Commonwealth. Even after the American giant moved in a year later, Holden still kept some outside contracts. Their last would be a series of Hillman Minx sedans put together in 1948. Interestingly, their 1935 "sloper" (four-passenger fastback coupé) for General Motors-built chassis would serve as the prototype for the two-door Chevrolet Fleetline of 1941.

After the Second World War, Australia found herself with an ever-growing demand for cars and better roads, and a chronic balance-of-payments problem. Thus, "Australia's Own Car" was born.

The technical genesis was, of course, anything but Australian. Rival schools of thought ascribe the origins to Vauxhall and to a rejected Buick compact laid down in 1938. Nevertheless, American-built prototypes received a 237,000-mile (nearly 380,000 km) workout on Australian roads before detail design was finalized.

The theme was simplified American – not far removed, indeed, from six-cylinder Vauxhalls or Opels. Dimensions were modest; the 2.2-litre pushrod motor was capable of propelling the car at close on 80 mph (130 km/h), and fuel consumption at normal driving speeds was in the region of 25–30 mpg (9.5–11 lit/100). A nationwide dealer network was

FX model. (The name was given retrospectively, and it has stuck.) People still argue over the Holden's origins. Some say it was an abortive compact Buick of 1938, others suggest Vauxhall ancestry, but essentially, it is an American theme adapted to Australian conditions and put into production at Melbourne. It is a compact – wheel-base is 105 in (2.7 m) as against the 116 in (2.9 m) of the contemporary Chevrolet, weight is a low 2,350 lb (1,066 kg), and suspension soft enough to cope with the appalling roads of the Outback. Over 120,000 FXs were sold in the 1948–53 period. Australia would, however, have to wait until 1956 for the first Holden of truly Australian design, the FC. Even then, grabbing brakes and peculiar handling were the price paid for a truly national automobile.

Anatomy of a Miniature, 1931. Tax loopholes as well as financial stringency could ensure cyclecar-survivals, and special reduced rates applied in the early 1930s in Britain (for three-wheelers only), in Japan, and in Germany, where, in the last years of the Weimar Republic, the owner of miniatures like this Goliath Pionier could dispense not only with circulation tax, but with a driving licence as well. The Goliath marked the first flowering of the empire of Carl Borgward, a man to be reckoned with in the 1950s, when he controlled two makes of truck and three of passenger car. From the outside his Goliath was quite good-looking, with single steering front wheel and drive to the rear wheels. Bodywork was the usual wood-and-fabric style also found on the famous DKW, the short snub nose suggested the popular Czechoslovakian Tatra (also available as a three-wheeler in 1930–31), and weight was a low 767 1b (350 kg). The car was also cheap – RM 1,460 (£73 or $375) in basic form and RM 1,510, if the more powerful 247-cc engine was specified instead of the regular 200-cc type. An electric starter was standard, and both open and closed variants were available. Photographs were even published of a coupé with a rumble seat. The rear view (*bottom left*), however, suggests that the engine room at the back would intrude too far to make this viable

188

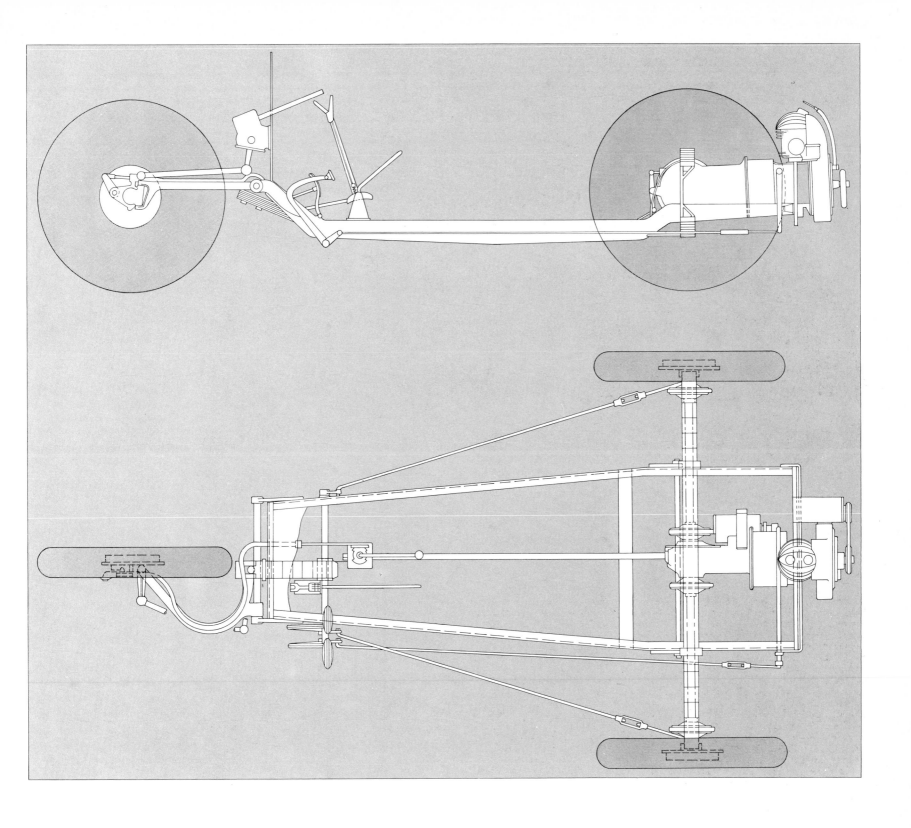

for any but small children. Some four
thousand Pioniers were made between
1931 and 1934, late cars featuring
aerodynamic coachwork. The Goliath
chassis (*above*) was somewhat crude. All
the works live at the rear, with the air-
cooled single-cylinder two-cycle engine
mounted over the rear axle, whence it
drives forward via a three-speed and reverse transmission and articulated shafts
to the wheels. Rear suspension is inde-

pendent by transverse quarter-elliptic
springs, and front suspension is by a
sprung front fork with car-type steering
gear. Also of car-type are the pedal controls, though once again we encounter
one of the inherent defects of rear-
engined automobiles: the lengthy linkages
connecting shift lever to transmission: not
that a "woolly" change would matter
much on a simple runabout capable of a
sedate 32 mph (50 km/h). Neither

diagram makes this wholly clear, but the
three-wheel brakes were of uncoupled,
early Austin Seven-type, with the pedal
working on the rear wheels and the lever
actuating a drum at the front. Borgward's
engineers ignored the then-popular
tubular backbone frame in favour of a
simple channel-selection affair which appears rather inadequately braced. It probably did flex too much: some cars had a
simple cruciform brace added amidships.

already there, and with a ninety-five per cent Australian content, the Holden could undercut the entire opposition. At peak, it would command forty-five to fifty per cent of the passenger-car market, and, even more incredibly, account for forty-one per cent of all new trucks, this at a time when the only commercial Holdens were pickups and panel vans based on the regular sedan. It would take over a quarter of a century – and an all-out effort by Ford's Geelong operation – to dislodge the Holden from its domination.

One species of automobile which might have survived from national conditions and prejudices was, however, doomed – the cyclecar. Its fate in Britain has already been discussed, and two seasons – 1914 and 1915 – had seen its mayfly-like cycle in the United States. All the appropriate tax concessions in France had been withdrawn in 1925. Thus, the cyclecar's impact in the 1930s was effectively confined to two countries – Japan and Germany.

Most of the Japanese species were, in any case, commercials. Datsun, however, did offer a single-seater, in 1932, to qualify for the annual motor-cycle tax, then a mere £1.50 ($7.50). The Datsun might be tiny; it was, nevertheless, a true car, for all its capacity of 495 cc.

German tax concessions survived into 1933, thus breeding all manner of oddities, such as the Framo, a restatement of the old Cyklon/Phänomobil theme dating back to 1902. The entire power pack – a 200-cc two-cycle motor and two-speed transmission – was perched over the front wheel, which it drove. Less barbarous were the same company's front-wheel-drive three-wheeler with a DKW car-type front end and the Goliath with two driven rear wheels and electric starting, but Hitler had other ideas, and by 1937, the sole survivors of this curious generation were light trucks and vans. Whatever his detractors might say of Hitler's *Kraft durch Freude* schemes, the Volkswagen was to prove itself as the best people's car since the Model T Ford.

Four wheels this time on another minicar from Germany, the 1934 Framo Piccolo. This one hailed from Hainichen in Saxony and was a private venture by J.S. Rasmussen, creator of the DKW and also of the great Auto Union combine (DKW, Audi, Horch, Wanderer). Framo tried various minicar configurations, among them a lethal three-wheeler with the engine mounted over the single front wheel, which it both drove and steered. Unlike the Goliath, the car used a forked backbone frame, at the back of which was mounted a 297-cc two-cycle single-cylinder power unit developing 8 hp. All four wheels were independently sprung, the vehicle weighed in between 750 and 800 lb (about 340 and 365 kg), and like the Goliath and the DKW, bodies were of wood with a fabric covering. Top speed was around 40 mph (60–65 km/h). The last Piccolos were cabrio-limousines bearing a marked external resemblance to the DKW, though the combination of a rear engine and a long dummy hood restricted carrying capacity and, on 300 cc, they could not hope to match the performance of Rasmussen's best-selling make with a 684-cc power unit. Nor were they significantly cheaper, which explains why total production of Piccolos in two seasons was 720 units, as against at least 30,000 DKWs in the same period.

Chapter 7

AFTER THE CONFLICT

As the tide of war swung in the Allies' favour, the press departments limbered up again. Hortatory paragraphs on rubber-saving gave way to hints of the future. Jensen showed an impressionistic and spectral shape which bore no relation to anything they would ever offer; there would be Fords in every American's future, and Buick, mindful that advancing GIs were now being exposed to the blandishments of the Volkswagen, headed their latest campaign with the punch-line, "Yes, the engine is still up front". According to Lagonda, "though the products of our company have always been fine, fast cars, it is worth reflection that they have not always been large cars".

But beneath the gathering euphoria, some awkward home truths were emerging. "The Ford in your future" might boast a "new ride", but in essence it was warmed-over 1942, and the unlucky Europeans hadn't even the 1942s to rehash. Across the Atlantic in England, Ford of Dagenham waxed nostalgic over such pre-war pleasures as "sixpence round the island" by boat. The only difference was that the copy-writer had inflated the charge to a shilling, and it was soon apparent that even this wouldn't be enough. Nor was Lagonda's 2.6-litre "small car", when it arrived in 1947, quite what a fuel-starved Europe wanted.

Everything was in short supply – fuel, rubber, sheet steel, manpower (demobilization took a long time), and above all, cars themselves. The United States was virtually the only country in which fuel was promptly derationed. France's sheet metal supplies had sunk to some forty per cent of the 1938 level, and too little of this, in the industry's opinion, was earmarked for automobiles. Italian factories were reduced to the salvage of wartime air-raid shelters. Britain faced a disastrous coal shortage which would close her plants during the hard winter of 1946–47. Bombing had neutralized many a company: among the worst hit were Alvis and Daimler in England, Daimler-Benz and Borgward in Germany, Peugeot and Renault in France, and Lancia in Italy.

Even in the United States, safe from the depredations of bomber and infantryman alike, production losses were running at some forty thousand cars a month in 1946. This, of course, highlighted one of the prevailing malaises of modern industry, and one that would get worse as the years progressed. The assemblers, it is true, had gone, but in their place had come the component specialists: Lockheed and Bendix for brakes, Corning for glass, and so on. These firms, unlike the purveyors of major units, were not owned by the automobile manufacturers and supplied more than one company. Sometimes, like Lucas in Britain, they enjoyed virtually a monopoly of their speciality. So if they were shut down, either through strikes or through sheer shortage of raw material, the whole industry could grind to a halt.

This, in effect, is what happened in Detroit during the latter half of 1945 and most of 1946. A shortage of door locks could bring body production to a standstill at Chrysler and Packard as well as General Motors. Once the flow was resumed, as likely as not there would be insufficient sheet metal, and so no doors to take the locks. It was not until mid-1947 that these problems had resolved themselves, and in the ensuing rush to cash in on the seller's market, their true implications were scarcely appreciated. Duplicated sources of supply, as a considered policy, were not a 1940s development, or even one of the 1950s. One has only to reflect what happened a few years later, when General Motors's principal automatic-transmission factory at Livonia, Michigan, burnt down, and this at a time when manual gearboxes had fallen from favour. Somehow the gap was filled, but it was touch-and-go.

In 1945–46, however, the car shortage was a more pressing headache. In Britain, it is true, registrations had slumped but mildly, from 1,924,394 in 1938 to 1,769,852 in 1946, but the exigencies of the export drive meant that the 2-million level would not be attained until 1949. In any case, a large proportion of those almost 1.8 million automobiles available at the return of peace were worn out and still commanding crazy prices. A 1931 Austin Seven, ripe for the scrapheap in 1939, might have made £15 ($75) on the strength of its low tax and upkeep costs. The writer was, however, asked £140 in 1946 for such a car, with sterling still nominally at $5 to the pound!

Elsewhere the situation was little short of desperate. Vehicles were scarce, and even where they existed, there were no tyres for them. Theoretically, there were still some two million passenger automobiles in France, but in 1945, it was reckoned that no more than 900,000 were usable. Transport in Germany had ground to a halt. Germans, of course, could not use their cars without permits from the Occupation authorities. Things had to carry on, but this was impossible with what was left. Only one in every six of Hamburg's pre-war car population had survived.

Nor was it a case of 1918 all over again. Now, the automobile was an integral part of life. What is more, there had been no real carry-over production, as during the first conflict. Everything had stopped with a bang in 1942. In the First World War, American involvement had not prevented the domestic production of nearly 950,000 units in 1918, sufficient to supply those neutrals and distant markets still accessible to shipping. This time, however, America "froze" her unsold stocks of cars, and though a certain number of civilian vehicles were made in Britain, Germany, and Italy, these were insufficient to supply even priority needs. Military vehicles were becoming more specialized, and

The spread of the American idiom. The calm of warmed-over 1942s was shaken in the summer of 1946, when Studebaker announced their 1947 line, the work of stylists Raymond Loewy and Virgil Exner. Here was the "coming or going" idiom with a short hood matched by a long rear deck. This meant, of course, the abandonment of the top-of-the-line straight-eights offered by the company since 1928, but Studebaker weren't alone in this policy, even before the first of the new short-stroke vee-eights appeared. Nash also decided not to reintroduce their Ambassador 8 family from 1942. Studebaker had, in fact, toyed with a rear-engine layout before opting once again for the conventional. The new cars were 7 inches (18 cm) lower than their predecessors, and everything was new save the motors, both flathead sixes, the 2.8-litre Champion seen here (*top* and *centre*), and the 3.7-litre 98-bhp Commander. Most spectacular of all the new bodies was the Starlight Coupé with full wrap-round rear window, not found on the more austere three-passenger Business Coupé.

Various forms of gas propulsion kept civilian traffic moving during the Second World War. Gas bags filled from city mains had been used during the first conflict and were again tried from 1939 onwards, as were cylinders of methane. The normal method was, however, the gas-producer plant which burnt coal or wood gas, the latter being obviously preferred in Scandinavia. On trucks it was either mounted behind the cab or on a trailer, but in the quest for more compact installations several makers tried to streamline it into the trunks of bigger cars. The

Swedish habit of placing the unit over the front bumper was not imitated. Producer-gas was an inefficient means of keeping the wheels turning, and caused a thirty-five to forty per cent loss of power: Volvo's six, rated at over 80 bhp on petrol, was down to 50 on wood gas. The Swedish manufacturer was the only firm who actually designed the system in: they furnished a neat, streamlined single-wheel trailer to carry the gas plant. This car (*opposite*) is an example of the PV53–56 series retained in production during the war years. Some vestiges of the unhappy Airflow shape of the 1935 Carioca are retained, but there are a projecting trunk at the rear and a 1939 Chevrolet-type grille at the front. The facia (*bottom left*) on the PV53–56 series was of a completely new design, the circular dial speedometer of the earlier models being replaced by a rectangular.

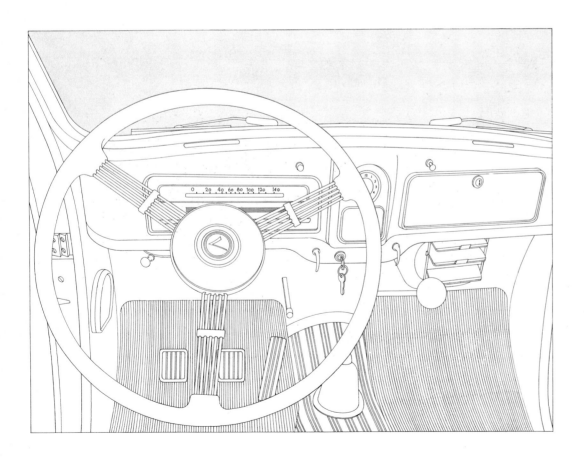

less adaptable to peacetime needs, as many people discovered when they acquired war-surplus Jeeps with a fuel consumption of 12–13 mpg (22–23 lit/100). Effectively the only country with a continuity of civilian production was Sweden, and here tight rationing (wood gas was hardly a practical substitute) held Volvo's deliveries down to less than 1,700 units between 1940 and 1945 – hardly enough for a country that had taken 14,000 cars from the United States alone in 1938. Switzerland, Australia, and New Zealand might have been untouched by the fighting, but they still needed transportation.

Worse still, their sources of supply were limited. The strongest industries in 1945 were those of the United States and Britain. Germany was under Allied military control and in process of partition. The American armed forces controlled Japan, not that her industry had ever amounted to anything. Italy and France had been fought over.

Technically and economically, the Americans had a head start of three seasons. One has only to compare their 1946 efforts (essentially 1942 models) with such parallel European sixes as Germany's Wanderer and Opel Kapitän, the French Viva Grand Sport Renault and 15CV Citroën, and Britain's 1939 quartet from Austin, Humber, Vauxhall, and Wolseley. Even allowing for their viability in a chilly economic climate – several of them vanished for good, notably the Wanderer, Renault, and Vauxhall 25 – they belonged, from one viewpoint or another, to a different generation. For all the Citroën's *avantgarde* thinking, its 1934 shape was not everyone's cup of tea – its complicated mechanics were ill-suited for emergent countries, and a formidable turning radius allied to heavy steering endeared it not at all to the ladies. Of the British contenders, only Humber and Vauxhall ran to independent front suspension, and the Austin's brakes, like those of the Renault, were innocent of hydraulics. Automatic transmissions, already available on 1940 Oldsmobiles, were unheard of in Europe, while the

still-common composite-body construction (not, admittedly, found on the unitary Citroëns and Opels) hardly lent itself to the pounding of washboard roads or monsoon rains. Thanks to the fiscal policies of the Old World, few of these offerings had an annual sales potential of anything like twenty thousand units, let alone a hundred thousand. Renault's average output of sixes ran at the three-thousand-a-year mark, while typical of form was the smaller four-cylinder Peugeot 402 (twelve thousand in a good season). In a higher price bracket, the Type 320 Mercedes-Benz, socially the equivalent of a Buick, seldom broke more than a couple of thousand units a year.

As for performance, nothing European in this category could cruise at over 70 mph (112 km/h), whereas a Buick or Ford V8, if not the lesser sixes, would hold 75–80 (120–130 km/h). Thus, the Americans should have been poised for the killing they made in 1919.

No such massacre eventuated. For one thing, the cars were too big – even the frugal and futuristic 1947 Studebaker Champion measured nearly 16 ft (4.6 m) from stem to stern, and a Chevrolet was crowding 5 metres, by contrast with the 4.45 m of a Humber Super Snipe and the 4.75 m of the big Renault with its obsolete American styling. The Citroën Six, regarded by Europeans as unwieldy, was appreciably shorter than a comparable Buick, Dodge, or Nash. Further, fuel consumptions were too high for those stringent days, a state of affairs which explains why the larger models faded from many a European catalogue. Under Pierre Lefaucheux's direction, Renault scrapped everything including their commercially successful 8CV range; Fiat offered nothing bigger than the 1500; and Vauxhall's biggest model between 1945 and 1948 was the 1.8-litre J Fourteen. Mercedes-Benz would not return to sixes until 1951, while in Sweden Volvo's thinking centred increasingly round the 1.4-litre PV444, a war baby.

But what really blocked an American renaissance – for all that chain

Hangovers and stopgaps, or how Britain's motor industry was back into production by the end of 1945. Both the exploded drawing (below) and the three-quarter rear view (bottom right) show 1946 Sunbeam-Talbots, though they could equally be 1940s, if not 1939s. The 2-litre shown in the drawing was just ready for production when Britain declared war. Both shape and engineering are conservative: an orthodox chassis underslung at the rear and hung on semi-elliptic springs, a side-valve engine set well back in its frame, a four-speed synchromesh transmission controlled by a long, willowy shift lever. Note also the big headlamps standing proud of the fenders, the twin trumpet horns (a Detroit fad way back in 1933!),

and the wheel discs concealing ordinary steel-spoke equipment. The trunk at the rear offered less room than would appear, thanks to the presence of the spare wheel. The differences between the 2-litre and the Ten (bottom right) were about 800 cc, 20 hp, a good length of hood, and hydraulic brakes (which you didn't get on the smaller car, which shared its mechanics with the Hillman Minx). Unlike the Minx, of course, it wasn't unitary: Sunbeam-Talbots would be made only with chassis right through to 1955. The leather upholstery wasn't always leather, either: on post-war cars Rootes used twin-trim, with the real thing only for the harder-wearing surfaces. Considering the conservative specification, the group did

well to unload nearly five thousand Tens between 1945 and 1948.

Germany returns to the fray. The Borgward Hansa 1500 sedan of 1949 was the first all-new design to rise from the ashes of defeat. It wasn't all that new, of course: the all-independent suspension and backbone frame with outriggers to carry the body had been found on Hansas of the 1934–39 period, and the 1.5-litre pushrod four-cylinder engine was a direct descendant of the old 1100. Ugly and slab-sided with a vee windshield, it was no best seller, either (22,500 in three seasons), but it paved the way for Carl Borgward's big success, the Isabella of 1954. Brakes were hydraulic, and the Hansa would top 70

mph (112 km/h). Column shift, alas, made its appearance early in the car's production run. The 1500 also accounted for a forgotten historical "first" – the first factory-fitted automatic transmission on a small European car at a popular price. The direct consequence of Herr Borgward's personal dislike for shifting gears, Hansamatic cost him dear. It worked well enough, but one had to stop dead before selecting reverse, and not everyone bothered. The ensuing expensive noises meant lots of guarantee repair claims in Bremen.

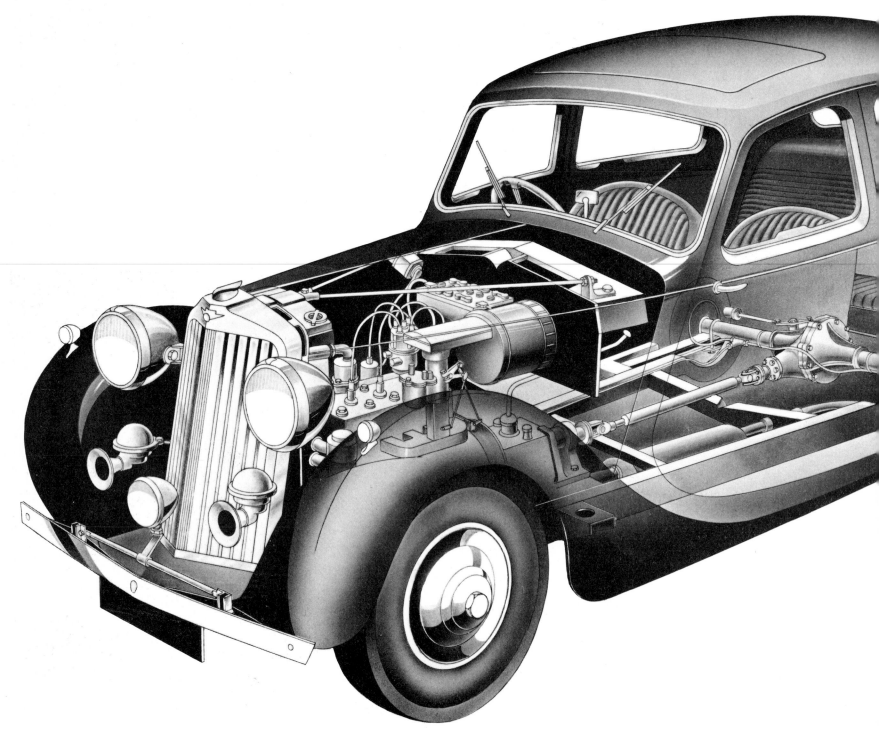

of assembly plants from Adelaide to Antwerp – was a worldwide dollar shortage, the price of being a creditor-nation. Ford, Chevrolet, and Plymouth were suddenly excluded from once-profitable markets. True, where currencies were strong and pre-war sales had been healthy, Detroit held its own. In Belgium, where Chrysler products, Ford, Mercury, Packard, Studebaker, and the entire native General Motors line-up with the exception of Cadillac were put together locally, American cars outsold all contenders, even in 1951. That year's figures showed 24,548 new American models registered, as against 14,949 from Germany, 11,485 from France, and 10,963 from Britain. In Switzerland, where imports tripled between 1946 and 1948, American cars virtually tied with British cars for first place in 1947. In 1950, they were still in fourth place, though by this time, Germany (which meant Opel and Volkswagen) had taken the lead for the first time since the war.

Australia represented the obverse, and commoner side, of the coin. As we have seen, the pre-war American car was tailor-made for Commonwealth conditions, yet in the three summer (i.e., Australian winter) months of 1949, when the Holden was as yet in its infancy, British factories furnished 3,741 new cars and their American rivals only 1,812. In 1951, the United States sent precisely 997 cars to Australia, 1,093 to New Zealand, and 7,735 to South Africa.

Somebody had to fill the gap, and that somebody was Great Britain. Suddenly, the tight little island found itself the general provider to the world, a role which called for rather more than the hasty translation of catalogues and manuals into foreign languages. Hitherto unknown breeds such as Armstrong Siddeley and Lea-Francis appeared on the streets of Ghent, Geneva, and Gothenburg, the process accelerated by a government which related steel allocations directly to export performances. Standard sent a small batch of cars to Peru, solely to claim another foreign outlet, but usually, there was a more energetic follow-through. Jaguar assembled cars briefly in Belgium to circumvent local import restrictions on luxury models, while the British Fords reached Stockholm within three months of VE-Day. Pre-revolutionary Prague housed Bristol and Allard agencies. At the first post-war Geneva Salon, in March, 1947, there were twenty-one British makes on show, as against eighteen from the United States, twelve from France, four from Italy, two from Czechoslovakia, and none at all from either of the Germanies.

Inevitably, "export or bust" had its miseries as well as its splendours. On the credit side, the 2,001 TC MGs shipped to the United States between 1946 and 1949 re-introduced Americans to the forgotten concept of fun motoring, as opposed to the euphoric sightseeing so ably promoted by Lincoln and others. Though Austin failed to hold their lead in America after the novelty (and 1940 Chevrolet styling) of the Devon sedan began to pall, they were still 1949's second best-selling foreign import with 3,642 cars, behind Ford of Dagenham with 5,087. True, the French Renault had crept up into third place, but behind them lay MG, Hillman, Morris, and Jaguar. Fiat, who distrusted the American market as "capricious", sold only 60 cars (they would try harder in 1956), and the first two Volkswagens to arrive occasioned scarcely a ripple. Other good British performances of the season were 13,887 sales in Belgium, 50,028 in Australia, and 17,960 in New Zealand, while a year later, Sweden would take nearly 10,000, an intriguing commentary on that country's total exports for the season – 154 cars and 356 commercial vehicles.

On the debit side, of course, was poor service. Small firms could not afford comprehensive dealer networks, much less elaborate pre-production testing programmes in their proposed markets. Not everyone offered left-hand drive, though the diehards were now in the minority.

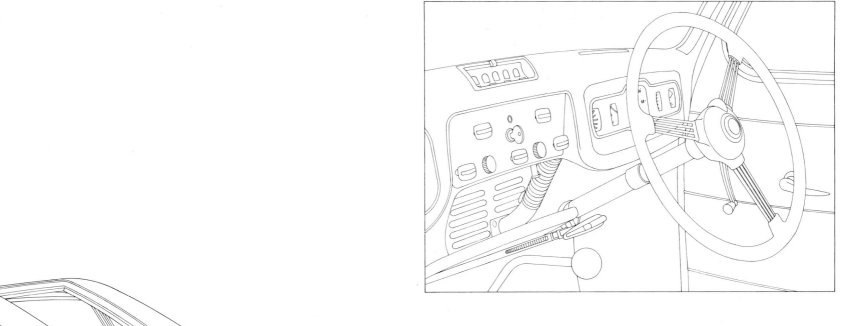

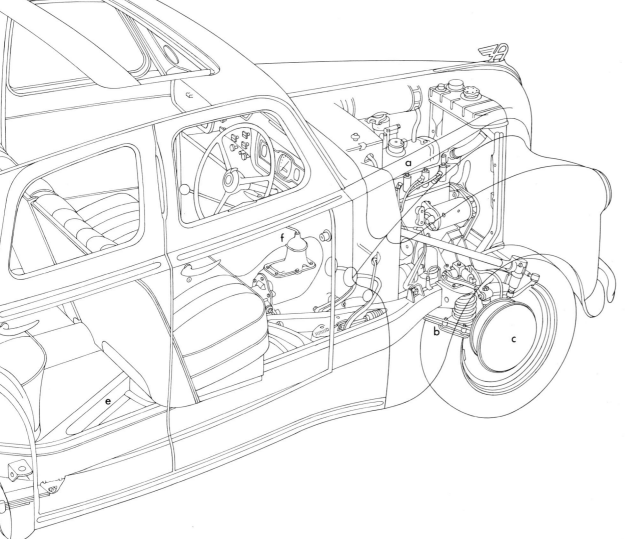

Britain Steps Out or, as Austin publicity put it, "Colour Comes Back Into Motoring" – a reference to the choice of pastel shades and light-tone upholstery (leather on de luxe models only) available on the 1,200-cc A40 announced towards the end of 1947. To the regret of home-market customers, it soon became the country's best-selling automotive export, appealing to Americans because its styling was close to the native product, until the real postwar models began to appear for 1949. The interior (*top left*) looks traditionally British. Less so is the dashboard (*top right*), with plastic much in evidence and instruments in the American idiom. The sectioned view reveals an element of compromise. The hood is of alligator type, and one immediately notices a valve-in-head four-cylinder engine (*a*), something only recently adopted for Austin's passenger cars, though they'd been using it on trucks since 1939. Coil-spring independent suspension (*b*) was also heretical by British standards in this class – neither Morris nor Ford had yet adopted it. The full disc wheel (*c*), standardized on American automobiles since 1937, had now supplanted the perforated type (which collected mud) in Britain, though the conservative engineers at Longbridge did not wholly trust hydraulic brakes (they were by no means alone in England), preferring the Girling "half and half" system with mechanical actuation to the rear (*d*). Austin preferred a separate chassis frame (*e*), though they did not offer a wide range of body styles: sedans, a pickup, a panel van, and a van-based station wagon represented their limit, tourers being a local phenomenon confined to the Australian assembly plant. Native influences remained in the floor shift (*f*), replaced by the column type during 1951, and in the sliding roof, with which Austin were to persevere until the mid-fifties. It was not, of course, specified in countries where monsoon rains and dust storms were prevalent.

True post-war Americans – the 1951 Ford convertible (*top right*). 1949 Studebaker Champion (*bottom*), and 1949 Town and Country Chrysler (*opposite, top right*). Studebaker were first off the mark with Raymond Loewy's revolutionary "coming or going" style, featuring a short hood and a long trunk. This one went on sale midway through 1946 and continued for three seasons without significant change. All the seats were firmly within the wheelbase. The little 2.8-litre six was a real fuel-miser, giving over 25 mpg (12 lit/100) with gentle driving and 21 mpg (13.5 lit/100) at a steady 60 mph (100 km/h). Also preoccupied with a better ride were Ford, who had cast aside all Old Henry's ideas on their 1949 line, which emerged with conventional springing (coils at the front, longitudinal semi-elliptics at the rear) and hypoid rear axles. The 1951 was little changed, apart from the twin-spinner grille and the option of an automatic transmission with three forward speeds to Chevrolet's two. A very different convertible was the Chrysler, dismissed by one unkind British critic as "stockbrokers' Tudor". By 1949, the full mahogany panelling of early examples had gone in favour of a mixture of wood and Di-Noc

appliqué. The engine was still the 5.3-litre 135-hp straight-eight: the legendary hemi-head vee-eight would be a 1951 innovation. The Chrysler dash (*opposite, top left*) is already safety-conscious, with leather-covered rubber padding extending right across the top. Note that there are still three pedals – Chrysler's Fluidrive was not a full automatic. The model also pioneered something we take for granted today – the key-start which eliminated the starter button. Finally, (*opposite bottom*), the limit of British stylistic heresy in 1946. Only the subdued sphinx mascot identifies the car as an Armstrong Siddeley. Thin pillars, disappearing running boards, recessed headlamps, and alligator hood date back to Cadillac's Sixty Special, and the grille is authentic 1938 Detroit, if a little more angular than the American idiom. In one respect, though, the Armstrong Siddeley Typhoon is a jump ahead of General Motors: it's an authentic hardtop, three years in front of Buick's Riviera.

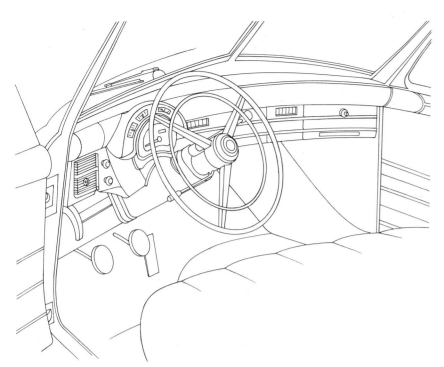

The Renault 4CV, 1946 (see also following page). The welded-up steel hull (*right*) follows orthodox unitary practice, and both front and rear "packs" are quick detachable – engine, radiator, drive unit, and rear suspension coming out in one piece. The engine (*far right*) is a conventional-enough little long-stroke pushrod four with down-draught carburettor, giving 19 hp. Initially, its capacity was 760 cc, but this was reduced early in the model's career to bring it into the smallest international competition category. The interior of the sedan (*centre*) was a little cramped, despite the hollowed-out doors with the inevitable, irritating concomitant of sliding windows, cursed by drivers of that future trend-setter, the BMC Mini. Rear engines call for some relocation of controls: the starter and the choke are out of sight between the front seats, although clearly visible on the sectioned drawing. A floor gearshift calls for linkages longer (if less complicated) than those associated with the column shifts of the later forties and fifties, and changes involve a soup-stirring action of surpassing woolliness.

Further, once the desperate phase had been passed, foreign buyers did not take kindly to vehicles not only designed for British conditions, but designed for such conditions according to the parameters of 1938. Whatever may have eventuated at London's first post-war Show in the autumn of 1948, it should be remembered that, of the wide selection of Family Tens and Twelves available in 1946, only Vauxhalls came with modern suspensions and hydraulic brakes. Austins, Fords, and Hillmans still lacked either. Leather upholstery meant nothing to a Swiss or an Australian, and sliding roofs let in dust and rain when exposed to more extreme conditions than the homeland's temperate climate. Coventry, Birmingham, and Cowley learnt this last lesson quickly; that most British of all gimmicks was on its way out, and virtually extinct five years later, only to be revived, years later, by Frenchmen and Americans deprived of their ragtops by the worldwide safety drive!

One great dilemma beset all the world's manufacturers: to continue an obsolete design or to take the proverbial clean sheet of paper. For those who chose the former way out, prospects were attractive. The tooling was there, and well and truly amortized. Some models, notably in Britain, had been in continuous production for the armed forces since 1939, a situation which explains why Austin, Hillman-Humber, and Vauxhall were so quick off the mark again in 1945. In the prevailing car shortage, almost anything would sell, provided the necessary raw materials and labour were to hand. Inevitably, however, there must be a substantial time-lag between the resumption of manufacture and the launching of all-new models. The first of Britain's new mass-produced generation, Austin's A40, did not appear until the winter of 1947–48. In France, Citroën, Peugeot, and Simca continued to offer nothing but rehashed 1939s for three whole seasons, the same going for Fiat and Lancia in Italy, and for Skoda in Czechoslovakia. The Americans, in any case, did not have to worry, as Studebaker led off in the summer of 1946 with their revolutionary "1947" line, followed over the 1948 and 1949 seasons by the rest of the industry.

Thus, the British lead in exports worked against Britons, once new

designs began to emerge – and the more modern 1939-type Continentals appeared in economic numbers. There was the astounding case of Germany, as yet not even a nation once more, yet recovering at a meteoric rate. In 1946, the Western Zone's total passenger-car production was 9,962 units, most of them Volkswagens, but three years later, output had broken six figures (103,997), and this would be more than doubled in 1950.

Though the best-selling DKW and the BMW six were as yet lost to the East, the surviving Germans, even in 1939 form, were entirely competitive. Spearhead of the national recovery was, of course, the Volkswagen – simple, aerodynamically efficient, and possessed of that indestructible little air-cooled *Boxermotor*. A useful second string was the American-inspired 1.5-litre Opel Olympia, the 1938 edition of a theme first encountered at the 1935 Berlin Show; it was better known than the parallel Vauxhall, if not a better car. Finally, for the middle-class market there was the stolid old Type 170 Mercedes-Benz, technically advanced beneath its conservative exterior, and available from 1949 with a diesel-engine option which returned 40 mpg (7 lit/100) on cheap fuel and cared not a whit for octanes. The Volkswagen appeared tentatively in export markets during 1947, but less than ten years later, it would be America's best-selling foreign import. Further, it had the right service backing; by 1953, the marque ran to over a hundred dealers in Switzerland. By contrast, Austin had thirty-seven and the Rootes Group thirty-four. And alongside Volkswagen's spectacular rise from nothing, there were the established houses of Citroën and Fiat, selling proven models little changed since 1936.

A clean sheet could pay, as witness the progress of another German group, Borgward, successors to the old Hansa firm and responsible for the lightweight Goliaths and Lloyds as well. During our period, Borgward were still recovering from bomb damage and the destruction of their entire tooling, but 1949 had seen the debut of their all-new 1500, Germany's first novelty for ten years, and a prelude to their best-selling Isabella of 1954. A more lasting triumph was scored by Renault,

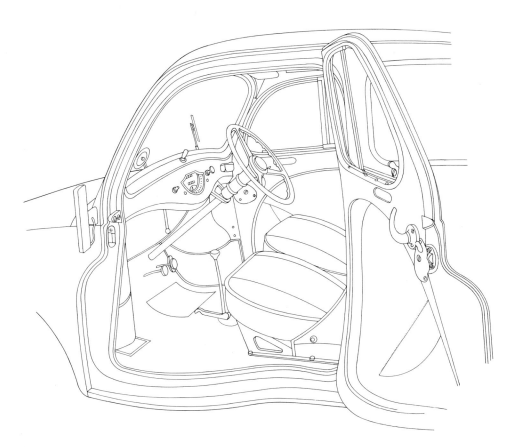

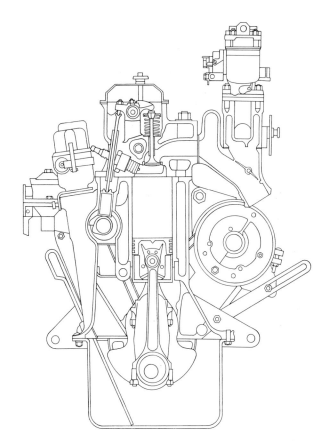

nationalized in 1945 under the direction of Pierre Lefaucheux. By opting realistically for the smallest viable four-seater, a 760-cc sedan, he launched an export best seller for which a black market still existed in 1950. It is fashionable these days to laugh at the cramped and noisy little 4CV with its alarming oversteer, but in 1946, a four-door model with no cyclecar attributes and a fuel consumption of 50 mpg (5.5 lit/100) was a major achievement; to get in into large-scale production within a year was a herculean effort. Further, the opposition had not as yet bestirred itself: the 2CV Citroën was still a secret, albeit a fairly open one; the Morris Minor would not take its bow until October, 1948; and Fiat's Dante Giacosa preferred to keep his *topolino* a two-seater.

By 1950, however, only the hardiest of pre-war themes – Volkswagen, Opel, and the evergreen Citroën *traction* – remained untouched by the hand of progress. Volvo's PV444 was edging the old sixes out of the limelight, Morris had a new all-unitary range with sophisticated handling characteristics, and the Hillman Minx had been updated as a six-seater with a squashed-Plymouth look. Fiat, while retaining its smaller cars in essentially 1940 form, had another miniature American in the shape of the 1400, and Standard were going all out for "colonial" markets with a staple model, the 2.1-litre Vanguard. Peugeot's unitary 203 had supplanted traditional themes. The new cars not only reflected American styling, they were modern underneath. New recruits to overhead valve included Standard and Renault, hydraulic brakes were general practice, and Detroit-type sheet metal had moved in with a vengeance. The separate fender and the running board were the main casualties, with proper luggage space as the principal bonus. In terms of hard fact, let us consider three European best sellers – Austin, Peugeot, and Renault.

The two former companies had long done brisk business in the 1,200–1,300-cc. sector. Peugeot's contribution had run to overhead valve since 1938, though the 202, still available in 1948, retained a separate chassis. The Austin had, however, been a copybook example of British tradition, apart from its integral floor, and its 1,125-cc flathead

engine developed a leisurely 32 bhp – more, curiously, than the contemporary valve-in-head Peugeot. Their synchromesh gearboxes were entirely in character – three forward speeds in France, and four in Britain. Performance was equally sedate; both cars were good for 62 mph (100 km/h) and took nine seconds to reach 30 (50 km/h). Only the French car had independent front suspension, and its hydraulic brakes were a post-war addition. The Austin Ten retained its rod-operated Girlings to the end in 1947.

Consider their 1949 equivalents. Engines were bigger in each case – 1,200 cc for the Austin and 1,290 cc for the Peugeot. Both were of short-stroke type, viable now that horsepower tax had been abolished in Britain. Outputs in the 40–42-bhp bracket meant top speeds of around 70 mph (112 km/h), while the Peugeot's gearbox incorporated an overdrive top to allow of high cruising velocities. The 0–30 mph acceleration time was now down to less than 8 seconds, and the Peugeot's unitary construction had saved nearly 30 lb (say 14 kg) on a car 10 in (25.4 cm) longer than the 202, and capable of carrying six people at a pinch. In the braking department, as before, only the French car had full hydraulics – Austin compromised with hydro-mechanicals. Nor was the Austin much roomier, but either way, the result was more car, with much the same fuel consumption – 30 mpg (*c.* 9 lit/100) with normal driving. Inevitably, however, costs had gone up – the norm in this class was £350–400 as against £160–200 in 1939. (Dollar comparisons are not valid, owing to the recent devaluations in Europe).

In the baby-car field, comparisons were far more dramatic, since a breakthrough had been achieved. Admittedly, the latest 4CV Renault was slower than the old Juvaquatre: 55–58 mph (90 km/h) as against 62 mph (the round 100). The smaller car had less room, thanks to an overall length some 6 in (15 cm) shorter. It also had all-independent springing, effective hydraulic brakes, and a tuning potential that would lead to victory in the Index of Performance at Le Mans. The Juva, by contrast, was a stodgy mock-Opel which bred no sporting variants. Its side-valve l-litre engine gave only 5 bhp more than the 760-cc overhead-

New methods and new shapes, 1946–50. In fact, only one of these cars, the 1949 Oldsmobile (*opposite, bottom right*) actually comes into our period, but you could buy (or at worst, join the queue for) all the others in 1950. Only the Oldsmobile had an orthodox chassis frame, and all the new trends are to be encountered. None of them, of course, retains a beam axle at each end, though orthodox rear suspension features on the Hudson Hornet (*top*), while Oldsmobile and the Peugeot 203 (*opposite, centre right*) have live-axle-and-coil suspensions at the back. The Hudson is the only flathead, while the two French babies, Renault's 4CV (*bottom*) and the Dyna-Panhard (*opposite, top right*), believe in putting all the works at one end. Renault favours a rearward location, while the Panhard, descendant of J. A. Grégoire's 1943 "people's car", features an air-cooled flat twin driving the front wheels. Transmissions range from a tricky four-speed crash set-up on the Panhard (rather dubious synchromesh had arrived by 1951) to the full automatic found on almost all 1949 Oldsmobiles and available on Hudsons two years later. Hemi-head design increased the efficiency of Oldsmobile's vee-eight and Peugeot's (*opposite, left*) engines, though the latter firm was always more interested in long life and content with 42 hp from 1,290 cc. Hudson, who couldn't afford a vee-eight programme, went to the other extreme,

with a massive side-valve 5-litre six: their reward was several years' domination of American stock-car racing, though this didn't help sales. Amortization was, as ever, the big problem. It mattered little in Europe, where styling was of secondary importance, hence the Renault, in a fifteen-year run, became France's first million seller, and the Peugeot accounted for 685,828 units in eleven years. The complex little Panhard found its niche with the enthusiasts, who weren't afraid of something difficult, fragile, and noisy,

while the small Panhard factory was content with sales of 10,000 in a good year. Oldsmobile, of course, had no problems; not so Hudson, whose clever unitary Stepdown design (the frame passed *outside* the rear wheels, and low build was allied to a wide tread) was inflexible and too expensive to replace. What looked pleasingly different in 1948 was outmoded five years later, even if the ancient engine could still give the vee-eights an excellent run for their money on a staggering 171 hp.

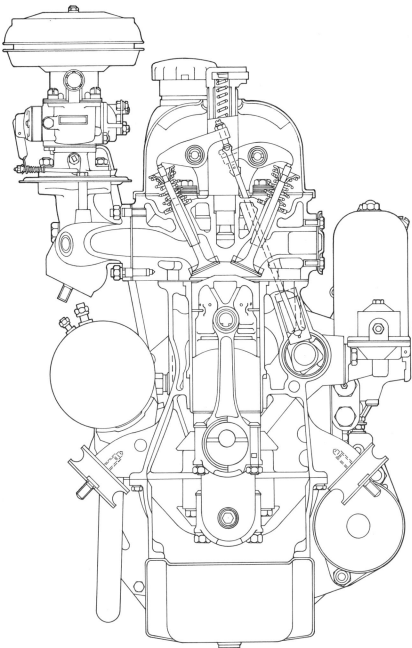

valve unit fitted to the 4CV, and it was not particularly compact. On the new model, the power unit was mounted at the rear. Driven hard, fuel consumption was around 45 mpg (6.2 lit/100), an interesting contrast with the Juva's mean of 36 mpg (7.8 lit/100). Already the shibboleths of the *système* Panhard were under fire.

But not as yet on a substantial scale. Renault was the sole important recruit to rear engines during our period – Fiat, Simca, and Hillman would follow much later. Nor did front-wheel drive make that many strides in the late 1940s, except in the realm of odd prototypes. DKW derivatives would appear in Denmark, Sweden, and East Germany, and the influences of J.A. Grégoire's lightweight Alpax structures would make their presence felt. Panhard in France actually got them into production, but plans for manufacture in Australia, Britain, and Holland came to naught. "Putting the works up one end" as a credo would be the consequences of growing congestion – and of BMC's inspired Mini.

There was other writing on the wall. In those days of appalling fuels, high compression ratios were largely academic. Fuel was rationed in most European countries as late as 1949, and branded fuels did not return to Britain until 1953; France was given them a little earlier. Before 1950 was out, however, there would be interesting developments in the United States, in the shape of a new generation of high-performance, short-stroke vee-eights with compression ratios the right side of 7.5:1.

Not that there was a lot to show as yet. On paper, increases in power did not look all that dramatic. The traditional flathead Cadillac gave 150 bhp to the new overhead-valve type's 160 in 1949, while the Oldsmobile Rocket's 135 bhp from 5 litres compares interestingly with the 4.2 litres and 110 bhp of their last inline type. The legendary 1951 Chrysler Hemi, which "sent Detroit's engineering staffs hustling back to their drawing boards", falls just outside our appointed limits. It also illustrates the shape of things to come, for the Corporation's new vee engine offered 33 per cent more power in return for a capacity increase of only 1.25 per cent.

The new eights featured short and rigid crankshafts of four-throw type with five main bearings, better balanced than earlier types. This paid off in terms of greater smoothness. Equally important was the fact that the latest units were more compact than the straight eights they supplanted, and the long-hood fashion of 1931 had been discarded many years ago, as it was a prime space-consumer. Nor was space the only commodity saved: once the new type had been tooled, chassis and body costs fell. Inline sixes and eights tended to call for two different chassis, though a degree of rationalization had crept in since 1940, with the additional length confined to the hood. Now, width was the sole problem, and a single type of running gear sufficed, whatever the motor. This cheeseparing would have its adverse consequences: all too often, the six-cylinder member of the family was painfully lethargic, while the eight, with all the performance options of the mid-fifties, would be too fast for the chassis and actively dangerous in the braking department, since 0–30 mph (0–50 km/h) times of four seconds odd were not matched by comparable retardation.

Also as yet confined to the United States was the spread of fully automatic transmissions. Before Pearl Harbor, such pain-killers had been available on Oldsmobiles and Cadillacs, and by the end of our period only Chrysler (who preferred a four-speed semi-automatic type incorporating a fluid coupling) still held out against the new idiom. Ford, admittedly, were still buying their automatics from General Motors, but then so did Hudson, Kaiser, and Nash. Studebaker chose the proprietary Borg-Warner unit, and Packard made their own.

Clutches and shifting were now eliminated for good, though there

was, of course, a manually selected low range, and Hydramatic offered a choice of four forward ratios. Inevitably, there was a certain amount of slip and consequent power loss, but this was of little import with an engine giving anything from 120 to 180 bhp and accustomed to doing most of its work in direct drive. Automatics could not be towed without first disconnecting the drive line, and the fluid in some early transmissions curdled, but the system's worst faults were reflected in the simpler two-speed types, such as Powerglide, offered on Chevrolets for the first time in 1950. Low range could not be selected below about 50 mph (80 km/h), and thus, there was precious little engine braking. Had Powerglide been limited to modest sixes with a maximum potential of 130–140 bhp, little harm would have resulted, but consequences could be alarming when the transmission was mated to a hairy vee-eight, and increasingly, wheel size limited the brake-drum diameter; it is salutary to remember that, as early as 1955, Chevrolet offered a 205-bhp option. Another hazard in early days was the absence of a positive stop between forward and reverse motion – a favourite early quadrant layout was P-N-D-L-R – park, neutral, drive, low, reverse.

The new shiftless motoring had no place in Europe. Already, there was a tendency towards smaller and more frugal engines. Even in the early post-war epidemic of "Vanguarditis" – of which more anon – the norm for a full-sized family sedan was 2,200–2,500 cc with outputs in the 60–70 bhp bracket, as against the four litres and 100–110 bhp of the simpler American sixes. In other words, European engines had insufficient power to absorb the inherent losses of automatic. Nor was there money to spare for experimentation, as the big battalions were wasting no time on a dubious starter while the seller's market was at its zenith and would not finally fade from the scene until early 1953. Borgward's 1950 Hansamatic proved a costly failure, since customers discovered the hard way that one had to come to a standstill before selecting reverse. The British Brockhouse single-speed system – tried only on the expensive Invicta – suffered from a temperamental, solenoid-actuated reverse, one of the reasons why only twenty-five cars were made, at a reputed loss of £100,000 ($280,000) in three years.

Americans, however, had the funds, and the public had never been enamoured of shifting. By the end of our period, it was well-nigh impossible to obtain a Cadillac or Lincoln with conventional transmission, while in the middle-class bracket the percentages of automatic-equipped models are illuminating: ninety-four per cent for Oldsmobile, the pioneers; eighty per cent for Packards; seventy-seven per cent for Buick; sixty-five per cent for Pontiac; forty-five per cent for Hudson; but only twenty-six per cent in the case of Nash, who did not offer it on their latest compact Ramblers. In Chevrolet's first "automatic" season, only one-fifth of all new cars were sold with Powerglide; within a year, this proportion had doubled.

Likewise on the march was unitary construction, largely because everyone who could afford it realized that the future lay in long runs, fewer changes, and bigger outputs. Hillman, Morris, and Renault were old supporters who converted wholesale to the new system, but interesting new recruits were Alfa Romeo, Fiat, Jowett, Hudson, Peugeot, Volvo, the new Swedish Saab, and, surprisingly, in view of their later, "Look, it's got a chassis" advertising campaign, Triumph, albeit only on their ugly little Mayflower launched in the autumn of 1949. Significantly, not all these breeds were mass-produced marques, though those who were not either made the big league or died.

With companies as big and secure as Fiat or Peugeot, survival was never in doubt, though the former firm's 1400/1900 family had become the despair of the stylists long before it eventually bowed out in 1958. Both Swedish companies chose right, the Volvo surviving an eighteen-year run and some 330,000 units, while Sixten Sason's wind-tunnel-

The two-speed Dynaflow automatic transmission (*bottom*) first seen on 1948 Buicks. The primary pump (*a*) is bolted to the engine crankshaft (*b*) and turns at engine speed. Directly opposed to this is the turbine (*c*) splined on to the gearbox input shaft and running (in direct drive) continuously at propeller shaft speed. The other three elements – secondary pump (*d*) and the two stators (*e*) – are each individually mounted on an over-running

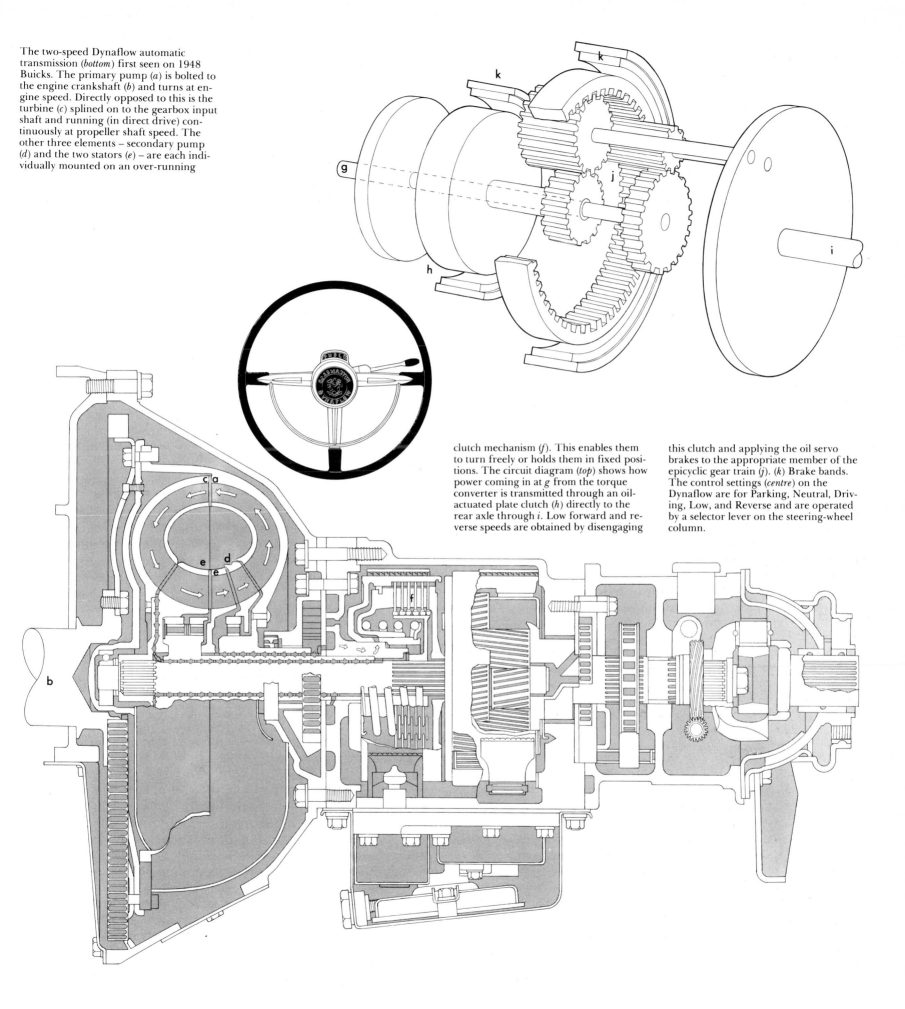

clutch mechanism (*f*). This enables them to turn freely or holds them in fixed positions. The circuit diagram (*top*) shows how power coming in at *g* from the torque converter is transmitted through an oil-actuated plate clutch (*h*) directly to the rear axle through *i*. Low forward and reverse speeds are obtained by disengaging this clutch and applying the oil servo brakes to the appropriate member of the epicyclic gear train (*j*). (*k*) Brake bands. The control settings (*centre*) on the Dynaflow are for Parking, Neutral, Driving, Low, and Reverse and are operated by a selector lever on the steering-wheel column.

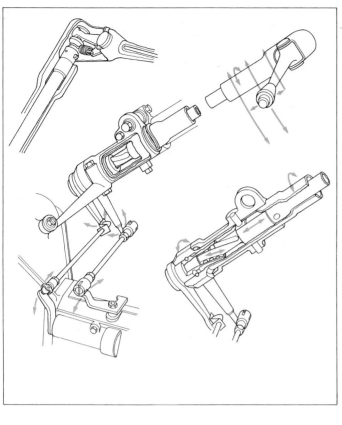

Unitary and fastback themes: the Volvo PV444 (*opposite, top*) and Jowett Javelin (*opposite, bottom*) were both on the road and largely finalized by the end of the Second World War, though it would be some time thereafter before the public could buy either – 1947 in the case of the Swedish car, and early 1948 for the Jowett. Both firms played with sports models, though the Gothenburg firm's interest was never more than halfhearted. Maybe this is why they survived and Jowett didn't.

In the Volvo we can see an outgrowth of the 1.3-litre Hanomag of 1939 (see pages 172–173). It has a conventional all-steel unitary structure, a similar fastback shape, and a modest 1.4-litre three-bearing overhead-valve four-cylinder unit giving 40 hp at 3,800 rpm. It looked a scaled-down American with the 1942 Ford-style box front fenders, and other features were notably American – the three-speed synchromesh transmission with the long and willowy central gear lever of pre-column-shift days, cam and lever steering gear, and a rear suspension by live axle and coils, adopted (as on Giacosa's 1400

Fiat) to give a good ride on poor surfaces. Also wholly American were the interior appointments, but in an era of fuel shortage (and rising prices) the PV444 furnished an excellent substitute for the old L-head Volvo Sixes, still around and destined to sit out another decade on the cabranks of Swedish cities.

Gerald Palmer's Javelin, by contrast, was intended as a British substitute for such established and well-handling sedans as the Lancia Aprilia, and (more specifically) the 11 *légère* Citroën. Like both its foreign rivals (still on the market in 1946), it was unitary, but unlike the Citroën, it had conventional drive, while it would never do on an English car to dispense with synchromesh, as Vincenzo Lancia had so successfully done on his Aprilia. Suspension was of a sophisticated all-torsion bar type, independent at the front, though it made do with the "halfway house" hydromechanical braking system until 1951. The low-mounted flat-four engine wasn't easy to service and had excellent self-drowning properties in wet weather. Early cars ran bearings, blew gaskets, and jumped out of third gear. The car at-

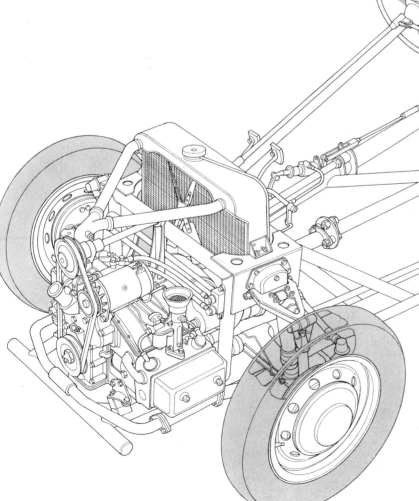

tained 80 mph (130 km/h), cruised at a steady 70 (112 km/h), accelerated to 50 (80 km/h) in 15 seconds, and returned as much as 28 mpg (10 lit/100).

(*Lower*) Jowett successfully transformed their Javelin theme into a sports car (the Jupiter) as had Fiat with their 1100: Lancia never officially marketed a sports Aprilia, leaving such things to tuners and custom coachbuilders. Here the Jupiter is seen in chassis form as exhibited at Earls Court in 1949. The multi-tubular frame was the work of a Ministry of All the Talents involving the resuscitated ERA racing-car firm, Laurence Pomeroy the younger, and Eberan von Eberhorst, formerly of the Auto Union Grand Prix *équipe*. The engine, gearbox, suspension, and transmission units are Javelin, and so

is the column shift (not visible here), though engine access was improved by the use of a swing-up hood-fender assembly in place of the Javelin's demountable front grille. Note the tubular sidemembers stoutly braced by a St. Andrew's Cross, and the robust triangulated structure at the rear.

(*Top left*) Volvo stayed with floor shift through the "column" era (except on their American-style sixes). The Javelin, however, preferred the column species, and though from the driver's viewpoint it was one of the better specimens, this exploded drawing shows why such a system was ill-suited to European four-speed transmissions. It also shows how the straight-line motion of the inner tube is converted into rotation.

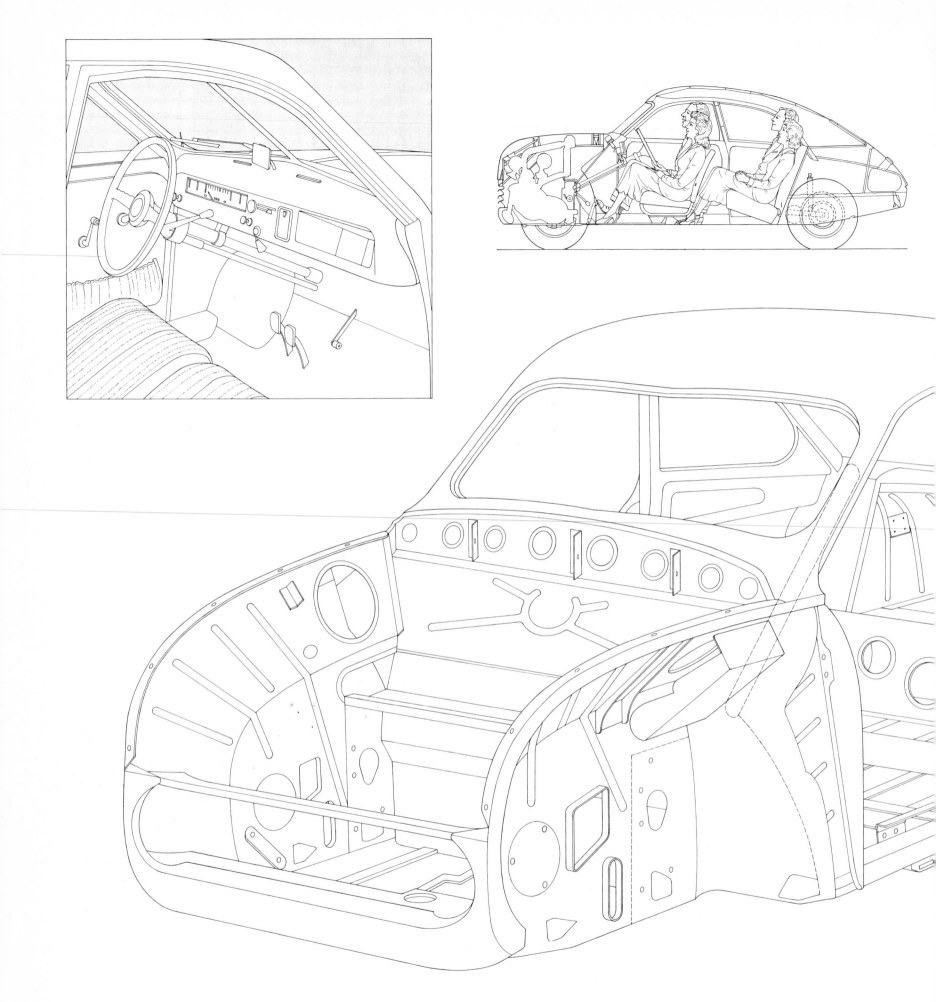

The "Other Swede" — or how Volvo lost their sole national-representative status from 1950 onwards. As yet, they were not really challenged. Though internationally respected for their aircraft, Svenska Aeroplan AB of Trollhättan were little known for automobiles outside their homeland. In 1950, their first full year of car production, they turned out precisely 1,246 units, all identical two-door sedans and all in the same shade of mid-green.

The Saab's genesis was interesting. Chief Engineer Gunnar Ljungström had little use for bulky American cars and considered even the Volvo PV444 too big (it was, for the less wealthy motorist un-committed to a big mileage). He favoured front-wheel drive, in any case, for its low build, so he took as his model one of Sweden's pre-war best sellers, the German twin-cylinder two-stroke DKW, now temporarily unavailable. The mechanics

of the new Saab were essentially DKW in layout. The water-cooled 764-cc engine was mounted transversely, and the three-speed transmission incorporated a free wheel: it also had synchromesh, some-thing no DKW had ever had. Other im-provements on the German prototype were an all-independent suspension by transverse torsion bars, and hydraulic brakes. Sason's shape offered minimal wind resistance and was quiet even at the 75 mph (120 km/h) attained by later three-cylinder developments of the theme. Prototypes had full-skirted fenders at front and rear: not a good idea, least of all in Sweden, where they proved to be magnificent mud-traps in the spring thaw! Rear-seat headroom was not very good, and rearward visibility on pre-1953 cars was nearly as bad as the Volkswagen's.

Heart of the Saab (bottom left) was its unitary structure. Aerodynamic influences

are immediately detectable in the shape of the floor pan, which doubles as a smooth undertray interrupted only by the exhaust pipe. Further, no individual unit of the layout reaches unwieldy proportions: the biggest is the pressing incorporating top, windshield, and firewall.

American influences are not wholly absent, as witness the facia (top left) with its stylized dials. Ljungström, however, pre-ferred orthodox column shift for his gears, where DKW had used an awkward handle projecting from the dashboard. Saab, likewise, followed its German pro-totype in having only three forward speeds, so the changes were reasonably easy and free of the horrible movements endemic to British four-on-the-column layouts. The spare-wheel locker (bottom right) in the tail had external access, though the back seat still had to be swung forward to get at the luggage.

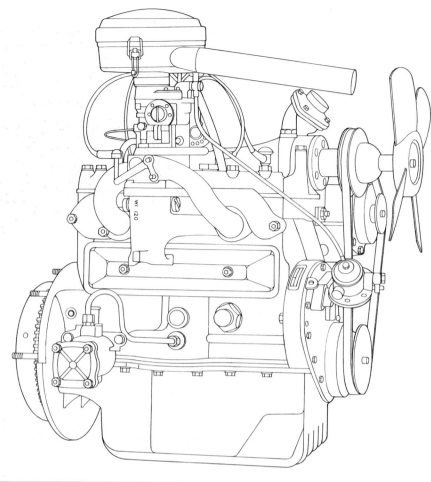

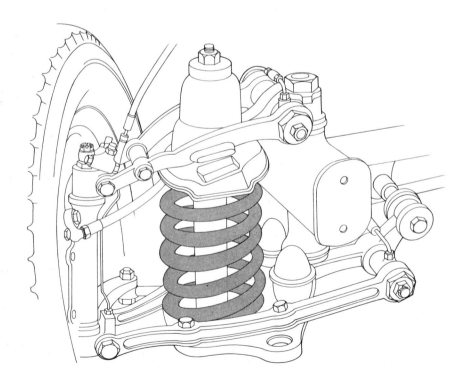

Well out of our period, but essentially 1930s in concept, is this Singer SM road-ster (*top left*) from 1954. The line began in 1939 with a 1,074-cc version featuring beam front axle, mechanical brakes, and three-speed transmission – no great per-former, and a disappointment to enthusi-asts nurtured on the "real" Le Mans Nines of the 1933–37 era. By 1951, the roadster had acquired independent front suspen-sion, and in its final guise with twin-carburettor 58-hp 1,497-cc unit (an overhead-camshaft four, like all post-1937 Singers), it would top 75 mph (120 km/h). Customers for "fresh air and fun", how-ever, wanted more performance or wind-up windows.

(*Centre, left*) Jeep in mufti. Created by Bantam (American Austin) and built in vast numbers for the Allied war effort in 1942–45 by Ford and Willys, the Jeep was taken over post-war by the latter firm. In-itially, few changes were made; retained were Willys's tough old 2.2-litre L-head four with roots going back to the 1927 Overland Whippet, the semi-elliptic springing, and the hypoid final drive to both pairs of wheels – front-wheel drive could be disconnected for street motoring. Top speed was 65 mph (105 km/h), and gentle driving was required to achieve the advertised thirst of 18 mpg (16 lit/100). By the end of our period, however, Jeeps were being made under licence in several foreign countries, and the first imitations were on their way. Britain's Landrover, the first of these, was on sale by mid-1948.

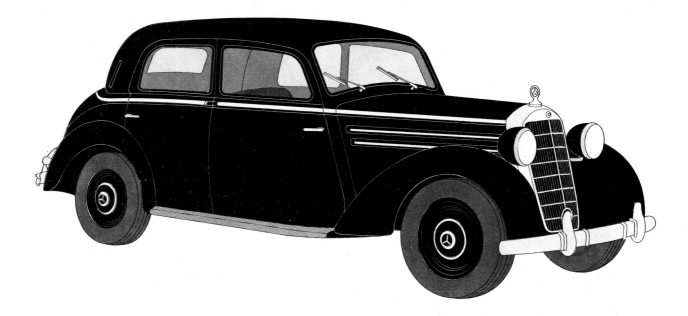

Among the most successful hangovers from the 1930s was the complicated Mercedes-Benz 170 range. There's nothing in the appearance of the 1951 170Da (*left*) to suggest either its date or the presence of its frugal four-cylinder diesel engine. The firm had pioneered these in passenger cars, the first being 1936's bigger 260D. The styling of the petrol-engined 170S (*top*) is different rather than more modern, though a careful look will reveal wider doors with centre pillars and an external-access trunk. Beneath the skin are a more powerful engine (*opposite, top right*) and coil-spring suspension at the front (*opposite, bottom right*), as opposed to the double-transverse-leaf arrangement on standard models of 1936–48. Rear suspension was, of course, by swing axles on all 170s. On S-series cars gravity feed had also given way to a rear tank with mechanical pump. Note, however, that the engine is still a sedate side-valve four with an output of 52 hp from 1.8 litres, and for all the sophistication of the tubular X-frame, weight-watching is not part of the deal. The S sedan turned the scales at 2,600 lb (1,180 kg), or 142 lb (66 kg) more than the companion diesel model with the old-type body. Performance played second fiddle to durability: if the 170S would stagger up to 75 mph (120 km/h), the diesel was flat out at 68 (108 km/h). But in countries where diesel carried a lower rate of duty, a 170D had its attractions, not the least of them an average fuel consumption of 40 mpg (7 lit/100). If Mercedes diesel taxis had yet to become a common sight in European cities, it was only because the war-torn factory had yet to get back into its stride. Both petrol and diesel 170s were, however, still being made in 1955, and when production ceased, total deliveries had topped the two hundred thousand mark. Nor was this the end of the faithful old flathead motor; adapted since 1953 to the unitary 180 series, it was not supplanted by a modern overhead-camshaft engine until 1957.

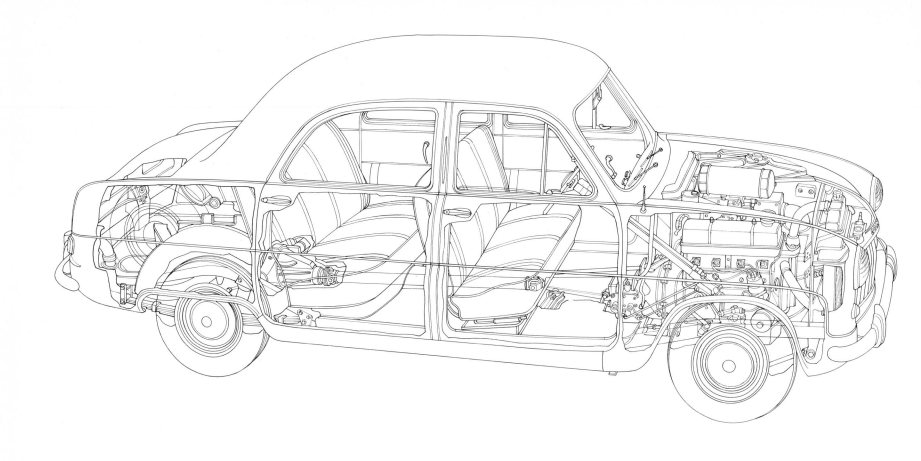

tested teardrop Saab, to be expected from an aircraft factory, was still around in the mid-seventies. Alfa Romeo, backed by liberal injections of American Marshall Aid, successfully transformed themselves from makers of specialist sporting machinery into second-division mass producers. Their twin overhead-camshaft four-cylinder 1900 sedan might look too like a Chevrolet for the purists' comfort, but annual production had broken the 11,000 mark by 1956 and was heading towards the quarter-million in 1975.

Jowett and Hudson, however, could not afford such bold steps. The British firm, accustomed to turning out five thousand sub-utility flat-twins a year in their small Bradford works, were forced to farm out the construction of their hulls to Briggs in Dagenham, mass producers geared to the demands of the nearby Ford plant. Teething troubles got the advanced 1.5-litre Javelin off to a shaky start. In principle, this should not have mattered, since to Britons (and to many Europeans as well) it offered standards of handling in the Citroën-Fiat-Lancia class, way above the native opposition. Alas! British purchase tax and a weak organization dogged the hapless Javelin all the way, and soon Briggs's production was outstripping sales. And one cannot ask a huge press-works to go slow... Hudson, who merged with Nash in 1954 after a comparable struggle, were stuck with an inflexible shape (they couldn't afford a vee-eight, either). Nor would "suddenly it's 1948 again" have been an apt slogan to help unload stocks of 1954 models scarcely improved by those refuges of the stylistically destitute, chromium plate and side flashes.

Power steering had yet to appear, but two other interesting trends, though slow starters in our period, were apparent to the discerning. These were the diesel engine and the light four-wheel-drive vehicle.

The former had already been tried commercially in pre-war Citroëns,

Hanomags, and Mercedes-Benz, though its appeal had been limited, just as it was later, in the late forties and early fifties, when the public was still thinking in terms of more and cheaper fuel – soon. In any case, the dieselization of commercial vehicles had yet to extend much below the 2/3-ton category, and such machinery utilized hefty fours and sixes with capacities of 4 or 5 litres – not wholly suitable for passenger cars, though Nash's English importers had offered the 4.7-litre Perkins P6 as a regular option in 1939. In any case, diesel "knock" was unacceptable in the price class in which such vehicles would have to sell. Only Mercedes-Benz offered a diesel model in 1950, albeit they would soon be joined by Borgward, Fiat, and Standard.

The legendary Jeep had introduced the world to four-wheel drive, and 1948 had seen the first of over a million Landrovers, closely based on the American prototype but using Rover's own 1.6-litre four-cylinder motor. Other recruits would include Alfa Romeo, Delahaye, Fiat, Nissan, and Toyota, but such makers relied heavily on military orders and the requirements of farmers. The 4×4's latter-day status as a "recreational vehicle" was a direct consequence of the emasculatory processes to which the true sports car was later subjected. In 1950, Jeeps and Landrovers were regarded much as station wagons had been in the middle and later 1930s.

The 1940s were no time for the second-division manufacturer. The casualties of 1946–50 – Chenard-Walcker, Imperia, Isotta Fraschini, and La Licorne are the names which spring immediately to mind – were mainly firms that were doomed in any case. Neither of the two French concerns made real attempts at a comeback, and Imperia's crossbred Adler-Amilcars stood no chance against the Anglo-French invasion of Belgium. As for the Isotta, a large rear-engined luxury car was hardly a suitable project for an impoverished aero-engine firm which had not

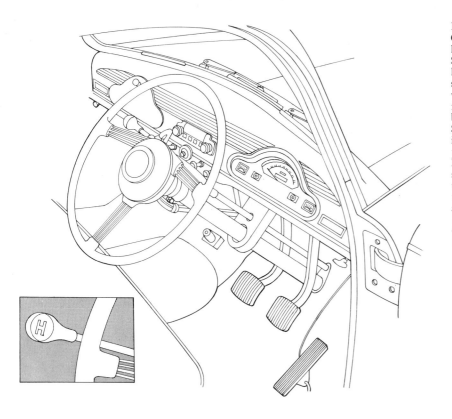

Modernizing the Ford. Britain's 1,508-cc Consul only just comes into our period, having been launched at the London Show in October, 1950. Thinking was, however, authentic late forties – an over-square four-cylinder engine set well forward in a classic unitary hull, independent front suspension by Earl McPherson's ball-joint system, and hydraulic brakes. Styling is slab-sided (Fiat would later copy it for their first true post-war 1100), with plenty of room for six people and their luggage. Further, it is a rationalized design, exploiting the unitary philosophy to the full, since Ford offered an alternative version with longer engine mounts to take a 2.3-litre six-cylinder engine sharing the Consul's dimensions. The Zephyr and this Consul were certainly the most advanced Fords you could buy at the time. The American and French species, though blessed with parallel suspension improvements, were still wedded to long-stroke flathead motors, while in Cologne the German factory was turning out the good old 1,172-cc Ten, even if their Taunus had been given hydraulic anchors way back in the summer of 1939. Less attractive is the driver's eye view (right). Pendant pedals are an asset and the new three-spoke steering wheel doesn't obscure the driver's view. The column shift is bearable only because Ford stayed loyal to three forward speeds, while styling has triumphed over ergonomics on the facia, even down to the motif of the matching glovebox lid. Just visible is the nasty umbrella handle actuating the emergency brake, a horror destined to stay with us for another twenty years.

built an automobile since 1934. More interesting were the casualties of the near future – the American Kaiser, the British Singer, and – a specialist case this – the remaining *grandes routières* of France.

The only obvious similarity between Kaiser and Singer is, of course, the body shape. The team which created Singer's 1948 SM1500 must surely have been influenced by Howard Darrin's Kaisers, first seen two years earlier. In other respects, the two concerns could hardly have been more different. Singer were an old-established outfit in Britain's Midlands, with roots going back to bicycle days. The Kaiser was the brainchild of a shipbuilding millionaire, Henry J. Kaiser, who dared to essay the "last onslaught on Detroit", challenging not only the Big Three but the still outwardly-strong independents – Hudson, Nash, Packard, and Studebaker. Kaiser made a frontal attack on his rivals; Singer, despite a strong bid in the lowest price class during the later 1920s, specialized in cars which were "a little different" and cost slightly more than a Morris or Austin.

The road to ruin was, however, a similar one, be it in Birmingham, England, or Willow Run in the United States. The juggernauts enjoyed comprehensive coverage of the market; smaller firms could not afford it. Once battle was joined, both Kaiser and Singer were doomed. The issue was exacerbated in the United States by Henry Ford II's all-out bid to beat Chevrolet, and in Britain not only by the Austin-Morris merger, but also by the powerful challenge of Sir John Black's Standard-Triumph empire.

The only real variables in the non-specialist automobile business are production and sales. The basic costs of tooling, manufacture, distribution, and publicity are the same. In the case of small firms there are simply fewer cars to sell and fewer dealers to sell them. Further, one is stuck with the same mechanical specification or the same shape (prob-

ably both), until one has paid for it. Diversification is risky and must succeed to pay off. Kaiser chose a true working-man's car, the Henry J, in preference to a vee-eight programme, and the Henry J was not a commercial success. The SM1500 story was just the same, only Singer's second string was a 1930s-style semi-sporting roadster of very limited appeal. As for their regular sedans, they were well-engineered automobiles with better than average handling. They could not, however, match Austin or Morris on price, and the factory's annual potential of perhaps 12,000 units was never realized. The SM's banner year was 6,358 cars in 1951; the design was obsolete by 1953, yet Singer were still making it, albeit with a new and more traditional grille, when they sold out to Rootes in 1956.

In any case, the public was becoming more critical, and so were the journalists who sought to educate it. All too many "road tests" of the 1930s were extensions of makers' advertising campaigns: criticisms were never very pungent. It would never have done to have dismissed an inefficient heater in the style of the late Laurence Pomeroy: "The designers ... appear to have missed a term owing to measles or the like." Of those infuriating American suction wipers, still general practice in the mid-fifties, he observed that "a comparable engine fault would be quietened at the cost of $100,000 worth of research". We were, however, a long way from the stern climate of 1963, when a British test team found it "impossible to be polite about the brakes" of a popular economy model.

Not that buyers could as yet afford to vent their criticism in any practical form. They took what was offered to them, which included all the American fads from the 1940–42 period. This included column shift, destined for a ten-year run in Europe, and found, incredibly, on early DB2 Aston Martins (it was not compulsory) and on every

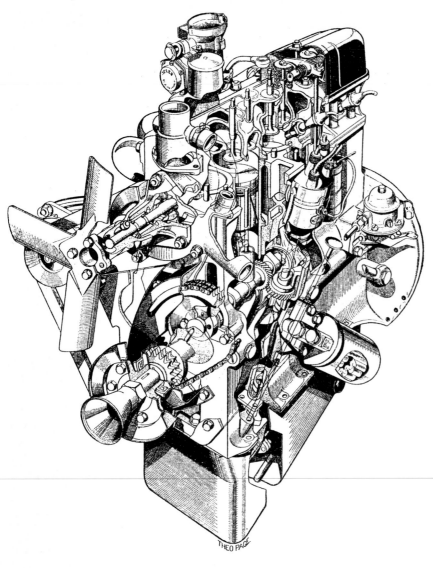

Because it was meant to look like a 1942 Plymouth, did look like a 1942 Plymouth, was ugly, and handled badly, the Standard Vanguard has suffered at the hands of posterity. By the mid-fifties, it was apparent that it was the wrong size of car for the world's markets, and Standard-Triumph were stuck with it for another seven years even then. But in 1950, this sedan with that season's new rear fender skirts, powered by a simple three-bearing wet-liner pushrod four (this is the 1.8-litre prototype, but production engines with 2,088 cc and 68 hp were identical in layout) was still a good seller: 185,000 customers in the first five seasons. And quite a few of these folk felt that Standard's 164-in (4.2 m) long compact was the logical replacement for their ageing Chevrolets, Willys, and Model A Fords. The Vanguard got itself put together under licence in such relatively unlikely countries as Belgium, India, and Switzerland, and it sold well in Australia, considering strong Holden opposition. Further, that tough old four would be around long after the Standard Vanguard was forgotten, powering the successful Ferguson tractor. As of 1950, it had only just found its way into a proper sports car (Morgan's Plus-4), but before production ceased in 1967, it had also been applied to Swallow Sorettis, Peerless GTs, and the first 150,000 Triumph sports cars to bear the TR label.

"Vanguarditis", Italian-style, or Ing. Dante Giacosa's American-type automobile for Europeans. Even by the standards of the Old World, the 1950 Fiat 1400, with 1,395 cc and 44 hp, was underengined, and thus at an immediate disadvantage against Standard's Vanguard (2,088 cc, 68 hp) and the later Renault Frégate (1,996 cc, 57 hp). Stylewise (*top left*), it was scarcely an inspiring object, the doleful egg-crate grille being hard to equate with the elegance of many a Torinese coachbuilder, but beneath the skin there was much of interest. One would expect good hydraulic brakes on a Fiat (they'd been using them since 1931), and Europeans had learnt to endure the company's transmission hand-brake, a sudden-death affair. The sectioned plan view (*bottom left*) shows that three of the parameters laid down by Giacosa's Board – good visibility, room for six people, and adequate luggage accommodation – were achieved. Here also was Fiat's first attempt at unitary construction, and they would use this method for many years. The body structure was welded to "frame" side members, and the engine and front suspension units were carried on "wheelbarrow" extensions as used by Citroën since 1934. Suspension arrangements (*right*) were a curious mixture: the conventional coil-and-wishbone setup was a logical development of the successful system found on pre-war 1100s. Less pleasing was the back end's combination of a rigid axle and coils. This gave a very soft ride at the price of some very peculiar roll angles in fast cornering, reminiscent of 1938 and later Buicks. (When Fiat upset the weight distribution by listing a diesel-powered option in 1953, the results were even more alarming.)

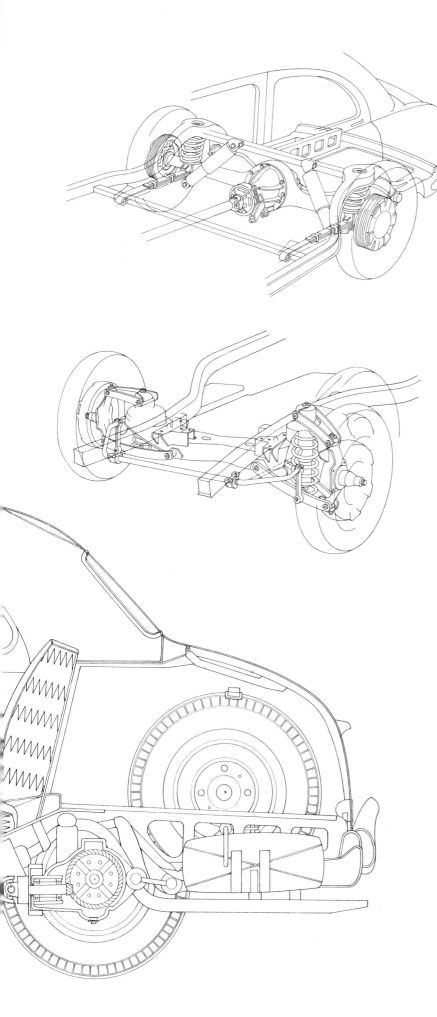

Mercedes-Benz sold to the public between 1950 and 1954. Alfa Romeo also fell for the blandishments of three-in-the-front-seat, though to their credit, Jaguar confined this fad to their automatic editions, first seen in 1953.

Four-on-the-column was frankly unpleasing, especially with the lost motion that comes with old age. Rootes, Peugeot, and Mercedes-Benz propably made the nastiest ones, though Triumph's right-hand column shift took a little acclimatization.

One concomitant of the European role as general providers was a curious attempt to revive the old American compact themes of the 1920s. If sedans with motors of 1,200 cc or 1,500 were right for the Old World, then for Africa, Asia, and the Antipodes the correct answer must surely be something a little bigger and roomier, an updated Model A Ford. A four-cylinder engine was imperative, since it was simpler and easier to maintain than a six and took up less room. Money could also be saved by using the same mechanical elements for a range of light trucks.

Thus, the trend from 2-litre sixes to comparable four-cylinder machinery, already detectable by 1938, moved on apace. Austin's pre-war Fourteen-Six gave way to their first overhead-valve passenger car, the 2.2-litre four-cylinder Sixteen. Alfa Romeo, Borgward, Fiat, Humber, Standard, Lago-Talbot, and Triumph – an interesting cross-section of makes – were others who made the changeover, albeit small-ish sixes were preferred by Nuffield, and by General Motors's two European houses, Opel and Vauxhall. In Czechoslovakia Tatra's big rear-engined automobiles were now flat-fours instead of vee-eights.

The rest of the new technical theme was more questionable and was typified by the Standard Vanguard. Styling was modelled, intentionally, on the 1942 Plymouth, and the car retained a separate chassis. In other respects it conformed to prevailing ideas, with a simple and tough 2,088-cc overhead-valve four-cylinder engine giving 68 bhp, a three-speed gearbox with (surprisingly) synchromesh on bottom, a hypoid rear axle, coil-spring independent front suspension, and full hydraulic brakes. It weighed 2,657 lb (*c.* 1,200 kg) and was far more compact than contemporary American cars, measuring only 164 in (4.2 m) from stem to stern. Handling was American, but the Vanguard would manage 80 mph (130 km/h) and had a modest fuel consumption, improved still further by 1950's overdrive option.

Others had the same idea. The Russian Pobeda was a sedate affair with a 52-bhp side-valve motor, a logical replacement for the old GAZ-A. Fiat's entry, the 1400 of 1950, was conceived by Dante Giacosa as "an American car of European type", which meant an ugly piece of bulboid with a rolling gait balanced by a first-class ride over rough surfaces. Alas, the dictates of economy had persuaded Giacosa to haul a 2, 486-lb (1,130 kg) sedan on a mere 1,395 cc and 44 bhp, a policy which led to ridiculous over-gearing and most un-American top-gear acceleration – or rather a total lack of it. Finally, in 1951, came Renault's 2-litre Frégate, a more sophisticated design, unitary like the Fiat, but with all-independent springing.

None were actually failures. All four survived into 1958, and the Vanguard – by this time a unitary structure restyled by the Italian Michelotti – was still around in 1962. The Fiat proved very popular in Spain, where it was chosen as the first product of the SEAT factory opened in 1953, while Vanguards were assembled in such countries as Australia, Belgium, India, and even Switzerland. The first four seasons' sales ran close to 185,000 units.

Unfortunately, the Vanguard and its rivals were not what the world at large wanted. Customers missed the smoothness of the two extra cylinders and soon discovered that one seldom actually needed to carry six people. And if the customer was not concerned with plenty of space, the frugal little 1,131-cc Volkswagen did the job much better. Further,

Miniatures: two failures, a moderate success, and one that is still succeeding. The 1948 Playboy (*top right*) was a baby only by American standards, with its 1.5-litre side-valve four-cylinder Continental engine, conventional drive-line, and unitary convertible body. But one paid the same for a "stripped" Chevrolet, and even the inclusion of a radio in the list price couldn't tempt the buyers. Far more basic were two contenders from 1948 and 1949 respectively, France's Rovin (*top left*) and Britain's Bond (*opposite, bottom right*). Though doorless and powered by a rear-mounted 260-cc single cylinder engine, the French contender had a backbone frame and all-independent suspension. Later models had doors and an extra cylinder – and more weight, hence sales never exceeded four hundred a year. The even simpler three-wheeled Bond used a two-cycle Villiers motor-cycle engine of 122 or 197 cc driving the front wheel, and its fat tyres doubled as suspension. Progressive improvement kept Bond in the minicar business until 1965, though unlike Rovin, they were untroubled by the all-conquering 2CV Citroën (*opposite, top left*), introduced in 1948. Cheap to make and to service, it possessed a frost-proof air-cooled flat-twin engine, interlinked self-levelling suspension, and all modern conveniences—save aesthetic appeal. The five millionth came off the lines in 1976, and there was no sign of its popularity diminishing.

Two generations of Americans from the 1940s. The 1946 Lincoln (*opposite, centre right*) was still the old flathead vee-twelve with 1942's box fenders and three-window styling. The 1948 Kaiser (*opposite, top right*) represents the new two-window (four-light to Englishmen) idiom dating back to the Cadillac Sixty Special, as well as the latest slab sides. The drawing of the Traveler version shows that it is the true ancestor of the modern hatchback. The idea was to combine the carrying capacity of the station wagon with the social acceptability of a sedan.

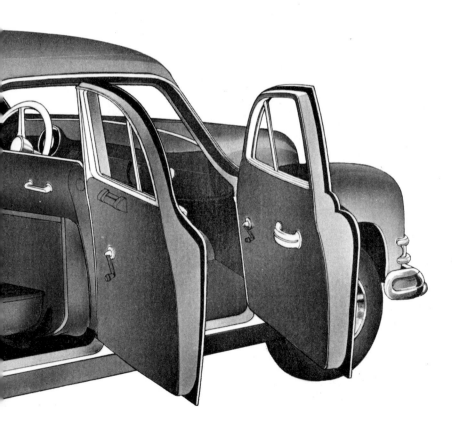

Ford's Model T theme up to date, or the New Universal Car, even if, numerically, the Volkswagen would stay ahead. On Citroën's 2CV, the unitary structure (*top*) was of the simplest. Body elements could be made with the minimum of press tools, there were no expensive curved panels to repair, and doors and hood used interlocking flanges instead of hinges. In the main drawing, by contrast, the remarkable roominess of the car must be the first impression. At 147 in (3.78 m) from stem to stern, it was a lot longer than the contemporary Fiat 500 and even longer than the more compact four-door miniatures such as the Austin A30 and the 4CV Renault. The simple tubular-framed seats are quick-detachable, and the convertible roll-top admits not only fresh air but indivisible loads. Doors can be lifted off, too. On the mechanical side, an air-cooled flat-twin engine drives the front wheels. The four-speed transmission with its facia-mounted shift has synchromesh: it also features a geared-up top to enable the little car to trundle along on level ground at 35 and even the maximum speed of 40 mph (65 km/h) without overstressing the tiny engine. Most ingenious of all is the interconnected self-levelling suspension – in effect, if not in design, a poor man's preview of the elaborate hydropneumatics for which Citroën would become famous in the mid-fifties. The horizontal coil arrangement (just visible under the driver's seat on the sectioned car) linked front and rear on each side.

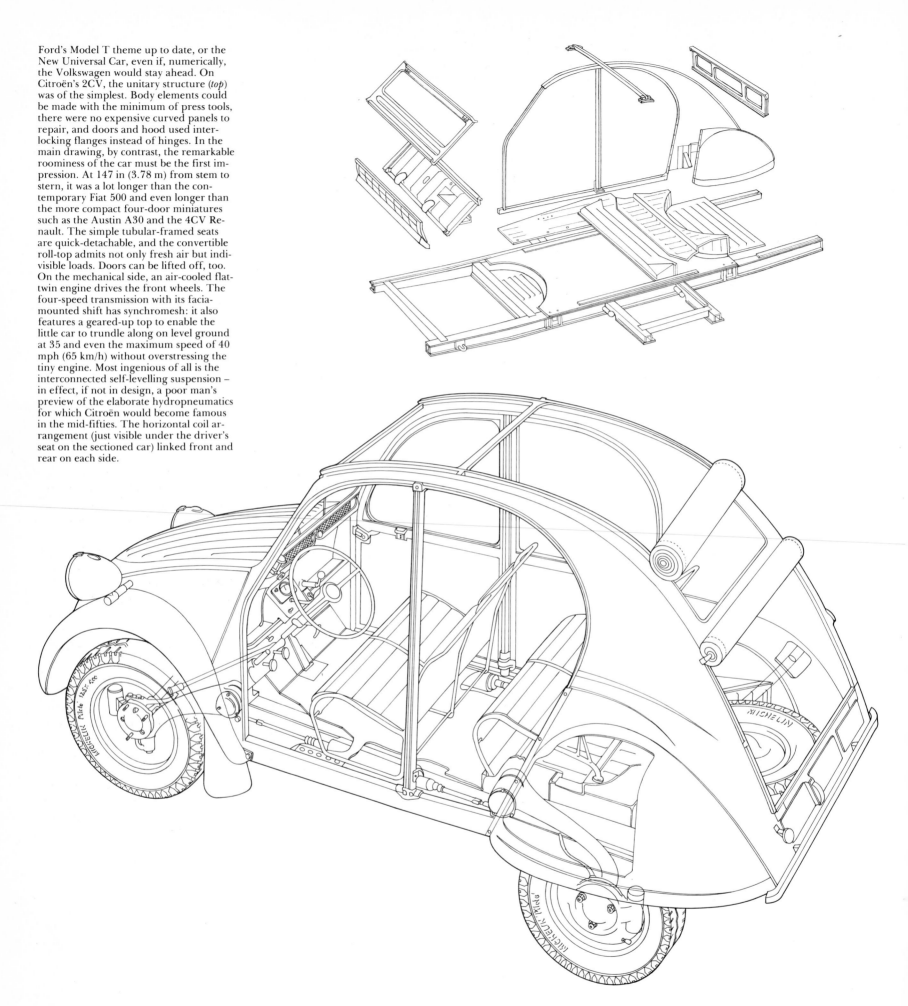

the introduction of the British Ford Zephyr Six at the 1950 Show suggested that the 2-litre class was moving up-market again, and so it proved. Renault and Fiat, to whom their "American" compacts were but second strings, suffered little; but Standard, committed too long to a one-model policy, would pay the penalty in due course.

There were other approaches to the chimera of a people's car. Minicars invariably arrive in times of economic stringency, and the late 1940s saw the usual assortment of oddballs: the Swiss Rapid, with its backbone frame and rear-mounted 350-cc motor; Britain's Bond, with unitary construction, a single chain-driven front wheel, and no suspension at all apart from fat tyres on tiny wheels; the 425-cc Rovin and the even more minimal Mochet in France; and sundry German devices such as Hermann Holbein's Champion, noted for a curious, spectacle-type steering wheel. Some survived; the Bond enjoyed a fifteen-year run, and both the French babies all but saw the fifties out, but they never enjoyed anything quite like the vogue of the next generation of "bubbles". There was no disaster comparable to 1956's Suez Crisis to administer the necessary shot in the arm. Fiat's domination of the Italian market ruled out any serious minicars in that country. Italians preferred scooters, their main contribution in the sub-utility sector.

In any case, Europe had her own basic transportation – without any cyclecar overtones. In Germany there was the standard Volkswagen, in Britain Ford offered the Anglia, and France had the 2CV Citroën. Both Ford and Volkswagen were pre-war designs with no amortization headaches, the formula being merely to reduce frills to a minimum. Throughout the 1950s, the cheapest Beetle lacked both synchromesh and hydraulic brakes, while the Ford reached its most rudimentary in 1953 with the 1,172-cc Popular – a single windshield wiper, and suction-operated at that, diminutive headlamps, the minimum of instruments, and scarcely any chromium plate. But the design was proven and the car sold for less than £400 ($1,120). Ford, like Volkswagen, contrived to hold prices down.

The Citroën was someting quite different, with front-wheel drive. It also took a leaf out of the Volkswagen's book, having a slow-turning air-cooled flat-twin engine, giving an untiring 9 bhp from 375 cc. The ingenious interconnected suspension gave an excellent ride over rough surfaces. Almost everything, the doors included, was easily removable, and parts were cheap. Admittedly, the thing was angular, it came in an unprepossessing corrugated grey finish, the overdrive top gear could not cope with even the slightest acclivity, and top speed was 40 mph (65 km/h). The ingenious rolltop convertible body was, however, an inestimable boon when handling bulky loads, and the 2CV was still available – and still selling – thirty years after the first one burst on a startled public in 1948.

There was, of course, no hope for parallel babies in the United States, though several firms tried. Playboys and Kellers used small proprietary four-cylinder engines, while Gary Davis toyed with a huge three-wheeler, and Powel Crosley revived his pre-war minicars, now with 722-cc, overhead-camshaft, four-cylinder units in place of the old air-cooled twins. Only Crosley enjoyed appreciable sales, working up to a peak of 25,000 units at the height of the seller's market in 1948. He survived as long as he did thanks to successful radio and refrigerator interests. The others were little more than hopeful stock-promotion schemes. Even when the Securities Exchange Commission turned a blind eye, Playboy and Keller stood no chance. They were dependent on proprietary firms for all their essential elements, and the only suitable small four left was the 2.2-litre Willys; all the others were conceived as stationary units and tended to overheat on the road. In any case, the bottom of the American market was where Ford and Chevrolet

prices began. Americans might buy Austin A40s and 4CV Renaults as second cars "because they were cute" and had the snob-value of being foreign, but they wanted no part of any such native offerings. George Keller tried a new tack by offering his car as a station wagon, a style he considered "the most wanted in America". But why buy an underpowered woody, when metal wagons were just round the corner?

There was also the case of the Aluminium Française-Grégoire, yet another people's car with an international history, albeit a sad one. Had all the licencees prospered, it might easily have anticipated the Ford Fiesta as a true car for all nations. Simca's initial involvement in France was made with Fiat's blessing, the Dutch Government was interested, and attempts were made to bring FN of Belgium back into the car business. Across the Channel, Denis Kendall's Grantham Productions Ltd., already exploring £100-cars, dropped their own radial-engined effort in favour of the Grégoire. They actually catalogued their English edition in 1946 for £37 ($185) less than a Ford Anglia, but the venture folded without delivering a single car. The Australian Laurence Hartnett bought the remains of Kendall's firm and tried to market the design in his homeland.

Alas! the Grégoire always seemed to miss out on promised government support. First it was France itself, where backing was withdrawn after Simca reneged on their original deal with the designer. Then the Dutch lost heart, and finally the Australian venture lost its backing both at federal and state levels after a change of administration. The last straw for Hartnett came when his body suppliers failed to meet their commitments, with the consequence that his Melbourne works had to content themselves with 120 handbuilt automobiles. Though Panhard would take the design up at home, and get it into series production by 1948, their modifications displeased Grégoire. They also transformed the image from people's car into a specialist machine, its distinguished competition record somewhat tarnished by a reputation for fragility in inexperienced hands.

This was a pity, for the AFG was an ingenious and logical development of the 1937 Amilcar Compound front-wheel-drive theme, with the same light-alloy unitary construction. This time, however, Grégoire had come up with an air-cooled flat-twin unit giving 18 bhp. Its four-speed overdrive transmission paralleled that of the 2CV Citroën, weight was in the 880–1,000-lb (400–500 kg) bracket, and the little four-seater sedan attained over 55 mph (90 km/h) with a staggering economy of 70 mpg (4 lit/100).

But if the Grégoire was too sophisticated for the role of international people's car, the Volkswagen had at least one rival in early post-war Europe: the old DKW-Front theme dating back to 1931. This one was, of course, a victim of the partition of Germany, the main factories in Saxony being lost to the East Zone, where production did not recommence until 1948. Even then, what emerged in the shape of the IFA F8 was unmodified 1937 and a little too primitive for most people, even at heavily subsidized export prices. The reconstituted Auto Union, now based in Düsseldorf, was not ready with their updated version until 1950, but numerous efforts were made to duplicate a well-loved theme. For example, Carl Borgward's LP300 Lloyd with its "Elastoplast" body fulfilled a need for sub-utility transport in the darkest years, and the Czechoslovak Aero-Minor, based on the 1938 Jawa, enjoyed a modest success. Attempts to market Danish DKW derivatives were foiled by the impossibility of obtaining engines, and the same fate attended Gunnar Philipsson's 1946 experiments in Sweden. In the latter case, however, the initiative passed to Saab (aircraft, electronics), a firm with sufficient resources to tackle the job from scratch. The first of their aerodynamic Type 92 sedans had reached the public by 1950, albeit the Saab would

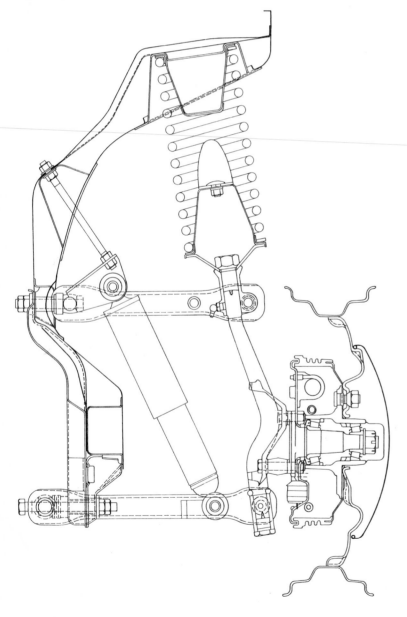

Post-war unitary construction. The American Nash Rambler (*top left*) and British Morris Minor (*top right*) typify true post-war creations from firms which had already abdicated from the traditional chassis frame, though earlier Nashes had not been full unitaries. Ingenious is the American car's coil-spring independent front suspension (*lower left*). The spring is mounted directly above the stub carrier and its abutment is formed on the body structure. This method dispensed with a heavy front cross-member; thus the engine itself could be mounted further forward and more passenger space made available on a true "compact" with a wheel-base of only 100 in (2.5 m). Also ingenious was Nash designer Ted Ulrich's solution of the problems of unitary con-

vertibles. By making the ragtop Rambler a cabrio-limousine with rigid sides, he added the necessary structural strength and achieved a higher degree of parts interchangeability, too. The Rambler was rather before its time as a compact, and sales got away to a slow start, though by 1953, it was outselling the full-size Nashes. Morris, of course, had marketed a fully unitary overhead-valve 1,140-cc Ten in 1939 and had been making it to military and civilian account ever since. The construction is seen on the opposite page, but despite the modest 27-hp output of the outmoded 918-cc side-valve engine used until the end of 1952, their new Minor handled better than almost all the opposition and was an immediate best seller.

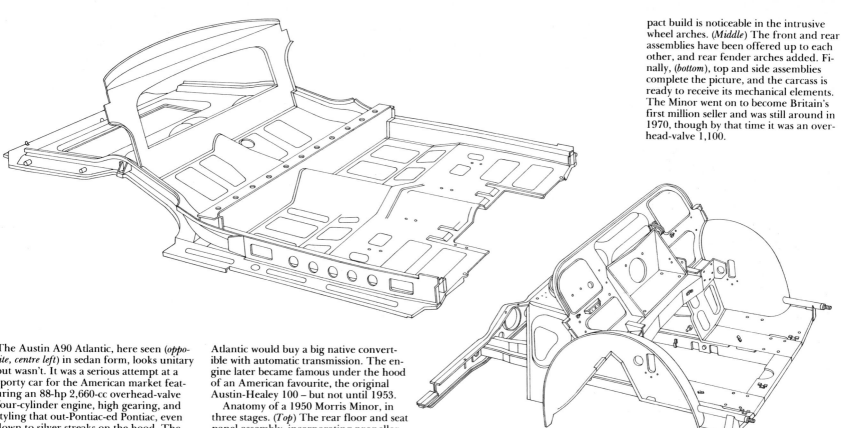

pact build is noticeable in the intrusive wheel arches. (*Middle*) The front and rear assemblies have been offered up to each other, and rear fender arches added. Finally, (*bottom*), top and side assemblies complete the picture, and the carcass is ready to receive its mechanical elements. The Minor went on to become Britain's first million seller and was still around in 1970, though by that time it was an overhead-valve 1,100.

The Austin A90 Atlantic, here seen (*opposite, centre left*) in sedan form, looks unitary but wasn't. It was a serious attempt at a sporty car for the American market featuring an 88-hp 2,660-cc overhead-valve four-cylinder engine, high gearing, and styling that out-Pontiac-ed Pontiac, even down to silver streaks on the hood. The original convertible had a power top, and this sedan was in the classical American hardtop idiom, but the A90 flopped. The short wheel-base made for a pitchy ride and a lack of stylistic balance, Americans wanted more than four cylinders, and in those days, the $2,300-odd asked for an

Atlantic would buy a big native convertible with automatic transmission. The engine later became famous under the hood of an American favourite, the original Austin-Healey 100 – but not until 1953.

Anatomy of a 1950 Morris Minor, in three stages. (*Top*) The rear floor and seat panel assembly, incorporating propellor shaft tunnel and body sills. The rear spring brackets have already been welded on, but the front end and firewall unit has been built up separately. The stout box cross-member is ready to take the upper members of the torsion-bar suspension, and already one of the penalties of com-

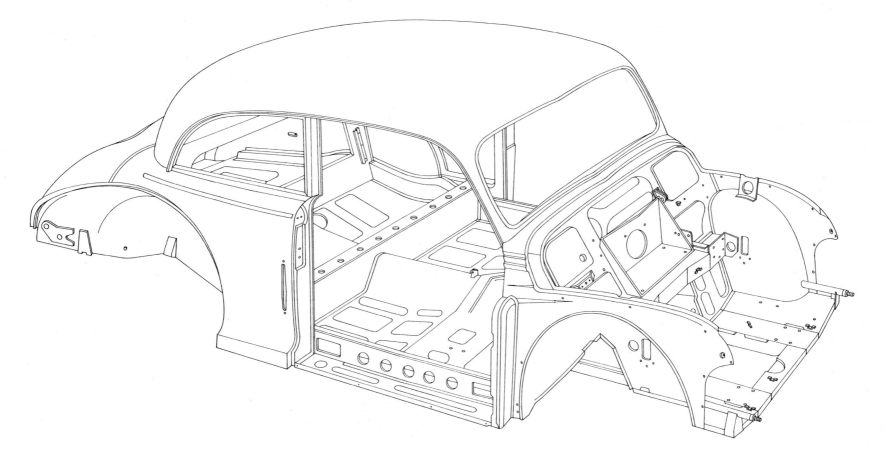

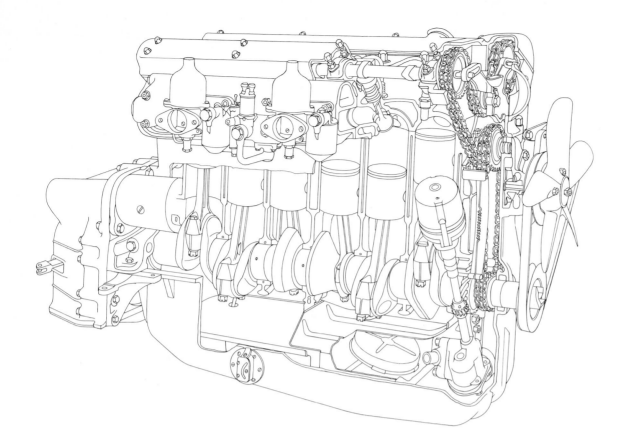

take some seven years to become known outside Scandinavia. Nor was the DKW theme exhausted; it would crop up again, outside our period, in Argentina and Poland.

Isolationism was truly on its way out. If the Pobeda, the Vanguard, and the 1400 Fiat represented three different approaches to the same idea, national characteristics were now confined to a few countries and a few specialist sectors. The Americans went their own sweet way, with a continuity undisturbed until the energy crisis of 1973. Compacts like Nash's Rambler were running firmly against the tide, which is why its makers offered it shamelessly as a luxury package ($1,808 inclusive of radio, clock, heater, and power top) and not as competition for Chevrolet. The same went for Japan, where the old regulations still obtained and 1930s themes were cloaked in unpleasing parodies of the post-war Crosley. Sheet steel had to be imported, and the handwork techniques dictated by short runs were only too apparent from the end-product's appearance. The Mercedes-Benz was typically German, every centimetre of it, and few of Britain's specialist offerings could have been made anywhere else. Jaguar's Mk V, new for 1949, featured semi-recessed headlamps, an umbrella-handle hand-brake, rear-wheel spats, and disc instead of centre-lock wire wheels, but there was still a polished wood facia with circular black-face dials, the radiator was unmistakably a radiator, and one sat on leather.

But a formula was evolving. The average small European sedan showed traces of its 1930s ancestry, but down-draft carburation was now general practice, and short-stroke motors predominated. If the Fiat 1400 was excessively oversquare at 82 × 66 mm, and some of the British hangovers still reflected the old horsepower tax (Vauxhall's 1.5-litre had dimensions of 69 × 95 mm right up to 1952), the Opel's 80 × 74 mm were more typical. The single-plate clutch was still with us,

hypoid final drives were gaining ground, and coil-spring independent front suspension was in the ascendant, albeit independent rear suspension was still largely confined to Germany and Czechoslovakia. (Only Renault of the other Big Battalions used it.) The disc wheel had supplanted most other types, and there was an increasing tendency to offer only sedan bodies. As yet, Volkswagen had no catalogued convertible, and all that Britain's Big Six could offer amounted to the Hillman Minx and the Morris Minor tourer in the low-price class. Floor shift was reserved for baby cars (Fiat 500, Morris Minor, Volkswagen, and 4CV Renault).

Fiscal policy still had its influence. While Britain's flat rate, enacted in 1947, was a bonus, the French balanced this unwonted official generosity by their sadistic and egalitarian ideas. Henceforward, there would be a gradual increase of impost up to 15CV (say, 3 litres), above which it was assumed that owners were rich men, and therefore, deserving of a swingeing rise, from about £20 ($56) to £78 ($220).

This was the end for the *grandes routières*. The Bugatti was a 17CV, Hotchkiss and Delahaye relied on 3.5-litre motors rated at 20CV, and Talbot, by that time offering the world's most powerful touring model with a 4,482-cc six-cylinder unit, found themselves saddled with 26CV. Until the rise of Jaguar, Ferrari, and a reorganized Daimler-Benz AG in Stuttgart, the *grandes routières* were the world's best-proven fast tourers. Contemporary British rivals such as Allard and Healey were produced only in penny numbers; but, deprived of their home market, the French factories could not bring export prices down to competitive levels. No foreign exchange was available to purchase leather from Britain; their bread-and-butter lines (Hotchkiss's excellent 13CV and Delahaye's 12CV, both with four-cylinder engines) were obsolescent and no match for the new Ford Vedette, much less for the indestruc-

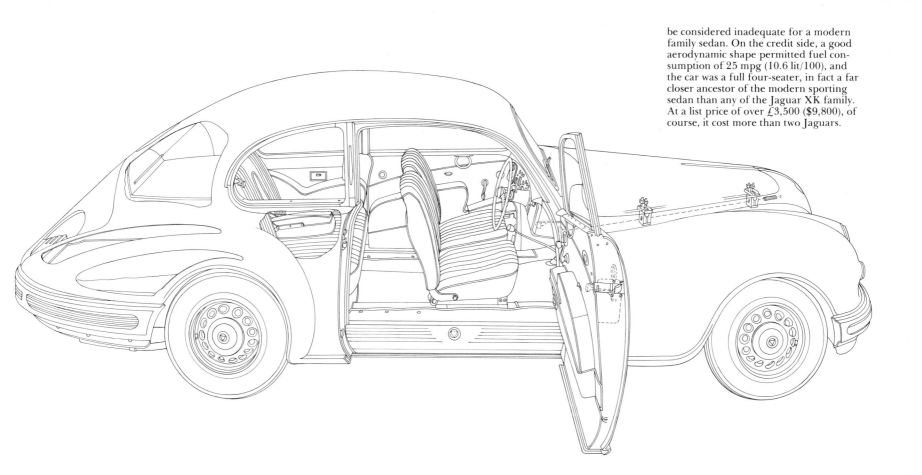

be considered inadequate for a modern family sedan. On the credit side, a good aerodynamic shape permitted fuel consumption of 25 mpg (10.6 lit/100), and the car was a full four-seater, in fact a far closer ancestor of the modern sporting sedan than any of the Jaguar XK family. At a list price of over £3,500 ($9,800), of course, it cost more than two Jaguars.

tible *traction*. There was no money for racing (which Talbot tried) or for new models to redress the balance. Hotchkiss could not afford Grégoire's 2-litre flat four (they made about 250 in three years), while Delahaye's light 4 × 4 was a complicated piece of machinery with which the army was soon disenchanted. It was all over, effectively, by 1953, though Talbots were still being made in small numbers as late as 1958.

In any case, there was precious little future for young firms. The fall of the Kaiser empire in the United States was a *cause célèbre*, but it was typical. Some ninety new manufacturers chanced their arm between 1945 and 1950, but of these, only eight were still in business in 1970, and of these, the British Bond and the Italian Abarth were on the verge of extinction. Another Italian specialist, Moretti, had abdicated into the custom-Fiat business. The remainder comprised two outstanding makers of specialist sports cars (Ferrari, Porsche) and three "national" cars which survived in the absence of serious competition. In addition to the Holden, these were Sweden's Saab (offering a smaller car than any pre-1975 Volvo) and the Hindusthan from India, essentially a Morris adapted to local conditions.

The "hopefuls" are a fascinating study. The Allard, last of the traditional Anglo-Americans, enjoyed a thirteen-year run, making hay while bigger producers stayed with sedans, and profiting from the sales of engine-less automobiles to the United States, where they could be fitted with the new vee-eights. In 1951, Allard's banner year, 337 units were delivered, but an attempt to diversify into smaller sports models with British Ford motors was frustrated by the Big Battalions. The Palm Beach coincided with the Austin-Healey and the first TR Triumph: that was that. Of the swords-into-ploughshares brigade, Britain's Bristol Aeroplane Company did well with their anglicized 2-litre BMW, but their Italian counterparts, Caproni of Milan, got nowhere with either

the attractive flat-four CEMSA-Caproni or with the rear-engined Isotta Fraschini Monterosa. Plans to make the former in Belgium foundered, and the ambitious Isotta was about as viable as Invicta's automatic Black Prince, a creature already encountered in our story. Most exciting of the *exotica* was undoubtedly Preston Tucker's rear-engined Torpedo, the fastest sedan available in the United States in 1948. Its specification embraced a modified Franklin flat-six helicopter unit and a Cord-like four-speed transmission, but even had the finance been forthcoming, one wonders how the long-cosseted American motorist would have coped with a projectile combining inherent rear-end breakaway with a top speed close to 120 mph (200 km/h). As less than fifty Tuckers were built, the proto-Naders never had the possibility to voice their indignation!

Styling evolved from the 1942 American shape. Fenders and grille were now firmly integrated, while slab sides added to the visual joys of the compound curve. Singer and Hillman in Britain and Borgward in Germany were among the staunchest exponents of the latest idiom, and the early 1950s would see desperate attempts to break up the monotonous areas of pastel paint, now edging blacks and browns out of fashion. To the inevitable chromium strip would soon be added a new generation of two-toning.

Of new body styles, the station wagon continued its upward move. This was reflected in American sales, always an anticipation of trends in the Old World. Only 4,551 wagons were sold in 1935, but over 30,000 had found buyers in 1941, and the six-figure mark was achieved for the first time in 1948. Though the style was now mandatory in middle-class ranges, Ford still outsold everyone else. The all-metal wagon, pioneered by Plymouth in 1949, was a timely improvement, since the 1946–48 period had seen a rash of quite hideous half-timbered sedans and

225

American success and failure. The 1950 Plymouth Suburban (*lower left*) is a copybook American automobile with a simple flathead six-cylinder engine (3.6 litres, 97 hp) in a conventional chassis, no frills, and a straightforward synchromesh transmission. Interesting, however, is the use of all-steel construction for the station wagon body at a time when woodies were still in fashion. The very "commercial" looks did not deter the customers, who bought over thirty-four thousand of this type in 1950, as against a mere two thousand woodies in Plymouth's de luxe line. The Tucker (*top left*) combined almost every possible heresy. The 5.5-litre flat-six engine (adapted from a Franklin helicopter motor) lived at the rear and drove the rear wheels via a four-speed transaxle with electric shift. All four wheels were independently sprung, and unusual features for 1948 included doors opening into the roof, a pop-out windshield, and a carpeted front compartment with no hazardous projections. Perhaps it's as well that the money ran out, for the average motorist could never have coped with a rear-engined monster weighing over 4,200 lb (1,900 kg), a tendency to hang its tail out, and a speed of 120 mph (192 km/h).

An altogether safer rear-engined proposition was the evergreen Volkswagen (*top right*), where the effects of a hoppity tail end were nullified by a top speed of 60 mph (100 km/h). This four-passenger cabriolet by Karmann was just beginning to reach the public in 1949; it would still be on the market thirty years later, having outlived the sedans in its native Germany.

Finally, four sports models from the late 1940s. The Allard (*lower right*) was lighter than pre-war "Anglo-American sports bastards", thanks to a trials ancestry. Engineering was somewhat rudimentary, and there wasn't a lot of room on a 112-in (2.8 m) wheel-base. Further, the faithful old 3.6-litre flathead Ford vee-eight engine gave an unspectacular performance. The car sold quite well, thought, at a time when the new generation of sports cars, such as the XK120 Jaguar (*opposite, bottom*) were in very short supply – though William Lyons's masterpiece was unveiled at the 1948 London Show, nobody got one until the following summer, and it was out of bounds to Britons until at least March, 1950. Its 3.4-litre six-cylinder twin overhead-camshaft engine developed 160 hp, and sizzling acceleration was combined with a 120 mph (192 km/h) top speed, civilized amenities, and a lack of temperament not usually associated with so complex a power unit. For real complexity the 166 Ferrari (*opposite, top left*) offered two upstairs camshafts, one per block of a small 2-litre vee-twelve designed by Gioacchino Colombo. Here it is seen in Mille Miglia trim with the minimum of road equipment: "street" Ferraris were the exception rather than the rule in 1949. Output was 130–140 hp; it was as fast as the Jaguar and could reach the ton (160 km/h) in well under half a minute. Snags were in the handling department: early Ferraris were not very forgiving and grew even less so as the original chassis was progressively asked to cope with 200–300 hp. Finally (*opposite, top right*) the car which re-educated the United States, MG's TC as made from 1945 to 1949. Stylistically and mechanically it is 1936, with a traditional chassis and beam axles. On the credit side the 1,250-cc pushrod four-cylinder engine gives a dependable 54 hp, and the owner got a lot of fun for his £528 ($2,640 in 1946). In those first euphoric months of peace, too, the British export drive had yet to gather momentum, and quite a few TCs stayed home.

convertibles. Most successful of these were Chrysler's Town and Country family, but Ford, Mercury, and Nash also jumped aboard the bandwagon, and Packard's Country Sedan was not much better than the others. All of these were killed by high manufacturing costs rather than by improving national taste. By the mid-1950s, the forests had receded, apart from the odd decorative strake, as affected by BMC in Britain for many years to come.

In Europe, wagons were still van-related, a cheaper way of tackling the problem than farming the style out to specialist coachbuilders. Vauxhall offerings wore Bedford badges, and the Hillman Minx Estate was sold as a Commer. Of the Continentals, only Fiat produced woodies in series, on the diminutive 500 chassis.

By contrast, there was the hardtop, first offered in series by Buick in 1949. This one can best be described as a convertible substitute; it shared the ragtop's sheet metal but sported a fixed metal top, sometimes vinyl-covered. It saved owners from the nuisance of renewing the top material at regular intervals, gave better rear vision through its wider rear window, and lent itself to two-toning. Every American maker had one in their range by 1951, and the effect of its impact is realized when one reflects that, in Chevrolet's first year in the game, 1950, hardtops outsold ragtops by more than 2 to 1. By the mid-1950s, such European makers as Fiat, Hillman, and Simca were offering similar styles.

The sports car stood at the crossroads. France's *grandes routières* faced extinction, German industry as yet lacked the strength to venture into the exotic, and the Italians alternated between Fiat-derivatives and super-cars in the Ferrari class. Thus, Britain assumed the role of general provider and was destined to remain in command of this sector for a good twenty years. Variety was still remarkable: for modest pockets there was the classic MG (real individualists might prefer HRG or Morgan). In support were the Ford-engined Allard, a new Frazer Nash based on BMW/Bristol ingredients, and Donald Healey's 2.4-litre, Riley-powered and featuring all-coil suspension. Jaguar, as yet, held back, so the interesting Europeans – both of them trend-setters – were the Italian Ferrari and the German Porsche.

The Ferrari took over where Bugatti left off, anticipating a revival in "street" Maseratis (not to eventuate on a serious scale until 1957) and also the exotic four-cam vee-eight Pegaso from Spain, though this latter would be one of 1951's débutantes. The Ferrari reflected the modern idiom in some respects. Early vee-twelve engines were of the overhead-camshaft type, with over-square dimensions (60 × 58.8 mm in the case of the 166, the first model to reach the public – in 1949) and coil-spring front suspension. Magnetos were reserved for racing versions, but Ferrari's synchromesh (when provided) was not of the best. Performance was, however, staggering by the standards of the day. Ferrari's 1949 sports car offered 140 bhp from two litres, and by 1951, the 4.1-litre America in catalogue form was "quite capable of breaking the unofficial speed records for production and sports cars by many m.p.h. on any decent stretch of road", which meant an easy 145 mph (230 – 235 km/h). Complicated twelve-cylinder machinery, unforgiving road behaviour, and prices in the region of £5,400 ($15,000) were not, however, for the many.

More important was the acceleration of design processes initiated by BMW in 1936. The sports car was becoming more habitable. Noise, draughts, and a tooth-shaking ride were no longer regarded as essential concomitants of the genre. By 1950, even the TD MG ran to coil-spring independent front suspension, though its disc wheels (and those of the XK Jaguar) were less appreciated by diehards. Jaguar, however, had the right ideas. The car, as its American importers observed, "sells itself because it's exactly what the American enthusiast has wanted for a long

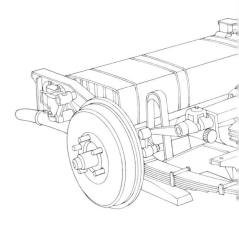

Spreading the British gospel of tradition, or pre-war engineering carried on into the 1950s. As long as there was a worldwide car shortage, almost anything would sell. Not that the 2½-litre Daimler of 1949 was entirely archaic when stripped of bodywork. Neither engine nor chassis were, of course, new: the former dated back in essence to 1933, while the latter had been unveiled at the 1937 London Show, when its coil-spring independent suspension was considered most advanced on an upper-middle-class British car. It gave high standards both of handling and ride. The frame has rigid cruciform bracing, though leaf suspension suffices at the rear. The engine is an entirely conventional long-stroke pushrod six, giving a sedate 66 hp in the single-carburettor form seen here, though as much as 90 could be had in sports guise with an extra carburettor. Sophisticated even in 1949 (when Europe still possessed not a single low-priced automatic) was the Daimler preselective fluid-flywheel transmission, with nineteen years of proven service behind it. It was probably the best compromise between manual and automatic, too, since the fluid flywheel eliminated the coarse and argumentative noises sometimes encountered on instant shifts on big engines incorporating the regular Wilson system. What one did not get, of course, was two-pedal drive: the left-hand pedal accomplished the actual shift. By now, the handbrake has been transformed into a nasty little umbrella handle under the facia in the cause of an unobstructed front compartment, though the battery has yet to move to the firewall, by now its normal location on the majority of cars.

time. It has the power to outspeed, outperform and outmanoeuvre anything built over here, and the price is right".

Though still an open car, the XK120 had adequate all-weather equipment. True, untemperamental twin overhead-camshaft, six-cylinder engines, a good ride, and speeds approaching 125 mph (200 km/h) had all been available in 1939, but only on expensive cars. Jaguar managed it all at a base price of less than £1,000 ($2,800), roughly double the old BMW's German list price in the 1930s, but a real bargain by 1949 standards. The car would accelerate through the gears to 100 mph (160 km/h) in 27.3 seconds, top-gear acceleration was a sensational 70–90 mph (112–145 km/h) in 9.9 seconds, and fuel consumption was a modest 18–20 mpg (13–14 lit/100). That this performance could seldom be utilized to the full was due to the fact that chassis and engine design had, for the moment, outstripped other technologies. The story of the disc brake and the radial ply tyre, essential concomitants of safe speed, lies just outside our period.

The first closed XK120 would be unveiled at Geneva in March, 1951. But already, the pre-war lead of Adler, Fiat, and the others had been followed up. The superb aerodynamics of Ferry Porsche's Volkswagen-based 1100s and 1300s were based on coupé themes, while the sports 1100 Fiat was back in improved form by 1947. The first post-war Aston Martin made in measurable quantities was 1950's DB2; its Bentley-designed twin overhead-camshaft six-cylinder motor accounted for much

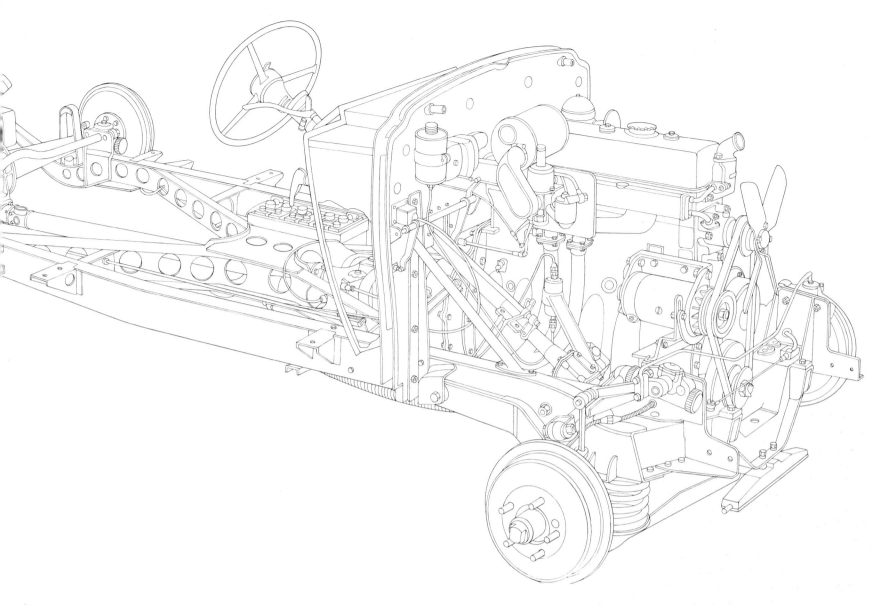

of the excitement, but pointers for the future lay in its aerodynamic two-passenger fixed-head coupé coachwork, and in a new variation on the alligator-hood theme: the entire hood, fender, and headlamp assembly tilted forward to give new standards of accessibility, even if (as latter-day Triumph owners discovered) dirt also gained access!

Also in the offing – and already visible, if not available in any quantity – was the true *granturismo* theme – offering indoor accommodation in a sports car for four at a pinch. The classic GT was, of course, the Lancia Aurelia, developed from Vittorio Jano's sophisticated 1,750-cc vee-six sedan, but the idea had been well expressed, in 1946, on the 2.4-litre Healey. This four-passenger sedan had excellent aerodynamics and a performance astonishing for its day, thanks to the 100-hp Riley engine, a light X-braced frame, and light coachwork in the Italian idiom. Weight was only 2,674 lb (1,215 kg). The car attained 104.63 mph (166.61 km/h) over a measured mile. That its commercial impact was small was due to the modest scale of operations at Warwick. A price of £1,598 ($7,990) simply could not compete with 3½-litre Jaguars at £1,100 ($5,500). None the less, the GT was off the ground, and 1952 would see a replacement for the lamented *grandes routières* in the 4.6-litre Bentley Continental – no wind noise, a speed of 117 mph (188 km/h), the effortless fast cruising available with a 3.077:1 top gear, and a fuel consumption superior to that of many 2-litre sedans. The price, of course, was prohibitive.

The traditional coachbuilders went into a sad decline. Fiscal savagery took its toll in France. Things were slightly better in Britain, where there were still some traditional chassis left – the Bentley, the Rolls-Royce, and the monstrous 5.5-litre straight-eight Daimler. Daimler boss Sir Bernard Docker enlivened London Shows with his exotic bodies on this car, such as the memorable Green Goddess, a power-top convertible with vertical headlamp clusters protected by perspex shields, and a single-panel curved windshield so vast as to call for triple wipers. Alas, the country was short of craftsmen and shorter still of cash: of twenty-three coachbuilders active at the outbreak of war less than ten made it into the 1950s. Vanden Plas sold out to Austin and Salmons-Tickford to David Brown's Aston Martin Lagonda Ltd.

Worse still, standard coachwork was often better-looking than bespoke efforts with price tags of £6,000 ($17,000) and more. It took a lot to match the balance of William Lyons's Jaguars, or, for that matter the razor-edge Triumph Renown and the latest Armstrong Siddeleys with a hint of 810 Cord at the front end. The coachbuilders did not help by their attempts to reconcile traditional shapes – especially the razor edge – with the latest slab-sided idiom from across the Atlantic, and some appalling creations graced Earls Court in 1948. Nor was it lost on visitors to the Show that the relatively inexpensive 4-litre Austin Sheerline sedan with factory bodywork (a true poor man's Bentley) was more attractive than the same chassis dressed up in aluminium panels

Hillman Minx

You think you are buying a brand-new post-war model, but ... Going clockwise from top left in this panorama of the 1948 Phase II Hillman Minx reveals how far improvisation may go. From the front end everything looks new, thanks to the recessed headlamps and three-piece grille in the 1941 American idiom, even if the alligator hood has been around on the recently defunct (1940–47) Phase I as well. Seen from three-quarter rear, however, it's 1940 from the firewall back, both the big projecting trunk and absence of running boards being familiar features. True, the wheels are full discs and not steel-spoke, but then Austin have just made the same change ... The facia would hardly puzzle a seasoned Minx owner, either, though the instruments have lost their plastic-wood surround and are grouped in front of the driver. Another heresy is the brand-new "Rootes Synchromatic Gear Change", no kind of an automatic, only public relations jargon for column shift. In the plan view from above, one could be looking at the 1940 car again: for all an overall width of 60½ in (1.53 m), there is

230

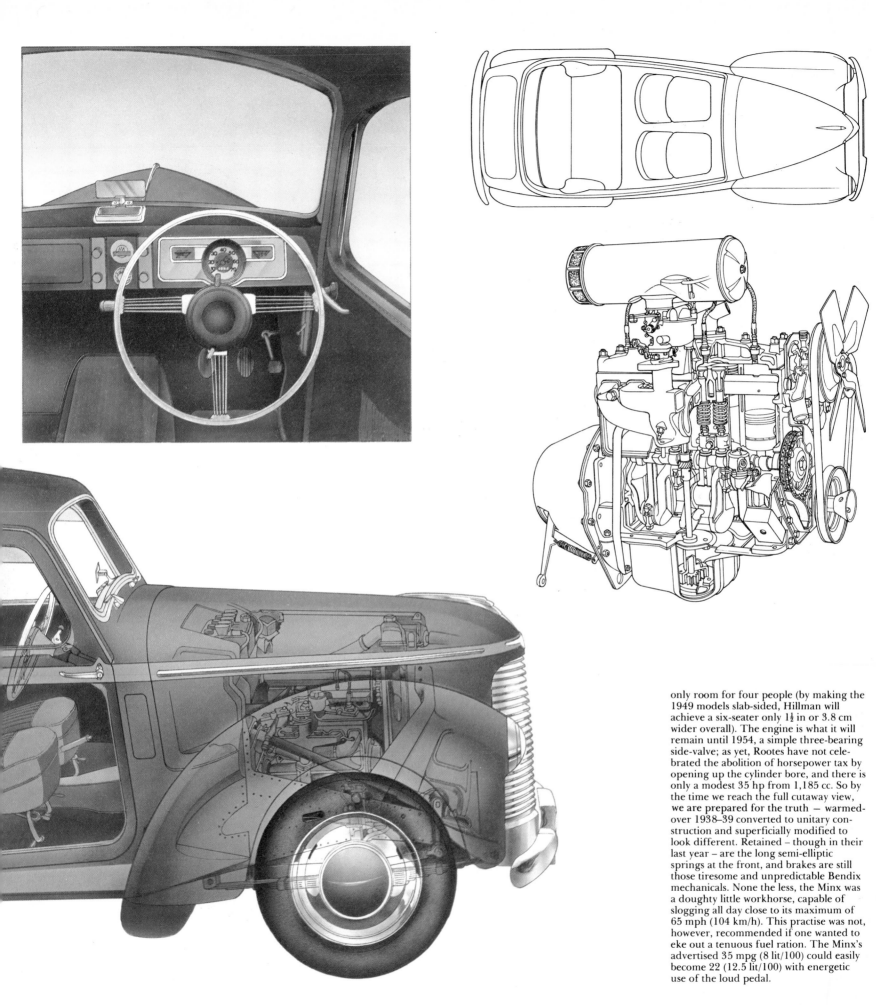

only room for four people (by making the
1949 models slab-sided, Hillman will
achieve a six-seater only 1½ in or 3.8 cm
wider overall). The engine is what it will
remain until 1954, a simple three-bearing
side-valve; as yet, Rootes have not celebrated the abolition of horsepower tax by
opening up the cylinder bore, and there is
only a modest 35 hp from 1,185 cc. So by
the time we reach the full cutaway view,
we are prepared for the truth — warmed-
over 1938–39 converted to unitary construction and superficially modified to
look different. Retained – though in their
last year – are the long semi-elliptic
springs at the front, and brakes are still
those tiresome and unpredictable Bendix
mechanicals. None the less, the Minx was
a doughty little workhorse, capable of
slogging all day close to its maximum of
65 mph (104 km/h). This practise was not,
however, recommended if one wanted to
eke out a tenuous fuel ration. The Minx's
advertised 35 mpg (8 lit/100) could easily
become 22 (12.5 lit/100) with energetic
use of the loud pedal.

231

and streamline fenders by Vanden Plas. Was it worth parting with an extra £825 (say $2,300) for the custom treatment, two extra carburettors, another 8 mph of top speed, and a fearsome rear overhang?

American custom coachbuilding was virtually extinct, while as yet, German shops confined their endeavours to making the Beetle look different: Hebmüller's two-passenger cabriolet was the best of the early ones. Only in Italy did the profession go from strength to strength. If, so far, the only significant design export was Pininfarina's sports cabriolet for Simca, one could already see why Nash would soon appeal to the maestro to make something of their tasteless 1949 bathtub shape.

One may well ask why this specialist industry throve in the impoverished trans-Alpine climate. The fact was that Italians – unlike the motorists of other countries – faced 1946 with virtually no choice of car at all. The Lancia was the economic equivalent of the Rover or the small Mercedez-Benz, and the 6C-2500 Alfa Romeo was beyond the reach of almost anyone. Thus, it was a Fiat or nothing, and all that Fiat offered were the two-passenger *topolino*, the 1100 in two wheel-base lengths, and the six-cylinder 1500. Better still, all pre-1950 Fiats retained the separate chassis.

So, one bought a Fiat and had the coachbuilder run up something different – no great problem, since experts of the calibre of Ghia, Pininfarina, or Vignale cared naught for stock grilles and fenders. And even if one doubled one's investment by opting for a *Millecento* coupé, it was still cheaper to buy – and to run – than an Alfa or Aprilia.

Pininfarina's 1100 Cisitalia fixed-head coupé stands out as the archetype of this generation. In fact, it was. But it was also the archetype of something entirely different from technical and sporting standpoints alike: the rise of the Fiat-tuners, who would progress from the provision of mere brake horses to being manufacturers in their own right, just as 1930's Standard Swallow had eventually bred the Jaguar. As a shape, however, the Cisitalia had few rivals – it was aerodynamically efficient, it was innocent of Detroit's beloved chrome-strip, and it did not date. Not all its contemporaries could be described as attractive: dreadful things were done with such American affectations as wheel spats and bumper-grille mergers worthy of a 1950 Buick. These, however, were usually one-offs because, as one Italian specialist put it, nobody wanted an expensive oddity that would be stylistically obsolete within a twelvemonth.

Fiat's unitary 1400 would serve as call-boy for the next act, and for the merger of tuners and coachbuilders into an integrated team. If Lancia placated the coachbuilders with a "platform", Fiat did not; a rolling floor pan with mechanical elements attached represented their limit. This, of course, gave the coachbuilder unlimited latitude. The tuners had already devised that characteristic of sports-car design of the 1950s, the multi-tubular space frame, and quite a few *topolino* mechanics had already found their way into such structures, even if such firms as OSCA and Stanguellini were as yet little known, and their wares not really suitable for street use. The tuners and coachbuilders now joined forces to camouflage the ungainly 1400 in some most improbable shapes. SIATA offered a brace of two-seaters, of which the Barchetta aped Ferrari and the Rallye the classic lines of the TD MG. Their Daina cabriolet anticipated Graber's later 3-litre Alvis, while their tuning shops worked the 1.4-litre 44-bhp motor up to 1,800 cc and 80 bhp. This, allied to the five-speed gearbox from Fiat's later 1900, added up to a formidable package with few Fiat affiliations. This trend would spread outside Italy: even if the Volkswagen/Porsche marriage had always been one of convenience, to be discarded as soon as possible, there would be cars like the Volkswagen-based Denzels from Austria, and Britain's Swallow Doretti, using the mechanical elements of Triumph's TR series.

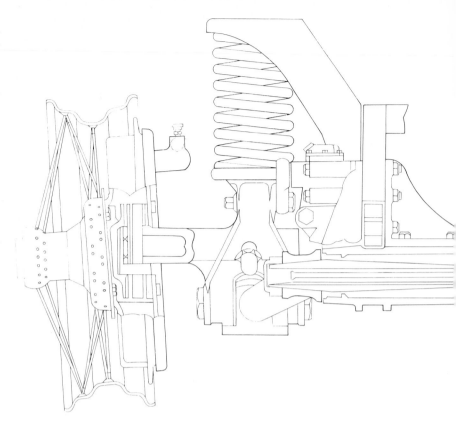

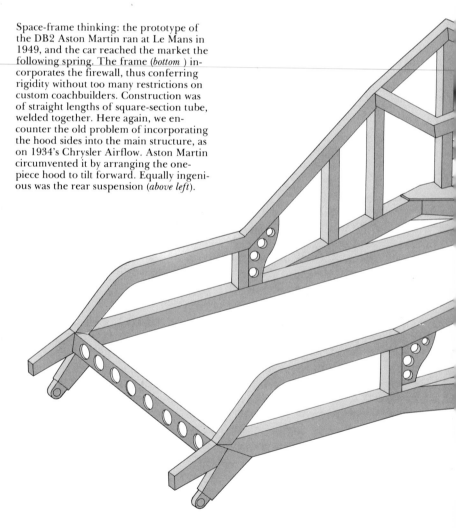

Space-frame thinking: the prototype of the DB2 Aston Martin ran at Le Mans in 1949, and the car reached the market the following spring. The frame (*bottom*) incorporates the firewall, thus conferring rigidity without too many restrictions on custom coachbuilders. Construction was of straight lengths of square-section tube, welded together. Here again, we encounter the old problem of incorporating the hood sides into the main structure, as on 1934's Chrysler Airflow. Aston Martin circumvented it by arranging the one-piece hood to tilt forward. Equally ingenious was the rear suspension (*above left*).

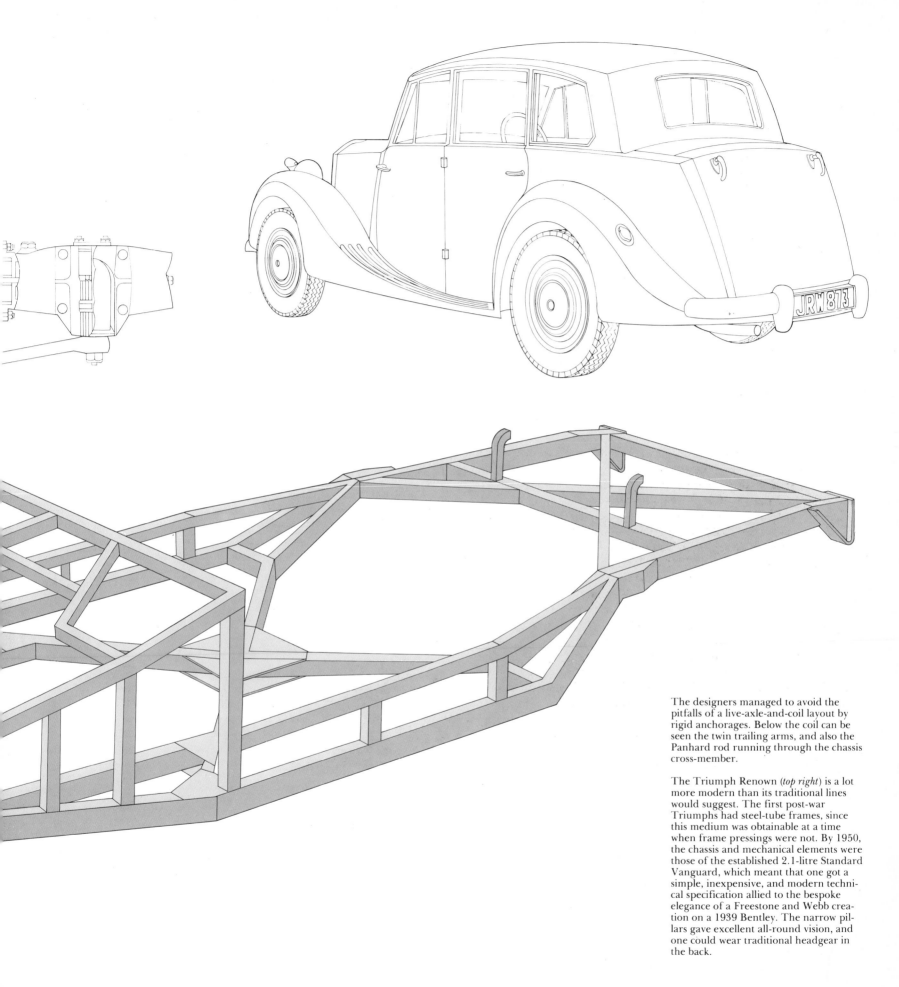

The designers managed to avoid the pitfalls of a live-axle-and-coil layout by rigid anchorages. Below the coil can be seen the twin trailing arms, and also the Panhard rod running through the chassis cross-member.

The Triumph Renown (*top right*) is a lot more modern than its traditional lines would suggest. The first post-war Triumphs had steel-tube frames, since this medium was obtainable at a time when frame pressings were not. By 1950, the chassis and mechanical elements were those of the established 2.1-litre Standard Vanguard, which meant that one got a simple, inexpensive, and modern technical specification allied to the bespoke elegance of a Freestone and Webb creation on a 1939 Bentley. The narrow pillars gave excellent all-round vision, and one could wear traditional headgear in the back.

The Motor Shows of the 1950 season were not, perhaps, the most inspiring. Power steering had yet to arrive, and Chrysler's much-touted disc brakes were confined to the enormous eight-passenger Imperials (precisely 414 sold that year). There was as yet no cheap and dependable automatic transmission suitable for engines of less than 3 litres' capacity. Neither Russia nor Japan boasted any significant export trade, and the Swedish Volvo had penetrated only as far as the Low Countries.

Yet a closer look showed that the turning point had been achieved. The trends apparent in the 1935–50 period had crystallized into a pattern that would follow through until the next phase of innovation, coincident perhaps with the début of the DS19 Citroën in October, 1955. Admittedly, some antediluvian elements were still around. Those who raved over the sophistication of the Morris Minor's torsion-bar springing were bored to tears with the gutless ways of its 1935 flathead engine, the Citroën was still the same car as it had been in 1934, and, of the traditional American inline sixes, only Chevrolets and Nashes ran to upstairs valves. The Volkswagen with hydraulic brakes had been available for less than six months, and owners faced another two seasons of double-clutch techniques. Of specialist cars, the Morgan, for all its newly acquired Standard Vanguard motor, was pure 1936, while the 2-litre AC combined a 1933 chassis with a 1919 motor.

On the credit side, some interesting new cars were in the pipeline. The Ford Zephyr pointed the way to a different norm in the important 2.5-litre class, Lancia's Aurelia, also a six, offered new standards of handling, and the Jowett Jupiter roadster marked the introduction of the Italian space frame to a production touring car. Perhaps the most sensational of 1950's débutantes was the Mk VII Jaguar, the marriage of the brilliant twin-camshaft XK motor to a full-size sedan. Better still, this sedan combined American proportions and baggage accommodation with European appointments and handling. Its 160 bhp were matched only by Detroit's latest vee-eights, its American price of $3,850 (£1,375) was less than $800 higher than the going rate for a Cadillac, and its fuel consumption was lower. All the Mk VII now needed was an automatic transmission – and this would be available by 1953.

The frontiers were receding, and demarcation lines were becoming blurred. From the back end, it was hard to distinguish the Alfa Romeo 1900 – deliveries of which were just beginning – from the 1952 Vauxhall line, which in any case consisted of nothing more than miniature Chevrolets. The 1900 sat six, thanks to a column shift, which appalled Alfa fanatics. It also made all the right noises associated with twin overhead-camshaft four-cylinder engines, steered "from the seat of the pants" in the best Alfa tradition, and it was nearly as fast on 1,884 cc as the big Jaguar on 3,442 cc. Once production had been worked up to a point at which competitive prices – and worldwide servicing – were viable, it would be a major challenger.

Even the ingredients of today's international cocktails were there, though they could not be bought in 1950, and one had to take a ticket to Idlewild and points west to see them – or rather it, for the NX1 Nash was strictly a one-off. This slab-sided two-passenger convertible was no beauty – the bathtub idiom did not take kindly to shrinking techniques. Nor can it have been much of a performer with its 570-cc overhead-camshaft *topolino* motor. It would, however, spark off an era of transatlantic cooperation, for, in 1954, when it reached the public as the Metropolitan, it combined a typical Nash unitary structure with the mechanics of Austin's proven 1,200-cc A40. Since Americans had no use for four forward speeds and Nash wanted to save the washing, the lowest ratio of the Austin box was blanked off. Construction was undertaken entirely in Britain, but virtually no cars were sold outside the United States before 1957.

The last link between past and present had been forged.

BIBLIOGRAPHY

Remarkably little has been written specifically on the period, and it is sad to have to record that the writer's own *Cars of the 1930s* (Batsford, London, 1970) is still the definitive work on the cars of this period and the background against which they were marketed. For the motoring atmosphere in the 1930s, I can strongly recommend John Dugdale's *Great Motor Sport Of The Thirties* (Wilton House-Gentry, London, 1977); the author was an *Autocar* staff member during this uneasy period and there's a lot in it beyond just racing. Another very personal account is J.A. Grégoire's *50 Ans d'Automobile* (Flammarion, Paris, 1974); make no mistake, it is strictly one man's view and largely concerned with the development of front-wheel drive, but none the worse for it. By contrast, the golden twenties have been written almost to death: in spite of this, the best introduction remains the oldest, *The Vintage Motor Car* by Clutton and Stanford (Batsford, London, 1954). It may be tendentious and a trifle snobbish in its outlook, but the essential background has never been explained more skilfully.

The traditional long-hooded "classics" have received a lot more attention, and for coachwork, the two best works are George Oliver's *History of Coachbuilding* (Cassell, London, 1962) and John McLellan's *Bodies Beautiful* (David & Charles, Newton Abbot, 1975). They cover all periods, of course. J.R. Buckley's *Cars of the Connoisseur* (Batsford, London, 1962) is a pleasing and well-balanced account of some of the "right" cars, while for German-speakers, there is the formidable *Klassische Wagen* trilogy published by Hallwag of Bern between 1972 and 1979. Hans Heinrich von Fersen did the Germans, Austrians, Czechs, and Swiss, Ferdinand Hediger the "Latin" breeds, and the present writer the British and American makes. All cover the official "classic" period of 1925–42 with only mild overlaps at either end, and though the story is hung once again round "selected" makes, there's a great deal of information to be extracted from it.

The post-war period is only just becoming fashionable, and there is a tendency to widen appeal by extending the story into the 1960s. Graham Robson's *The Post-War Touring Car* (Haynes, Yeovil, 1978) concentrates again on the more sporting machine but is a first-rate reference work, while my own *The Motor-Car 1946–56* is a sequel to *Cars of the 1930s* and is planned on the same lines. Lord Montagu of Beaulieu's two volumes of *Lost Causes of Europe* (Cassell, London, 1969 and 1971) gave me a lot of background on the decline of the smaller European makers.

For the United States generally, the standard work of reference must remain *Automobile Quarterly's The American Car Since 1775* (New York, 1971), the long chapters on the big mass-producers and on custom coachbuilding in the United States being outstanding. No real history of the Belgian motor industry has yet been written, but much was culled from the *Livre d'Or du Salon de l'Automobile et du Motocycle*, by de Barsy and Frère (E.P.E., Brussels, 1970). Being bilingual (French-Flemish), it isn't as long as it looks.

Autotypenbücher (a German word which defies translation) are admirable short cuts to knowledge on the cars, though all too often they give types and specifications and not much more. An exception is Werner Oswald's immensely detailed *Deutsche Autos 1920–1945* (Motorbuch Verlag, Stuttgart, 1977), which is packed with facts on the German industry (including the coachbuilders and the bigger foreign importers) under the Weimar and Nazi administrations. His *Deutsche Autos 1945–*

1966 (Motorbuch Verlag, Stuttgart, 1966) is more concise but nevertheless the best guide to early post-war efforts in the two Germanies. David Culshaw's hard-to-find *Motor Guide to Makes and Models*, 1945–1956 (Temple Press, London, 1959) performs the same service for the early post-war British cars, while for the last pre-war decade in the United States there is James Moloney's *Encyclopaedia of American Cars*, 1930 to 1940, (Crestline, Glen Ellyn, Ill., 1977), which makes up for a fairly sketchy text with lots of good pictures. And no student of American cars should be without Tad Burness's two *American Car Spotters' Guides*, covering respectively 1920–39 and 1940–65 (Motorbooks International, Osceola, Wisc., 1973 and 1975). These were constantly at my side, especially when captioning pictures. H.P. Rosellen's *Deutsche Kleinwagen* (Motorbuch Verlag, Stuttgart, 1977) is mostly about the "bubbles" of the 1950s but is very good on small German cars of the late 1940s. I also drew on two of Blandford's attractive little colour guides, Tim Nicholson's *Sports Cars 1928–39* and my own *Passenger Cars, 1924–42*: not a lot of perspective information, but all manner of odd facts on individual makes you won't find elsewhere.

One-make histories are limited in their value, and too many an author shoots apologetically through the 1930s (and even more through the 1940s) with an air of disdain. Others deny the existence of rival makes – to the detriment of their own information-value. For the specialist industry in the uneasy thirties (and in the United States as well), *Triumph Cars* by Langworth and Robson (Motor Racing Publications, London, 1979) should be a bible, while two books I leant on heavily for the post-war part of the saga were Richard Langworth's *Last Onslaught on Detroit* (Automobile Quarterly, New York, 1975), the tragic account of the rise and fall of Kaiser-Frazer; and Tom Lush's *Allard: The Inside Story* (Motor Racing Publications, London, 1977), a blow-by-blow account of the tribulations of a small manufacturer trying to thread his way through the world of permits, steel allocations, and "short supply". J.L. Elbert's *Duesenberg: The Mightiest American Motor Car* (Post Publications, Arcadia, Cal., 1951) is redolent of the atmosphere of the Four Hundred and Beverly Hills, while a book that ought to be read more than it is, is S. Kamiya's *My Life With Toyota* (Toyota Motor Co., Tokyo, 1976), a first-hand account of the formative years of Japan's automotive industry.

In addition, the following are recommended for in-depth, if specialized, information on the period:

Davey, A., and May, A. *Lagonda – A History of the Marque* (David & Charles, Newton Abbot, 1978)

Hendry, M.O. *Cadillac: The Complete 70 Year History* (Automobile Quarterly, New York, 1973)

Kimes, B.R., ed. *Packard: A History of the Motor Car and the Company* (Automobile Quarterly, New York, 1979)

McComb, F.W. *M.G. by McComb* (Osprey, London, 1979)

Beaulieu, Lord Montagu of *Jaguar: A Biography* (Cassell, London, 1961)

Price, B. *The Lea-Francis Story* (Batsford, London, 1977)

Robson, G. *The Rover Story* (Stephens, Cambridge, 1977)

Sedgwick, M. *Fiat: A History* (Batsford, London, 1974)

If I seem to recommend too much of my own work, it is only because I have always studied this period and sought to remedy the gaps in published information the very hard way!

Finally, there is, of course, G.N. Georgano's *Complete Encyclopaedia of Motor Cars* (Ebury Press, London, 1973). Nick Georgano has written the reference book to end all reference books, and even if the information given in this masterpiece is cursory, no writer ever shows up any work without a final look through Georgano to make sure he hasn't missed anything out.

INDEX

Names of models are indexed in alphabetical order, even when some names are themselves numbers. Page numbers in italics indicate an illustration.